Praise for *Black Power*

"What Fujino and Harmachis have done with this collection of articles is comparable in scope to Charles Jones's *The Black Panther Party (Reconsidered)*, and Judson Jeffries's *Comrades*, both superb and deeply critical anthologies, but with a provocative twist: what would be the historical impacts of the Black Panther Party half a century hence? As a young member of the original collective, I can say without contradiction, we were so busy, and often so nerve-wracked that we barely thought about the next fifty minutes, much less fifty years! Fujino and Harmachis show us that history is never done. It runs like a river, sometimes rushing, sometimes meandering, but always moving."
—MUMIA ABU-JAMAL, author of *We Want Freedom: A Life in the Black Panther Party*

"*Black Power Afterlives* constructs an urgently needed bridge between the Black Power era and the Black Lives Matter movements of today. Deftly sidestepping well-trod ground, the authors trace how the Panthers' international engagements, artistic practices, ideological frameworks and community organizing have continued to influence new generations of activists. By locating the Panthers' richest legacies in the work of students, poor Black folks, and Black queer feminists, and in the sustained commitment of political prisoners, it reminds readers of the transformative possibilities of struggle."
—ROBYN C. SPENCER, author of *The Revolution Has Come: Black Power, Gender, and the Black Panthers Party in Oakland*

"The Black Panther Party's 1966 armed actions against police brutality in Oakland's Black community reorganized mainstream consciousness in the United States. The BPP exposed entrenched notions of gun-ownership as the exclusive right of white Americans. The Party's armed cop-watch, aesthetic exaltation of Blackness, and challenges to capitalism also released Black resistance from the state's ideological grip. *Black Power Afterlives* is the first book to explore this post-60s reorganization of Black consciousness, resistance, and humanity. Its intervention is as urgent and rich as the legacy of the Black Panthers."
—JOHANNA FERNÁNDEZ, author of *The Young Lords: A Radical History*

"*Black Power Afterlives* gives us concrete insights into the continuing significance of the Black Panthers without the common iconization and stereotypes. Through carefully chosen writings and interviews we are reminded of the transformative power of movements and real people that envision a far more just and equitable future for humanity and the planet."
—CLAUDE MARKS, director, the Freedom Archives

"The vivid, engaging, and compelling testimonies that Diane C. Fujino and Matef Harmachis have collected in *Black Power Afterlives* offer unparalleled insights about the origins, evolution, and continuing influence and impact of the Black Panther Party. This is an indispensable book, one that demonstrates how oppositional social movement organizations fuel future struggles long after they seem to have departed from the scene."

—GEORGE LIPSITZ, author of *How Racism Takes Place*

"Tender and determined, these meditations on the enduring afterlives of the Black Panther Party illuminate the incandescent dreams of freedom joining one revolutionary generation to another. The essays and conversations—on art and prison, ecology and the spirit—focus on the lessons rank-and-file Panthers have to offer today's rank and file. They remind us of the eternal dedication and determination required of us all."

—DAN BERGER, author of *Captive Nation: Black Prison Organizing in the Civil Rights Era*

"*Black Power Afterlives* shares important insights about the Black Panther Party and radical activism. Examining an inheritance that bridges two centuries, it explores mobilizations against poverty, exploitation, imprisonment, violence, and war. Fred Hampton's Rainbow Coalition sought to wrest victories from police in order to secure "Power to the People." With prescience, Hampton warned that he would not die slipping on icy Chicago streets, and that we either organize with radical intent or forget him. *Black Power Afterlives* remembers Fred and the sacrifices of those who fought and fight for their communities—especially political prisoners. Recognizing the need to free them all, and our communities, *Black Power Afterlives* builds an archive and a foundation for continued struggles."

—JOY JAMES, author of *Shadowboxing: Representations of Black Feminist Politics*

"There are more stories of the deep and continuing legacy of the Black Panthers than can be contained in any one book, but *Black Panther Afterlives* does a good job at beginning to fill the gap. Editors Fujino and Harmachis present us with a must-read book, essential to a true understanding of the positive ways in which Panther politics can and do enrich our lives today."

—MATT MEYER, secretary-general, International Peace Research Association; coeditor and author, *Look for Me in the Whirlwind: From the Panther 21 to 21st Century Revolutions*

BLACK POWER
Afterlives

The Enduring Significance of the Black Panther Party

Edited by Diane C. Fujino and Matef Harmachis

Haymarket Books
Chicago, Illinois

Published in 2020 by
Haymarket Books
P.O. Box 180165
Chicago, IL 60618
773-583-7884
www.haymarketbooks.org
info@haymarketbooks.org

ISBN: 978-1-64259-126-2

Distributed to the trade in the US through Consortium Book Sales and Distribution (www.cbsd.com) and internationally through Ingram Publisher Services International (www.ingramcontent.com).

This book was published with the generous support of Lannan Foundation and Wallace Action Fund.

All royalties from this book go to the Yuri Kochiyama Fund for Political Prisoners in support of former Black Panthers and other political prisoners and liberation struggles broadly.

Special discounts are available for bulk purchases by organizations and institutions. Please email orders@haymarketbooks.org for more information.

Cover design by Eric Kerl.

Printed in Canada by union labor.

Library of Congress Cataloging-in-Publication data is available.

10 9 8 7 6 5 4 3 2 1

CONTENTS

INTRODUCTION

The Enduring Significance of the Black Panther Party

Diane C. Fujino and Matef Harmachis

There is a paradox in writing about the Black Panther Party for Self-Defense fifty years after its founding. The instant recognition of the Black Panther Party (BPP) contrasts with the sparsity of any sustained study of the Party's continuing influence on later generations of activism. As is broadly acknowledged, the BPP is one of the most significant organizations of the twentieth century. There is now a sizeable literature of rigorous studies of the BPP, but nearly all of these, by design, examine the party during its existence. Yet even a cursory review of some of today's most visible activist and cultural productions are revealing of the Black Panthers' ongoing impact. The widely covered Black Lives Matter protests against police violence call to mind, in different form, the BPP's famed police patrols. Mega-celebrity Beyoncé's 2016 Super Bowl halftime performance was a clear reference to and celebration of the BPP. Football star Colin Kaepernick's widely covered—and controversial—"taking a knee" against police brutality during the national anthem at NFL games harkens back to John Carlos and Tommie Smith raising the Black Power fist at the 1968 Olympic Games in Mexico City, with all three athletes inspired by the BPP. The 2018 smash hit movie *Black Panther*, a filmic version of the Marvel comic strips, invokes images and themes raised by the BPP. More quietly, an entire social service infrastructure has been developed since the 1960s, inspired in part by the BPP's community survival programs. The influence of the BPP also continues in the children of former Panthers, most notably through the famed rapper Tupac Shakur, son of New York Panthers Afeni Shakur and Billy Garland, and the prominent Black intellectual Ta-Nehisi Coates, author of the award-winning *Between the World and Me* and son of Baltimore Panther Paul Coates, founder of Black Classic Press.[1] Forty-five years after the decline of the BPP's most active period, the Black Panthers maintain an influence in mainstream culture, sports, social service delivery, activism, knowledge production, and beyond, and have always had a presence in Black and alternative communities. Yet to our knowledge, there is no extensive study of the continuing impact of the BPP on later generations of political and cultural justice work. We thus call *Black Power Afterlives* into being to re-narrate the significance of the BPP, beyond its iconic image and symbolic meanings, to reveal how the party—through former Panthers and direct lineages with later activists—continues to impact and inspire social justice and racial liberation movements to the present.[2]

That the BPP has captured the imagination of today's youth, as well as multiple generations of activists, is understandable enough. The BPP was the largest Black Power organization of the era, with an estimated two thousand to five thousand members at its peak in forty chapters and branches across sixty-eight cities, including Los Angeles, Seattle, Milwaukee, Kansas City, New Orleans, Winston-Salem, Baltimore, Philadelphia, and New York. By late 1968 and at least into 1970, the *Black Panther* newspaper sold more than one hundred thousand copies weekly. Even prominent mainstream institutions acknowledged that the Panthers garnered widespread support. An ABC-TV poll in 1970 showed that 62 percent of those surveyed admire the work of the BPP, and the *Wall Street Journal* in January 1970 wrote that "a clear majority of blacks strongly support both the goals and the methods of the Black Panthers."[3] Internationally, BPP groups formed in at least eight countries, including Algeria, Bermuda, India (Dalit Panthers), England, Palestine, Israel, Australia, New Zealand (Polynesian Panthers); BPP political delegations traveled to China, Japan, North Korea, North Vietnam, Sweden, Denmark, Germany, France, Palestine, and elsewhere; and the Panthers influenced struggles in Cuba, Vietnam, and beyond.[4] Their national and international influence was so remarkable that Judson Jeffries asserts that the Black Panthers were not just an organization but "a movement" and "a cultural happening." Joshua Bloom and Waldo Martin saw the BPP as the "center of the revolutionary movement in the United States," while George Katsiaficas called the BPP "the most significant revolutionary organization in the United States during the latter half of the twentieth century."[5]

The Panthers were masterful at capturing the image of Black militancy in photograph after photograph of Black men and women in leather jackets, berets, and sunglasses facing down the police with guns and with provocative drawings in the *Black Panther* newspaper of pigs on two feet as symbols of the police and the entire apparatus of state power. But the BPP's significance exceeds its sensationalist representations. The party, especially in its early years, was serious about ending the multiple violences of the police, poverty, and racism against Black communities. They popularized the ideas of Frantz Fanon, Robert F. Williams, and others about armed struggle in bold tactics that worked to reduce police violence in Black communities, even as it created other kinds of problems. They studied revolutionary theorists from Malcolm X to Mao Zedong to Fidel Castro. They worked to build a far-reaching organization that implemented numerous community survival programs, most famously the free breakfast program, but also the Oakland Community School, health care clinics, tuberculosis testing, ambulance services, senior escort services, and many more.[6] The BPP also committed major errors and engaged in dangerous internal conflict, fomented by brutal FBI and police repression. The BPP needs to be studied in its totality and in terms of its impact, some still unknowable, on future generations of activists. Whatever its shortcomings, it is clear that the work of the BPP transformed knowledge of Black history, culture, and resistance, and inspired new cultural expressions that awakened Black pride and undercut the internalization of white supremacist and colonial images of Black subordination. The BPP rarely gets credit for certain major achievements, including recruiting gang youth fixated on neighborhood rivalries into a united struggle on behalf of Black people. Becoming a Panther heightened pan-Black consciousness and reduced the salience of neighborhood identities. The Panthers also forged cross-racial and cross-class alliances that created unexpected affiliations (such as among medical students, sickle cell patients, and teenage militants) and opposed both the middle-class respectability politics of civil rights organizations and the narrow nationalisms of groups like the US Organization and the Nation of Islam. Theirs was a bold experimentation in community organizing and in the deployment of Black revolutionary ideas, images, and practices.

Even as the BPP's historical significance is widely acknowledged, we offer a cautionary warning not to overstate the singular importance of the Panthers. To the contrary, we view the philosophy and programs of the BPP as building *vertically* through the long history of the Black radical tradition from Harriet Tubman to Martin Delany to the African Blood Brotherhood to Malcolm X as well as *horizontally*, developing knowledge and activist practices in collaboration with other Black Power organizations such as the Student Nonviolent Coordinating Committee and the Republic of New Afrika. Together—as well as through the clashes and contradictions among these groups—the varied Black radical organizations, including the BPP, helped to develop the ideology and practice of Black Power focused on unabashed and unapologetic opposition to the power of the state to dominate and oppress Black communities. We also recognize how other moments, especially the radical groups of the 1990s, notably the Black Radical Congress, Critical Resistance, and INCITE!: Women, Gender Non-Conforming, and Trans People of Color Against Violence in Barbara Ransby's astute formulation, provided the most immediate political genealogy to the current Movement for Black Lives.[7] Taking a longer view of history, Erik McDuffie, Dayo Gore, Ashley Farmer, Carole Boyce Davies, and Jeanne Theoharis make arguments for the influence of Black feminist organizing since the 1930s and 1940s on today's struggles.[8] We agree with this longer historical contextualization and in fact have promoted this "long" radical movement framing freedom elsewhere.[9] The point of *Black Power Afterlives* is not to negate these other important histories, but to make an argument for the critical importance of the BPP to today's intensive social movements.

The Black Panther Party's Relevance to Current Social Movements

In the second decade of the twenty-first century, the world is witnessing an outpouring of protest activities, the most exhaustive and widespread resistance, domestically and globally, since the time of the BPP. The groups and breadth of issues is vast, from Black Lives Matter and the Movement for Black Lives demanding an end to police violence, to Standing Rock water protectors and Mauna Kea activists fighting for Indigenous land rights and the need to protect our shared resources, to the environmental movement issuing an alarming warning of tipping points and climate catastrophe, to Latinx and Asian American immigrant rights movements opposing the deportation of undocumented people and an end to the cruel separation of parents and children, to efforts to stop the travel ban and racist targeting of Muslims and Arabs, to the women's movement raising up the #MeToo hashtag and struggling to oppose violence against women, to the Occupy movement's popularizing the "99 percent" slogan to highlight issues of economic inequality and class struggle, to efforts to cancel the debt of student and taxi workers, and much more. A number of important books have been written about these various movements that reveal the influence of the BPP and Black Power, yet there remains little by way of a sustained discussion of the impact of this history on the present movement.[10]

This book's focus on the continuing impact of the BPP raises several questions in relation to today's struggles. At a time when it seems like nothing has changed (in terms of poverty, racist policing, and sexism) or have gotten worse (in terms of mass incarceration, the growing austerity state, gentrification and houselessness, the expanding wealth gap), many ask: Have we not gained anything as a result of the massive social movements of the past fifty years? How would we characterize what has changed and why? How are present-day movements different from the Black liberation struggles of the 1960s and '70s, yet, in what ways are contemporary struggles influenced by Black Power? How does the study of the past inform today's social movement organizing? In what ways does the analysis of structural racism, racial capitalism, imperialism, and heteropatriarchy emerging today build on or depart from the work of the BPP?

The Movement for Black Lives (M4BL), as one of the most extensive and comprehensive Black political formations of today, offers a lens through which to begin to address such questions and to examine the significance of the BPP's continuing impact. The M4BL, a collective of more than fifty organizations, issued a vision statement in 2016 that echoes the BPP's insistence on self-determination and "all power to the people." The vision statement begins, "Black humanity and dignity require Black political will and power." Like Frantz Fanon or Paulo Freire, M4BL views its work as the humanization of society and the removal or diminishing of structures of domination so that Black communities can not only survive but also flourish. It, like the BPP before them, embrace a Black-centered, but never Black-only, analysis. The M4BL platform states, "We are a collective that centers and is rooted in Black communities, but we recognize we have a shared struggle with all oppressed people; collective liberation will be a product of all of our work."[11]

The M4BL and its collective participants, including the Black Lives Matter network, Black Youth Project 100 (BYP100), Dream Defenders, National Black Food and Justice Alliance, Southerners on New Ground (SONG), and many other Black organizations, deploy a Black-centered, intersectional politics that emphasize at least three significant commitments. First, M4BL seeks "not reform but transformation." Its goal is not to advance the so-called best and brightest (the talented tenth philosophy) at the expense of the most vulnerable sectors of the Black community who are, in fact, the very groups most susceptible to the violence of prisons and of poverty. The M4BL views the multitude of problems facing Black communities—including sexual violence and hyperpolicing; lack of proper housing, education, health care and jobs—as interconnected and rooted in structural racism, patriarchy, capitalism, and militarism. M4BL writes: "Together, we demand an end to the wars against Black people. We demand that the government repair the harms that have been done to Black communities in the form of reparations and targeted long-term investments. We also demand a defunding of the systems and institutions that criminalize and cage us."[12] The M4BL seeks an end to the overt violence of policing and prisons, but also to the less obvious but insidious structural policies and practices that strip assets, wealth, and resources of Black people, resulting in enduring and exacerbated poverty across the generations.[13] The M4BL thus calls for "reparations for the historic and continuing harms of colonialism and slavery." Like the famed BPP Ten-Point Platform and Program of 1966 and the even bolder, more radical documents emerging from the BPP-led Revolutionary People's Constitutional Convention in 1970, which attracted an estimated twelve thousand to fifteen thousand people, M4BL's vision statement is radical in its critiques of racial capitalism and global in its analysis.[14] But in ways that exceed the Panthers' ideology and practice as a whole, the M4BL issues a rejection of heteropatriarchy—that is, a critique of patriarchy and assumptions of heterosexuality and heteronormativity.

Second, M4BL seeks to promote and develop the leadership of the most marginalized within Black communities, "including but not limited to those who are women, queer, trans, femmes, gender nonconforming, Muslim, formerly and currently incarcerated, cash-poor and working-class, [people with disabilities], undocumented, and immigrant."[15] They recognize that without an intentional focus on developing leadership, it is too easy to rely on the leadership of those already more advantaged by way of education, class, race, gender, citizenship status, and able-bodiedness. Many of the groups came to M4BL as already youth-based and working-class Black feminist organizations. This insistence on the leadership of the most vulnerable sectors represents both a departure from the BPP's more hierarchical and male-centered leadership *and* an affirmation of the BPP's emphasis on working-class Black leadership.

Third, M4BL adopts what BYP100 calls "radical inclusivity" that "emphasizes the importance of addressing the varied identities, needs, and experiences of *all* Black people." This requires an intersectional analysis so as not to reproduce the ways, for example, that Black men's issues tend to stand in for the near totality of the Black community and marginalize the forms of violence directed against Black women.[16] In 1982, Akasha (Gloria T.) Hull, Patricia Bell Scott, and Barbara Smith captured this idea in the title of their book, *All the Women Are White, All the Blacks Are Men, but Some of Us Are Brave*. While most of their work focuses on local communities, M4BL's analyses and values, like the BPP's, are global in focus: "We stand in solidarity with our international family against the ravages of global capitalism and anti-Black racism, human-made climate change, war, and exploitation. . . . We also recognize and honor the rights and struggle of our Indigenous family for land and self-determination."[17] The BPP earlier rehearsed the broad inclusivity of the Black community as well as alliance building with multiple formations, including the white left, albeit with shortcomings, as addressed below.

While some have been critical of M4BL's focus on working within the system, M4BL made the decision to develop and promote more than thirty policy briefs that are far-reaching and intersectional in analysis. Their demands include: "an end to the war against Black people"; "investment in the education, health, and safety of Black people [and end to] the criminalizing, caging, and harming of Black people"; "economic justice for all and a reconstruction of the economy to ensure Black communities have collective ownership, not merely access"; "community control"; and "independent Black political power and Black self-determination." Surely these ideas echo the BPP's Ten-Point Platform's demands for "full employment," "decent housing, fit for shelter of human beings," "an immediate end to POLICE BRUTALITY and MURDER of black people," and ultimately, "power to determine the destiny of our Black community." The M4BL organizations also implement programs that build from BPP's programs of free breakfast for schoolchildren, free health care, support services to the elderly, and liberation schools as well as the BPP's engagements with global anticolonial struggles.[18]

Still, this book does not merely assert that M4BL and today's other radical movements emulate the BPP without critique. To the contrary, the BPP exhibited both a visionary model of Black liberation and devastating flaws dangerously fomented by police violence and the FBI's COINTELPRO (Counterintelligence Program). The COINTELPRO was devised to disrupt and destroy left movements through surveilling, harassing and discrediting leaders and members, provoking conflict through the fabrication of false information, and extinguishing the movement through raids, bombings, and targeted killings. The FBI directed its greatest fury and attention on the Black Panthers, implementing 233 of its 295 official COINTELPRO actions against the BPP.[19] The Panthers clearly faced a nearly impossible situation, targeted by state repression and aggravated by the constraints of the times and their own internal contradictions. One would hope that today's movements improve on the past, while also recognizing that the changes in the political economy, racial structures, collective knowledge, and state surveillance since the 1960s and 1970s create new opportunities and new constraints that require the development of analyses, tools, strategies, and tactics for today's social context and racialized political economy.

The most significant ways today's movements are extending and advancing the politics and practice of the BPP and other "long sixties" groups is in their prioritizing of gender and sexual liberation, in combination with racial and economic justice, and in their radical inclusion of the leadership of queer and trans people, women, and other people of color. There has been much written and spoken about how three Black, queer, feminist women originated #BlackLivesMatter and the ensuing movement. The BYP100 was, from its inception, with intentionality, "building a Black politic through a Black, queer, feminist lens" and gathered "the Black queer and trans community along with artists and labor unions" to its founding meeting in July 2013. Southerners on New Ground (SONG), since 1993, has been "a regional Queer Liberation organization made up of Black people, people of color, immigrants, undocumented people, people with disabilities, working class and rural and small town, LGBTQ people in the South." These three organizations and many more form M4BL as a Black youth-, women-, and queer-led formation that is rooted in the Black feminism, queer politics, and the Black radical tradition's critique of capitalism and colonialism.[20]

It may seem paradoxical that, in our analysis, the promotion of feminist and queer leadership and the intersectional analysis of M4BL and other transformative movements can trace a lineage to the BPP, other radical organizations, and academic efforts to decolonize knowledge and advance intersectional theories.[21] It's more straightforward to see how the BPP's Ten-Point Platform's focus on multiple and interconnected issues provided a framework for M4BL's intersectional analysis demanding democratic education, food security, fair housing, jobs with living wages, and the ending of police violence, militarism, and gendered and racist violence as interconnected issues. While it appears contradictory to assert a genealogy from the BPP's policies and practices to today's M4BL's focus on Black feminist queer politics, the

BPP, notably BPP cofounder Huey Newton, wrote one of the earliest statements on gay oppression/liberation by any Black political organization. Ten days after his August 1970 release from prison, Newton issued an open letter on "The Women's Liberation and Gay Liberation Movements." In that letter he viewed "homosexuals and women as oppressed groups" and called for the forging of coalitional politics among the Black, women's, and gay liberation movements. He acknowledged the psychological insecurities that form the basis of antigay beliefs. Just as "[m]any times the poorest white person is the most racist because he is afraid that he might lose something, or discover something that he does not have," Newton acknowledged the limitations of his analysis and affective understanding in that "male homosexuality is a threat to me" and "to our manhood." But Newton was also self-reflective, "Maybe I'm now injecting some of my prejudice by saying that 'even a homosexual can be a revolutionary.' Quite the contrary, maybe a homosexual could be the most revolutionary."[22]

It appears that Newton did not go on to champion Black gay liberation, in part because of the ways the FBI's COINTELPRO exploited tensions within the BPP on this issue, including fabricating letters to create divisions within the BPP and to undermine Newton's credibility. In response to Newton's open letter, the San Francisco FBI office sent a fictitious letter, allegedly from a Black community member to the BPP chief of staff, David Hilliard, which included: "Huey is wrong. Something must have happened to him in prison. Panthers got enough things to do in the Ten-Point Program and fighting for niggers without takin up with m... f queers."[23] Given the ways the Black movement had an emphasis on reclaiming Black manhood, especially in terms of protection of the heteronormative family, community, and nation, it is not surprising that there was opposition within the BPP to Newton's support of gay liberation. But Newton's statement also generated internal teach-ins on homosexuality and a differing gendered response. According to BPP leader Ericka Huggins, "The [Panther] women did not have a problem with it, but the men were not down."[24] Moreover, Newton's letter was significant, given that, as Alycee Lane observed, it "was the first time any non-gay black organization whether mainstream, like the NAACP, or radical, like Ron Karenga's US, recognized the oppression of homophobia; connected that oppression to the plight of black people; and attempted—based on that connection—to build coalitions openly with lesbians and gay men."[25] While the M4BL and other groups today have certainly advanced much further the intertwining of Black, feminist, and queer liberation, there is recognition that today's intersectional politics build on the work of earlier activist organizations and scholarly thinkers, including Claudia Jones and Esther Cooper Jackson in the 1930s and 1940s, the BPP and Combahee River Collective in the early 1970s, and the surge of women of color theorizing in the 1980s. In 2017, the National LGBTQ Task Force hosted a session on "Lessons Learned from the BPP," in their annual Creating Change conference to recognize the BPP's contributions to racialized queer rights and much beyond, including that "the Black Panthers are the reason we currently have free breakfast programs in public schools today." In this volume, Mary Hooks discusses the impact of the BPP on her own political development as a Black queer feminist activist.[26]

Why Study the "Afterlives" of the BPP?

In titling this book *The* Afterlives *of Black Power*, it is not our intention to imply that Black Power or the BPP has died. To the contrary, just as afterlife suggests a continued existence absent the original physical body, the BPP remains very much alive, not in organizational form but in the ongoing activism of former Panthers and in the party's persistent influence on today's struggles. This is precisely the objective of this book—to examine the enduring presence of the BPP. In doing so this book also expands the historiography of Black Power in at least three significant ways. First, *Black Power Afterlives* **extends the time frame** typically associated with Black Power, with its origins in 1966 (Stokely Carmichael's call to "Black Power" in Greenwood, Mississippi, and the formation of the BPP in Oakland, California) ending by the mid-1970s. Scholars Cedric Robinson, Gerald Horne, Robin Kelley, George Lipsitz, Penny Von Eschen, Nikhil Pal Singh, Glenda Gilmore, and many others have challenged the conventional narrative of the civil rights movement in ways vital to the production of scholarship in the past two decades.[27] The call for a "long civil rights movement" (Jacqueline Dowd Hall) or a "long Black Power" (Peniel Joseph) framework extends the earlier writings about the "classic" or "short" civil rights movement (mid-1950s to mid-1960s) back at least to the intensive social movements of the 1930s and forward to Black Power.[28]

In a recent review essay in *American Quarterly*, Diane Fujino argues for the need to expand Black Power forward in time and space. Rigorous studies of Black Power leaders Kwame Ture (formerly Stokely Carmichael) and Robert F. Williams, for example, focus intensively on their work in the US context yet give disproportionately light attention to their significant activism following their most famous activities. This refers, in the case of Ture, to his thirty years of global Pan-Africanism occurring after his ten years in the civil rights and Black Power movements, or, in the case of Williams, his decade spent in exile in Cuba and China subsequent to his creating an NAACP rooted in self-defense in Monroe, North Carolina. Given the ways that today's Black Lives Matter and M4BL clearly borrow from Black Panther and Black Power politics, it is ever more imperative to expand the long sixties forward in time. Let it be clear: We are not arguing that the Black struggle of the 1960s and '70s is the same as the Black struggle today. Even as we often hear laments that "nothing has changed"—and on many days it certainly seems so—we do recognize differences in political economies, with the neoliberal austerity trumping the welfare state of the past, and differences in racial discourse, with more voices for racial equality and against explicit racist language than in the past, even with the rise of the alternative right, or Alt-Right movement, during and also before the Trump era. This book does not call for a replication of the 1960s but rather a study of the past to create theories and models of organizing today that enable us to create a new future.[29]

Second, in addition to expanding the time frame of Black Power studies, this book **expands the geography** of how Black Power is conceptualized. The formidable intellectual-activist Grace Lee Boggs references a Black journalist who stated that, "It would have been better for the movement if Malcolm had spent the year after his split with Elijah [Muhammad] organizing and staying with us in Detroit rather than running all over the country and the world."[30] While one can read this as the understandable wishes of Boggs, a Detroit activist, to have one as monumental as Malcolm X organizing in her city, it also signals the tendency of US activists and scholars to privilege the United States as the site for organizing. Likewise, much of the writings on the BPP, with intentionality, examine activism in local or national contexts. While *Black Power Afterlives* is not intended as a study of the international impact of the BPP per se, it is in conversation with the literature examining the global context of Black liberation, including writings by Gerald Horne, Brenda Gayle Plummer, Yuichiro Onishi, and Robeson Taj Frazier; and the internationalism of the BPP, including writings by Sean L. Malloy, Kathleen Cleaver, George Katsiaficas, and Elaine Mokhtefi.[31] In this volume, such an international impact is evident in the chapter on Emory Douglas, former BPP minister of culture, whose artwork inspired the introduction of the new word "Zapantera" to signify the intertwining of Zapatista and Black Panther ideologies and practices. This book also includes a rare essay exploring the activism of Panther icon Assata Shakur during her exile in Cuba and further examines the global Pan-African politics of several former Panthers.

Third, the histories, stories, and analyses provided in *Black Power Afterlives* **produce new ways of thinking about the meanings of Black Power and its impacts into the future**, thus working to reframe the public discourse about activist struggles. Much has been written about the ways the "long civil rights movement" or a "long Black Power" historiography, by expanding beyond the "classic" civil rights period (1954 to 1965), does the important work of critiquing the conventional narratives of linear progress, the "Great Man" story, a racist South and noble North, and the still-looming unexamined focus on integration, formal equality, and legal discrimination to raise questions of self-determination and power.[32] This book addresses both the widely known and the rarely discussed areas of social justice work influenced by the BPP. Policing and prison activism are some of the most recognized Panther-influenced areas of struggle, with the resistance against police killings invoking Panther police patrols and the rise in prison abolitionist activism, especially since the 1998 Critical Resistance conference in Berkeley, California. The Panther impact in music, arts, and culture is notably visible in the hip-hop music of Public Enemy, dead prez, and The Coup, in Boots Riley's audacious film *Sorry to Bother You*, and in the murals of Bay Area writer REFA 1 (Revolutionary Educator For Africa).[33] But, this volume, with intentionality, also examines the scarcely recognized areas of post-Panther influences, including the spiritual practices exemplified in the lives of former Panthers Ericka Huggins, Dhameera Ahmad, and Hank Jones; the Pan-African internationalism of David Brothers, Dedon Kamathi, and Akinsanya Kambon; and the ongoing work of young activists today, as seen in the chapters on Southerners on New Ground (SONG) in Atlanta, the African Black Coalition in California, the ecosocialist movement from the East Coast to South America, and the Chinese Progressive Association in San Francisco. *Black Power Afterlives* thus intervenes in the study of Black Power by showing complex dimensions—meditation and nurturance, connections with Mother Earth, art and music, self-defense, queer feminism, prison abolition, and community building—that shape new thinking about the legacy of the BPP.

Writing About the Black Panther Party

The writings on Black Power have worked to challenge the "declension narrative" that holds Black Power culpable for the decline of the "noble" civil rights movement.[34] Black Power studies thus narrate not declension but the emergence of a different kind of struggle, one that centered Black nationalism *and* internationalism, self-defense and armed struggle, and theories of Black oppression and strategies for Black liberation that in many ways harken back to earlier resistance within the Black radical tradition.[35] This section provides a brief historiography of the writings on the BPP, while locating the Panther literature within the larger Black liberation scholarship.

Moving away from the near singular Black Panther image in the popular imagination of militancy, masculinity, and the gun, the new writings on the BPP reframe the party in important ways. First, the new studies examine the BPP's work over the entirety of the Party's existence (1966–1982). This longer trajectory still focuses on self-defense, political education, and ideological struggle, but also shifts—as the BPP did itself—to include greater attention to the community survival programs and organization development.[36] Second, the more recent scholarship, especially by Black women scholars and former Panther women, centers gendered analyses of the BPP. These studies show how the BPP enabled political opportunities for and contributions by women, even as the BPP—and some Panther women themselves—both contested and reinforced patriarchal structures within the party.[37] Third, there is also greater attention to the study of local histories and local chapters,[38] art and culture,[39] and cross-racial and coalitional politics.[40] Together, the surge in publications, including Panther memoirs and biographies, scholarly studies, and primary source documents, produce a multifaceted and polyvocal examination of an organization that spanned sixteen years, forty chapters and branches across the nation, an international section, and had significant shifts in its focus and programs.

In thinking about historiography, or the study of and writings about the BPP, several of the most influential books have been written by Black Panthers. It is only in the past decade or two, especially since the fortieth anniversary of the BPP in 2006, that a substantial number of scholars have taken up the task of examining the history of the BPP. Creating different "periods" of BPP scholarship or writing has its inherent risks, including the problem of creating seemingly rigid boundaries between time periods, but we nonetheless find it productive to think about the historical context for the publication of writings on the BPP and thus offer this historiographical framework. The pioneering literature on the BPP dates back to late 1960s and early 1970s. The most famous of these were writings by Black Panther leaders, now viewed as "classic" BPP texts, notably Bobby Seale's *Seize the Time*; Huey Newton's *To Die for the People* and *Revolutionary Suicide*; and Philip Foner's edited volume of BPP writings, *Black Panthers Speak*.[41] Other books in this "first phase" (late 1960s to mid-1970s) focused on overall BPP history as well as BPP political prisoner cases, reflecting the intensity of police and FBI repression and the imprisonment cases of prominent Panthers in the party's earliest years.[42] Bobby Seale's and Assata Shakur's widely read memoirs were published in the "second phase" of Panther writings (the late 1970s to the late 1980s), as was Ward Churchill and Jim Vander Wall's study of FBI repression against the BPP.[43] But this period is generally characterized by a lull in publications on the BPP in the context of rising neo-conservative politics in the nation and the diminishing of Panther programs, membership, and activities by the mid-1970s. It coincides with a notable inactivity of writings on other social movements.[44]

The death of Huey Newton on August 22, 1989, in Oakland, California, brought together former Black Panthers in ways not seen since their departure from the party and spurred the production of writings on the BPP. In this "third phase" of Panther writings (1990–2009), for the first time, scholars began to publish books on the BPP in sizeable numbers, including the two most influential edited volumes in this period: Charles E. Jones's *The Black Panther Party Reconsidered* and Kathleen Cleaver and George Katsiaficas's *Liberation, Imagination, and the Black Panther Party*.[45] There was also a growth in Panther memoirs, most significantly by Elaine Brown and by David Hilliard, and biographies of former Panthers that added local and (auto)biographical histories to a former Panther historiography that had primarily, but not exclusively, focused on the national organization's base in Oakland.[46] Important primary source books of BPP documents and books of photography on the BPP, accompanied by essays, were also published in this period.[47] In 1996, while preparing for the thirtieth anniversary of the BPP, former Panther Billy X (Jennings) created an online archive to preserve the party's legacy and keep former Panthers connected. The virtual clearinghouse of Panther information matched the actual museum-like space that his house had already become.[48]

Admittedly, it is not entirely clear where to draw the line between the third and fourth periods of BPP historiography, except that we wish to call attention to the surge in writings about the BPP sparked by the fortieth and fiftieth anniversaries of the BPP. Given that the research and writing begin years, or in some cases decades, before a book's publication, we decided not to begin the "fourth phase" at the moment of the 40th anniversary. Instead, we selected 2010 as the starting point for the "fourth phase"—as a year halfway between the 40th and 50th anniversary of the BPP and one that saw a rise in publications on the BPP. This most recent period (2010–present) witnessed, by far, the greatest outpouring of scholarly writings on the BPP.[49] The writings by former Panthers continue to be autobiographical,[50] while also discussing self-narratives within larger historical and social contexts.[51] Children's fiction based on the BPP has also emerged.[52] In short, the now sizeable literature on the BPP includes scholarly monographs, edited volumes, memoirs, primary source documents, and photographs and artwork that create a complex narrative of the BPP that focuses on national and local histories, global contexts, self-defense philosophies and community survival programs, theoretical perspectives and grounded praxis, a gendered analysis and Panther women, and media portrayals and representations of the BPP.

An Overview of *Black Power Afterlives*

Black Power Afterlives picks up where the BPP's organizational history ends, after the closing of the BPP's Oakland Community School in 1982, and places a primary focus on the study of the ongoing impact of the BPP on today's social justice struggles. The book is not intended as a comprehensive study of all trajectories after the BPP. Instead, *Black Power Afterlives*, by design, examines less recognizable impacts of the BPP in the areas of Pan-African internationalism, environmental justice, and spiritual practices as a basis for social justice work while also studying the more familiar but nevertheless important post-Panther themes, notably prisons and policing, art and culture, and youth activism. The book further includes: a) lesser known Panthers as well as some of the most renowned members; b) an intentional focus on Panther women to counter the predominant focus on Panther men; and c) geographic range, even as there is a heavy focus on California and New York. The chapters in *Black Power Afterlives*, authored by former Panthers, activist-intellectuals, and academic scholars, contain a variety of formats, including essays, analytically oriented biographical essays examining the ongoing activism of former Black Panthers, and interviews. All chapters speak to the strong impact of BPP ideology or practices. We deemphasize nostalgic reflections on the BPP, but instead seek to explore the circuits, social networks, ideas, practices, and ongoing social movement activities that can trace a clear lineage from the BPP to later activism. We also explore creative tactics, strategies, and ideas that draw from the BPP, or deviate from them in productive ways, and experiences that help us think theoretically and practically about social justice organizing—always with an eye to the Panthers.

The essays in part 1, "The Persistence of the Panther," reveal the complexity of post-Panther activism through the lives of three former Panthers, Assata Shakur, Hank Jones, and Kiilu Nyasha. Teishan Latner examines a topic that has been scarcely studied—the life in exile of renowned revolutionary Assata Shakur. There were certainly challenges in conducting the research and in making decisions on what could be included, and what excluded, for the safety of Shakur, who lives in hiding in Cuba under a $2 million bounty from the state of New Jersey. Latner's article tackles the difficult topic of exile, the laments of one forced out of her community, and the ways Shakur has worked to retain her activist commitments in a country known for its revolutionary movement. Diane Fujino deploys W. E. B. Du Bois's concept of abolition democracy—requiring not just legal emancipation but the establishment of new institutions and new social relations to create a liberatory society—to frame the philosophy and activism of the San Francisco 8 Black Panther defendant Hank Jones. It is ironic that Jones, who spent time in clandestinity, would represent the building of community institutions, but this chapter raises questions that compel a discussion about the uses of violence and the meanings of fugitivity and confinement. Paradoxically, it was in spaces of confinement that Jones found the greatest reserves to fight for freedom and to strengthen his spiritual practices. Tina Bartolome's tender letters to the late Kiilu Nyasha, written posthumously to Nyasha, are revealing of the remarkable influence former Panthers have had on younger activists. In Bartolome's letters are discussions of support for political prisoners, the challenges of a lifelong physical disability, and the joys and struggles of writing and living a life of persistent activism.

Part 2, "Sustainability and Spirituality," addresses a little-studied area of post-Panther activism—the spiritual practices used to sustain one's activism and one's humanity as well as to heal the planet. In *The War Before*, former New York Panther Safiya Bukhari wrote a chapter titled, "We Too Are Veterans," that examines the connections between the sufferings experienced by soldiers in war to the traumas experienced by Black Panthers—what Bukhari viewed as a war for Black liberation against centuries of Black subjugation. To Bukhari, after witnessing the police shoot one of her comrades in the face, while a store manager and his son "stomped" another comrade to death "in front of my eyes," the traumas that she and other Panthers (and Black radicals generally) experienced was not unlike the flashbacks suffered by her brother, who was a veteran of the US war in Vietnam. Bukhari makes a convincing argument for the need to address the posttraumatic stress experienced by many Panthers.[53]

Perhaps more than any Panther, Ericka Huggins represents the excesses of police and FBI repression and the possibilities for healing and political sustenance through meditation and a spiritual practice. She is best known in the context of the murder of her husband John Huggins and Alprentice "Bunchy" Carter at UCLA on January 17, 1969, and four months later, for her arrest and subsequent trial with Bobby Seale in New Haven, Connecticut. The pain of her multiple traumas, especially the separation from her infant daughter, was nearly unbearable. In an interview with Diane Fujino, Huggins reveals the meanings of her spiritual practice, begun inside that Connecticut prison and practiced daily to the present, as a process not only of personal self-care but a "collective self-care" that requires one to attend to one's own healing and the collective struggle as intertwined and indispensable components of revolutionary justice work. Maryam Kashani's essay on former rank-and-file Panther Dhameera Ahmad shows the compatibility of a Muslim faith and radical politics—or rather for her, the essentialness of her faith to extending her post-Panther activism and support for political prisoners—and the ways her life challenges what gendered, racial, class- and religious-based justice movements look like.

Quincy Saul's powerful chapter on ecosocialism adds a different dimension of restoration—that of healing Mother Earth through a radical environmental justice movement that carries on in the legacy of the BPP's critique of racial capitalism and colonialism that, in Saul's formulation, underlie today's crises of climate catastrophe. Borrowing from former Panther Safiya Bukhari's statement that "the prisons of America were the universities of revolution" and Masanobu Fukuoka's statement that "gradually I came to realize that the process of saving the desert of the human heart and re-vegetating the desert is actually the same thing," Saul asserts provocative ideas about the role of prisoners and political prisoners in advancing the environmental justice movement and about the humanization that occurs through political struggle.

In part 3, "Sankofa: Pan-African Internationalism," *Black Power Afterlives* engages discussions of internationalism in ways that both reflect and diverge from the ideas of certain Panther leaders. The book calls attention to the fact that Black Panther activists did not adhere to a single ideology, nor did they follow any single trajectory after the BPP. There were, indeed, many paths in and many paths out. It is widely known that there were sharp ideological differences within the BPP. There were intense internal debates about whether to refocus on community survival programs in the aftermath of massive police and FBI repression or to continue the struggle for self-defense and even armed offensive strategies. And the New York Panthers expressed Black nationalism in their self-naming, dress, cultural expression, and politics to a much greater extent than did West Coast Panthers.

While largely absent from the BPP literature, a noteworthy minority of former Panthers adopted Pan-Africanist politics, particularly through the influence of Kwame Ture, whom top Panther leaders partnered with and then sharply criticized. In April 1970, Ture expressed that, "the highest political expression of Black Power is Pan-Africanism." In response, in September 1970, Huey Newton denounced Pan-Africanism as "the highest expression of cultural nationalism," arguing instead that "[t]he Black Panther Party is internationalist." Yet this is curious given that Ture was an internationalist and socialist—similar to Newton in many respects. In 1970, Ture framed Black oppression within the systems of "capitalism," "racism," and the conditions of the "settler colony," called for community control of political institutions and the development of an independent economic basis, and consistently argued for the intertwining of the problem of slavery in the US and colonialism in Africa. Ture, like Newton, further insisted that Black liberation be based on a unity of politics and not racial identity per se, calling for Third World solidarity with the people of Vietnam and opposed the "genocide against the traditional owners of the land." These ideas resonated with the BPP's ideology and created a basis for the movement of former Panthers into global Pan-Africanism.[54]

In part 3, Matef Harmachis examines the relationship and tensions between Black Power and Pan-Africanism through the lives of David Brothers, former chairman of the New York BPP, and Dedon Kamathi, former San Diego Panther, both of whom worked closely with Kwame Ture for decades in the All-African People's Revolutionary Party.[55] In doing so, he illuminates why these former Panthers view Pan-Africanism as "the highest political expression of Black Power." Diane Fujino studies the importance of African history and culture in the Pan-African art of former Sacramento Panther Akinsanya Kambon. She uses the concept of "fugitivity" to discuss the meanings of Kambon's literal and figurative escapes and marronage practices and his use of art to promote pan-African culture and consciousness as well as to heal from the traumas arising from his experiences as a US Marine in Vietnam and from the constancy of police harassment and violence since his Panther days.

Part 4, "Art, Revolution, and a Social Imaginary," examines the impact of the BPP on the cultural visualizations and sonic imaginings about what Black liberation looks like. The BPP iconography is popularly captured in the *Black Panther* movie, Beyonce's NFL Super Bowl halftime show, and the enduring fame of rappers like Tupac Shakur, son of Panthers Afeni Shakur and Billy Garland and stepson of political prisoner Mutulu Shakur. The impact of the BPP on music is widely recognized in the hip-hop lyrics and beats of KRS One, Digable Planets, and San Francisco-born rapper Paris who refers to himself as the "Black Panther of Hip-Hop" and invokes the Ten-Point Program in his piece "Panther Power." The BPP has impacted other sonic categories as well, including the martial arts operas of Fred Ho and the genre mashup of the Prophets of Rage, a band made up of members from Public Enemy, Rage Against the Machine, and Cypress Hill. The comic strip and TV cartoon character Huey Freeman in Aaron McGruder's *Boondocks* is an encomium to the BPP and its founder Huey P. Newton. Even Michael Jackson digitally appears as a feline black panther in his video for "Black or White" before he metaphorically joins in the destruction of Los Angeles after a jury acquitted the police officers in their brutal beating of Rodney King. Mary Hooks, in her interview for this volume, noted the significance of the "swag" that the Panthers brought to the movement in their walk and talk and dress and style. They inspired generations to imagine and see as possible the creation of a new society that values Black humanity and radical democracy for all and to participate in the struggle for liberation.

In contrast to the Panther's voluminous influence in hip-hop, this book addresses less visible influences of the BPP on art and culture. In the chapter on the former BPP minister of culture Emory Douglas, Diane Fujino examines the current global impact of Douglas's iconic Panther artwork, including with the Zapatistas in Southern Mexico, Aboriginal artists in Australia, and in support of Palestinian liberation. Fujino emphasizes the community-based nature of Douglas's art cocreation from his Panther days to the present, with his explicit acknowledgment of the ways his ideas and artwork emerges from the everyday experiences of Black people and from the revolutionary activity of the BPP and Black liberation struggles. Ben Barson, himself a musician, activist, and musicology scholar, examines the inspiration and influence of the BPP and of Black Power as vital to the development of

Fred Ho's avant-garde jazz and revolutionary politics and writings. Barson argues that "Ho's ability to defy the expectations of genre occurred precisely because he was driven by a vision of communally centered work inspired by the BPP, the Black Arts Movement, and the Asian American Movement" and further reveals the long history of continuities between Black and Asian American art and activism.

Part 5, "The Real Dragons Take Flight: On Prisons and Policing," explores one of the most visible arenas of post-Panther activism called into being by the FBI and police attacks on the BPP. In 1968 alone, the BPP reports that the police killed twenty-eight Panthers. In 1968 and 1969 the party paid $4,890,580 in bail following 739 arrests.[56] Many have written about the nefariousness of the FBI and police repression against the Panthers designed to destroy the BPP and discredit ideas that were increasingly popular among working-class Black communities and radical movements.[57] In the face of massive state repression and the imprisonment of scores of former Panthers and other radicals, former Panthers and younger activists have taken up the work to support and free incarcerated Panthers and other political prisoners, to work for prison abolitionism, and to protest anti-Black and racist policing and state violence, sparking today's Black Lives Matter and Movement for Black Lives struggles. The writings and broadcast journalism of former Philadelphia Panther Mumia Abu-Jamal, the most renowned US-held political prisoner, continues to shape the present movement's understanding of prisons and broader political analysis. Former Panthers such as Albert Woodfox, released in 2018 after forty-three years in solitary confinement, worked inside prison to stop violent attacks on prisoners and to assist prisoners with legal defense. Fred Hampton Jr., son of assassinated Chicago Black Panther Deputy Chairman Fred Hampton Sr. and Comrade Mother Akua Njeri, founded both the Prisoners of Conscience Committee and Black Panther Party Cubs to continue the work of the BPP. Through these and other efforts, 2018 alone saw the release of political prisoners former Panther Herman Bell and MOVE activists Debbie and Michael Africa.[58]

In this section, Sekou Odinga, former New York Panther released in 2014 after thirty-three years in prison, and déqui kioni-sadiki, member of the New York–based Black Panther Collective, offer their own biographical sketches to illuminate the indispensable influence of the BPP on their political ideas and activities and long-standing political prisoner support work. Matef Harmachis discusses the history and current work of Black August organizing in multiple US cities to recognize the killings by state apparatuses of numerous Black Power and prison activists in the month of August. Jalil Muntaqim, former Panther, current political prisoner, and inspiration for the Jericho rally in Washington, DC, in 1998, discusses the history of Jericho as a street demonstration and subsequent movement to free US-held political prisoners. joão costa vargas examines the activism of former Los Angeles Panther Michael Zinzun, whose lawsuit victory in the case of his own brutal beating by the police and whose work with the Los Angeles–based Coalition Against Police Abuse (CAPA) in the 1970s to 1990s provides a longer arc to the current movement against anti-Black police violence. vargas's chapter engages theoretical critiques of CAPA's work as prioritizing multicultural coalition building over analyses of Black autonomy and Black genocide in ways that diminish how the particular atrocities and animosities against Black people function differently from a rubric of racism against people of color. While offering the important framework of anti-Blackness, vargas's ideas contrast in ways with other essays in this book that examine the deployment of Black-centered but never Black-only analyses, the intertwining of nationalism and internationalism, and the possibilities for an analysis of Black genocide alongside Third World solidarity practices. Just as the BPP was not monolithic in its ideology, *Black Power Afterlives* includes varied ideas, which we hope will spark discussions and critiques that enable the advances in thinking and activism required in today's urgent struggles.

The last part, part 6, "Black Panther Legacies in a Time of Neoliberalism," explores the impact of the BPP on present-day activism. The part title acknowledges that today's organizing takes place in a different racialized political economy, with the welfare state of the 1960s and 1970s (including the War on Poverty office where Huey Newton and Bobby Seale wrote the Ten-Point Program) being replaced by neoliberal austerity. Even as it seems like nothing has changed, there have been both noteworthy gains and painful rollbacks such that the problems of anti-Black police violence, poverty, prisons, joblessness, and houselessness stayed the same or became worse, partly because of the funding of militarism over human services and the diminishing of ideas promoting public spaces and the communal good. But the hardships produced by neoliberalism have also motivated today's activists to revitalize and transform ideas about shared resources and to build collective institutions. So while we face many of the same problems as the Panthers did fifty years ago, we argue for both continuity and disruption of political conditions, ideas, and organizing praxis that require not only generalized and understandable laments ("nothing has changed") but also more precise analyses of the enduring influence of the Black Panthers as well as departures in theory and practice from the BPP.

In this section, Mary Hooks, codirector of SONG in Atlanta, in an interview with Diane Fujino and Felice Blake, advances the politics of Black queer feminism as the antidote to white supremacist heteropatriarchy in ways that build on and exceed the work of the BPP. She makes clear that it is one's politics and not one's pigment that forms the basis of Black liberation theory and practice. SONG seeks to build an "ecosystem" that connects the multiple issues of local, national, and international movements, one that borrows from and critiques the long struggles in the Black radical tradition. Yoel Haile in his examination of the African Black Coalition's work on numerous California college campuses shows the ongoing influence of the BPP and Black Power on Black student organizing today as well as the ways students translated that into specific campaigns and achievements. Blake Simmons explores his own family lineage from a former Panther and the ways the BPP in general shaped his work as a former student activist and a current community organizer in Oakland. Alex Tom's discussion of the Chinese Progressive Association in San Francisco extends the BPP's influence into the Chinese American community, noting the ways the Panther legacy directly impacts an Afro-Asian solidarity, while also provoking seeming contradictions in work around immigration rights with Chinese immigrant elders and queer rights with Chinese American youth.

Black Power Afterlives is unique in offering a multifaceted examination of the enduring impact of the Black Panther Party shaping a new iteration of Black liberation and beyond. By deploying a "useable past" that informs present organizing and visions of a new future, the intervention of this book is more important than ever given the urgency of the current moment and the development of the largest, most profound, and vibrant social movements since the sixties. The book asks that we not simply evoke the BPP for inspiration or nostalgic remembrances of an earlier time, but that we engage in a serious study of the ongoing activism of former Panthers and the BPP-inspired work of current-day organizers, so that we can build on and advance the past to create a better present and future. The Black Panthers would ask no less of us.

I.

THE PERSISTENCE OF THE PANTHER

Melanie Cervantes and Jesus Barraza of Dignidad Rebelde, a graphic arts collaboration of Oakland-based artists, created this poster in 2013 to protest the state of New Jersey's increased bounty for the return to the United States of Assata Shakur in exile in Cuba.

CHAPTER ONE

Assata Shakur:
The Political Life of Political Exile

Teishan A. Latner

I n early summer of 2005, Assata Shakur moved out of her two-story home in Havana, in whose backyard garden she had tended tropical flowers and grown collard greens and, for the second time in her life, disappeared from public view. On the evening of May 10, Fidel Castro had appeared on Cuban television and denounced the actions of the FBI and the New Jersey State Police, which had announced a reward of $1 million for information leading to the apprehension of Shakur, Cuba's best known US political asylee.[1] Newspapers in the United States reproduced translated portions of the speech. "They wanted to portray her as a terrorist, something that was an injustice, a brutality, an infamous lie," the Cuban president affirmed, referring to Shakur as a victim of "the fierce repression against the black movement in the United States" and "a true political prisoner."[2]

A former member of the Black Panther Party and the Black Liberation Army, Shakur had lived in political exile in Cuba since 1984, where she had been known within the intellectual circles of various research institutes throughout Havana for her insights into US political life and her connections with US Black radical movements, and where she had been a frequent speaker to delegations of visiting American students, academics, and solidarity activists. Although Shakur and her contacts in the Cuban government had long been aware of the danger of bounty hunters enticed by the reward—the May 2005 announcement represented a tenfold increase from the previous

$100,000, active since 1998—she had managed to live a semblance of a normal life in Havana, where her phone number and home address had once been listed in the telephone book, and where she had regularly been seen at public events throughout the city. Now, all this would change. Living at undisclosed locations for the indefinite future, Shakur would now be protected directly by the Cuban government's security apparatus. Limited in her ability to move freely and with little contact with her friends and family, Shakur now lived in an exile within an exile.

In the long afterlife of the Black Panther Party, few living figures descending from the Black Power era occupy as prominent a place within the radical imagination as Assata Shakur. Due in part to the enduring critical success of her 1987 autobiography, *Assata*, Shakur remains one of the best-known living Black radical activists among today's younger generations. Convicted of killing a New Jersey state trooper in 1973 despite significant evidence of her innocence, Shakur was sentenced to life in prison in 1977 by an all-white jury during a heavily politicized trial. To police, it was a long-awaited victory: a conviction, albeit on scant evidence, after six prior legal cases against her on unrelated charges in the State of New York had resulted in acquittals by trial juries or were dismissed by courts, with an additional trial resulting in a hung jury.[3] To many observers, the unrelenting legal charges brought against Shakur, who had become one of the most visible faces of clandestine Black liberation struggle, was emblematic of state repression against radical activists, and of the virulence of "COINTELPRO," the FBI's Counter Intelligence Program, whose targeting of left-wing movements had been exposed by antiwar activists in Media, Pennsylvania, in 1974, but was suspected to have continued under other auspices.[4] Shakur's legal persecution was known in Cuba, prompting the state-run *Granma*, Cuba's largest newspaper, to describe her as a "political prisoner" the year of her sentencing.[5] Liberated in 1979 from a New Jersey prison by comrades in an audacious, carefully planned prison break that made headlines and unleashed a national dragnet, Shakur attained folk hero status among supporters, who framed her as a refugee from anti-Black political persecution. Surfacing in Cuba five years later, she was granted political asylum, joining approximately a dozen other American political exiles living on the island.[6]

Yet while Shakur remains a powerful symbol of resistance to anti-Black police repression, COINTELPRO, mass incarceration, and the afterlives of slavery, the full dimensions of her significance as a historical figure have often been obscured. Little has been written about Shakur's life in Cuba, and the nature of her time in exile, now enduring for more than three decades, is not widely known. The iconography surrounding Shakur is largely derived from her political acts, real and alleged, prior to her arrival in Cuba, and her autobiography devotes only seven pages of its postscript to her life on the island. As a result, the significance of Shakur's exile, in which the trajectory of her political life as a Black woman revolutionary has become intermingled with the complex political project of the Cuban Revolution and its historical confrontation with US global power, is often overlooked. This chapter provides a brief portrait of Shakur's political life in exile in Cuba, paying particular attention to the resonance between the internationalist legacy of the Black Panther Party and the praxis of her political engagement on the island. Examining the period from 1984, when Shakur arrived in Cuba, to May 2005, when she withdrew from public sight and, by all accounts, became unable to participate in direct political activity, this chapter explores the routes through which Shakur sought to maintain her political commitments in exile.

It should be noted that this brief rendering of Shakur's life in exile is conspicuously incomplete. The tenacity of the US government's efforts to secure her return to prison, together with the Cuban state's protection of her as political asylee, pose unique methodological challenges. Shakur cannot be contacted by researchers, much less interviewed, and she has been unable to speak publicly since 2013. Her safety is regarded as a matter of state security by the Cuban government, which has acted accordingly, protecting her with formidable layers of security and secrecy. With the increase of the FBI and New Jersey State Police reward to $2 million in May 2013—the fortieth anniversary of the New Jersey Turnpike shooting—US pressure on Cuba increased.[7] Due to both the diplomatic ramifications of Cuba's provision of political asylum to Shakur and the intensity with which the US has sought to achieve her extradition through state diplomacy and monetary enticement, the question of her political asylum has historically been enormously politically sensitive.

While Shakur's protection constitutes a high priority for Cuba's government, which remains, as of this writing, committed to ensuring the security of Shakur and other remaining US political exiles as a matter of political principle, the Cuban state has simultaneously been keenly aware of the diplomatic repercussions vis-à-vis Washington. Indeed, the status of the US political asylees in Cuba has long been imbricated within US-Cuba relations. Washington has repeatedly attempted to make the return of the US political asylees in Cuba, including Shakur, Nehanda Abiodun, Víctor Manuel Gerena, Charlie Hill, and William Morales, a key requirement for the full normalization of relations, with Shakur's extradition always assuming the greatest priority for US negotiators.[8] There is no evidence that the Cuban government has ever succumbed to these diplomatic overtures, despite frequent speculation, false claims, and misleading media reports, and Cuban officials have repeatedly reaffirmed their commitment to protecting Shakur and the other US political exiles.[9] Nonetheless, a cloud of wariness hovers over the topic in Havana, making it an intensely fraught area of research.

This essay is therefore a tentative historical sketch, constructed from available sources. It does not presume to speak for Shakur, who has the right to speak for herself. Rather, it is intended to generate greater understanding about the nature of Shakur's political exile, with the hope that she will one day be free: free to tell her own story publicly and free to engage the world on her own terms. Moreover, this chapter contains certain silences and omissions, some due to the unavailability of source information and others intentional. The practice of critical scholarship, and of historical writing in particular, in which the past is analyzed and interpreted is, at times, in direct contradiction with efforts to ensure that those who hope to send Shakur back to prison will never be successful.

Political Life in Exile

The Cuban cultural theorist Roberto Zurbano, a researcher on themes related to race and identity in Havana and a friend of Shakur's, notes that US political exiles in Cuba such as Shakur and Nehanda Abiodun fought continually to avoid "political death" in exile, in which a revolutionary or activist is unable to maintain their political commitments and lapses into a permanent state of apathy, despair, or inactivity.[10] Shakur's clandestine arrival in Cuba in 1984 signaled the end of her former political life and the beginning of a new one. The Cuban government, assuming the role of a surrogate state guardian, provided Shakur with housing and a living stipend, and assigned to her a staff person tasked with liaising with the Cuban government and ensuring that her needs were met as she adjusted to life in Cuban society. According to Shakur, her priorities during the early months and years in Cuba centered on adjusting to life in Havana, learning Spanish, reuniting with her daughter, who had been born in prison, and writing her memoirs.[11] Shakur also enrolled in graduate studies at the Escuela Superior del Partido

Comunista de Cuba, a specialized university institute affiliated with Cuba's Communist Party, where she received a master's degree, and where she began her association with members of the Comité Central, the central committee of Cuba's Communist Party, the nation's highest political body.[12] The Cuban government helped facilitate these aims and placed upon Shakur no requirement to participate in any political activity, nor did it limit her associations with either Cubans or foreign visitors to the island.[13]

Shakur's political engagement from exile in Cuba assumed several broad forms. Shakur authored a number of statements for public audiences, including political communiqués and open letters, in ways that represented a continuation of her communications from prison and while "underground" as she eluded capture by US law enforcement after her escape. She granted interviews to foreign journalists in Cuba, taking advantage of these opportunities to communicate her ideas and defend her positions to a global audience. She granted interviews to visiting left-wing activists and intellectuals, using these forums as a means through which to communicate with political movements and communities in the US, particularly the Black radical left. She met with visiting political delegations from the US such as the Venceremos Brigade and Pastors for Peace, to which she gave presentations or held informal discussions with participants. She advocated on behalf of US political prisoners remaining behind bars, including Mumia Abu-Jamal, Marilyn Buck, Sekou Odinga, and Mutulu Shakur. And she worked with the Cuban government in the capacity of an informal adviser of issues of race and the Black freedom struggle in the US. As Shakur's exile in Cuba progressed, her political work evolved with it, incorporating Cuban sensibilities and aspects of the nation's singular revolutionary identity and historical memory, particularly its ethos of internationalism and anti-imperialism. Nonetheless, Shakur's new political life preserved many elements of her former identity in the United States, one that had been shaped in significant ways by her participation in the Black Panther Party and its clandestine offshoot, the Black Liberation Army.[14]

A Panther in Cuba

The resonance between the internationalism of the Black Panther Party, which discursively linked the varied freedom struggles of African Americans to those of oppressed people globally, and that of the Cuban Revolution, which situated Cuba's historical impulse for national self-determination within the history of the wider decolonizing world, and which envisioned the Caribbean nation's presence in the world as one of solidarity with the poorest and most vulnerable, has been the subject of much scholarship.[15] Moreover, the mutual embrace between the Panthers and Cuba's revolutionary leadership was itself rooted in the fertile ground of earlier political engagements between African American activists and Cuba. The Cuban government's provision of formal asylum to Robert F. Williams in 1961, for instance, had done much to make Cuba visible to US Black radical activists as a potential sanctuary from political repression, even after Williams abandoned Cuba for China after becoming disillusioned with the Cuban leadership.[16] The multiracial Fair Play for Cuba Committee, with which Williams had been affiliated along with a number of prominent African American intellectuals, had defended Cuba in the US public sphere against mounting US hostility in part by contrasting the Cuban government's efforts to promote racial equality on the island with the Kennedy administration's tepid support of the civil rights movement and the continuation of Jim Crow and anti-Black terrorism in the American South.[17] The Cuban government's work with boxer Joe Louis to encourage African American tourism to Cuba beginning in 1959 had been premised on the Cuban government's claims to have eliminated racial discrimination through desegregation, and itself drew upon prerevolutionary encounters between African Americans and Cuba during the previous decades.[18] Coming at the height of the sixties era of Black freedom struggle, engagements between Cuba and the Black Panthers at the end of the decade therefore drew upon a longer US Black radical gaze toward Cuba, the Caribbean, and the Third World.

Certainly too there were dis-affinities: the Black nationalism of the Panthers, however internationalist and embracing of coalitional politics, nevertheless remained somewhat in contradiction to Cuba's historical emphasis on a multiracial nationalism, which sought to unite all Cubans in the pursuit of "raceless" national self-determination, subsuming or repressing Black political demands within a larger multiracial nationalist project.[19] Nonetheless, the Black Panther Party, among all the large formations within the milieu of the African American freedom struggles of the long sixties era, was among the best suited for collaboration with Cuba's revolutionary project because of a range of parallel political commitments. Both shared an internationalist orientation and a commitment to principles of decolonization and Third World national self-determination. Both adhered to variants of Marxism and identified as socialist, despite their different understandings of its theory and practice. Both were explicitly antiracist, even if their analysis of the nature of race oppression grew from very different historical circumstances. Both shared commitments to opposing US imperialism, particularly the unfolding horror of the US war in Vietnam, itself situated within a longer history of US Cold War and colonial interventions. Both believed in the right of oppressed peoples to deploy political violence in the service of their liberation, even if in Cuba's case it had taken the form of direct participation in revolutionary and anticolonial movements throughout the Third World, while the Black Panthers' deployment of violence was almost entirely symbolic and vernacular, not actualized.[20] Finally, Cuba and the United States were geographically close, unlike the United States and China, Algeria, and Vietnam, with which the Panthers also established political connections, leading some Panthers to perceive Cuba as an attractive destination for political asylum, including Huey Newton and Eldridge Cleaver, both of whom obtained sanctuary there years before Shakur's arrival.[21]

Although Shakur's treatment of her life in Cuba in *Assata* is brief, it nonetheless provides a reference point through which to understand her early impressions of Cuban society upon arriving as a political asylee in 1984. These impressions confirm that the Cuban Revolution, which she had admired prior to her exile, continued to embody for her key elements of the Black Panther Party's political platform, particularly during the organization's later years, when the party began to emphasize its "survival programs" in the arenas of community health, nutrition, and education. Like the Cuban Revolution's socialist conceptualization of housing, education, and health care as universal human rights—not the social services, often for-profit, of a liberal but capitalist democracy—the Panther's community programs were rooted in revolutionary theory that framed them, as Joshua Bloom and Waldo E. Martin have noted, as "part of a broader insurgency to change the American capitalist system into a more equitable socialist one."[22]

Urban poverty and the spatial consequence of institutional racism are recurrent themes in *Assata*, and her descriptions of Havana at the close of her memoir stand in stark relief to the book's earlier descriptions of US cities. Contrasting urban development in Havana and Manhattan, for instance, Shakur notes that the new buildings being erected in Cuba are "schools, apartment houses, clinics, hospitals, and day care centers," not the "exclusive condominiums or luxury office buildings" of New York.[23] Socialism was clearly visible in Havana, creating on a large scale what the Panthers had sought to implement at the community level. "Medical care, dental care, and hospital visits are free," she observed. "Schools at all educational levels are free. Rent is no more than about ten percent of salaries. There are no taxes— no income, city, federal, or state taxes."[24] These early portrayals of Cuban society in Shakur's writing from exile are confirmed and deepened in her subsequent interviews and public statements, which repeatedly affirm the value of Cuba's socialist achievements in providing for human needs, despite the effects of the US embargo.[25]

Shakur's early impressions of Havana, as described in *Assata*, similarly confirm that the internationalist strains of her political consciousness, already shaped by her formative years as a student activist and honed during her time in the Black Panther Party and Black Liberation Army, had become far more prominent as a result of her immersion in her new adoptive country, deeply influencing her political commitments. The brief postscript in *Assata* about her arrival in Cuba is immediately preceded by a paragraph describing the role of internationalism within the larger struggle for Black liberation. "Any community seriously concerned with its own freedom," Shakur writes, "has to be concerned about other peoples' freedom as well. . . . Imperialism is an international system of exploitation, and, we, as revolutionaries, need to be internationalists to defeat it."[26] The following section of the book's text notes the consequences of US policy in the Third World amid the Cold War at the hands of the US and its allies, including "death squads in El Salvador," the "bombing of hospitals in Nicaragua," and "Namibian children who had survived massacres," arguing that "too many people in the u.s. support death and destruction without being aware of it."[27] Echoing the Panthers' commitment to rendering visible the linkages between local and global systems of oppressive state power, these sketches of Havana in the final pages of *Assata* suggest linearity between her prior life of Black internationalist freedom struggle in the US and anti-imperialist socialism in Cuba.

As Shakur's Cuban exile lengthened into years and then decades, the resonance between the internationalism of the Black Panther Party and that of the Cuban Revolution remained a recurrent theme in Shakur's public statements to reporters and foreign solidarity and academic delegations. Meeting with a visiting delegation of the humanitarian organization Pastors for Peace in November 2000, for instance, Shakur's comments suggested that for her, Cuban society continued to exemplify many of the ideals of the Panthers. "I was a member of the Black Panther Party, and we used to say, 'Power to the People,'" Shakur told the sixty Pastors for Peace delegates, "but here in Cuba is where I've seen that put into practice, where I've seen that internalized by people in such a way that people feel empowered to build this planet and to change it. And to contribute and feel privileged to do that. Feel that when they go to sleep at night that all is not in vain. There is some sense in living on this planet. That there is some beauty in constructing something better and giving to other people . . . It's another way of looking at the world and another way of living on this planet."[28]

Activism in Exile

Shakur's political praxis in Cuba occurred through both her independent work and through her collaborations with government-sponsored educational and political entities. Working regularly with the Cuban Institute for Friendship Among the Peoples (ICAP), meeting with visiting solidarity and academic delegations from the US or giving presentations to them, Shakur became a small but important part of Cuba's foreign relations with US social movements. ICAP was founded in 1960 to facilitate solidarity and goodwill between Cuba and its global allies and to counteract US attempts to isolate Cuba from the international community, a significant part of its work centered upon the coordination of the innumerable solidarity delegations arriving from abroad, many of these delegations composed of foreign leftists, including US Americans, who traveled to Cuba to learn about Cuban society and contribute to the revolution's social programs through volunteer work. The largest US solidarity delegations to Cuba were organized by the Venceremos Brigade, launched in 1969 as an anti-imperialist travel and political education initiative that provided an avenue for US activists to travel to Cuba, in intentional violation of the US travel ban, to assess Cuban socialism and take a public stand in opposition to the embargo.[29] From then on, the delegations traveled to Cuba every summer, where itineraries sometimes included presentations and informal discussions with US political exiles living in Cuba. These exiles, including William Lee Brent, a member of the Black Panther Party from Oakland, California, who had hijacked a commercial airliner to Cuba in 1969; Michael Finney, a member of the Republic of New Afrika (RNA) who had hijacked an airliner from New Mexico to Cuba, and his comrade, Charlie Hill, a Vietnam veteran and member of the RNA; and Nehanda Abiodun, a member of the Black Liberation Army and RNA who had come to Cuba in 1990, met with the Venceremos Brigade repeatedly, sharing their experiences living in Cuban society and their perspectives on the US movement.[30]

Shakur's meetings with the Venceremos Brigade appear to have left powerful impressions on participants from the group from 1987 to 2004. Shakur met regularly with contingents of the organization or made herself available for informal conversations with members of the group when it visited Havana. Just a year after Shakur's presence in Cuba was publicly confirmed to the outside world by a *Newsday* reporter, the legendary political activist Yuri Kochiyama, herself a longtime advocate on behalf of US political prisoners, traveled to Cuba as a member of the Venceremos Brigade. There participants met Shakur, whom Kochiyama described as "the highly esteemed, recognized folk hero, Black revolutionary. . . . Seeing Shakur and her daughter looking well and strong was heartwarming."[31] Members of subsequent Venceremos Brigade delegations often recalled group meetings and informal encounters with Shakur, in which she answered questions about Cuba and shared her thoughts on the US movement, as experiences of great personal significance. My own brief encounter with Shakur occurred in this manner in 2004, as a member of the Venceremos Brigade, while attending a public event in Havana about health care and human rights organized in association with Pastors for Peace. Shakur, who was also attending the event, embraced us and graciously answered questions about her life in Havana, revealing that she was working part-time as a translator and continuing to write a sequel to her autobiography, and permitted the group to take photographs with her. In the evening, as a Cuban salsa band took the stage and the Cubans and foreigners in the audience mingled and drank mojitos, Shakur and a small group of friends spent the evening by the side of the stage, dancing and looking relaxed and happy.

Shakur's praxis of freedom struggle in exile has been visible in other ways, some of which broaden conventional notions of activist practice. While exile foreclosed prior avenues for political engagement, forced separation from her US community enabled new opportunities to reflect upon the psychology of oppression and resistance. Prompted by an interviewer in 2000 to describe the extent to which she had been able to "continue being the political person you were in the United States," Shakur's response focused not upon traditional political struggle, but upon recovery from it. "For me personally Cuba has been a healing place. When I first got here I had no sense that I had to heal or anything. When you're struggling for your life and you're in the midst of things, you don't feel all the blows."[32] Shakur's observation echoes others who have sought to understand the psychic wounds inflicted by white supremacy and oppression, from Frantz Fanon to James Baldwin, as well as

Audre Lorde, whose much-quoted exhortation of self-care as "self-preservation," and therefore "an act of political warfare" suggested that self-healing was integral to sustaining political struggle.[33] As Shakur noted, "The obvious racism before had affected me, and in addition to that, prison, torture . . . my whole life had created wounds, scars in me that in Cuba I was able to find a space to begin to heal."[34] Asked by a reporter from *Essence* magazine a decade after her arrival in Cuba what life had been like for her in Cuba, Shakur replied that she had been able to "rest. . . . Being in Cuba has allowed me to live in a society that is not at war with itself. . . . Political struggle has always been a 24-hour-a-day job for me. I felt I could never take time out for myself. Now I feel I owe it to myself to develop in ways I've been putting off all my life. I'm crafting a vision of my life that involves creativity. And Cuban society allows me to do this. I know it's harder in the US where so many people are just grateful to have a job."[35]

For the US political exiles in Cuba, radical praxis sometimes drew as much upon the nurturing of intentional communities of struggle as it did from traditional political activism. While forced exile had severed some of the ties that had bound Shakur to the US environs in which she had lived and struggled, it opened others. Like US political exile Nehanda Abiodun, who mentored visiting US students and Cuban hip-hop artists in the late 1990s and throughout the 2000s, Shakur also developed informal mentoring relationships and friendships with Cuban youth and with US students, artists, and activists visiting Havana. For several years in late November, the beginning of a holiday season that often left US exiles in Cuba feeling particularly vulnerable to homesickness and the pain of separation from family and loved ones, Abiodun and the students, often joined by Shakur, organized gatherings on the third Thursday of the month. Nostalgic for the community and seasonal flavors of home but with no intention of reifying a holiday rooted in genocide, they playfully dubbed the yearly gatherings "anti-imperialist thanksgivings," celebrating them with Cuban and US friends and comrades. Featuring American-style Thanksgiving fare prepared by Abiodun, the menu was cobbled together from what was available in Cuban markets, supplemented by North American ingredients such as cans of cranberry sauce brought by visiting US friends. On one occasion, ICAP hosted the event, which drew two hundred US, Cuban, and foreign guests.[36] Through this mixed milieu of visiting foreigners and Cubans, Shakur's radical community in exile took shape in myriad small acts of solidarity and camaraderie.

Focus on the Carceral State

Despite the distance imposed by exile, the impact of Shakur's life and words continue to be felt within the contemporary iteration of the historical movement against anti-Black and racist police violence. In the United States, activists in the Black Lives Matter (BLM) movement have read lines from Shakur's poetry at street protests and donned T-shirts featuring the words "Assata Taught Me," and BLM cofounder Alicia Garza has repeatedly invoked Shakur's 1973 public statement, "To My People," in her organizing work.[37] To many activists, the arc of Shakur's political life, embodying struggle, hope, resistance, and triumph over confinement and police terror, continues to serve a powerful symbolic purpose.[38]

These deployments of Shakur's words and iconography within contemporary political struggles echo older engagements between Shakur and movements for prison abolition. In September 1998, as activists and scholars converged in Berkeley, California, for the historic Critical Resistance conference organized at the height of the Clinton era of imprisonment to draw attention to the escalating crisis of mass incarceration, Shakur sent a public statement of solidarity that linked the incarceration apparatus in the United States to intertwined legacies of white supremacy, capitalism, colonization, and slavery. "The Prison-Industrial Complex is not only a mechanism to convert public tax money into profits for private corporations," she wrote, "it is an essential element of modern neo-liberal capitalism. It serves two purposes. One to neutralize and contain huge segments of potentially rebellious sectors of the population, and two, to sustain a system of super-exploitation, where mainly black and Latino captives are imprisoned in white rural, overseer communities."[39]

As a number of scholars have noted, Black prisoners played key roles in elevating the issue of incarceration and political imprisonment in public consciousness, making it a central feature of the African American freedom struggle and broader radical left during the long civil rights and Black power eras.[40] Shakur's relatively early recognition of the crisis of mass incarceration in the late 1990s United States and its links to racial capitalism, an analysis that was probably enriched by her contact with US activists and intellectuals well before the issue became a focus of mainstream civil rights organizations during the presidency of Barack Obama, foreshadowed the adoption of her iconography and words by activists in movements against incarceration and police brutality in the 2000s, a movement that achieved unprecedented visibility and mainstream awareness with the rise of the Black Lives Matter movement in 2013.

Perhaps the most consistent theme in Shakur's political work from exile has been her advocacy on behalf of US political prisoners. Shakur maintained close ties with former comrades affiliated with the Black Liberation Army and Black Panther Party and repeatedly called for the release of imprisoned US political prisoners and prisoners of war.

Exile within Exile

Shakur's sustained personal engagement with social movements in the United States, together with her presence within Havana's intellectual and political milieus, and within broader activist and intellectual communities of struggle, was not to last. With the FBI's announcement in 2005 that the reward for information leading to her extradition to the US had been raised to $1 million, fears for Shakur's safety necessitated her retreat from public life in Cuba, effectively severing her contact with US social justice movements at the height of the George W. Bush era and the global "war on terror." Shakur's isolation increased in 2013 with the raising of the reward to an extraordinary $2 million for her "safe return," and the FBI's cynical designation of her as a "most wanted terrorist," inaugurating an indefinite period of heightened vigilance for those in Cuba tasked with protecting her from bounty hunters.[41] Shakur now entered a period of almost total isolation, including from most friends and loved ones, with whom she was now able to communicate only through Cuban government security staff. A 2015 statement bearing her name, although few of the hallmarks of her political analysis and writing style, entitled "Listen up! The European is not your friend," ostensibly written by Shakur in solidarity with the "Rhodes must fall" protest movement in South Africa, which sought to remove statues of British colonial politician Cecil Rhodes, is likely fraudulent and appears to have been written by someone impersonating Shakur.[42]

Nehanda Abiodun, a US political exile living in Cuba and one of Shakur's longtime comrades and friends, recalls the last time she saw her prior to 2013. Abiodun was hosting a dinner at a private house for a visiting political delegation from the US, a group that included a former US political prisoner, a respected radical archivist, and a former member of the Black Panther Party's inner leadership, together with a group of US medical students studying on scholarship at Havana's Latin American School of Medicine. As the group ate plates of rice and curried chicken, a knock came at the door. To the surprise and happiness of the group, it was Shakur, who had arrived unannounced for security reasons. In the years after the first $1 million reward of 2005, Shakur and Abiodun had talked by telephone nearly every weekend, giving the two a chance to catch up even if personal meetings were no longer feasible. After the second $1 million reward of 2013, the calls ended. From then on, the two friends communicated only intermittently, via the government security personnel protecting Shakur.[43]

Once a familiar face in Havana's public sphere, Shakur now lived in the shadows. US political exile Charlie Hill recalls seeing Shakur in early 2005 at the funeral for Hill's former RNA comrade, Michael Finney, who had died following a struggle with cancer. Speaking before those assembled about her friendship with Finney, she then accompanied the group to the sea, where she helped spread his ashes. A few months later, with the FBI's May announcement of the increased bounty and her addition to the list of "domestic terrorists," Hill wondered whether he would ever see Shakur again. However, several years later, while walking along a quiet street one day, Hill was startled to come almost face to face with Shakur, disguised and virtually unrecognizable, as she walked in the opposite direction, although not alone.[44] Other friends of Shakur encountered her after 2005 under similarly covert circumstances. Joining Shakur in a car one afternoon, with plain-clothes security personnel present, one friend was driven around Havana with her before parking on a quiet street facing the city's winding sea-side promenade, El Malecón, where the two shared a beer and talked. Then the car dropped him off on a side street and drove away, leaving him pained and wondering how Shakur, apparently cut off from many of her comrades and friends, was able to cope with the social isolation of a double exile.[45]

While Shakur has suffered as a result of political persecution, imprisonment, and forced exile, her more recent isolation in Cuba for reasons of security amid US efforts to engineer her extradition has perhaps been a less recognized loss for the US social justice movements that have been influenced by her life and words, movements that have been unable to maintain contact with her after her disappearance from the public sphere. What remains is a formidable Black revolutionary iconography, one that offers a set of images and narratives that have significant radical pedagogical power, yet sometimes work to obscure Shakur herself. As Joy James has observed, "Assata Shakur's power as a narrator of black struggles and freedom movements [has] become eclipsed itself as she evolved, along with the BPP, into an icon. The reified thing, the icon, replaces the dynamic human being who changes her mind, her practices, her desires as a living entity."[46] This is not to suggest that Shakur has strayed from her convictions and political commitments. None who know her seem to be able to imagine that possibility. Asked in the summer 2018 what she would like to say about Shakur for this chapter, Nehanda Abiodun, who had managed to maintain intermittent contact with Shakur, spoke unequivocally: "If I can say one thing, it is that Assata absolutely remains a revolutionary. She is still completely committed to the principles of anti-imperialism, Black freedom, internationalism, and the liberation of all people everywhere. Even though she is mostly cut off from the world, she has never backed down, she has never given up."[47]

Today's activists would undoubtedly benefit from Shakur's perspectives and unique vantage point as a Black woman political exile, a revolutionary and a former political prisoner who has survived, and even thrived, in Cuba for more than thirty years, making herself a unique asset to Cuba's revolution through her commitment to the ideals of freedom and justice for Black people and for oppressed and poor people the world over. The lack of avenues for dialogue between Shakur and the US social justice formations that have embraced her iconography and words, such as the Black Lives Matter movement, have foreclosed important opportunities for dialogue and comparative reflection that might illuminate important concerns related to people of African descent in both Cuba and the United States, particularly concerning the nature of race, poverty, gender, incarceration, policing, and education, which have unfolded in Cuba and the United States amid very different historical and political conditions, yet have points of mutual legibility.

Shakur's political sanctuary in Cuba, a Caribbean nation with a singularly unique place in the revolutionary history of the Americas and the modern world, remains an under-explored avenue through which to understand the legacies of the Black Power era within an international context. Cuba retains significant aspects of its internationalist, socialist, and anti-imperialist heritage, even as the country continues to undergo changes after the "special period" of the 1990s, and even as daily life for most Cubans remains materially precarious amid the weak economy, dampening the populace's once palpable revolutionary fervor. Shakur's political exile, which has merged her trajectory as a revolutionary activist within the historical arc of the US Black freedom struggle with Cuba's revolutionary history, remains a vitally important point of intersection between these two significant forces of the twentieth century whose effects continue to reverberate today.

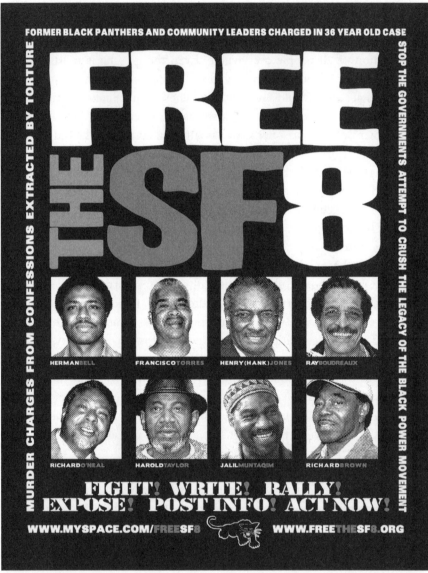

A poster created for the campaign to gain the release of the former Panthers targeted as the San Francisco 8 in 2007, reopening a cold case from the 1970s. The defendants, their lawyers, and supporters worked not only to win the legal case but also to expose the policies of the FBI's counterintelligence program, which used illegal tactics in efforts to terminate the Black Panther Party and other activist groups. Courtesy of the Freedom Archives

CHAPTER TWO

"We Had Our Own Community": Hank Jones, Spaces of Confinement, and a Vision of Abolition Democracy

Diane C. Fujino

H ank Jones's entire life has been shaped in the historic struggles of Black people stretching from Mississippi to California. The brutality of racism in segregated Mississippi and the contradictions of living in the alleged paradise of postwar California established the foundations of his worldview. But even in Depression-era Mississippi, Jones's memories are also filled with being loved and cared for by his family as well as by a nurturing Black community desiring to—and forced to—support one another for survival. The lessons he learned about mutual support and collectivity in his small rural town of New Albany later found resonance for him in the grassroots struggles to secure the freedoms that Black people had long fought for, but that had been continuously denied or turned back. Like today's youth animated by anti-Black violence, he found himself propelled into action by the brutal murder of Emmett Till. That incident produced a burning rage in him that in the early 1960s compelled him to organize with the Student Nonviolent Coordinating Committee (SNCC) and then the Black Panther Party (BPP).

Paradoxically, it was in spaces of confinement that Jones found the greatest reserves to fight for freedom. In the aftermath of 9/11 sweeps of '60s-era radicals, he and seven other former Panthers, known as the San Francisco 8 (SF8), were arrested for a three-decade-old unsolved police killing. Though little discussed in the Black Power literature, he relied on a growing spirituality and introspective meditation to fortify his political resolve while in prison. Spurred by the FBI's actions and a grand jury investigation of the SF8, Jones reconstituted his political activism to expose the FBI's counterintelligence program used against the BPP and the SF8. In 2007, he spent nine months in jail, all of it in isolation, before the court reduced his bail. The charges were later dropped and he was released a free man. But for Jones, it was never enough to be "free" in a society premised on domination and genocide. It was not justice to win his case but leave in place the conditions of structural oppression that created the situation of mass incarceration with prisons disproportionately filled with working-class Black and brown people. He was resisting the racism that Ruth Wilson Gilmore articulated as "the state-sanctioned or extralegal production and exploitation of group-differentiated vulnerability to premature death."[1]

Jones's dissatisfaction with being released from prison into the unfreedom of society invokes a desire for the abolition democracy called forth by W. E. B. Du Bois in *Black Reconstruction*. To the newly freed, it was not sufficient to gain legal emancipation into a society founded and built on "a vision not of work, but of wealth; not of planned accomplishment but of power."[2] The newly emancipated were released into a society premised on what Du Bois called "the American Assumption" that wealth was created through individual effort and that anyone through thrift and hard work could gain upward mobility. The brilliance of this narrative is its erasure of the structural oppression that produces and reproduces Black subordination across time and form. While the American Assumption's ideology ostensibly applies to all, its benefits were disproportionately blocked to Blacks. So at the moment of their greatest hope for freedom, at the formal ending of slavery, their liberation was betrayed by the implementation of Black codes and lynchings, the removal of federal protections, and the creation of a new slavery and a new subordination in the form of sharecropping and convict leasing.[3] More than a century later, the massive rise of the prison population, disproportionately Black and poor, reveals prisons as the new form of slavery and "the new Jim Crow," as Michelle Alexander observes. It was precisely the contradictions in the Thirteenth Amendment—which made "slavery" and "involuntary servitude" illegal, "except as a punishment for crime whereof the party shall have been duly convicted"—that created in Jones the need for abolition democracy. To him, laws and the legal system, while an area of necessary struggle, were severely constricted by the establishment system and thus required the cocreation of the kinds of democracy institutions and community structures that allowed for the possibility of a society premised on the ideals of justice and liberation to actually enact such freedoms.[4]

In this chapter, I am making the argument that Jones's life and activism represents the cocreation of an abolition democracy. This may seem contradictory. Certainly, his time in SNCC campaigning for fair housing and in the BPP working on the free breakfast program align with normative ideas about the development of community institutions. But his time in clandestinity in the 1970s creates a more complicated connection with the ideas of abolition democracy. The claim that Jones's activism promotes abolition democracy requires the disruption of normative thinking about what is noble and readily comprehensible versus what is illegitimate and illegible. Through the study of Hank Jones's activism, this essay examines one of the least written about aspects of Black Power studies, Black radicalism's belief in armed resistance as a legitimate form of struggle.[5] As I will argue, Jones's beliefs and practices reflect the lessons of the BPP (a politic of Black liberation intertwined with Third World decolonialization) and of organizing (that people most affected by issues ought to determine and lead their own campaigns). His experiences with racism and with grassroots organizing shaped his belief in the capacity of ordinary people to collectively contest power and to create the communities and institutions, paired with radical critiques of racial capitalism and imperialism, that abolition democracy seems to require if we ever are to get truly free.

Mississippi: Banding Together Out of Necessity

Henry Watson Jones Jr., known to all as Hank, was born on July 28, 1935, in New Albany, in northern Mississippi, the birthplace of his parents and grandparents. All four of his grandparents were born between 1872 and 1887, the first generation of Black people born after the ending of formal slavery. His paternal grandmother, Tommie Rose Taylor, was mixed race and inherited her father's land in the Black part of New Albany, and her husband, Hank's step-grandfather, George Taylor, was a brakeman in the railroad industry. For Hank's first five years, he lived with his paternal grandparents, his parents, Henry W. and Annie L. Jones, and older sister Clair Jean in his grandparents' home in New Albany. His grandparents already knew that the legal abolition of slavery did not bring about true freedom for Black people and even his family's relative wealth provided rather partial protection from the system of white supremacy developed in the Deep South. Hank's most vivid memories of growing up in New Albany center on living in daily terror in a strictly segregated town under the reign of the Ku Klux Klan. His parents taught him to never look a white person in the face, to get off the sidewalk when a white person passed, to go to the back door of white people's homes, to not ever stare at a white woman, and to never, ever walk alone at night. These were behaviors that Black parents taught their children as a matter of survival.[6]

But in New Albany, Jones also found a flourishing and nurturing Black community. "I felt loved and cared for and protected," he recalled. "Out of necessity, we were forced to band together and to work together. We had our own professionals. We had our own artisans and craftsman. We had our own community."[7] So even though the paved roads stopped at the railroad tracks that separated the Black neighborhood from the white one, those living in poorer sections of town didn't merely survive, they thrived by building a community that supported a generative social life. To Jones, the key to liberation revolves around building community as a place where people have autonomy over their family and social lives, where people have economic self-determination, where people can cocreate a participatory democracy, and where children can not only access public schooling, but also learn about their own histories. These were lessons that drew Jones to the BPP in San Francisco in 1967. But his ideas also reflect a longer trajectory of the Black radical tradition and of the Du Boisian concept of abolition democracy to argue that beyond legal abolition, Black people, in solidarity with others, need to build (and be allowed to build) the democratic institutions and social structures that would end their racial subordination and economic exploitation to approach a truer emancipation.[8]

California Contradictions

Jones's life reflects the rhythms and patterns of Black history. He came to the BPP already schooled in community organizing in SNCC's urban programs in San Francisco. His family's journey from Mississippi to California was part of the Depression-instigated Second Great Migration that brought the families of other Black Panthers from the South to the West, including BPP cofounders Huey Newton and Bobby Seale. Hank's father, Henry Watson Jones Sr., born in 1900, was educated at Fisk University in Nashville, was a singer with the famed Fisk Jubilee Singers, and worked as a public school teacher in a segregated Black school in New Albany. But, responding to the ways the Great Depression exacerbated the ongoing racist repression of southern Blacks and to the economic lure of shipyard jobs in California, he relocated his family in 1941.[9] Hank and his older sister first lived with relatives in Santa Monica, west of downtown Los Angeles, while his parents looked for work in Northern California. To Hank, his new town, with its streets lined with fruit trees and its bright schools and nearby beaches, seemed like "paradise" compared to New Albany. Within a year, he and his sister were reunited with their parents and living on Grant Avenue in San Francisco's Chinatown. Living in a residential hotel above Chinatown storefronts, Hank loved the sights and sounds and aromas of his new neighborhood. But he learned that racism didn't end at the borders of the South nor was it solely a Black and white problem. He was one of three Black students, one being his sister, among the predominantly Chinese and Italian American students at Jean Parker Elementary School. The other kids gave Hank a rough time, teasing him about Little Black Sambo and taunting him half the way home.[10] The next year, his parents transferred him to Raphael Weill Elementary School located in the predominantly Black area of Fillmore, a neighborhood that overlapped with the heavily Japanese American Western Addition. By still living in Chinatown, Hank was an outsider to the Fillmore and the daily hassle for lunch money and other kinds of harassment continued—that is, until he fought back. This was an early lesson for Hank in the efficacy of self-defense. He also remembers his shock when in 1945, Japanese American kids suddenly appeared at the school. It was only then that he came to understand that the Japanese had been rounded up and put into concentration camps in spring 1942. To his delight, he fell "immediately in love" with the Japanese American girl who sat next to him but seemed to barely notice his existence. In school, Hank had gotten actively involved as the president of the student body and captain of the traffic squad.[11]

Jones recalls his father as a "race man" and a professional who wasn't about to stay in his place and who taught his son about Marcus Garvey and the politics of self-determination. But, like most young men of his generation, Jones was also influenced by the construction of masculinity during the unprecedented military buildup of the early Cold War. He joined the Reserve Officers Training Corps (ROTC) in junior high school and served in the Marine Corps from October 1954 to October 1957. He was fulfilling the military service mandated by the Universal Military Training and Service Act of 1951, while also performing the martial masculinity that linked the achievement of manhood with patriotic service.[12]

He vividly remembers the moment of his political awakening. He was stationed in Japan in September 1955 and received his regular copy of *Jet* magazine.[13] There, on the inner pages, were the gruesome photos of Emmett Till taken at his funeral in his hometown of Chicago. The article explained that, for the act of whistling at a white woman, the woman's husband and brother-in-law abducted the fourteen-year-old from the home of his great uncle and aunt in Money, Mississippi. Afterwards, he was found with a bullet hole above his right ear, "the left side of his face . . . crushed to the bone," and a grotesquely distorted face, after being pulled out of the Tallahatchie River with a 200-pound gin fan tied around his neck. Till's mother decided to hold an open casket funeral to show to the world the horrors of white terror in the South. It shook Jones to the core. He had grown up in Mississippi about a hundred miles from where Till was murdered, and Till was only five years his junior. Jones started questioning, "What are you doing over here in this people's country? You're supposedly bringing them democracy, but you never had it yourself." The US military base town in Japan was racially segregated. "But after Emmett," Jones recalled, "I remember thinking that they were going have to kill me too because I wasn't going to put up with that anymore. We were a small number of Blacks in a marine company, but we started integrating that town. We integrated everything. Wherever we had been denied before, we went in. And if we weren't welcomed there, we tore the place up."[14] It's important to Jones to make clear that the Black marines were fighting fellow US servicemen and not the local Japanese people, with whom they had no problems. Moreover, they were not fighting to be close to white people per se and in fact were content enjoying drinking, dancing, and socializing in the Black clubs, but they did not want to be denied access on the basis of their skin color. The intense rage that Jones felt about Till's killing and all it represented stayed with him throughout his life, so much so that for twenty years "it was to the point where I couldn't even talk," said the outwardly mild and soft-spoken Jones of today. This fury fueled his actions to desegregate that base town in 1955 and his activism a decade later.

A Knock on the Door: The Roots of Activism

In the early to mid-1960s, living again in San Francisco and now married with children, Jones got involved in political organizing with a knock on his door. There before him stood a young white man, a SNCC organizer and housing activist, who had recently been the student body president at

San Francisco State College and would go on to support the campus's Third World Strike of 1968–69. Tom Ramsey asked if Jones knew that city officials were getting ready to bus his kids to a white neighborhood. Jones hadn't heard a thing but showed up at the next planning meeting and soon got immersed in that campaign. He and another parent would later issue a statement on behalf of the parents at Dudley Stone Grammar School to protest the busing of their children and indict the school board for failing to provide quality educational facilities at predominantly Black schools. At a parents' meeting in early 1966, when the Dudley Stone principal, who showed up uninvited, portrayed their children as "culturally disadvantaged," Black parents responded with compelling arguments and with anger. "We've got a culturally disadvantaged government," countered one parent. "Our kids are being bussed and theirs aren't," charged another. Jones, holding his young daughter, was featured in a photo accompanying an article on the bus boycott in the Bay Area SNCC newspaper, the *Movement*. Jones explained that they couldn't stop busing, which was federally mandated, so they strategically demanded two-way busing requiring white students to also be bussed as a way to ensure that the schools in Black neighborhoods improved.[15]

From this experience Jones learned the organizing methods of SNCC and Saul Alinsky. SNCC in the South had developed a strategy of going to the homes and community places where Black people congregated to listen to their concerns and to connect with them. SNCC stressed developing local leadership and nonhierarchical and participatory organizing. Alinksy was famous for devising creative tactics and strategies for provocatively exposing social injustices. It was Tom Ramsey who introduced Jones to Alinsky's *Reveille for Radicals*. When a few of the San Francisco activists returned from SNCC's Mississippi Freedom Summer in 1964, Jones recalled that they implemented SNCC's campaign for urban centers in the North. Their "End Slums" campaign sought to end not only race discrimination but also poverty. Implementing SNCC's organizing strategy, Jones, with SNCC organizer Danny Brown, knocked on the doors of seemingly "every housing unit in those little Victorians in the Western Addition" discussing code violations, inferior heating, absentee slumlords, and other housing problems. They also deployed an Alinsky-style tactic, taking roaches and rats to the affluent neighborhoods of absentee landlords to publicize the substandard living conditions in Black communities.[16]

Their work for decent housing coincided with efforts by the City of San Francisco and other US cities to mark for redevelopment areas deemed to be blighted. In 1964, the San Francisco Redevelopment Agency, headed by Justin Herman, began the second phase, A-2, of its urban renewal plans for the Western Addition. The board of supervisors implemented its first phase of redevelopment in 1956 designed to turn the overlapping Western Addition and Fillmore districts, predominantly Japanese American and Black, into a space filled with luxury apartments and modern businesses. The first phase proceeded with little opposition, but, by phase two Project A-2, residents began protesting the bulldozing of their homes and businesses and the lack of adequate replacement housing. In 1967, a coalition of progressive ministers and community activists, primarily Black (like Mary Helen Rogers) but also Japanese (like Yori Wada) and white, formed the Western Addition Community Organization (WACO) to address issues of housing, education, and racial discrimination in hiring in their neighborhood. As Jones distinctly remembers, "SNCC rounded up the community activists and religious leaders to start WACO" and, as was SNCC's model, promoted the leadership of local activists to the point of "organizing yourself out of a job." WACO won an unlikely federal lawsuit that placed residents' rights on the negotiating table in urban redevelopment plans. They managed to delay redevelopment and to demand that residents' needs be considered in some fashion, but by then 20,000 to 30,000 residents had been displaced, almost 900 businesses closed, and 2,500 Victorian houses that lined the streets demolished. Justin Herman, the head of the redevelopment agency, strategically invited Black Fillmore residents to work at his office and had them oversee the razing of their own neighborhood, including one highly placed staff person responsible for demolishing the church his own father had built.[17]

Jones worked as a SNCC volunteer organizer for five years, devoting every moment he wasn't doing his paid work to the organizing campaigns. But when each of their efforts was outmaneuvered by Herman and other pro-development forces, it became a lesson in disillusionment for him. As he viewed it, "It took us a year of daily organizing and a day for the government to co-opt all of it. They paid off the tenants' rights groups and offered the parent watchdog groups that we had organized jobs as teacher's aides and things like that." From this experience, Jones discerned two crucial political lessons that propelled him into Black Power politics and the BPP. First, this experience solidified in Jones a critical view of integration as the unquestioned goal of civil rights campaigns. For many, integration seemed like a reasonable antidote to racial segregation. But Black Power advocates, in particular, raised critical questions that challenged this seemingly noble objective.

SNCC leader Stokely Carmichael expressed that if integration meant uni-directional movement from Black spaces to white spaces, then integration was in actuality "a subterfuge for the maintenance of white supremacy."[18] To Jones, integration represented a loss—a forgoing of the kind of cohesive Black community of his New Albany childhood and the relinquishing of "our minds" in the process of trying to fit into the overall society. The famed author bell hooks, having personally experienced busing to "integrated" schools in white neighborhoods, writes about the power of all-Black spaces prior to desegregation as well as the difficulties of forced integration and its continuing spatial segregation.[19] Second, Jones came to the conclusion that the system required more than fixing; it needed to be completely transformed. Like Du Bois, he would soon argue for the development of an alternative system to advance abolition democracy. Still, to the present, Jones retains his belief in community organizing and in SNCC's model of developing local leadership among those most affected by a particular issue. Significantly, it was when he became engaged in community organizing that he turned from a state of rage to learn to "love all oppressed people and their struggles for humanity."[20]

Panthers, Prisons, and Possibilities

The Black freedom movement has always been more complicated than the way it has been portrayed, as if integration were the singular goal and as if legislative victories signaled the death knell to racism. Jones was increasingly drawn to the politics of Black Power, to its critique of power and its goal of radical transformation of social, economic, political, and racial relations, to ideas of Black pride and self-determination. So after SNCC, he helped to establish two Black nationalist organizations, the Independent Action Movement (IAM) and the Black Panther Party of Northern California (BPPNC), based in San Francisco. It was through this work that he came to know the Oakland-based Black Panther Party for Self-Defense (BPPSD), famously founded by Huey Newton and Bobby Seale, when the two Black Panther groups provided security for Betty Shabazz, Malcolm X's widow, for a program on February 21, 1967, the second anniversary of Malcolm's assassination. Like Eldridge Cleaver and Emory Douglas who relay a similar pathway from this incident into the BPPSD, Jones was awestruck when the BPPSD entered the San Francisco International Airport, walked all the way to the gate, and provided armed escort for Betty Shabazz. After that, Jones gravitated toward the BPPSD in San Francisco, one of the first chapters of the BPPSD and the publication site of the Panther newspaper, headed by Eldridge and Kathleen Cleaver and Emory Douglas.[21] Joining the BPPSD in 1967, Jones did the work of a rank-and-file member, including securing food from local businesses for the BPP free breakfast program and serving meals to schoolchildren.

Jones joined the BPPSD in a period of intensive police and FBI attacks on the party. At the time, neither he nor any of his Panther comrades understood that the FBI was launching in August 1967 its counterintelligence program, COINTELPRO, to "expose, disrupt, misdirect, discredit, or otherwise neutralize the activities of black nationalist, hate-type organizations." In February 1968, FBI agents began round-the-clock surveillance on the San Francisco Panthers. In July 1969, FBI director J. Edgar Hoover announced that the Black Panther Party represented "the greatest threat to the internal security of the country." The FBI was determined to stop the BPP by any means at its disposal, whether inside or outside the bounds of legality. Of the FBI's 295 official COINTELPRO actions, 233 were directed against the BPP.[22]

From the start, the Panthers promoted and practiced a politic of self-defense, expressed as a desire to defend the Black community from police violence and advocated the Second Amendment right to bear arms, including while patrolling the police, as stated in Point #7 of their Ten-Point Platform. The Panther leaders reasoned that violence and the threats of violence had long been used in the process of creating the US empire by seizing Indigenous lands and by maintaining slavery and the continuing subordination of Blacks after formal emancipation. To many Panthers, armed self-defense was an antidote to the violence of the state. In this, the BPP followed in a long history of Black and Indigenous armed resistance to the violence of slavery, colonialism, and white supremacy.

In the 1920s, the African Blood Brotherhood advocated the creation of paramilitary self-defense units. In the 1950s, ex-marine Robert F. Williams reconstituted an unusual chapter of the NAACP in Monroe, NC, teaching its members to fight back with gun power against the Ku Klux Klan. While Williams acknowledged that "nonviolence is a powerful weapon in the struggle against social evil," that it depended, as he saw it, on the conscience of one's adversary meant that "nonviolence is no repellent for a sadist." In the early 1960s, Malcolm X condemned the hypocrisy of nonviolence: "How are you going to be nonviolent in Mississippi, as violent as you were in Korea?" Why was it that Black people were asked to be nonviolent against the violence of white supremacy, while the US government enlisted Black soldiers to kill in wars overseas?[23]

As with so many men of his generation, Jones had already learned how to shoot in the US military as well as a rationale for the use of guns in defense of the nation. In the BPP, Jones learned a political analysis that advocated armed self-defense in protection of Black communities against the violence of the state and its military and police apparatuses. The Black Liberation Army (BLA), as an underground and armed wing of the Black Liberation movement, arose in this context. The most common account presents how the BLA originated in the BPP as a result of external repression by the state and the internal conflict within the party. Others, however, contend that the Black underground existed prior to and was broader than the BPP. Whatever its origins, the BLA apparently did not function through any centralized command. Its work intensified in 1971. In that year, the public break between Huey Newton and Eldridge Cleaver that took place during and after a San Francisco television show led to deadly internecine fighting within the BPP. One major component of the struggle centered on whether the BPP should continue to promote self-defense and armed struggle (Cleaver's position) or whether, as a way to counter mounting police and FBI repression, the party should focus exclusively on community survival programs and electoral campaigns (Newton's position). Another major aspect of the struggle centered on Newton's unprincipled expulsions and purges of the nineteen New York Panthers, Los Angeles Panther Geronimo ji Jaga Pratt, and others he perceived as opposing him. A few days after the televised Newton-Cleaver break, Panther Robert "Spider" Webb was killed in an ambush near the Harlem BPP office, followed by the killing of Panther Sam Napier. Meanwhile, the police and FBI violence against Black communities continued. An article in the BPP newspaper estimated that the police had killed nearly a thousand Black people between 1971 and 1973. Before this, the police had killed a total of twenty-eight Black Panthers in 1968 alone, according to BPP lawyer Charles Garry.[24]

In this context, the BLA viewed offensive campaigns against the police as part of a combat strategy needed to defend and protect Black communities. In August 1971, the BLA claimed responsibility for attacks on police stations in San Francisco and New York, in retaliation for the killing of George Jackson—BPP field marshal and prison activist with growing influence—on August 21, 1971, in the San Quentin prison in Northern California. The BLA was responding to FBI and police violence as well as to a longer history of anti-Black violence, and in turn, the FBI and police heightened their campaigns against the Black militants, with a particular vengeance against the BPP. In that tumultuous year and fearing for the safety of his family, Jones made the difficult decision to go underground, leaving behind his wife and four children, while he endured the difficult daily struggle for survival in clandestinity.[25]

In 1973, the FBI, working with local police departments, arrested Black militants in New Orleans, Los Angeles, and Georgia. Jones, who had been living in New Orleans, fled town and was traveling in Alabama when he heard an all-points bulletin issued for his arrest. He was being indicted for the killing of the unsolved police killings in San Francisco two years earlier. He took off to Atlanta but was caught a few months later. He and others had robbed a bank, what many would condemn as criminal activity, but what Jones viewed as necessary for their survival while underground. After a circuitous and months-long journey that took him from prisons in Atlanta, to Leavenworth in Kansas, to El Reno in Oklahoma, and to Lompoc in Central California, Jones finally ended up at the McNeil Island federal penitentiary in Washington State.[26]

When Jones was released from prison in 1977, he immediately went to work. In prison he had received training as a machinist, so he took the first job offered to him, a machinist job in Berkeley. He had hoped to attend graduate school to become a psychoanalyst, but he had recently remarried and his new wife hadn't gotten to attend college, so they prioritized her schooling while he worked, and they jointly raised her daughter and later had a daughter together. His wife had worked with the BPP and understood the importance of struggle, but she also understood the dangers involved. Knowing that Jones had emerged from clandestinity and then prison, she didn't want him to resume his activism. Jones felt immense guilt from leaving his first family. And there were costs. He acknowledges never having formed a bond with his fourth child and only son, who was only eighteen months old when he went underground. Only in the past several years has he reestablished relations with his two oldest daughters. He vowed he wouldn't leave his family ever again. So, despite his ongoing social justice longings, he lived a life of quiet domesticity in Oakland, attending to his family, working steadily as a machinist, and putting his kids through college—a life devoid of Panthers, prisons, and politics.[27]

Still, there were a few moments of reconnection with former Panthers. When he emerged from prison he reunited with a few Panthers, notably John Bowman and Wayne Thompson, dedicated community activists in Spencer, Oklahoma, who had continued the kinds of survival programs initiated by the

Panthers. In the early 1990s, he reestablished contact with Ray Boudreaux and traveled to Los Angeles to attend a New Year's Eve party at Boudreaux's home in 1993. This was the first time in fifteen years, since exiting prison, that he had seen Boudreaux, one of his closest friends and comrades, with whom he had shared many years of prison time and underground space. And in the late 1990s, following the fatal stabbing of the daughter of a former Panther in East Oakland, Jones interacted with his former Panther comrades. But these interactions, while meaningful, were the exceptions to his life.[28]

Propelled into Action: COINTELPRO and the San Francisco 8

The FBI propelled Jones back into activism. In 2003, they came knocking on his door. He was expecting them. Following the attacks on the World Trade Center and Pentagon on September 11, 2001, the government had heightened its surveillance and repression against sixties radicals. Immediately after the Twin Towers fell, prison officials moved into the "hole" or isolation long-held imprisoned radicals, including Black Power activist Sundiata Acoli, Puerto Ricans Antonio Comacho Negron and Carlos Alberto Torres, and white activists Marilyn Buck, Ray Levasseur, Richard Williams, and seventy-seven-year-old Phillip Berrigan. Most had their visiting and phone rights to family and legal counsel revoked. For Richard Williams, that was the beginning of a fifteen-month stint in solitary that led to a dramatic decline in his health and his dying in prison at age fifty-eight. These varied prisoners had one thing in common—they were all militant resisters, but they had nothing to do with the attacks of September 11. Particularly since 9/11, the FBI began doubling down on 1960s–'70s cold cases, especially those involving police killings allegedly by militants, Black, white, or otherwise.[29]

When the FBI knocked on his door, Jones let them in, knowing, he says in retrospect, that you should never talk to the FBI without an attorney present. But he was curious about what they had to say. Their first question bordered on the ridiculous: "Do you know any white people?" They proceeded to ask him about the Weather Underground, environmental activists, and other white militant organizations. When they got to the BPP, Jones asked if they had any legal documents to hold him and, finding none, ended the conversation. In 2005, the FBI returned, this time with a subpoena for Jones and other sixties activists to appear before a grand jury in San Francisco. Grand juries are legal proceedings that investigate potential criminal conduct and can compel documents and sworn testimony in order to determine whether to proceed with criminal indictments. Critics argue that grand juries are a method for the government to require people to testify, without the presence of an attorney, and otherwise produce information in order to gather broad and nonspecific information. Six former Panthers, including Jones, were subpoenaed and all six refused to testify. They were held in contempt and jailed for about thirty days. Then in 2006, the FBI came around for DNA samples of Jones and the other targeted former Panthers.[30]

The FBI came a fourth time, this time with warrants for arrest. On January 23, 2007, police in California, Florida, and New York arrested six former Panthers, Hank Jones, Ray Boudreaux, Richard Brown, Richard O'Neal, Harold Taylor, and Francisco Torres on charges related to the 1971 killing of a San Francisco police officer and on conspiracy charges centering on police attacks from 1968 to 1973. They also charged Herman Bell and Jalil Muntaqim (née Anthony Bottom), both already serving thirty-year prison terms. Two others would have been arrested, but John Bowman had died a month earlier and Stanley Bridgeforth hadn't been seen or heard from in over thirty years. They were given excessively high bails of $3 million, effectively guaranteeing a jail stay.[31]

The possibility of spending the rest of one's life in prison would be debilitating for most. But for Jones, as with the other SF8 defendants, the arrests and especially the grassroots mobilization for their defense had the opposite effect. It propelled him back into political activism. Along the way, support came from unlikely places, such as the two white women, complete strangers, who put up their homes as collateral for Jones's bail. It also came from predicable places, notably sixties radicals and younger activists as well.[32]

When the FBI first knocked on his door in 2003, Jones had been married to his third wife, Ann, for not even a year. He was now living in Altadena, northeast of downtown Los Angeles, and close to Ray Boudreaux and his wife. In 2005, when the two San Francisco police inspectors from the original case, Frank McCoy and Ed Erdelatz, began interviewing the people allegedly involved in the 1970s incidents as well as family members, they went to Ann's workplace in an attempt to interview her.[33] Jones felt like they put "a knife to my neck." His wife knew "none of this," said Jones, referring to COINTEL-PRO. She understood that he had been in the BPP and did time for a bank robbery, but she did not know about his time underground, the extent of FBI and police repression, or Black militant counteractions to police violence. He feared the end of their marriage. When Ann returned home after the FBI visited her, she and Hank sat in their backyard and talked extensively. She was terrified that he would be imprisoned for the rest of his life. When Hank was arrested in January 2007, Ann responded in an unexpected way—organizing on her husband's behalf. She had been active in her church community but was no political activist and in fact was rather "apolitical," as Hank noted. Yet she organized the entire block in their well-groomed Altadena suburb as well as her church in support of Jones and the SF8. She went where she had relationships, but this also entailed a certain risk. Her valued social circles might reject her husband's history of radical politics—and herself as well. Her support and organizing work deeply touched Jones, who a decade later, quietly expressed, with tears in his eyes, his gratitude to her.[34]

After the 2005 grand jury subpoenas, Jones and his Panther comrades decided to go on the offensive. They felt that the murder and conspiracy charges alleged against them would be incomprehensible outside the context of the FBI's program of counterintelligence. The FBI's COINTELPRO was a series of covert and often illegal operations designed to surveil, infiltrate, discredit, and neutralize activist organizations and leaders. COINTELPRO acted with a vengeance against the BPP, resulting in daily harassment, imprisonment, and deaths of Panthers, bombings of Panther offices, and fomented conflicts—some turned deadly—within the BPP and between the Panthers and other organizations. So the former Panthers and grand jury resisters began speaking out about the broader context of FBI and police strategies to destroy the Black liberation movement and the broader progressive movement. They discussed the anticipated charges against them. And they spoke publicly about the torture of Panthers Harold Taylor, John Bowman, and Ruben Scott by the New Orleans police in 1973 used to extract statements that implicated them in the 1971 San Francisco police killing. In 2007, Taylor recounted his experience in the New Orleans jail:

> Immediately, when we got in the jail, they started beating us. They never asked us any questions in the beginning. . . . They put plastic bags over my head and held me back while five or six police officers stood around me, hitting me and kicking at me. . . . They were hitting each other trying to hit me. . . . [They used] the slapjacks across the back of my shoulders, all down my legs and on my shins, between my knees. It was so painful that all you could do was try to scream. . . . And they says, "You're going to talk, or we're going to continue" . . . They did that all day. It went in shifts. . . . They'd come in there with a hot blanket . . . real soaking wet . . . they'd throw it over my head. And one would pull my head back, and I'm trying to breathe, and I'm sucking in water from the blanket. And, you know, you feel like you're going to drown.[35]

The decision of the former Panthers to go public involved personal risk and possibly jeopardizing their legal defense. But they had reasoned that remaining silent also entailed risks and that their speaking out could make visible the history of COINTELPRO to new generations of activists then battling the "war on terror," attacks on Muslims, and the USA PATRIOT Act's abrogation of civil liberties affecting virtually every American. Jones observed at the time: "The climate in the country is much like it was back in the late 1960s and early '70s. It's designed to squash any form of dissent. . . . Some of us have taken a stand and we've decided that whatever the consequences, we're not going to cave into this."[36] They wanted to create a visceral experience for people to understand the extent of FBI and police brutality and the viciousness of anti-Blackness and to understand the parallels with present-day state violence. So they deployed an innovative but disturbing tactic to not only tell their stories but to reenact the torture techniques used by the New Orleans police in 1973 against Taylor, Bowman, and Scott. For these "live demonstrations," they had to carry with them a cattle prod to replicate the electric shock administered to their genitals, anus, feet, and underarms; the blankets dripping hot and wet wrapped around their heads to simulate drowning; and the plastic bags used to suffocate. The New Orleans police directed these torture methods against the three Panthers, while beating, kicking, and knocking them unconscious, only to arouse them for more torment. The beatings stopped only so that police inspectors from San Francisco and New York could interrogate them about the 1971 police killings in their respective cities. The brutality went on for a few days. In the end, the police got their torture-induced "confessions." Doing the live demonstrations over and over again at different places was particularly painful to the men who had suffered the torture and its ongoing post-traumatic effects, but it was also hard on everyone involved. So, working with the Freedom Archives in San Francisco, they decided to make a documentary of their case. *Legacy of Torture: The War against the Black Liberation Movement* features five of the eight Panthers subpoenaed before the grand jury in 2005, including Hank Jones, and contextualizes their case within the Black liberation struggle and the FBI's COINTELPRO operations. The torture scenes are narrated by Bowman and Taylor to accompany dramatizations in black-and-white video footage. The plan was to use the documentary in place of the live demonstrations in their speaking engagements around the country. But that was not to be.[37]

On January 23, 2007, five days before the documentary's scheduled premiere in San Francisco, authorities arrested the eight former Panthers. The two years of organizing since the grand jury resistance had raised public awareness, particularly in activist circles, of the government's efforts to reopen the 1971 case. The film's premiere went on as scheduled but was used to educate and rally people in defense of the SF8. The Committee for the Defense of Human Rights organized community backing for their case and further helped to galvanize a number of activist organizations already doing prison, political prisoner, and antiracist organizing.[38] With his typically dry wit and understated demeanor, Jones remarked, "The SF8 organizing community did incredible work. All we had to do was go to jail."[39] His statement reveals his recognition of the tremendous work that goes into grassroots organizing—and its power to create change. It further recognizes that his arrest was not a reflection of his individual actions or ethics, but rather part of a larger struggle premised on repression and resistance. The breadth of the grassroots organizing for their case is revealed in this statement by SF8 defendant Herman Bell, admittedly gushing with gratitude:

> I am so proud of you and all the work you've done on our behalf and in waking our movement from its lethargy—proud of your speaking, proud of your fund-raising, proud of your organizing (the Labor Council, the City Supervisors, the caravan to Sacramento, such a sweet piece of 'mainstream' organizing, and the tribute to Panther women). So very proud that you were in court to smile your greetings whenever we appeared; proud that you made bail for those of us who could bail-out, and that you routinely visited those of us who could not.[40]

Based on the work of the legal team as well as the grassroots campaign, the SF8 gained reductions in bail from the initial $3–$5 million down to $200,000 to $660,000 that made possible their release from jail on bail. The conspiracy charge was later dropped.[41] Finally, in early July 2009, two and a half years after their arrest, all charges were dropped against Jones and three others. Two others, both already serving life sentences for a 1971 New York police killing case, made plea bargains that resulted in no additional prison time and helped lead to the release of their codefendants. Richard O'Neal's charges had been dropped earlier, while the charges against the final defendant, Francisco Torres, were finally dropped in 2011.[42] The defendants and activist community consider the case of the SF8 to be a "people's victory"—not only in terms of the legal case, but also in mobilizing the grassroots and educating a new generation about the impact of state repression in the 1960s–'70s. It was a lesson from history that was particularly relevant in the post-9/11 environment. Their case also anticipated the need to once again retell their story in the current context of the Movement for Black Lives and its work to connect anti-Black police violence with poverty, colonialism, environmental degradation, and the collapse of the public institutions and communal spaces as well as the post–2016 election context of unbridled capitalism, neoliberal austerity, white supremacy, xenophobia, misogyny, and neofascism.

Health and Healing, Spirituality and Struggle

Around the time of the SF8 case, Jones began attending the monthly Black Panther breakfasts, started by former Los Angeles Panthers Marvin Jackson and Roland Freeman and held on the second Sunday of each month, at restaurants in the Crenshaw and Slauson areas, west of the original Panther office at Forty-First and Central.[43] According to Jones, the breakfasts started as a "place of healing" for former Panthers to connect and share about their lives as well as to make brief announcements about political or community events. But in time, especially after a microphone was brought in, it became a place where people "pontificated" about all kinds of matters, particularly political ones, and the sense of intimacy was lost. They have recently revised the format, and while non-Panthers continue to be welcome, the public talking is now kept to a minimum. As political as Jones is, he prefers the more personal atmosphere. To him, many Panthers, himself included, have been traumatized by their time in the party, especially owing to the intensity of police repression, and the difficulties for many former Panthers of growing up in tough neighborhoods encapsulated in violence, poverty, and structural racism.[44]

The healing process for Jones began many years ago. He describes himself as having been filled with an inconsolable rage after finding out about Emmett Till's brutal murder, one that lasted for twenty years and left him with a quick temper to the point where, as he recounts, he couldn't even talk without filth coming out of his mouth. Even as early as the 1960s, he had begun to read about healing practices and began to do "internal work" and meditation. While in the Marine Corps at age nineteen, he had wanted to be a psychoanalyst and was briefly enrolled in a graduate program in psychology at San Francisco State College. But his spiritual practice intensified during his time in prison in the mid-1970s, beginning with his arrest and incarceration in Georgia in 1973. He engaged in a process of introspection and practiced meditation to the point where he could "shut out the other eleven people in the cell." He also discovered that he had a heightened spiritual radar. He recounted:

I had a manner of blocking negative stuff that I had devised from my readings. I could sense if you're negative, I could stop you six feet from me, and
I would often try to extend that further. I could ward off that stuff. I know
from the spiritual realm, like attracts like and negative attracts negative. So
I utilized that and it worked for me.

Jones found himself attracted to Taoism because of the freedom he found
in it and at different times identified with Taoism, Shintoism, and Islam. While
in the federal penitentiary at McNeil Island in the mid-1970s, Jones became
an imam-in-training, connecting other prisoners to the teachings of Warith
Deen Mohammed (the son of Elijah Muhammed, the long-time leader of
the Nation of Islam), after Mohammed moved from the Nation of Islam to
more orthodox Islam. Jones managed to survive in prison by doing meditation,
studying the Koran, and running half marathons on the weekends—all practices that took him to another state of consciousness and removed him from
the physical and mental confinement of prison.[45]

Then in 2007, while in prison on the SF8 charges, Jones found the spiritual path he had been searching for most of his life. The Ausar Auset Society,
founded in 1973 by Ra Un Nefer Amen, author of the seven-volume *Metu
Neter*, promotes a Kamitic (ancient Egyptian) system of spiritual cultiva-
tion.[46] It was his lawyer who introduced him to this spiritual practice, which
Jones views as "a blueprint for the spirit." To him, "It explains how you nurture that spirit and move towards your divine state." For Jones, spirituality
represents the path to liberation. In prison, "what I discovered is that when I
tapped into spiritual power, the supreme intelligence that created everything,
there was nothing they could do to me. I was in control. I shifted the power
from them to myself." Inside prison Jones participated with a group of other
Muslims in monthly three- to five-day, water-only fasts. For him, after the
third day, he found himself on a spiritual high where "all kinds of things
occur to you." Even as Jones views himself as a student of spiritual growth—
and not one ready to teach—one thing is clear to him: "If you get the spirit
right, pretty much everything else will fall into place."[47]

It was in moments of imprisonment, when Jones's need for physical and
spiritual protection was greatest, and when he had time free from work and
family, that he made qualitative leaps in his spiritual practice. He remarked
that from the time he was a child, he had been deeply spiritual but not in a
religious institutional way. While in the BPP, he did not know of any other
Panthers who were meditating or engaging in non-Western and noninstitu-
tional spiritual training.[48] The meaning of spiritual life, especially outside of

conventional Christian or Muslim religious beliefs, is rarely discussed in the literature on the Black Panthers or Black Power struggles. Yet the traumas experienced by many Panthers meant that the monthly Panther breakfasts and other spaces that cultivated community convening and personal sharing were crucial to what it means to create a nourishing afterlife of the BPP.

An Elder in the New Black Liberation Struggle

It was through the SF8 case that Jones not only reconstituted his activism but also gained the greatest public prominence of his life. He had not sought any iconic recognition, but young activists were eager to meet sixties-era elders, and he was grateful to reconnect with the grassroots movement. The early 2000s was a time of heightened contradiction. On one hand, the state repression following the events of September 11, 2001, and its calls for uncritical hyperpatriotism, led to the FBI pursuit of sixties activists for decades-old cold cases and also silenced the social movements rising in the late 1990s. On the other hand, the calls for a perpetual "war on terrorism" and polarizing views of good versus evil coming from the highest levels of the US government provoked a resistance movement to the US attacks on Afghanistan in 2001 and especially to the US "preemptive" bombings of Iraq in 2003. In 2011, the Occupy movement challenged the contradiction that exists between the 1 percent (Wall Street corporate owners) and the 99 percent (everybody else) that reflected, but did not necessarily endorse, a Marxist analysis of class struggle. Around 2013, the grassroots movement of resistance to police killings of unarmed Black people, spurred by the killings of Trayvon Martin and Michael Brown, launched the Black Lives Matter slogan that grew into the broader Movement for Black Lives (M4BL), as well as the mounting alt-right anger and organizing. Since the November 2016 elections, there has been a groundswell of grassroots activism against climate catastrophe, white supremacy, violence against women, heteropatriarchy, neoliberal austerity, houselessness, and deportations and family separations, and for economic and ecological sustainability, labor rights, truth and science, and much more.

In this milieu, Jones found himself being invited to speak about the SF8 case and the BPP at community and campus venues, often accompanying the showing of *Legacy of Torture* or the newer documentary, *COINTELPRO 101*, also produced by Freedom Archives. He spoke at an anarchist conference in Los Angeles in 2007 that connected the FBI raids on animal rights and anarchist activists with the arrests of Black militants. He spoke on a panel of Third

World sixties radicals, featuring Brown Beret Carlos Montes, Asian Hardcore and Eastwind activist Mo Nishida, and American Indian Movement activist Tammy Blacklightning, at Glendale Community College in 2013. He was also interviewed multiple times on the radio, including Pacifica (KPFK) in Los Angeles and "LA Live." In February 2016, he organized a Southern California speaking tour that extended from Santa Barbara to Los Angeles and San Diego for Sekou Odinga, former BPP, Black Liberation Army, and Republic of New Afrika radical, recently released from thirty-three years in prison. He further coordinated, with Mo Nishida, a series of film showings and discussions on activist history and issues at Pasadena Community College and Occidental College, and on spirituality and revolution at Pasadena Community College. These are but a small representation of the talks Jones began doing, primarily in Southern California, but also in the San Francisco Bay Area and beyond.[49]

Jones views the M4BL as one of the best indicators of the growth and promise of the US-based liberation movements. At the first national M4BL convening, held in Cleveland, Ohio, in July 2015, he, along with about two thousand others, gathered to reflect on the state of the Black movement for liberation and to collectively reimagine the future. It was a gathering of youth and elders; of queer, trans, and cisgender people; and of the differently abled coming together across difference to reclaim Black humanity. One participant was most inspired by its creation of intergenerational spaces that invoked "collective memory," or "a people's understanding of the world and themselves throughout time as formed by the group's constituents."[50] Jones spoke on a panel with three other former Panthers, Ashanti Alston, Pam Hannah, and Dhoruba Bin Wahad, who reminded the audience of the ongoing activism of former Panthers and raised questions about intergenerational continuity and rupture. More than a gathering of individuals, the M4BL convening was an assemblage of more than fifty *organizations* that came to discuss and strategize, to commune and heal as a collective gathering, and ended up executing a generative process of collaboration from which emerged a far-reaching set of demands. From the discussion came a mandate to articulate a vision and set of strategies. Over the course of a full year of deliberations, the different participating grassroots organizations met to create a document, "A Vision for Black Lives," that is extraordinary in its breadth and interweaving of issues and for its collectively conceived and written demands to promote Black humanity and dignity and to end the war against Black people.[51]

The M4BL articulated a broad view of violence that connected police brutality with economic impoverishment, militarism, environmental degradation, racial capitalism, colonialism, patriarchy, and heterosexism:

> Cleveland reaffirmed what we already knew. Neither our grievances nor our solutions are limited to the police killing of our people. State violence takes many forms—it includes the systemic underinvestment in our communities, the caging of our people, predatory state and corporate practices targeting our neighborhoods, government policies that result in the poisoning of our water and the theft of our land, failing schools that criminalize rather than educate our children, economic practices that extract our labor, and wars on our Trans and Queer family that deny them their humanity.[52]

Jones, who was already working with and attending meetings of the Los Angeles Black Lives Matter group, was inspired to participate in the M4BL convening, which included but extended beyond the Black Lives Matter formation and that connected many of the issues important to him since his days organizing with SNCC and the BPP.

Like the Panthers, the M4BL sought "an end to the wars against Black people" and recognized that the injuries of history reverberate in the present, as recognized in their statement: "We demand that the government repair the harms that have been done to Black communities in the form of reparations and targeted long-term investments." Moreover, like the Panthers, the M4BL was rooted in a politic that saw anti-Black racism intertwined with all forms of oppression locally and globally. The M4BL platform states: "We are a collective that centers and is rooted in Black communities, but we recognize we have a shared struggle with all oppressed people; collective liberation will be a product of all of our work. . . . We stand in solidarity with our international family against the ravages of global capitalism and anti-Black racism, human-made climate change, war, and exploitation." The M4BL articulates a demand for transformational change to create "a fundamentally different world," but also recognizes the necessity "to address the current material conditions of our people and will better equip us to win the world we demand and deserve." The document includes specific policies and strategies to create that change. Jones hadn't seen anything like this since the sixties. Indeed, the M4BL explicitly recognizes its roots in the Black Power movement: "This agenda continues the legacy of our ancestors who pushed for reparations, Black self-determination and community control." But the M4BL also recognizes the shifts in thinking and in practices that build on and advance the sixties generation, including linking Black liberation to struggles for "reproductive justice, holistic healing and reconciliation, and ending violence against Black cis, queer, and trans people."[53]

Jones, now an octogenarian, graciously accepts his responsibility to speak as an elder in the movement, but also repeatedly states his unequivocal desire to learn from the younger generations. At a public program at UC Santa Barbara, Jones shared his views about giving "advice" to young people: "I belong to a different era, so I try not to influence the thinking about the kind of world this generation will produce. We didn't like anyone telling us what to do. I try to give the benefit of our generation's experiences, our successes and failures, and then try to get out of their way. We want them to be better, faster, better organized. That's what progress is all about. I don't try to tell them what to do. If I design it, it'll look like what we created and probably with similar outcomes." He further encouraged young people to get involved: "It'll take everything we got. Find someplace to plug in, do what you do. If you're not a street soldier, don't try to do that. If you're a teacher, writer, whatever, do it the best you can and in the interest of our people, of all oppressed people globally."[54]

This view, rooted in Third World solidarities, further propelled Jones to participate in a ten-day delegation to Palestine, convened by Dr. Rabab Abdulhadi, professor at San Francisco State University, in spring 2016. He was part of a nineteen-person delegation of anti-prison, labor, and scholar activists, which included former Black Panthers and former political prisoners, that met with a variety of activists, former political prisoners, and families of young people killed in the struggle as well as human rights organizations. They observed Palestinian towns devastated by Israeli occupation and an Israeli military tribunal. Jones went because he wanted to see for himself the conditions of life and struggle facing a people whose land was occupied and colonized by Israel in 1948 and whose daily lives are marked by "racialized arrest, segregation, settler violence, land confiscation, forced relocation, home demolitions and civil rights violations" and where 40 percent of the male population has been imprisoned.[55] Jones recalled one particularly heartbreaking moment when meeting with the parents of Palestinian youth and children killed through settler violence. The parents of Muhammad Abu Khudair talked about how their sixteen-year-old son was abducted, beaten unconscious, awakened and forced to drink kerosene, and then burned alive by three Israeli settlers.[56] In that meeting, Jones disclosed how his mother used to tell a story of a Black father in Mississippi forced to bring the kerosene that white supremacists used to kill his son. It seemed to him that Khudair was another Emmett Till.

The conditions Jones witnessed in Palestine were eerily familiar to him, reminding him of growing up in 1930s Mississippi and of current-day police violence against and imprisonment of Black people. It served to strengthen his resolve to fortify international solidarity and to fight not only racism, but all forms of colonialism as well. Jones's experiences as a former Black Panther and former political prisoner elevated his stature in the eyes of many in Palestine. The knowledge gained from his activist and prison struggles as well as his ability to eloquently and concisely articulate poignant stories and ideas meant that he had many speaking invitations to fulfill. Jones saw it as his responsibility and was happy to oblige. On several radio programs, on multiple campuses, and at community venues, including at the Black Panther breakfast and at a Black August program (annual commemorations of Black prison martyrs held in multiple US cities), primarily in Los Angeles, he spoke about what he witnessed in Palestine, taking seriously the Palestinian people's request to the delegation to tell the world about what's happening in Palestine.[57]

Jones's commitment to Black liberation intertwined with Third World internationalism is further revealed in an art exhibit that he co-organized. Jones worked with the curators and artists of the RISE Arts Collective to develop an art exhibition inspired by the BPP. "RISE: Love. Revolution. The Black Panther Party" was launched at Art Share L.A. in Los Angeles on February 21, 2014, and traveled to Oakland; the Chicago exhibit opened in November 2018, followed by plans for New York and London. The exhibit featured art by over thirty artists, including former Panthers Emory Douglas and Akinsanya Kambon; art featuring images of Panthers Bobby Seale, Assata Shakur, Eldridge Cleaver, and the BPP free breakfast program; and general Black- and African-themed art, including a Black Madonna and an enlightened Black Buddha. The exhibit was Black-centered, but not Black-only. In fact, a stunning painting of legendary Japanese American activist Yuri Kochiyama, a fierce advocate of Black liberation associated with Malcolm X, was included after curator Jimmy O'Balles convinced artist Shuji Nakamura to paint a portrait of her for this exhibit.[58] When Kochiyama died in June 2014, Hank Jones traveled to her Oakland memorial to show Nakamura's painting to her family and four weeks later at her Los Angeles memorial, through Jones's introduction, Nakamura presented his portrait as a gift to the Kochiyama family.[59]

Based on his life experiences, Hank Jones came to see history and society rife with contradictions—incongruities that signaled problems but also the possibilities for liberation. In the fertile soil of Mississippi, the seeds of his political consciousness were sown through the brutality of anti-Black violence and racial segregation as well in the nurturing Black community surrounding him. While raising young children in San Francisco, he discovered that he had a knack and a passion for community organizing. But in the struggle for fair housing, he also discovered the limitations of grassroots organizing in the face of power. One might not expect a community organizer to turn to armed self-defense and move into the Black liberation underground. Yet it was because of the SF8 case, rooted in the violent exchanges between the police and the Panthers, that Jones revitalized his activist practice. Arising from the Panthers' insistence on solidarity and radicalism and Jones's own experiences, including growing up in San Francisco's Chinatown, Jones created a politic of Black liberation intricately linked to Third World anticolonialism. His life not only reveals a complicated relationship between civil rights and Black Power, it also raises questions about the meaning of abolition democracy. Could Nat Turner's slave rebellions or John Brown's armed insurrection to overthrow slavery be part of a society rooted in abolition democracy? Does spirituality play a role in revolution? What will it take to get us to move beyond legal emancipation? Based on Jones's experiences, there is no one best model. "It'll take everything we got," Jones urged.[60] Still, without being mechanical or reductionistic, it seems like Jones's life signals two fundamental bases for social change. First, he holds a fierce belief in the capacity of ordinary people to collectively contest structural oppression and to develop the communities and institutions needed to create the conditions for freedom. For Jones, this requires political *organizing* to develop long-term strategies, alternative institutions, deep participatory democracy, and transformational change—beyond the *activist* tactics of signing a petition, liking a post, or going to a rally. Second, in the genealogy of W. E. B. Du Bois, the BPP, and the broader Black radical tradition, grassroots organizing needs to be paired with radical critiques of racial capitalism and imperialism.[61] While we may never create a truly free society, how we envision freedom matters. Raising up abolition democracy, and its requirement for collective knowledge and collective struggle, as a goal and method of liberation suggests the ongoing significance of the Black Panther Party in the life and work of Hank Jones.

Kiilu Nyasha, journalist and former New Haven Panther, known for her print, radio, and television journalism spotlighting injustice and raising local and global issues and struggles for liberation. Photograph by Eric Norberg

CHAPTER THREE

Kiilu Taught Me:
Letters to My Comrade

Tina Bartolome

Kiilu Nyasha joined the New Haven chapter of the Black Panther Party as a thirty-year-old single mother in the winter of 1969.[1] The party offered her a set of principles and tools to fight for her own survival and she dove into rank-and-file duties with passion. She made her apartment and car available to Panthers and pooled resources to make more time to devote to the work. Her strong writing skills and work ethic soon got her recruited to serve fulltime on the Panther legal defense team, and she helped organize a successful national campaign to gain the dismissal of charges against Ericka Huggins and Bobby Seale in New Haven. In the spring of 1971, when internal divisions became intolerable, Kiilu left the party, moving across the country to cover the Marin Courthouse Rebellion pre-trials of Ruchell Cinque Magee and Angela Davis as a journalist for the *San Francisco Sun Reporter*. This set of experiences solidified Kiilu's approach to movement work and personal practice for the rest of her life. As COINTELPRO effectively waged its war and the political landscape continued shifting to the right, she gave birth to her second child, took up studying Wu Shu kung fu and then developed polymyositis, a chronic muscle disease that left her permanently disabled by 1980.

Continuing through adversity, Kiilu blossomed into a prolific print, radio, and television journalist, exposing injustice and amplifying local and global struggles for liberation through the *SF Bayview* newspaper, various radio programming (KPFA, KPOO, SF Liberation Radio, Free Radio Berkeley), and her longest-running media project, *Freedom Is a Constant Struggle*, a bimonthly television show.[2] She earned a reputation as a news junkie, staying current with an impressive range of world events and as a sharp critic of nationalist and capitalist tendencies within the Black liberation movement. Her articles were meticulously researched and carried the weight of urgency and ultimatums, always pushing toward bold collective action and divestment from the system.

Kiilu used art and culture to gather, inspire, and express solidarity with, among others, the people of Haiti, South Africa, Palestine, and the Philippines. She worked to popularize the revolutionary tradition of Black August, a month to embrace the principles and spirit of Black resistance and to remain steadfast in the struggle to free political prisoners within the United States. Her body of work includes beautiful charcoal portraits of numerous international freedom fighters accompanied by over four decades of correspondence with comrades behind bars, including George Jackson, Hugo "Yogi" Pinell, Ruchell Cinque Magee, Mumia Abu Jamal and Geronimo ji Jaga Pratt.

She was a resident of Ping Yuen North, San Francisco Chinatown's largest housing project, for almost four decades and was recognized by her neighbors as a tenant leader. She demanded rights and dignity for the poor and homeless and successfully fought to make the building ADA-compliant through rent strikes, grievance letters, and raising hell at tenant meetings.

Her spirit thrived as a mentor to countless young people, candidly sharing her lessons and wisdom earned through decades of principled struggle as a contribution to the next generation of freedom fighters. She lived on her own terms and never compromised her dignity under a system she despised. Kiilu loved the people, believed in the people, and fought tirelessly for our collective liberation. She joined the ancestors on April 10, 2018.

I met Kiilu in 1996 after moving a block up the street from her in San Francisco's Chinatown. I was a twenty-one-year-old newly radicalized organizer. She was a fifty-seven-year-old force of nature. I started out as one of her home care workers, and over the next twenty-two years we became close comrades and chosen family. I came through in times of crisis. I was her company for music concerts, marches, and birthdays. An extra pair of eyes for her drafts. Though she participated in organizing meetings and actions, with her limited mobility, most of her political work took place inside her ninth-floor apartment. She needed loving and dependable relationships with people who could be trusted to practically support her capacity to remain active in the struggle. I became one of them.

I realize that my grief lies between these lines. Her death in April 2018 is still very much with me. Stories not mine to tell lie between these lines. In the spirit of dignifying her life and especially her invisible labor, I have chosen to write this reflection in her preferred form: letters. I want to speak to her rather than about her so that I may continue to invite her spirit to impact my own. I share these letters as an offering to anyone willing to let her spirit impact them too.

Read at her memorial at the African American Art & Culture Complex in San Francisco, California, on May 20, 2018.

Dearest Kiilu,

It feels fitting to write you a letter now. You taught me about the power that letters have to connect with people we love who are out of our reach. I am, we are, left here feeling you out of our reach. It aches. This city feels truly done without you.

I am, we are, also left with your teachings. I thought I knew most of them by now. You led so clearly and consistently by example, you never minced words and always made yourself accessible. I remember how you purposely stayed listed in the yellow pages because you wanted people to be able to find you. How you'd often leave your door unlocked in case someone wanted to visit. If I know anything about you, it's that you will insist on this same policy as an ancestor. And same as when you were alive, it's on us to stay connected with you. And so begins our correspondence.

It's hard to accept your passing. In part because you are irreplaceable. No one will ever possess both your disarming smile and your razor-sharp commentary, your fierce independence alongside your deep belief in community. But also hard to accept, because there is so much work left to do to take down this system and we are so far from the discipline, the steadfastness, the rank-and-file boldness that you humbly embodied. That is so necessary if we are to stand a chance at winning.

And just when I'm about to let another layer of despair settle into my bones, I am flooded with memories of you and your love of being in water, hot as you could take it. You'd take up any opportunity to get in a swim at North Beach Pool. A hot bath at least three times a week, maybe with P Funk, Earth, Wind & Fire and Tupac playing loud so you could feel the bass enough to move your limbs and exercise. I remember hearing the joy in your voice, the joy of your limbs defying gravity. A regular hot bath was not a luxury, not just a way to get clean. It was one of your tricks to keep the despair from settling into your bones. You were full of tricks to maintain your humanity. I'm so grateful to have witnessed them up close. I'm so grateful for the time I got to spend with you in this city, for how you shaped my walk and my talk in this place where we are against the odds.

Until next time,
daring to struggle, daring to win,
Tina

August 1, 2018

Dearest Kiilu,

I kept a few of your things. Your key remains on my key ring and goes with me everywhere. A part of me is glad you were spared the burden of relocating when your apartment gets demolished this fall for redevelopment. I am sure your place will show up in my dreams defiant and fully intact as pre-gentrification San Francisco sometimes does. Your many voicemails are still on my phone. I just listened to the one you left me on New Year's Eve wishing us both a year of more art and creativity. I remember the delight on your face as you jotted down the art date we set on your wall calendar. Acts of accountability were always your jam.

The object I cherish most, however, is the little red book you always kept bedside, faded, worn and marked up with notes in the margins.[3] I gave it to you fourteen years ago to replace your previously worn copy. You quoted from it often, but I never saw you write in it, something you must have done alone in your quiet evening hours. The little red book was your touchstone, from the day Dougy Miranda and Robert Webb came to your New Haven apartment to recruit you into the party to the morning you died in your bed at the age of seventy-eight in San Francisco. I don't know anyone else who embodied its principles more.

You came up in a historical moment when Mao's writings had become shared language to support national struggles for liberation around the world. You were brought into amplified purpose through your own praxis in the company of millions. Then the moment passed. You went from living in the Bayview and Fillmore surrounded by Black community to living in isolation in the Chinatown projects, the only place the city claimed was wheelchair accessible when you got out of the hospital. Over many years you built community with other tenants to meet your mutual interests. After demanding that tenant meetings solely conducted in Cantonese also be translated into English, you joined efforts to collectively demand hot water when it ran cold and to make sure the elevators got fixed when they were broken. Even Housing Authority staff grew to respect how you wielded your power. When In-Home Support Services paid less than a living wage for your home care providers, you worked the system as long as you could to pay them a higher wage and gain more control over your own care. "Use what you have to get what you need," you used to say. "Preserve the style of plain living and hard struggle," Mao wrote.[4] So you did. And slowly it became known that there was a bona fide Panther living in the Ping.

In the absence of vibrant international mass movements for liberation, you continued to advance the Panther legacy, always striving to eliminate contradictions between your personal practice and political principles. I never told you this, but it's why I wanted younger Black and Brown organizers that I mentored to meet you in person. They were sometimes starry-eyed about the party's heyday and the trajectory of its surviving visible leadership. Your intellect did not come with a professor's title from a prestigious university. You preferred being single over being married. You had not extended your leadership into electoral politics, in fact you advocated boycotting elections entirely. You lived unapologetically in a twelve-story housing project, not in a nice big house in the hills. You proudly served the people and were of the people.

Each summer I'd bring a new crew of organizers over for an informal "PE session" as you liked to call them.[5] We'd pile into a tight circle in your cozy living room, their eyes lingering over your freedom fighter portraits lining the walls and the titles on your bookshelves, stealing more cautious glances at your hospital bed and weed stash. They would be awestruck by your stunning and unobstructed view of the Bay Bridge, remarking on how much people paid to have this kind of view. They would later see it with new eyes when you described it as a saving grace because you spent so many hours unable to leave your bed.

Before sharing your story, you wanted to learn their names and hear about their organizing work, curious to ask them follow-up questions if you were unfamiliar with a term they used or a campaign they mentioned. I would watch their bodies relax and settle in your presence as you candidly shared, the good, the bad, and the ugly of your time in the Panthers with generous sprinklings of profanity, health advice, and revolutionary agitation. Sometimes you would quote Fanon, "Every generation must, out of relative obscurity, discover its mission, fulfill it or betray it."[6] You acknowledged the sacrifices that came with committing your life to serve the people and fight their enemies. You intervened in respectability politics by emphasizing that "to be attacked by the enemy is not a bad thing but a good thing."[7] And that they must never forget to defend our comrades behind bars. You urged them to study movement history but use tactics that respond to current conditions. You spoke as one generation of freedom fighters speaks to the next, to their hearts, rooting for them to achieve the victory that you knew you would never get to see. Kiilu, so many young people, many now full grown like myself, credit a conversation with you or a series of conversations, with deepening their understanding of protracted struggle and their own role in carrying it forward. You always told me how much these visits "recharged your batteries" and "lifted your spirits." These visits were part of my role. You always looked forward to the next one. So did I.

Missing you,
Tina

August 21, 2018

Dearest Kiilu,

There are so many deaths you've suffered over the decades, and here I am looking to your example for how to survive yours. When George Jackson was murdered on this very day forty-seven years ago you smoked your last cigarette outside San Quentin and vowed to become the female version of him. When Yogi was murdered inside New Folsom Prison in 2016, you were so heartbroken you got sick with pneumonia and stopped corresponding with prisoners altogether. So many times when I came over in the morning, I found you shedding tears upon receiving the news of a loved one's passing. Still you rolled out into the sun for Lil' Bobby Hutton Day and Malcolm X Jazz Arts Festival and you rooted for Serena Williams and the Spurs from your bedside. You got dressed up to meet Oscar Lopez Rivera and celebrate his long-awaited release. You continued hosting *Freedom Is a Constant Struggle* and turning out for Palestine, Haiti, the Philippines, Frisco Five, SF8, and World War II comfort women. You faithfully promoted the origins of Black August. Year after year, you marked their birthdays and death anniversaries, both privately and publicly, committed to saying their names and honoring their spirits. When death piled up you met its weight with resolve. You assessed the damage and figured out what new discipline was needed to stay alive.

You looked to your heroes for inspiration. You saw George Jackson make prison a time to study, train, and organize so you used the same approach for the three painful and abusive years you spent inside the medical system when you first got sick. You smiled when you would show up to the courtroom extra early for the SF8 trials and Yuri Kochiyama would already be there. Yuri's daughter continued to check on you after her mother passed, bringing you soup when you were sick. When Grace Lee Boggs came to town for a film screening and study group, you were the only one who raised her hand when she asked who had done the readings. I remember how touched you were to sit side by side in your wheelchairs, and she reached for your hand when it was time to take a photo. Kiilu, you were on the same level as your heroes.

I know it was sometimes frustrating to deal with the rest of us. Those of us who said we would visit but didn't. Those of us who didn't give you the credit due for your work. Those of us who ignored your suggestions but took them seriously coming from an able-bodied man's mouth. These things told us more about ourselves than they did about you.

Your bullshit detector was impeccable. Your face was incapable of masking shade in untrustworthy company and you were quick to keep a fool at arm's length. You had high expectations of anyone with basic decency and you were a practiced master in the art of giving second, third, and even fourth chances. Part of cultivating people power required not discarding one another, trusting in our capacity to do better next time. You often spoke of how we were all in lifetime training to become our best selves, the new men and women that were needed to build a new society. Even in interpersonal conflict you could point out precisely where there was individual accountability and where the system was to blame.

Nedzada and I came through the days before you died because you were short on regular help.[8] You had been suffering through the poor care of a home care worker you had started calling "Evilina." She often would not speak one word to you during her whole shift and ignore your requests for basic things. You fired her, even though this left you stranded for the weekday mornings to come. You told her to her face that she didn't care about you as a human being, that she was mean and you didn't need to put up with treatment like that in your own home. More important than safety or belonging was your dignity. You would not let anyone compromise your dignity, not a caretaker, not a man, not your children. Still, you signed off on her timesheet for the rest of the week. In-Home Supportive Services was designed to fail. None of your home care workers could afford to live in the city. "Traveling from Antioch to San Francisco to work half a day for $13 an hour is a joke," you said. Kiilu, I did not understand what dignity was until I met you.

Unlike so many of the other struggles you were famous for championing, the ongoing struggle to get your basic needs met while living with a disability was most often waged in private. This contradiction sits in my heart as I mourn you. You taught me how to ask for help with dignity and how to give help without taking away someone's agency. How to follow through on my word or else not give it at all. How to put in the work that showing up requires and listen deeply without an agenda. How to believe more in people's capacity to grow than to fail. The kind of training I got through caring for you is foundational for how to be an ally for all bodies and relationships that make up our movements for liberation.

You made it clear to us, your circle of chosen family, how fiercely you valued your independence and preferred death over institutional assisted living. So we came together in the spirit of interdependence with your self-determination at our center. We practiced our love for you with many verbs, but it wasn't enough. Only a new world, the one that people power can deliver, the one we continue to fight for now in your honor, will be enough. We get there by doing better now. I know there are others who have already been answering this question and so I join them: What would it look like if disability justice was as central to our analysis, demands, and work ethic as racial, gender, and economic justice?[9] Who and what do we stand lose by not doing so? Kiilu, I am trying to assess the damage and figure out what new discipline our movements need to stay alive. This, and these letters, are how I survive losing you.

Love & solidarity always,
Tina

II.
SUSTAINABILITY AND SPIRITUALITY

Erika Huggins, former Los Angeles Panther and longtime director of the BPP Community School. Her spiritual practice, begun inside prison in a BPP case in New Haven, is the foundation of her work for restorative justice and healing. Photograph by Lisbet Tellefsen

CHAPTER FOUR

A Spiritual Practice for Sustaining Social Justice Activism: An Interview with Ericka Huggins

Diane C. Fujino

E ricka Huggins, one of the longest-standing members of the Black Panther Party (BPP), joined the Los Angeles chapter with John Huggins in late 1967, after traveling from Lincoln University in Pennsylvania, to support the Huey Newton defense committee. She remained a member of the BPP until 1981. After exiting from Niantic Prison in 1971, she served as an editor of the *Black Panther* newspaper, director of the BPP's Oakland Community School from 1973 to 1981, and was a member of the BPP Central Committee.[1] She is most widely known as the wife of Panther leader John Huggins, who was killed with Alprentice "Bunchy" Carter at UCLA's Campbell Hall in January 1969. Ericka was subsequently arrested and stood trial with Bobby Seale in New Haven, Connecticut—a trial that was eventually declared a mistrial.

She speaks in the interviews about the heartbreak of separation from her daughter, Mai, only three weeks old at the time of John's murder and three months old upon Ericka's arrest in New Haven. A poet since age ten, writing helped her survive prison not just physically but emotionally and spiritually, as did the spiritual practices of meditation and yoga, which she began in prison. She was incarcerated from May 22, 1969, to May 25, 1971.[2] To this day, her daily practice of meditation helps to focus her mind, preparing her to face the challenges of human life and the pressures of social justice activism, while enabling her to walk in the world with extraordinary compassion, humanity, dignity, and self-power.

The following is based on two interviews I conducted with Ericka Huggins on April 17, 2018, at her home in Oakland, California, and on October 5, 2018, by phone. The dialogue is edited to reduce the lengthier ways of oral conversation. To focus the interview and for space considerations, I did not include the first part of the April interview. That interview began with a common practice of Ericka's—asking the interviewer questions. Scholar Mary Phillips writes about her own interview experience with Ericka. Ericka told her: "I care about your work and I know that you've read many books and articles that party members have written. So before we begin, do you understand where I'm coming from? Because I do not want you to think I am picking apart your work or anybody else's. I just want you to understand how it feels to be written about while we are still alive."[3] Ericka's questions claim her own subjectivity and agency, rather than being the object of another's interview and writing. She is direct and clear about her expectations, but also compassionate and connects in the ways of women. Her questions to me included: Who is in the book? What other women activists are included? She offered well-placed criticism: "If the book doesn't have a balance of women and men, it makes me feel uncomfortable to contribute to it. There is such a hole. It's not a blame or critique about the party or writers. What's needed is a shift in perception about the history of the party, and *why* it has an impact today." She made clear the two areas that she wants emphasized in any interpretation of BPP history: "I'm happy you're doing this [book] . . . to move from mostly men to a balance of women and men" and to "show how the community survival programs were a form of self-defense . . . a form of community health and well-being."

The interviews focus on Huggins's spiritual practice as a basis for social justice work.

◊ ◊ ◊

Diane Fujino: *You began a practice of yoga inside prison, in that very traumatic environment. I'm interested in how you use your spiritual practice—you meditate every day, what you're calling self-care—and how it relates to social justice work.*

Ericka Huggins: (pause) I know you know about COINTELPRO. I know you know that John Huggins and Alprentice "Bunchy" Carter were murdered at UCLA on January 17, 1969, just three weeks after my daughter's birth in December 1968. When John and Bunchy were killed, I became a widow and single mom in a single breath. To say I was heartbroken doesn't suffice. Bunchy was the dearest friend to me, other than John. There was something about both of them. John was absolutely a feminist man. Bunchy was chivalrous, but open in a way I know few men are today. I felt he saw me as an equal. He was brilliant. Both of them gone in one moment was a lot. I had my baby daughter to care for—and I was very young, just twenty-one.[4] Then, three months later, I was arrested, and my daughter had to be taken from me. Prisons don't have a setup where women can live with their children. So I was forced to stop breastfeeding, which was traumatic in and of itself. The Huggins family was so kind, they lived an hour from the prison and brought my daughter to see me every week, every week for one hour, for two years. My daughter's life became the catalyst for me to shift something. I'll explain. When I recognized I could only see my new baby for an hour once a week, my heart felt like shattered glass. Just shards everywhere. There wasn't any thought I could have or feeling that made me feel okay.

So I spoke to my friend Charlie Garry, one of the main attorneys in our legal team. People don't know that Charlie practiced yoga for a good part of his life. Before he entered any courtroom, he'd do a full headstand, dressed in his suit, with his fancy tie-clip, and big topaz ring.

When I said, "Charlie, I don't think I can live like this." He knew what I meant. I asked him if he'd bring me a book on yoga. He did. The book included pictures of a woman doing yoga poses with clear descriptions of how to do them. I laughed, thinking, *I always loved to move, but if I snap or break something, oh well.* So I began to teach myself those poses, *asanas.* I felt energized and rejuvenated, which is the whole point. But the thing that got my attention was that, after a series of poses, the book encouraged me to sit still a while and notice my breath. So I did. Then I sat still, in meditation, not just after I did yoga poses, but every morning to face the day. On days when there were court hearings an hour away, I meditated to face being in a caravan of cars, handcuffed, and on trial for my life—without any friends to talk to—because I was in isolation.

For a few months, I was in isolation with four other women. They were all released. Thank goodness, they didn't keep those women incarcerated. Then I was in isolation by myself in a wing locked away from the rest of the population. I existed in this cloistered environment for fourteen months before the trial started. The trial took six months, and, after the jury hung twice, the judge declared a mistrial. The hung jury was due to one jurors' bias about the BPP and Bobby and me. The day the mistrial was declared Bobby Seale and I were released from prison.

Meditation made me capable of shifting my experience in that carceral site. I became self-reflective. What is the kind of world that I have been envisioning and speaking about? How can I create programs for people that change inequities? And what is the world that I want to know from the inside out? How will I heal the woundedness I'm feeling right now? I didn't talk to anyone about my deep self-inquiry.

I wrote poetry, as I had done all of my life. Some of those poems are in a book that's out of print, *Insights and Poems*, coauthored with Huey Newton.[5] Meditation kept me resilient, aware, and awake in a good way. I didn't want to be hypervigilant and paranoid. I wanted to be aware of my circumstances. I wanted to be able to trust people when I needed to. It was necessary to trust people and not let everyone's stuff in. COINTELPRO was literally trying to kill us. Every day in the courthouse I wished for Bobby the awareness of this infinite power inside him, inside every human being. We're born with it, but we're not taught about it, which is a shame. But it is there, and it's meant to help us through challenging times, to face the day, to face the night, to face anything. So I began to shift my perception of the world and what freedom really is—its source. I came to an understanding that *I will never be free if I don't feel free here, in prison*. Free of being raised by my alcoholic father. Free of blaming myself for every decision I'd made. I realized there, in that tiny cell, that every part of our lives impacts us, nothing gets left behind. Nothing is unimportant. We need to heal old wounds, so we can walk forward and continue to be of use. We can't be walking wounded. I came to this understanding sitting there in solitary confinement. I was just temporarily restricted or with other women in an isolated wing. I was intended to be in one cell, twenty-three hours a day, for the duration of that time I was incarcerated. That was a profound experience, having no one to talk to other than prison guards who brought my meals. Not only did my perceptions shift, the quality of my thoughts shifted. I stopped asking myself, *What if I'm convicted and I'm forced to live here for the rest of my life?* I knew the government could do anything it wanted. Eddie Conway was recently released after almost four decades. Albert Woodfox was released from solitary confinement after almost forty-five years! So I didn't take lightly that that could happen to me.

My meditation practice helped me. Instead of becoming depressed about being away from my daughter, I tried to see everything in the here and now. When I visited with my daughter for an hour, no matter where I was, what I was doing, no matter the circumstances of my life, I could face her and remain balanced. After a few months I was less sad, my heart was healing, my body—because of the daily yoga—was not succumbing to the challenges of the physical cold, damp cement, and steel building.

In 1970, the State of Connecticut agreed to release me from solitary confinement. I was released into the main population of women. It wasn't until I was engaging with all of the women that I could see the difference in myself. Women would reflect back to me: "You're so calm, so peaceful, how do you do that?" A friend and I set up a collective that people don't know about. It was called Sister Love. The prison didn't mind us getting together to do each other's hair. Black, brown, and a few white women doing hair. The white women were who there were very poor. I was there for conspiracy with the intent to commit murder. When the women met me and befriended me, they said, "Something is not right. What are you doing here?" And I said, "What are you doing here? None of us belong in prison."

Prison didn't mind us doing hair together. What the authorities didn't know is that when women get together for any reason, that's when real conversation happens. We started to talk about the concept of a pimp.

So, I'm braiding someone's hair, and I asked,

"How is it the pimp gets to put you on the street, but you don't get the money he gets? Your work is sex, which is fine, but how come you don't get the money he gets? What's really going on?"

"You right, Ericka. I asked my pimp, 'Why you get more?' and he just said, 'Shut up, bitch.'"

This is how we would begin to talk. The woman who did check fraud said, "How is a person to survive? I'm a single mom. I want to feed my children. How am I to buy groceries, pay rent? There's no cash flow, so I have to get from Tuesday to Friday." I said, "I know. Do you think there's something wrong with you, or something bigger going on?" This conversation while washing or blow drying someone's hair.

In these conversations we decided we could do a lot for each other by talking. And we could do more for the women coming in. There were many recovering heroin addicts at Niantic. First idea an elder woman in Sister Love shared, "We can help women kick heroin, so they don't have to go cold turkey—because they die from doing that." I was isolated, so I didn't know women die in a kick cell, a special isolation cell where they were deprived of the drug—and medical attention and human contact. It was supposed to be rehab, but it wasn't. They got no medication, no support, we could hear them screaming at night. So we'd smuggle in cigarettes and candy. The nicotine eased the muscle spasms and pain, and sugar helped to balance the cravings. Not healthy, but it saved their lives. We could talk. We could talk through the open vents that went to the kick cell and just say kind things. "Can we get you a lawyer?" "Where are your children?" "Who has your children?" Through my legal team, we got lawyers for many women. This was an organic thing, Sister Love. No one encouraged us to do this. It is what was needed—love. My training was in the Black Panther Party. I knew what to do, you serve people wherever you are. There, I made lifelong friends.

I've continued to mediate every day. Why? Because it gives me the same resiliency I experienced when I was incarcerated. Over the years I've become more and more grounded in myself. I've become less swayed by external circumstances. I've learned to protect my heart in order to keep serving. That's why one topic I speak about is the importance of spiritual practice in sustaining social justice activism. "Radical self-care" is what we call it. It's about individual and collective healing and how that relates to social justice. Did you read the article in the *New York Times* on the importance of self-care, "Black Stress Matters"?[6] The article talks about Black women activists who died in the last year. Two were suicides. The third woman, twenty-seven years old, died of a heart attack.[7] At an event on a campus, a young woman came to me in tears, saying, "I have no time for my partner, no time for my family, no time for myself." How are we nurturing each other? We act as if we're supposed to do everything, keep doing everything, without any recharge to the inner battery. It's a male idea that you serve the people until you fall on your face.

DF: *One of the things you mentioned is how this work is an ongoing practice and must be applied to your life. I'm wondering how you do that in your personal practice.*

EH: I meditate every day, and I do this before the day begins early each morning, which fosters and supports self-inquiry. When you are in a calm and steady state, things arise for you to look at: "Why am I having that thought?" or "Hmm, that thought may be the resolution to a problem," or "Maybe if I speak to so-and-so, it will clear the air."

DF: *What strikes me, Ericka, isn't that it's a humane process, which I expected. But I am struck by the ways you really work with honesty and candidness. I know that would be necessary because it just can't be superficial or false kindnesses.*

EH: No! Because that really isn't kind! We can't keep this stuff inside and never speak our truth. That's why we're in the horrific situations we keep finding ourselves in as humans. It really isn't just about who's in the Oval Office or who wants to be the judge. It's about discerning what it is that we've allowed for centuries. What we've taught the children decade after decade. What we have allowed to happen to children in our education, health care, and prison systems.

DF: *I agree with you about the kinds of personal wounds and injuries that people have, but I also see it as structural and systemic in that this is—*

EH: That's the point I'm making. These are infrastructures that we've allowed to rot, and we pretend that it's still holding us up. These systems of race, gender, and class hatred started with the inception of this country.

I'll never forget when I was at a conference after Tim Wise spoke. He says, "I'm white. I'll talk about what it means to be white." He lays it out. Two women came to me after he spoke, two white women. One was a middle-age white woman who lived in Toledo, doing restorative justice work in local prisons. Her world was limited. She came to me in tears and said, "Why does Tim yell at us?" I looked at her, and she was really sad. I got her a tissue, and I said, "I didn't hear Tim yelling." She said, "No, he didn't raise his voice, but he's making us (white people) all wrong." I said, "I didn't hear that. As a matter of fact what I felt when Tim spoke is that my breath evened out and I felt relieved."

She looked at me in shock like it had never dawned on her that there was another perspective than hers. She continued to cry but said, "You really feel supported when Tim talks?" I said, "Yes! He's a white person talking about what it means to be white. It's so honest. It's so clear. He talks about race structurally; how it works. He also talked about how the prisons work and who gets arrested—and who doesn't." He also encourages all of us to do our personal work.

DF: *I'm wondering how you've seen prisoners change as a result of the restorative justice circles that you've done.*

EH: Well, I didn't facilitate them. I was invited into them. Here's one way that they work. The circles are for incarcerated men or women. They last sometimes anywhere from a year to eighteen months. During that time every man or woman in that particular circle gets to tell their story. Restorative justice asks for three things, or two: accountability, responsibility, and, if possible, asking for forgiveness. Each person in the circle is scheduled to tell their story without making excuses, being entirely accountable and responsible, knowing that the circle is a brave circle, that everybody in the circle is willing to do the same thing.

The day that I went to San Quentin, which was the first circle I sat in, the man who was scheduled to speak was to share his story of how he beat and robbed someone. He said that the week before he was to speak he was sick to his stomach every day. He had restless nights because he knew he was going to have to make his story clear to all the men he knew, the men he supported, and he had to trust that they would support him. He'd never told this story until that day. He cried as he moved through the story of the person he harmed. I mean, he could barely get some of the words out. And midway through he says, "One of the things that made me sick when I was preparing to tell this story was I remembered how my father beat me." He wasn't making an excuse. He said he was having a flash of how his childhood and his adulthood were connected. The men in the circle were nodding their heads. Every single one of them, Diane. They nodded their heads in recognition of the connection. Hurt people hurt people. My experience is that this is a familiar story for incarcerated women and men.

That day the facilitator asked me to go in and share my story of harm done to me and the healing that occurred for me when that person asked my forgiveness. The men told me that they felt uplifted and encouraged. They felt, if that could happen with me and the person who asked my forgiveness, maybe someday they would be able to speak to the person they harmed. Or, that at least in their heart they could ask forgiveness in the hope that it would reach the people that they harmed. I felt transformation happening in those two hours. I saw the result of the healing in that circle. The healing had been continuous for a year or more. It was palpable and tangible to everyone.

I had a *completely* different experience when I went to a prison for women to sit in a restorative justice circle. It was just as difficult for the women to share their stories. When a woman shared her own story of harming a family member, the women on either side of her were holding her hand as she talked. It was beautiful. Everyone appreciates the speaker for doing the hard-ass work of healing from the heart. They are continually offering their forgiveness. That is the intent that circles had centuries ago in parts of the world where this was the natural way communities would restore and thrive.

DF: *How do you see this spiritual practice, this work of restorative justice and meditation and other practices, as enabling social justice work?*

EH: It's important if we're wanting to uplift humanity that we uplift ourselves. They're not mutually exclusive. They're necessary. They're powerfully important. You know, if my body is in harm, how can I make it move down the steps out the door to do the work I must do? I have to take care of my body. If my heart is hurt by something or my thoughts are scattered, I must do something about it before I go to the next part of my work, especially if it's talking to people or standing up for something. But this isn't something, generation after generation, we've been trained to do because activism has been seen through a very male lens.

The antithesis to the old perspective is a conversation I had with Alicia Garza some years ago. She told me that among the Black Lives Matters networks—she was talking about herself and locally here, and also about many of the activists across the country—people take care of each other before they go out to their next action or after they leave a protest. They are very much aware of the toll that activism takes on the spirit of a human being. That energy can determine the wellness of a human being, and it shows up in our bodies, expresses in our thoughts and words.

I said, "Alicia, I'm so happy to hear you say that. I wish we'd done that in the movements of the sixties and seventies. I wish we'd been able to do it." When somebody was killed among us we just pulled out that black dress and went to a funeral. And then it was, "Next action!" And we didn't process it. How healthy is that? Young activists want to know how to do it differently. They know we made mistakes, at least I tell them that we made mistakes. If they don't know the movement history before them, it's our duty to tell them how it really happened. There is the romanticized version, and there's the reality.

I remember talking to an activist and mother who asked, "Is it fine for to me to take a pause?" I was like, "Oh, sweetheart, is it fine? It's urgent that you do so!" She said, "You know, I have children and I work and I'm an activist. I just don't have time for anything. I'm not as clear as I used to be. I'm not sleeping well." I said, "You must stop—pause." "Is that okay, Ericka?" she asked again. I had to convince her. Isn't that amazing, Diane? That I would have to convince her that rest was alright, important. So, yes, we all know our work is to abolish systems of violence, like prisons. However, it's interrelational and personal. It's all these things at once. It's not one or more of those things instead of another one. It's a Western and male paradigm that puts parts of our lives and work in boxes. But being a person who was a single mom raising children while being an activist, I know that men don't have to consider raising the children when they say, "You don't stop, you keep going for the revolution."

People must take care of themselves because our bodies, minds, and hearts are the vehicle for real transformation in our world. It's not a self-referenced taking care. Cars cannot run without fuel. The human body needs a different kind of fuel. Not just food. But we need to fuel our hearts and fuel our minds with great things. We need to have people around us to support us. I want younger people to know that there are people, whom they will never see, who are proud that they are doing the work they're doing. I want them to know that we support them in taking care of themselves while taking care of our world.

Dhameera Ahmad, educator and former Oakland and San Francisco Panther, lived as if religion and revolution are one because they are both expressions of a people's culture. Photo courtesy of Nisa Ahmad, daughter of Dhameera Ahmad

CHAPTER FIVE

Serving the People and Serving God: The Everyday Work and Mobilizing Force of Dhameera Ahmad

By Maryam Kashani

When I think of Sister Dhameera, I see her sitting on a gray metal folding chair, her long skirt and coat draped majestically on either side, her face illuminated—framed by a neatly pinned blue or white headscarf. She sits quietly reading the Qur'an, smiling, or more likely, she is attending to the women and children who assemble around her for hugs and greetings of peace. It is before or after the Friday congregational prayer, *Jumu'ah*, at Lighthouse Mosque, a small, but all-encompassing storefront mosque in North Oakland. But it could also be any number of places—the diner on MacArthur, the Thai restaurant in the Tenderloin, the Islamic retreat in San Jose, or along the walking paths around Lake Merritt. Everywhere I went with Dhameera, she was greeted by people she knew, whether from her years as an Oakland schoolteacher, principal, and parent; her activism as a Black Panther, as a student organizer at San Francisco State, or on behalf of political prisoners; or as a devout Muslim and organizer in Bay Area Muslim communities.

It is difficult to convey the force of this woman who meant so much to so many, who spoke so little of herself, but who profoundly impacted—materially and spiritually—the people around her. How do we recognize leadership that keeps people moving, pushes them along, that makes them feel like the struggle

91

for justice is worth it and possible, not through grand speeches and fervent campaigns, but through the everyday work of being present, getting people in order, gathering them together, and reminding them of what came before and where we are trying to go? How can I describe the affective and mobilizing force that was Hajja Dhameera Carlotta Ahmad?[1]

In my research I often discuss Islam as a mobilizing force that moves people in dynamic ways, but as I think about Dhameera, I am forced to rethink this.[2] Perhaps it is actually the people who embody Islam in their ways of being and their actions who transmit and exude that force. The Islam that Dhameera embodied also carried within it the knowledge and experience that she gained as a Black Panther; the way she carried this history is just one of the many lessons that I learned—and continue to learn—from her in ways that extend the expansive arc of Black Panther Party legacies and lessons. Through the example of the way she lived and what she believed, Dhameera taught me that one could serve the people and God at the same time, that there was no negotiation between the spiritual and the political if we recognize that in a "continuing practice of serving . . . part of our responsibility is to look and see, 'What can we do?' to make a difference."[3] Indeed, her life was lived as one who believed that one could not serve God unless one was serving the people. Dhameera was consistently committed to the goals of both the BPP and her life as a practicing Muslim woman within a sociopolitical context in which religion, especially Islam, and revolutionary politics are often positioned as oppositional, contradictory, and threatening forces. She found this consistency by focusing on what she could do and by mobilizing others to also "look and see" and then *do* toward making a difference.

Ahmad, born Carlotta Basseau Simon (aka Nisa) was born into a legacy of activism by way of her Louisiana and Oklahoma roots on January 11, 1950, in San Francisco, California. She was the first of five children born to the late Bettye Opal Simon Johnson, a community builder and matriarch, and to the recently deceased Joseph "Bunny" Simon Sr., a widely known Bay Area entrepreneur and activist. At sixteen years old, while attending the Catholic, all-girls Presentation High School, Dhameera (then known as Carlotta) joined the Black Panther Party for Self-Defense. She was drawn by "these movement people. I just thought they were sharp, you know, well-read, good discussions, people that I had a lot of respect for. They worked hard, I worked hard. We worked."[4] After her day at school, she would "go check in down at the Panther office. Put my uniform in a paper bag and put on my black pants and a blue shirt . . . either work down at the office, or go out selling papers, or serving breakfast that morning, working on food distribution, getting people to rallies, getting people to health clinics. All the work that was involved in the early movement days of taking care of the people."[5]

Dhameera was active in both the Oakland and San Francisco chapters from about 1967 to 1971, and she also spent time with the New York chapter when she traveled there around 1968. Dhameera "was strictly a foot soldier," yet she was "deemed an asset" because she was a Catholic schoolgirl with "advanced skills" from her college-preparatory education. Kathleen and Eldridge Cleaver recruited her to work on the newspaper after Huey was arrested, yet lacking the "basic" skill of typing, she wielded a razor to cut and lay out articles as she listened to the humorous and "rich tales being told" by her movement elders.[6] Her other service ranged from doing security—"reading my book, studying for my exam, having my gun because I am supposed to be keeping the place safe"—to traveling across the Bay Bridge regularly to participate in the Oakland-based breakfast program before her own classes.[7] Entering San Francisco State in fall 1968, she immediately joined the Black Student Union (BSU) and its movement to establish Black studies and also participated in the Third World Strike, which began on her campus in November 1968. Dhameera was known as a Panther on campus and applied her Panther skills and knowledge as she worked with other students in the BSU presidium to staff classes, write class descriptions, and do the administrative and communicative footwork to develop the emerging Black Studies program.[8]

Dhameera stepped away from the Panthers in 1971 to focus on her studies and being a mother to her Panther baby, Nisa Leila. In Arabic, "Nisa" means "woman" and was the name Mutulu Shakur, then with the Republic of New Afrika and current political prisoner, gave Dhameera (then Carlotta) when they met in New York. Dhameera passed the name on to her daughter and added "Leila" for Palestinian freedom fighter, Leila Khaled, symbolizing the internationalist commitments and solidarities that she and the BPP held. Although Dhameera would enter the Nation of Islam (NOI) in the mid-1970s, she had been introduced to Islam as a global faith in the 1960s through her interactions with African American Muslims (some of whom were members of the Black Panther Party and Black Liberation Army) and through her study—of the Palestinian struggle, of Algeria in Frantz Fanon's *Wretched of the Earth*, and of the speeches and autobiography of Malcolm X, El-Hajj Malik El-Shabazz.

Movement histories say little about spirituality and faith, often setting up false dichotomies between revolutionary politics and "religion" or situating religion-based organizing as inherently reformist. People's faith is often marginalized as false consciousness, "the opiate of the masses," or regarded as peripheral to the political in the case of the Nation of Islam. For example, many people misinterpreted Malcolm X's departure from the NOI and move toward socialism as a disavowal of his faith and religious commitment, or at least a clear fissure between the two.[9] Dhameera's life assists in demonstrating the compatibility of Muslim faith and radical politics, putting pressure on our assumptions of what justice, or movements for justice—gendered, racial, class-based—can look like.

Taking on a new Islamic or African name (rejecting one's "slave name") was an important part of a sociopolitical self-identification that rejected the (Euro-American and Christian) West and claimed a connection to and historical depth through, a global community of Muslims and an Islamic cosmology that was a critical part of the Third World project of the 1950s and '60s.[10] Many Black Panthers became Muslims in their post-Panther lives; some took deep dives into the faith, others engaged it as a continuation of their social and political activism with an Islamic veneer.[11] For many young African Americans in cities throughout the United States, the decision was often whether to join the Panthers or the Nation.[12] Dhameera was a part of both movements, leaving the Panthers in 1971 and beginning her association with the Nation in the mid-1970s as it was beginning to transition to al-Islam.[13] Counter to claims—both then and now—that women and men who fought for their communal liberation were giving something up or were losing their radical politics by becoming Muslim, Dhameera and others found that they and their movements had something to gain through this radical reorientation that required a practice of submission (Islam) prior to and in the name of liberation.

In the BPP and the BSU at San Francisco State, Dhameera felt empowered to speak her mind, yet she was also cognizant of how her relationships with particular Panthers sheltered her from misogyny in the party. When she joined the Nation of Islam, she had to negotiate a different set of patriarchal gender dynamics. The patriarchal tenets of the NOI located the Black Muslim family and the respective roles and responsibilities of Black men and women within it as the foundation for a Black nation.[14] While women's responsibilities to *their* homes and children were foregrounded (as opposed to the domestic labor Black women performed for white families), Black

Muslim women extended this form of leadership and kinship into their communities as well. Dhameera's commitment to social justice and movement-building for Black people motivated her participation in the NOI; she was one of the first teachers at the Clara Muhammad School, and she took on a leadership role in Muslim Girls Training (MGT) where women trained in the domestic sciences, but also found sisterhood, opportunities for leadership, and mentorship.[15]

Dhameera, like other women who joined the Nation or converted to Islam, embraced and took pride in the gendered roles she took on. Muslim women revalued these roles as essential for the reproduction of social, spiritual, and material life, and they revalued the labor of the men in their lives as well. It was important to Dhameera and her family that people recognized that "she was a good Muslim, a good wife, and a good mother."[16] Though Dhameera worked outside the home for much of her forty-one-year marriage, she took these responsibilities seriously. Educating and feeding her husband and children, while also educating other children in Oakland and organizing food distribution and feeding programs, were a part of her social justice vision, informed by both Islam and the Black radical tradition, in which people had roles and responsibilities to each other that both re-inscribed and challenged capitalist and patriarchal relations. Her kinship network extended horizontally beyond her blood ties and across racial and ethnic identities to all those whom she felt a responsibility toward as someone who was able, an elder, and who had survived state violence and its aftereffects. It was for this reason that she often focused so much of her energy on the most vulnerable and disenfranchised in society—Black and brown children, the unhoused and hungry, and the imprisoned. She enlisted her friends in the everyday caretaking for Marilyn Buck when a cancer-stricken Buck was finally released from prison, and she often brought her husband and children with her on prison visits across the country. In remembering her forty-plus years of support to political prisoners, former political prisoner and fellow Muslim Sekou Odinga states that Dhameera "always took it seriously that her comrades from the Black Panther Party, the Black Liberation Army were political prisoners. She always did what she could to help us whether it was sending money, sending a letter of encouragement, a call, or information about what was going on in the streets. She was always looking out for us, you know." While she performed much of this service with humility, she mobilized others to get involved for maximum effect—toward building a movement and for their own moral and spiritual edification and salvation.

Many popular accounts of Black Panther history discuss the period from 1968 to 1972 as a "conservative shift from revolution to reform." Scholar Donna Murch suggests that "a more useful framework for understanding this new development was the Panthers' attempt to create a long-term organizing strategy to ensure the party's survival in the face of massive state repression."[17] Having experienced the state's policing and counterintelligence against the BPP and the Third World Strike firsthand, while also recognizing the significant need for and contribution of the BPP service programs, Dhameera, in her post-Panther life, applied herself toward the long-term sustenance and survival of communities that would fuel movements for social justice. Developing a spiritual relationship with Islam was a critical part of ensuring survival and longevity, not only for Dhameera herself but for those around her. As her friend and writer asha bandele describes, "Dhameera was deeply rooted in her own spiritual traditions, deep in practice. . . . This was a woman who has seen so many of her comrades, her peers and contemporaries, devastated by the FBI's war on the Black Panther Party. . . . She went further and further into the regions of her own spirit and soul to strengthen herself."[18] While the Panther organization was deeply disciplined and disciplining, the introspection, self-restraint, and daily practice of Islam was a significant draw for Dhameera, as was the possibility of taking on a new name, an oppositional politics, and building self-determined communities and institutions.[19]

Like so many other women organizers, rather than a spokesperson, she was a "centerperson"; she built and maintained the communications and spatial infrastructures through which Black and brown lives could thrive, from Oakland's public schools to its mosques and Islamic schools.[20] She did this work intentionally, as she went from foot soldier to leader, carrying her Panther history and knowledge into the Muslim community through her spiritual rigor and organizing. It was important for her that Muslims, especially in Oakland, "have a base where . . . people can benefit and . . . learn about their Lord."[21] Because she believed that these spaces should be community-run— meaning accountable to the people's needs and visions, rather than subject to the whims of a few imams and spokespeople—she organized community meetings and provided critique and advice to religious leaders. She pushed Muslims to recognize themselves as a community that could be mobilized and to take on leadership and determine "the direction of the *masjid*."[22] This was painstaking and frustrating work, but Dhameera persevered, encouraging young women and men to join mosque boards, participate in and support feeding programs, continue their study of Islam, organize and participate in protests against police surveillance and violence, and build a self-sustaining and thriving community—amidst and against resurgent state intervention and rapid gentrification—that could envision and implement social justice.

Her experience and knowledge became especially significant during the Gulf War (1990–1991) and then again after September 11, 2001, when Muslims were targeted by forms of anti-Muslim racism ranging from assaults on women and men in headscarves and turbans to state-sanctioned preemptive surveillance, entrapment, policing, and incarceration.[23] Dhameera's fearlessness, defiance, and continued organizing reminded the multiracial Muslim community that attacks on Muslims were part of a longer history of racism, dispossession, and oppression, and she was a living reminder of how Black people resisted, organized, and survived.

There are two Qur'anic verses that describe the actions of believers, those beloved to God that describe Dhameera's expansive political and spiritual embodiment well. Firstly, Dhameera would "fight them on until there is no more tumult or oppression, and there prevail justice and faith in Allah altogether and everywhere" (Qur'an 8:39).[24] From the first time she read Frantz Fanon's *The Wretched of the Earth*, Dhameera recognized "that oppression was universal, and I wanted to be a part of the chapter that struggled to end oppression worldwide."[25] By showing up and getting things done, Dhameera never faltered from this commitment, whether for a protest march, mosque fundraiser, or her five daily prayers for "she was a lady of action."[26] At the same time, the Qur'an speaks of feeding with pure intentions to serve God by serving the people; while Dhameera did indeed feed people with food, she also fed those around her with her spirit, amassed from the things she had seen, done, and inherited—the wisdom she gained from victories and missteps; the secrets she kept; and the comrades and history she honored. As to the Righteous, "They feed, for the love of Allah, the indigent, the orphan, and the captive. Saying, 'we feed you for the sake of Allah alone: no reward do we desire from you, nor thanks'" (Qur'an 76:8-9).

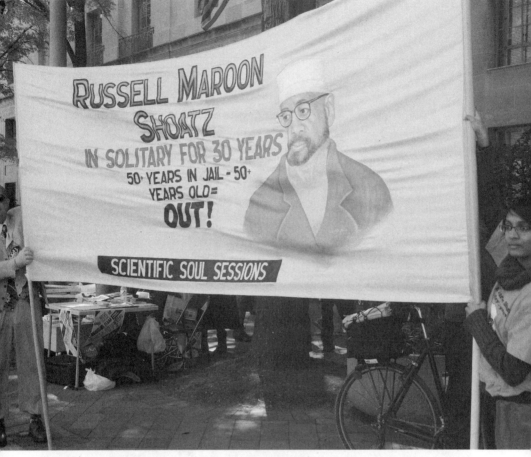

Fred Ho, left, musician, activist and writer, pictured here with fellow Scientific Soul Sessions comrade Kanya D'Almeida holding banner promoting freedom for political prisoner and former Panther Russell Maroon Shoatz. Scientific Soul Sessions helped win a campaign to release Maroon into general prison population ending twenty-two consecutive years of solitary confinement. Photo courtesy of Quincy Saul from his personal collection

Author Quincy Saul and Kanya D'Almeida visiting former Panther Russell Maroon Shoatz at SCI Graterford in Pennsylvania after his release from solitary confinement.

CHAPTER SIX

Ecosocialism from the Inside Out

Quincy Saul

This essay emerges from five years of organizing around political prisoners in the United States.[1] In the process I have been honored to meet and correspond with remarkable individuals in prison, and also to share relations and revelations with those on the outside who support them. In the same time period, I have also been involved with writing and organizing around ecosocialist politics, ranging from global climate justice initiatives to local urban gardening. I hope to recognize here and record the synthesis of these struggles, which already exists in practice but has not yet been theorized. Any errors in this analysis may be blamed on me, but I hope that its insights may be shared by all.[2]

Mass Extinction and the Matrix

If you have not accepted that we are experiencing a mass extinction, like the one that wiped out the dinosaurs, then count yourself amongst the Real Walking Dead.

—Russell Maroon Shoatz[3]

The people I know who seem most concerned about climate change and the sixth mass extinction are locked up in prison, where they can't do anything about it. On the outside, where we seem free to do many things about it, people don't seem so concerned. Everyone seems to know about it, but if we weigh this knowledge against action, then we come up short.

What's going on here? We have to understand these two things at the same time: (1) our crisis, and (2) our ongoing denial and disavowal of the crisis. As Ashley Dawson writes, "human experience itself is undergoing a form of extinction."[4] If we don't understand how these crises are interrelated, we have little chance of surviving either. The kingdom of extinction is all around us but also inside of us. We face not only climate catastrophe but a zombie apocalypse.

Why is it that these prisoners seem to care more than anyone on the outside? Is it that they can't enjoy the springtime weather in February? On some level it may be that simple. Capitalist modernity is a matrix that has trapped its constituents in a consumer trance that lasts lifetimes. This matrix is what makes us zombies, what keeps us from caring and/or acting about mass extinction. Those excluded from it have a better chance of seeing it clearly.

On one hand, we face unprecedented dangers and feel an appropriate sense of dread. On the other hand, the total crisis of society and ecology presents us with an unprecedented project and sense of liberation. We have been cursed/blessed with an existential crisis so profound that it drives us to the heights of what it means to be human: for in order to solve our immediate problems, we have to solve the most ancient problem of all—humanity's alienation from nature, and thus from our own nature.

Ultimately, the way to fight climate catastrophe and the zombie apocalypse is the same. As Masanobu Fukuoka writes, "Gradually I came to realize that the process of saving the desert of the human heart and re-vegetating the desert is actually the same thing."[5] In the terms of Frantz Fanon, the struggle for human nature is the mission our generation will fulfill or betray.[6] The central thesis of this essay is that prisoners are already leading the way.

Prisoners as Organic Intellectuals and Revolutionary Subjects

The prisons of America were the universities of revolution.
—**Safiya Bukhari**[7]

We have been transformed into an implacable army of liberation. . . . Believe me, my friend, with the time and incentive that these brothers have to read, study, and think, you will find no class or category more aware, more embittered, desperate, or dedicated to the ultimate remedy—revolution.
—**George Jackson**[8]

As Safiya Bukhari and many others knew from lived experience, prisons were once the universities of revolution. The list of people who developed revolutionary intellectual leadership inside prison is long. Many were radicalized for the first time in prison; others who were already politically conscious used the time to study and sharpen their politics. But in the United States, in the aftermath of the Attica uprising and other rebellions, starting in the early 1980s, the US prison system recognized the threat and developed a new technique to stifle and destroy this.[9] The control unit model of systematized isolation has been highly effective over the last forty years in destroying revolutionary organization within prisons and in eliminating the political education that was once central to the prison experience.[10] This has enabled the mass incarceration system to grow with relatively little resistance compared to forty years ago. Today the system designed to control political prisoners is redeployed on a mass scale. In order to break the spirits of millions of innocents (over two million in prison in the USA), it has been necessary to isolate between eighty thousand and one hundred thousand people in solitary on any given day.

Nonetheless, despite the systematized torture of solitary confinement as a control technique, there is still great potential for organization and education inside the prison system today. The conditions of prison life reveal the contradictions and realities of our system and society in ways that those on the outside often fail to understand. To see the world from the inside out is to understand that, as Assata said, "inside and outside / is just an illusion."[11] Or as John Clark has written, "Prison is designed to crush the soul, deaden the mind and destroy the spirit, but it becomes for some . . . a place for new awakening, deeper insights and expanded solidarity. . . . The awakened prisoner understands the contradictions of the state, capitalism and patriarchy in a way that most of us, living in our larger and more comfortable prisons, can hardly begin to understand. We are living in Babylon and Babylon must be destroyed. Our brothers and sisters in prison are uniquely gifted to help lead us out of captivity."[12]

Lenin wrote and argued that revolutionary leadership comes from the outside in.[13] But it is not a contradiction to suggest that in our times, it comes also from the inside out—that today's ideological and political leadership will come from our sisters and brothers behind bars, whose life experiences and labor processes strip away the illusions and smoke screens that continue to zombify and blind even the revolutionary-minded on the outside. Throughout history, incarcerated women and men stand out as some of the most consistent revolutionary subjectivities. At the height of decolonization, many heads of state were former prisoners![14] Antonio Gramsci in his prison notebooks theorized the historical and political formation of intellectuals, arguing that revolution could only be achieved as the working class developed its own "organic intellectuals" to replace the "traditional intellectuals" of the previous regime.[15] This essay understands political prisoners in these terms as organic intellectuals and revolutionary subjects particularly suited for leadership in the twenty-first century. Thus we repeat Ho Chi Minh's prophecy that "when the prison doors are opened, the real dragon will fly out."[16]

Today and the Need for New Theory

There'll come a time / when the world won't be singin' / Flowers won't grow, bells won't be ringin' / Who really cares? / Who's willing to try / to save a world / That's destined to die.

—Marvin Gaye[17]

Today we confront a structural crisis of capitalism in which the world system cannot sustain itself internally and is also up against the final fatal contradiction of the ecological catastrophe it has precipitated. Immanuel Wallerstein wrote in 2009, "The crucial battle . . . in the middle run (next 15–25 years) . . . is a battle not about capitalism, but about what will replace it as an historical social system."[18] Who will lead the next wave of decolonization? In this context, the search for revolutionary subjectivities to lead the coming struggle to define and build the new world becomes an urgent priority. And the identification of prisoners as among these, indeed as what George Jackson called "an implacable army," takes on an extra, existential weight.

The current global crisis is qualitatively distinct from previous crises in several respects. Unlike the world-historical crisis of feudalism in the Middle Ages, today we suffer not from underconsumption but from overproduction. And unlike the world historical crisis of the 1930s, today's crisis of overproduction cannot be resolved by a further retrenchment of state capitalism, debt, and the growth of military spending, which are already at astronomical heights. Finally, today's crisis is unique in its ecological dimension, in which life as a whole is under attack from the global to the cellular level, in which the collapse of human civilization as we know it is implicit, and in which the survival of the human species and all others are at risk.

In this context, it has become obligatory to not only build revolutionary movements and organizations but also to revamp and qualitatively revise previous revolutionary theories. The theories of the eighteenth, nineteenth, and twentieth centuries have proven largely unsuccessful in guiding revolutionary practice, and have also almost universally failed to account adequately for any ecological dimension. These failings have their reasons, but the twenty-first century is the last chance to make amends.

In the last three decades, ecosocialism has emerged as a worldview, ideology, and line of reasoning that has been successful in unifying and consolidating (to a preliminary degree) a wide range of mass movements in the global South. It has brought us closer perhaps than we have ever come to finding ideological unity between the revolutionary ideas of the proletarianized, industrialized, and urbanized world, and the indigenous, eco-centric, and spiritual dialectics and cosmovisions of first peoples. This unity found organizational expression recently in the foundation of the First Ecosocialist International, whose program connects the struggle to free political prisoners with the emergence of a new mode of production.[19] (It's no coincidence that two members of the Black Panther Party, Charlotte O'Neal and Dhoruba Bin Wahad, took part in this gathering.[20]) In this sense, ecosocialism emerges as an owl of Minerva, which spreads its wings at twilight, just in time, to lead us toward the horizon of an ancient future. Ecosocialism is a movement of movements, unified by a common worldview, which may help us toward the Lakota medicine man and warrior Black Elk's vision of a return to the Sacred Hoop.[21]

But What Do Prisoners Know about Ecology?

Prisoners are confined in perhaps the most artificial environment on the planet. But as ecologists and prisoners both know, outside and inside are an illusion! Everything is interconnected. Prisoners are revolutionary subjectivities uniquely gifted not only to understand the full nature of the capitalist system but also the ecosocialist alternative. When I use the word *prisoners* here, I am in agreement with Russell "Maroon" Shoatz's concept of "potential political prisoners." Against those who define political prisoners narrowly as only those who have been incarcerated for their participation in overt revolutionary actions, Shoatz argues that

> what's becoming clearer every day is that in addition to the "real political prisoners," there are literally hundreds of thousands of other "potential

political prisoners" being held in prisons in this country! . . . We cannot reach a consensus on a definition of just what makes one a PP, which leaves this author to adamantly insist that we view all in the ten categories as potential political prisoners! Clear political realities overshadow the alleged criminal acts that landed these individuals in prison.[22]

We wouldn't expect every single prisoner to develop ecological consciousness, any more than we would expect every single prisoner to recognize the political conditions of their confinement. As political prisoner Mumia Abu-Jamal broadcasted, "Most of us have heard of jailhouse lawyers—guys and gals who battle in court for themselves or others. But I'd wager few of us have ever heard of a 'jailhouse environmentalist.' Truth is I didn't think such a thing existed. Well, it's real."[23]

After years of being repeatedly surprised that the prisoners I was in touch with seemed to know and care more about our ecological crisis than those of us on the outside, I was led to formulate the following list of conditions, which prepare prisoners for ecosocialist leadership:

1. In addition to understanding the political economy of the prison-industrial complex, prisoners may also see firsthand its political ecology: the immense environmental footprint of its construction and maintenance. From the use of productive farmland to build prisons on to all the resources necessary for the maintenance of the prison (water, food, electricity, heating oil, etc.), prisoners may understand the connections between social justice and environmental injustice, as victims of both.

2. With mass-produced and factory-farmed food, limited pretense to health care, along with cruel and unusual manipulation of temperature, light, and other environmental torture techniques, and limited access to intellectual stimulation, the prison cell and the prisoner's body are a microcosm and an epitome of ecological destruction. In addition to understanding the real totalitarian nature of this regime, and its basis in the preservation of the institution of slavery, prisoners may thus also understand how capitalism is ecocidal ("the enemy of nature," as Joel Kovel argues), because of how this plays out on their bodies in the prison system.[24] Prisoners may thus understand capitalism and the emancipatory promise of ecosocialism on a literally physiological level.

3. All prisoners who are held even briefly in solitary confinement experience at the most extreme level imaginable the meaning of alienation. For these prisoners, alienation is much more than

something that happens in the labor process, but can be recognized as something that is destructive of the human body as a natural organism. A prisoner in solitary confinement is alienated at the ontological and existential level. We are social animals who evolved outdoors, and to confine us in a solitary confinement cell is to alienate us from what Marx called our species-being, our social essence that in southern Africa is called *ubuntu*.[25] To understand this is to understand truly the depth to which capitalism is ecocidal: the prisoner in solitary can understand themselves as part of nature and understand the prison system as the enemy of that nature. (This experience also exposes the capitalist myth of the "rational utility maximizer"—the isolated individual decision maker explained by neoclassical economics as the model of humanity—by revealing its true form in the control unit.) But those whom solitary doesn't kill, it makes stronger. As Jack Henry Abbott wrote, "A kind of genius can come from this deprivation of sensation, of experience. . . . *The composition of the mind is altered.* . . . It is Supersanity."[26] The list of those who suffered solitary confinement only to emerge as intellectual leaders goes back decades if not a century, and while it would be a gruesome mistake to romanticize torture, the fact that genius emerges from solitary confinement is upheld today not only by Russell Maroon Shoatz in the United States but also by Abdullah Öcalan in Turkey.[27]

4. The mass incarceration system is a historical continuity from the era of legal slavery, and the prison industrial complex also inherits the legacy and disciplinary techniques of the Native American reservation system. Prisoners may thus often understand and identify with the peoples of the First Nations, who are the global and historical standard bearers for the preservation and protection of ecosystems, and the indispensable guides to an ecosocialist future. It's worth noting here that all Native prisoners, who are disproportionately incarcerated in every state, should be understood as political prisoners.

5. Prisoners are forced to understand the dual nature of capitalist exploitation and control, which has two forms: both physical (of bodies, ecosystems, territories, etc.) and metaphysical (of the spirit, the soul, memory, imagination, etc.). This understanding is essential to fully grasp both the full gravity of capitalist exploitation and also the full depth of the ecosocialist revolution necessary to overthrow

and overcome it. Prisoners are uniquely gifted to understand how "everything holy is profaned," and thus how the struggle for the sacred must be at the heart of any liberation struggle which seeks to restore ecological balance.[28]

6. In 2005 during Hurricane Katrina, in 2012 during Hurricane Sandy, and in 2017 during Hurricane Harvey, prisoners were left inside locked up throughout the storms. These prisoners, and prisoners everywhere, thus may understand not only climate change but the use to which it will be put politically, and the real face that this regime will take in the coming era of climate chaos. They have been told as Leonard Cohen wrote, "Get ready for the future: it is murder."[29] They should have no illusions here, unlike so many of us on the outside, about the necessity of what George Jackson called the ultimate remedy.

7. A mass migration beyond biblical proportions is already under way, but catastrophic climate change will exponentially amplify this exodus. Given current political realities, millions of climate refugees will inevitably wind up in mass detention camps. We know that these camps are already being built and prepared. Combined with everything already mentioned, we can predict at the very least the possibility of the emergence of a revolutionary movement of incarcerated climate refugees, who understand ontologically that capitalism is the enemy of nature and that "the future will be ecosocialist, because without ecosocialism there will be no future."[30] To prepare for this moment now is the final point at which this very preliminary list will end.

So What Is to Be Done?

Only by establishing a core of professionally trained, matriarchal, ecosocialist, conscious, and fully committed individuals, can an effective foundation be laid to reinvent the commons in a world where the potential for overwhelming violence on the part of others is ever-present.
—**Russell Maroon Shoatz**[31]

The most advanced and focused theory of ecosocialism will likely come from the inside out: the theory and analysis that develops from inside what Jack Henry Abbot called "the belly of the beast" is likely to be the most free of illusions about the real nature of the enemy and about what is required to overthrow it.[32] Maroon has set the standard for ecosocialism from the inside out. Others are following his lead. This author has received at least half a dozen requests for copies of Joel Kovel's *The Enemy of Nature* in Pennsylvania alone, and these copies are circulated and studied closely—or at least more closely than they seem to be on the outside.

Other authors have written about the alliances that are forming between movements for prison justice and environmental justice.[33] In the past five years, consciousness and action around convergence seem to have accelerated, reflected in various articles and organizing projects, including a Fight Toxic Prisons conference and a Prison Ecology Project.[34] Remembering the prophecy of Ho Chi Minh, we can make an educated guess that in terms of environmental and climate justice as well as for revolutionary anti-imperialism and anticolonialism, the real dragons will not fly out until the prison doors open. This understanding makes prison abolition an ecosocialist struggle, and the liberation of political prisoners a central strategic orientation for the climate justice movement.[35]

In the face of catastrophic climate change and mass extinction, almost all the institutions of modern civilization—from nation-states to corporations to NGOs to places of worship—are succumbing to zombie apocalypse. Perhaps prisoners are the ones we have been waiting for: the Implacables. None of this is destiny, only possibility. Prisoners like everyone else have the capacity to play the roles of heroes, fools, cowards, villains, and more (or less). As Eduardo Galeano says, "We are all half-gold, half-rubbish."[36] And as Hugo Blanco summarizes, "it is possible, but not inevitable."[37] May the explosive potential of this possibility lead us to listen and learn from the leadership of political prisoners, real and potential. The destiny of the human species, not to mention the meaning of our own lives, could depend on it.

III.

SANKOFA: PAN-AFRICAN INTERNATIONALISM

David Brothers, former New York Panther and All-African People's Revolutionary Party cadre member, right, sitting with Matef Harmachis in a New York restaurant across the street from the college campus where original New York AAPRP cadre privately met before the Pan-African organization publicly emerged in 1972. Photograph by Diane Fujino, 2000

Former San Diego Panther Dedon Kamathi, far right, with from left to right, Tsehai Kidane, Muhammad Ali and Kwame Ture holding Ali's daughter, Laila. Photograph from Dedon Kamathi's personal collection, courtesy of Tejvir Grewall

CHAPTER SEVEN

The (R)evolution from Black Power to Pan-Africanism: David Brothers and Dedon Kamathi at the Bus Stop on the Mountaintop of Agitprop

Matef Harmachis

Pan-Africanism is the highest political expression of Black Power.
—Kwame Ture (Stokely Carmichael)

Campfire Intro

It was June 17, 1966, when Stokely Carmichael called for Black Power. Everything that happened after that within the civil rights movement and its heir, the Black Power movement, was a response to that moment.[1] Just ten days before, James Meredith had begun his solo March Against Fear, an attempt to walk from Memphis, Tennessee, to Jackson, Mississippi, to promote voter registration and defy the violence of racial capital. On the second day of his march, an unknown gunman shot Meredith. Immediately every civil rights organization of import moved to continue the march. Carmichael was on that march as an organizer for the Student Nonviolent Coordinating Committee (SNCC).

The night before Carmichael's call for Black Power, he had been arrested—again. He arrived from jail just before it was his turn to speak at that night's outdoor rally in Greenwood, Mississippi. Mukasa Willie Ricks had already primed the crowd that it was time to claim Black Power. Carmichael was furious from his ill treatment by the police—again—and hit the microphone running. By the time he finished, the crowd was blaring, "Black Power!"[2]

The next summer Black Panther Party (BPP) cofounder Huey Newton recruited Carmichael into the BPP as part of a move to mesh the party and SNCC, pulling together the upstarts on the West Coast with the veterans in the South. The party had suddenly become nationally notorious in May with their brazen armed demonstration at the California capitol to protest the Mulford Act, which would outlaw the open carry of loaded weapons, a party staple in its police patrols. In February 1968, the BPP named Carmichael honorary prime minister. While the linking of the two organizations failed, Carmichael nevertheless showed himself on the cutting edge of African liberation in the US working to bridge the most radical strains of resistance.[3]

By the summer, Carmichael would still be at the forefront of the movement. He would relocate to West Africa to study with the premier theorists and practitioners of Pan-Africanism and then help Black Power give birth to a new heir apparent. From 1968 until his transition in 1998, Carmichael—now Kwame Ture—worked tirelessly to build the All-African People's Revolutionary Party (AAPRP), the revolutionary political party that Osageyfo Dr. Kwame Nkrumah discussed in his *Handbook* as the logical means to bring about liberation, unity, and socialism in Africa.[4]

Academic Intro

This chapter is an example of the myriad paths Black Panther Party members took out of the party into continued service to the movement for self-determination, focusing on the Pan-African route as, for them, the next logical step in revolutionary praxis. While Carmichael's call for Black Power in 1966 is viewed as the beginning of the Black Power movement, activists and scholars are increasingly noting that the ideas of Black Power, notably self-determination, radical critiques of power, and the centering of Blackness long preceded 1966. The histories of Black Power and Pan-Africanism are both long and complicated and each concept has multiple and contested meanings.[5] Still, this essay seeks to illuminate Kwame Ture's statement that "Pan-Africanism is the highest political expression of Black Power."

While there were several ways former Panthers took to work in their communities, the leftist ideologies and philosophies upon which their actions were based did not necessarily agree any more than when comrades were still in the BPP. This article attempts to delineate some of those principled ideas in disagreement and give historical background to each, culminating in the lives of two comrades who chose the Pan-African pathway out of the party. While the question of which path to take to African liberation is complex and beyond the scope of this article, we can point to a wide range of arguments and the motivations behind each.

Historic Background of Pan-Africanism

For Osageyfo Dr. Kwame Nkrumah, first president of a liberated Ghana, the revolutionary nationalism of Pan-Africanism was not the petit nationalism promoting a single state at the expense of neighboring nations. It was the legitimate cry of an oppressed people using the vehicles of independence and sovereignty to fundamentally change and uplift their condition.

True, there are myriad conceptions of Pan-Africanism, just as there are a multiplicity of definitions for Black Power. And it fully depends on how one defines these philosophies as to whether there is compatibility or contention. Some say Pan-Africanism means no matter where a Black person is that person belongs to the African Family and owes his/her allegiance to Africa. Others say it stands for putting the building up of Black folk first and foremost. There's also the notion of the land question; Africa for the Africans at home and abroad; the primacy of Africa. Plus, some want independence of thought and action; if anything is to be done for Africa and Africans it must be done by Africans. And still there's more; or all of this together and more.

To this day the ideological/philosophical and strategic differences among and within nationalism, socialism/communism, and Pan-Africanism persist. Within the BPP alone, all of these tendencies rose and waned across time and geography. For example, Huey Newton was so disgusted with George Padmore's definition of Pan-Africanism he said, "It is not only outdated, it sets back the liberation of all oppressed people."[6] Yet Padmore is a man whose ashes are buried in Ghana and was considered by C. L. R. James as standing next to W. E. B. Du Bois as a champion of Pan-Africanism.[7]

In our trek to liberation, Booker T. Washington had differences with Du Bois and Du Bois disagreed with Marcus Garvey. The Negritude or cultural nationalism of Léopold Senghor, Senegal's president, stood against the Pan-African internationalism of Dr. Nkrumah, as did Côte d'Ivoire president Félix Houphouët-Boigny's insistence on reliance on the former French colonizers clash with president of Guinea Ahmed Sékou Touré's determination to make a clean break with all invaders and occupiers.[8]

Ideological Ruptures at Home

These personal ideological splits represented African continental and later global cleavages. While the anticolonial struggle raged, some semblance of unity could be had against a common enemy. But the seeds of neocolonialism are planted right at the point of independence, which led to groupings represented by the multiplicity of conferences, congresses, and other continental meetings in Africa beginning in 1960 with the series of crises in the Congo.[9] True, there were political differences expressed among Pan-African organizers preceding the first Pan-African conference in 1900.[10] But postcolonial African unity had its first major test when rival leaders Patrice Lumumba and Joseph Kasavubu could not reconcile, leading to the United Nations intervention and implosion of the new state of the Congo.

The Brazzaville Group, made up of former French colonies, was moderate and pro-French. Even in the radical Casablanca Group, led by revolutionary Ghana and Guinea, there were different strains of thought and strategies. The United Nations' (mis)handling of the Congo crises in 1960 split the radical Casablanca Group and alienated other independent states that would join the Brazzaville Group in 1961 to form the more moderate Monrovian Group. The Casablanca Group eschewed anything that smacked of colonialism/neocolonialism, created the ideal of an "African Personality" to uplift their people's moral and cultural well-being, proposed plans for economic and social development, and "pinned their faith to socialism" because this was how precolonial Africans lived.[11] Meanwhile the Monrovian Group saw the radical Casablanca Group nations as unreasonable and their ideas as a dead end. Unfortunately the so-called moderate states of the Monrovian Group never stated any political ideology nor a cohesive philosophical program for moving forward in the postcolonial era.[12]

The schisms in Pan-Africanism were getting so deep that at a Positive Action Conference in 1960 nations that would become the Monrovian Group actually agreed that independence should be achieved through nonviolent means. The Monrovian Group were the "traditionalists," "sluggards," "stooges and agents of imperialism." They were for gradualism, could not see a unified Africa until each of their nations had overcome its unique individual problems—opting for "cooperation" rather than outright unity. For them nationalism was itself the goal instead of a means to an end. Forty years before this, the Pan-African nationalist Joseph Casely-Hayford referred to these individualistic stalling methods by saying the Almighty was already "weary" of "wranglings, disputations and quarrels," which slowed progress and kept Africans from their Creator's blessings.[13]

The Casablanca Group were the "radicals," "progressives," and "militants." Ghana, Guinea, and Mali already had a secret pact since 1959 to become a single nation prefiguring "One Unified Socialist Africa." In their minds, all social, economic, and political indicators became strengthened through a collective convergence of land and people, that is, all resources of each "nation" whose borders were created by outsiders in the first place. To them all problems from political backwardness to poverty stemmed from imperialism and could only be solved through the unity of revolutionary Pan-African nationalism.

The Effect on the Movement in the US

Eldridge Cleaver, writing from exile in Algeria, exemplified the move in the US of Black nationalism away from the BPP's original ideological underpinnings of Marx, Lenin, and Mao, later referred to as MLM Thought. In the October 1971 issue of *Black Scholar*, Cleaver explained how following the class analysis of Marxism-Leninism led the BPP away from Black nationalism; and how their struggles against cultural nationalists also moved them away from their connectedness to Africa and nationalism.[14] Their ideas around cultural nationalism would also play a part in the West Coast–East Coast divide in the party; BPP membership on the East Coast, New York as the main example, were much more tied to and influenced by traditions and organizations that upheld African culture. This even led some West Coast members to lump their East Coast comrades in with "pork chop nationalists." Yet in these debates, there was often confusion or conflation of a "narrow nationalism," denounced by BPP leaders as "pork chop nationalism" or mistakenly as "cultural nationalism," with a "revolutionary nationalism" that could incorporate analyses of class struggle and national oppression and that could be both nationalist and internationalist.[15]

What happened inside the BPP exemplified the ideological struggles throughout the left regarding nationalism and Marxism. But watching the wars for African liberation taking place in Namibia, Angola, Azania/South Africa, Mozambique, Guinea-Bissau, and the Cape Verde Islands carried out by Africans with unabashed calls for socialism through Marxism-Leninism caused Africans and other leftists in the US to rethink their brand of nationalism. The weight of freedom fighters like Amilcar Cabral, Robert Mangaliso Subukwe, Samora Machel—who were anti-oppression, never anti-European—forced thoughtful leftists to wage unrelenting written and verbal struggles over the question of the relationship between class struggle and nationalism.[16]

Revolutionary theorists in and out of the party attempted to address opposing tendencies and construct a more balanced view that incorporated the science of Marxism-Leninism with the concrete experience of Africans at home and abroad.[17]

In this vein, Amiri Baraka would embrace both Ghana's Convention People's Party of Kwame Nkrumah and Maulana Ron Karenga's US Organization to promote the blended solution to oppression of nationalism, Pan-Africanism, and ujamaa (African scientific socialism) in the formation of the Congress of African People in New York, which influenced local BPP members.[18]

The Crux of the Matter According to Bro Kwame Ture

It was Kwame Ture writing from Guinea who would explain the necessity for a scientific, complex, cohesive approach. "The All-African People's Revolutionary Party knows that the correct ideology for Africans the world-over is Nkrumahism. Nkrumahism does not and cannot negate the universal truths of Marxism-Leninism; it merely incorporates these truths," he said. He reasoned that any divisions between Nkrumahists and Africans claiming Marxism-Leninism was based in misunderstandings of ideology. He was clear that there were those who "do not understand the importance of race in the class struggle today. Consequently they are unable to comprehend the world socialist revolution in general and the Black Revolution in particular." This is what Bro Kwame meant when he said, "We Black revolutionaries, who are Nkrumahists, know that the highest political expression of Black Power is Pan-Africanism; and the highest political expression of Pan-Africanism is Nkrumahism."[19]

For Bro Kwame there is an ideological evolution moving from civil rights to Black Power to Pan-Africanism.[20] His coauthor of *Black Power*, Charles Hamilton agreed, "Pan-Africanism is clearly the next viable stage of the historical struggle of black people to assert themselves on the world scene."[21] Bro Kwame understood not everyone was going to Pan-Africanism with him any more than everyone had moved forward from civil rights to Black Power. True, on a timeline each of these movements has a much longer history and exist concurrently.[22] However Bro Kwame is speaking about ideological growth. And as a student of Ahmed Sékou Touré, Bro Kwame comprehended it is the duty of leadership to walk with the people, behind the people and—sometimes—ahead of the aspirations of the people in order to construct the conditions for liberation.[23]

Again, Pan-Africanism was not new in 1968. Some argue that Pan-Africanism finds its origins as soon as West Asians start invading the Continent in the 1670s BCE; just as the American Indian Movement begins in 1492, the moment Cristobal the Colonizer sets foot in what was the New World to Europeans. Pan-Africanism is also part of the international workers' struggle against imperialism and has its roots in the class phenomenon of the colonial subjugation of African labor and African people by international capitalism, that is, racialized class oppression.[24]

More modernly the Pan-African concept began as an expression of solidarity between Africans at Home and in the Diaspora as advocated by Henry Sylvester-Williams, a Trinidadian barrister, in the last quarter of the nineteenth century. By 1900 Sylvester-Williams helped organize the first Pan-African Conference. His Pan-African vision would be expanded by the writings and actions of Garvey and Du Bois, both of whom worked internationally for African unity.

At the Fifth Pan-African Congress held in Manchester, England, in 1945, the leaders of the African revolution would meet, plan, and create the major push that heralded decolonization to the African continent just a decade later.[25]

This is the background to the context in which members of the BPP would be bombarded with an ideological smorgasbord from which some would choose the revolutionary Pan-African path.

Two Pan-African Lives

David Brothers (December 25, 1919–June 25, 2007) was already steeped in community activism and revolutionary organizing before establishing a BPP branch in Brooklyn, New York, in 1968. He was influenced by the Honorable Marcus Garvey's Universal Negro Improvement Association and African Communities League of which his mother was a member. The struggles of Father Divine's followers to maintain basic needs for downtrodden Africans throughout the Great Depression impressed him. He joined the support for Paul Robeson against state repression and mobilized advocacy for Marian Anderson when the Daughters of the American Revolution banned Ms. Anderson from performing at Constitution Hall in Washington, DC, simply for being African. He stumped for Adam Clayton Powell and campaigned for socialist and communist candidates like Ben Davis for elected office.[26] Like other BPP members he had already been seeking the most advanced formation to join in order to foment African liberation specifically and uplift humanity generally.

Dedon Kamathi (August 19, 1949–August 25, 2015) also had already been an organizer against the US invasion of Vietnam and against the draft. He had already cofounded both a Students for a Democratic Society chapter and the Black Student Union at San Diego University. But in 1969 the police beat him unconscious. At nineteen years old he joined the BPP declaring, as did so many Panthers, that the police beat him into the party.

Because the BPP founded with students who had been attempting to put into practice the theories they'd been discussing in progressive organizations and who had been observing the liberation struggles in the Third World, the party could attract like-minded students and observers.[27] David Brothers and Dedon Kamathi, although three decades apart in age, were of that same mind.

Both Brothers and Kamathi would progress to revolutionary Pan-Africanism, the next step in the development of Africans in the US from civil rights to Black Power and beyond. Nevertheless, while in the BPP both men worked tirelessly to move forward the party. David Brothers, as chair of the New York BPP, held the chapter together when New York state falsely accused party members of planning bombings and shootings then jailed the "New York 21" for more than two years, from 1969 through '71.[28]

In San Diego Bro Dedon lived communally as did many Panthers in order to prefigure a socialist future and accomplish more party work. "[The police] would always wreck our house. They'd come crashing in through the windows, smash in the doors and arrest everybody. They could have just knocked, but they wanted to exponentially increase the fear and intimidation factors," he said. For the BPP, the harassment was constant. In one year alone, the police arrested Bro Dedon more than forty times.[29]

Bro Dedon said his rebellious nature started early on watching his Indian mother's family from Trinidad ostracize his African father. The hypocrisy of their supposed devotion to Islam disgusted him. Also he could not abide what he called his father's playing Uncle Tom to move up the ranks of the US Navy to become one of the first Black commanders.[30] When the family moved to the Philippines following his father's reassignment, Bro Dedon told his parents he could not in good conscience go with them. "As a revolutionary, it'd be my duty to sabotage the base," he said.

The BPP in New York fractured and finally succumbed to COINTEL-PRO attacks, the internal divisions represented by the Huey Newton–Eldridge Cleaver split, and the anger and distrust throughout the party produced by Newton's purge of nineteen of the New York 21 while comrades were still in jail. Other members felt forced out, some drifted away, a few formed the Black Liberation Army underground fighting formation. Chairman David—the title would follow him the rest of his life—would be recruited into the All-African People's Revolutionary Party by past chair of SNCC and former honorary prime minister of the BPP, Kwame Touré.

The AAPRP initially organized in Guinea in 1968 under the guidance of Osageyfo Dr. Kwame Nkrumah, first president of Ghana, which had already fallen to a CIA-directed coup in 1966. President Ture on behalf of the citizens of Guinea invited Osageyfo to be copresident. Osageyfo refused the honor but not the hospitality and remained in exile in Guinea. When Bro Kwame moved to Guinea in 1968 he worked and studied with both presidents Touré and Nkrumah. It was Osageyfo who tasked Bro Kwame with taking the AAPRP to the US. Bro Kwame started quietly gathering the most progressive persons from his organizing days in the US. "I immediately started calling all the formers: former NOI (Nation of Islam); former SNCC folk; some Rastas; former Panthers. . . . And in New York the first person I called was Chairman David Brothers!" Bro Kwame said.

Bro Kwame would follow Osageyfo Kwame Nkrumah's instructions and pull together the first AAPRP work-study circles in the US to build Pan-Africanism, defined by Osageyfo as the total liberation and unification of Africa under scientific socialism. The AAPRP began publicly recruiting in 1972.[31] In 1973, Bro Dedon was one of the first California recruits.

Chairman David was on the first central committee of the AAPRP. His AAPRP New York chapter members entrusted him to represent them and serve on the central committee 'til his dying day. Bro Dedon would also earn the respect of his California chapter organizers—with a heavy preponderance of former BPP members—to represent his chapter on the central committee.

Both men would organize for the AAPRP across the US and internationally: Chairman David mainly in Africa; Bro Dedon in Brazil, Belize, India, and also in Africa. Chairman David had strong coalition ties on behalf of the AAPRP with organizations like the December 12th Movement, the Nation of Islam, the Patrice Lumumba Coalition, and the New Afrikan People's Organization among others. He was a founding member of both the African Anti-Zionist Front and the World-Wide African Anti-Zionist

Front. Both men represented the AAPRP in Cuba, Libya, and other revolutionary nations when it was against US policies to even visit such places.

Bro Dedon, a self-described joiner, not only worked with brother and sister organizations for the AAPRP, but joined any group with whom he perceived an ideological affinity, for example, the American Indian Movement, the Filipino Farm Workers, the Brown Berets, the Kerala Dalit Panthers, Belize Rural Economic Development of Agriculture through Alliance, the Jericho Movement, and many more. He helped found Born Free Die Free, which supports our oldest political prisoners/prisoners of war, many of whom are former Panthers. His *Freedom Now!* radio show on KPFK-FM still brings together the strongest Pan-African and revolutionary voices to Los Angeles airwaves through the collective of programming talent he brought together. He also cochaired the Crack the CIA Coalition (CCC).

When CCC pronounced its original objectives, many said none of CCC's labor would bear fruit. But after Gary Webb's *San Jose Mercury News* articles exposed CIA complicity in drug sales to illegally support the Contras in Nicaragua, the CCC succeeded in getting then CIA director John Deutch to testify before the people of Los Angeles regarding the CIA's role in chemical and biological warfare against African and other depressed neighborhoods through cocaine importation.[32] In addition, many of the founders of the CCC, including Bro Dedon, had been long working for the freedom of imprisoned former Panther Geronimo ji Jaga (Elmer Pratt). The CCC was instrumental in getting Geronimo's murder conviction vacated and he exited prison in 1997 after twenty-seven years inside for a crime he did not commit."[33] These are but two examples of the ways Bro Dedon, a global pan-Africanist, forged community alliances to address local campaigns that connected seemingly disparate issues.

Chairman David and Bro Dedon, just like Bro Kwame, each spent time in multiple organizations. But each spent most of his organizational life in the AAPRP struggling toward the Nkrumahist-Touréist objective of Pan-Africanism. Clearly these comrades were always moving forward to the most ideologically advanced groupings they could find in order to do the most effective work they could. Their internationalist vision of the destruction of all forms of capitalist oppression—imperialism, zionism, apartheid, neocolonialism, sexism, racism—found its clarity in revolutionary Pan-African formations at home and in the diaspora.[34]

These comrades came into the BPP in different ways. And while there was an incredible array of paths by which members left the BPP—but continued to serve the people—an important progression of revolutionary work was through Pan-African structures like the All-African People's Revolutionary Party. Based in their devotion to Africans everywhere and their commitment to the oppressed internationally, Chairman David and Bro Dedon pledged their lives to the ideals of Pan-Africanism. "Whether it is the Black Student Unions, the Black Panther Party, the All-African People's Revolutionary Party or *Freedom Now!* I made a principled commitment to use whatever educational vehicles are available to challenge the US Empire," wrote Bro Dedon. "My weapon is media, lectures, protest, and organization."[35]

"We should not get discouraged," wrote Chairman David.

We are working for the next generations. . . . We are planting seeds. Seeds don't bloom when you plant them. . . . It is a process. Kwame Ture didn't see what he was fighting for. . . . Kwame Nkrumah was fighting for the United States of Africa. He did not live to see that. Seku Ture, Patrice Lumumba, George Padmore, didn't live to see what they were fighting for. What we are fighting for will not be for us to see.

Akinsanya Kambon's painting, *Trophies*, shows the aftermath of one of the largest slave rebellions in US history, in 1811, near New Orleans. A militia of slave owners killed and decapitated the rebels and placed the heads on posts to announce their power and as a method of terror and intimidation. The horrified Black men, women, and children represent members of Kambon's own family as they fled Louisiana and found their father among the heads on the posts. *Trophies*, 2018, Watercolor, 18 x 24 in.

Opposite page: Akinsanya Kambon's *Detroit Blue* is one of his art pieces based on his experiences as a US Marine in the Vietnam War. Detroit Blue is depicted reading the newspaper to his fellow Black soldiers when he discovers that weapons banned for use in Vietnam were deployed against the Black community in Detroit. *Detroit Blue*, 1973, Oil, 21 x 26.

"BLACK IS BEAUTIFUL"
"MOTOWN"
"SOUL POWER '67"
"SMOKEY"
RIOTS
DETROIT
BLACKS
1967
USA

Akinsanya Kambon's bronze casting skills, developed in Africa, were enhanced working with the bronze casters in Burkina Faso in the city of Bobo-Dioulasso. Working with other artists in the city of Ouaga-dougou, Kambon added the patina to this art piece. *The Moor*, 2008, Bronze sculpture, 15 x 13.

CHAPTER EIGHT

States of Fugitivity: Akinsanya Kambon, Pan-Africanism, and Art-Based Knowledge Making

Diane C. Fujino

My part has been to tell the story of the slave. The story of the master never wanted for narrators.

—Frederick Douglass[1]

Art can only deal with the truth. You have to tell the truth whether the people like it or not. The truth is the basis for setting you free.

—Akinsanya Kambon

Introduction

In May 1987, Akinsanya Kambon held a press conference in Chicago to announce that he was turning himself in. Behind him, his artwork, symbolic of his suffering and state of captivity, was on display. One reporter observed: "[There] were several busts he had sculptured of black men with expressions of agony. In a corner sat two huge oil paintings of young males with chains around their necks, hands and feet. The faces were those of Kambon's sons."[2] Kambon had been single-parenting two sons, who were with him throughout his eighteen months underground, in Mexico, Long Beach, California, Washington DC, New York, and finally Chicago. From Chicago, he returned to Sacramento, California, where he surrendered. In November 1985, he had skipped his sentencing hearing and begun life as a fugitive. The first two trials had resulted in hung juries and mistrials; the third jury convicted him of drug and gun possession. Kambon explains that he was visiting a friend when the police raided his friend's apartment. His friend handed him one of the dishes of cocaine to flush down the toilet. Kambon refused, but in the attempted exchange left four fingerprints on the dishes. Kambon states, "Anyone who knows me knows that I don't drink or do drugs." He was facing up to five years in prison. Kambon told reporters that he felt his life was endangered given the constancy of the police harassment and brutality he faced in his hometown of Sacramento, especially since the Oak Park Four won a dismissal in a 1970 case involving Black youth accused of killing a white police officer. When arrested in the Oak Park Four case, Kambon recounts that the police had chained him to a radiator pipe, pulled down his pants and underwear, and threatened to castrate him with a razor. When he refused to sign a waiver to remain silent, they beat him and kicked out two teeth. From that time to the mid-1980s, he reports having been stopped by the police seventy-eight times and beaten numerous times. This kind of police violence and harassment prompted Kambon's flight.[3]

Kambon's time underground raises questions about the meanings of fugitivity. Does it involve any kind of escape, or specifically an escape from criminality (as in outlaws) or from conditions of oppression (as in runaway slaves)? Is it largely a physical condition, or are there political, cultural, psychological, and spiritual elements? How might we understand the multiple meanings of fugitivity? For Kambon and family, the physical escape, as expected, posed innumerable challenges. Angela Davis recounts her life as a fugitive rife with fear and anxiety. She decided to flee after being charged with aiding Jonathan Jackson in an armed courtroom takeover in an effort to free Jonathan's brother, prison movement leader and Black Panther George Jackson. Of her experiences in 1970, Davis writes: "[F]ugitives are caressed every hour by paranoia. Every strange person I saw might be an agent in disguise, with bloodhounds waiting in the shrubbery for their master's command. Living as a fugitive means resisting hysteria, distinguishing between the creations of a frightened imagination and the real signs that the enemy is near."[4] Like Davis, Kambon experienced the exhaustion arising from the need for constant hypervigilance to avert capture. Physical conditions were also difficult. But for one who survived the Vietnam War and who understands the hardships endured by fugitive slaves before him, Kambon could handle the meager conditions. What concerned him most was how to care for his two children while on the lam, including registering them for school while remaining undetected.[5] He worried constantly about their futures and, if found, the possibility of their being killed as "collateral damage" in the police pursuit of Kambon. In fact, the media coverage and press conference were strategies to stay alive when relinquishing himself to the authorities, based on advice from the renowned human rights attorney William Kunstler.[6]

What may be most surprising about his fugitivity is the way Kambon continued a kind of normalcy while in hiding. Some would say this was foolish, but he had a friend ship some seven hundred pieces of his artwork to him in Chicago. When the reporter met him at his Chicago home in May 1987, he observed:

> I walked into a scene as strange as any I have encountered in many years covering the vicissitudes of urban warfare. The ground floor of the house had been transformed into a secret African art gallery. Hundreds of paintings . . . hung on the walls over the decaying wallpaper. There were paintings of slave markets and paintings of starving black women staring hollow-eyed as their dying children suckled at their dry breasts. There were statues—hundreds of proud African heads with patinas of bright green and black and red. There were unfinished statues—clay molds in the making . . .[7]

Kambon recalls that when he turned himself in, he brought about fifteen hundred art pieces with him from his Chicago home. The creation of art while on the lam was more than a way to occupy his time; it allowed him to express his political and cultural beliefs, focus his fears, and connect to a liberation movement of utmost importance to him.

Fugitivity represented for Kambon not only escape from the law, but, more so, a kind of marronage or creation of a life outside of mainstream capitalist society. He already knew about the numerous slave rebellions that had taken place (including one in which his great-great-grandfather participated) as well as the maroon societies established by runaway slaves throughout the Americas. Whether called *palenques, quilombos, cumbes, mocambos, ladiera,* or *mambises,* whether ephemeral or complexly structured, maroon societies represented a freedom through the creation of autonomous Black communities.[8] Like Assata Shakur, Eldridge Cleaver, Russell Maroon Shoatz, Safiya Bukhari, Sekou Odinga, Kuwasi Balagoon, Hank Jones, and other Black Panthers, Kambon's resistance exceeded escape from specific criminal charges.[9] He viewed the entire US legal and criminal "justice" apparatus as functioning to reproduce racial capitalism's inherent inequalities of race, class, gender, and nation—one that was particularly ruthless against descendants of Africa. "I don't think there's any justice for Black people," observed Kambon.[10] No matter how harsh the conditions and the level of hypervigilance required, the creation of an alternative society, outside the strictures of white supremacist, colonial logics made sense to him. In fact, throughout his life, he had lived a kind of maroon existence from his early years in poverty, to prison, to homelessness, to the establishment of the Pan-African art studio in Long Beach, California. Akinsanya and his wife S. Tamasha Ross Kambon (Susan Ross) have created what Barbara Tomlinson and George Lipsitz call "insubordinate spaces" that can transform spaces of oppression into spaces of transformation.[11] His life's work is to make art that tells the story of African captivity, escape, marronage, and resistance. His sculptures, paintings, and drawings—and accompanying storytelling—tell the story of African creation of art, knowledge reclaimed from the ancestors, revolutionary theories and practices, transformed social relations, and emancipatory imaginations. Akinsanya states strongly, "I am a maroon!"

Early Years

Akinsanya Kambon was born Mark Anthony Teemer on Christmas Day 1946, in Sacramento, California, to Laura Ella Hackett (née Wells) and David Mike Teemer. His parents divorced when he was two years old. His mother married two more times. Kambon was the second oldest of nine children. There was poverty in his early years, but his tenacious mother, who was an avid reader and high school valedictorian, saved enough money to buy a boxcar, place it on concrete blocks, and creatively transform it into a home. In 1960, his mother was able to buy a two-story house on Sixth Avenue across from McClatchy Park, in the predominantly the Black neighborhood of Oak Park.[12] Kambon's life experiences taught him about the harsh realities of racism and impoverishment and about the need to defend oneself—lessons he would carry with him into the Black Panther Party.

Kambon recalls a childhood made difficult by his disability. At age three, he contracted polio and was paralyzed on the left side of his body, including his face. The children at North Avenue Elementary School teased him unmercifully. One student stood out. This is a story Kambon tells to explain how he became aware of US racism.

I was in kindergarten, and only four years old. There was a little white girl named Becky with Shirley Temple curls. I'd be sitting outside at school and everyone would tease me. I'd be crying and she'd come and put her arms around me, "Don't cry, Mark." We lived in a boxcar across the street from Becky's house that had shrubs and fences. One day, Mama [ed.: Kambon's maternal great-grandmother] and I were walking down the street and Becky came out to the gate and started waving at me, "Hi, Mark." I went to wave. But my great-grandmother grabbed me by the ear, twisted it so hard, she twisted my head around, and said, "Boy, that's fire and rope. Fire and rope." I didn't know what she was talking about. All I knew was just looking at that little white girl made my ear hurt.[13]

Kambon would soon learn that the threat of Black lynchings was not confined to the South. When he was about twelve years old, after seeing his white neighbors getting ready to go camping, he begged his mom to join their Boy Scouts troop. His mother objected, but he was so deeply disappointed that she relented. When they joined, he and the four other Black boys integrated that all-white troop. None of the Black scouts could afford the uniform and had to settle for a little cap as a stand-in to signify their inclusion. At one meeting, Kambon relayed how his excitement to learn to tie a variety of knots turned into tragedy.

The Scout leader said, "Now I'm going to show you how to tie a knot that all scouts should know how to tie." I tied my little knot and wrapped it around thirteen times and it slipped up and down. Then he said, "And now we'll show you what it's used for." So he comes to the back of the room and grabbed me by the arm and took me up on the stage. I was a little guy for twelve or thirteen. I'm all proud and all these people are looking at me. He gets me to the edge of the stage, stage is about four foot up, and he puts that noose around my neck and then he kicks me off. The knot hit me in the neck and I couldn't breathe and I started crying. I could see people laughing. And then I passed out. When I woke up somebody was massaging my neck. And there was two white men back there fighting. The guy that told us about the Boy Scouts and let us join was fighting with this other guy. I was scared! When I could breathe again, I started throwing up. I jumped off that stage and I took off and I ran out in the field. I laid down in the field and I cried. I said to myself, "My mother told me not to join the Boy Scouts." I didn't know nothing about the South and lynchings, nothing about racism.[14]

As Kambon heard family stories, he came to realize how the lives of his own ancestors intertwined with the history of Black oppression and Black resistance. Years after his great-grandmother's "fire and rope" warning and the Boy

Scout incident, Kambon learned that his maternal great-grandmother, had a son who was lynched in Texas. During a short visit with his father, shortly after the Oak Park Four case ended in dismissal, Kambon heard stories about family rebels on his father's side. His father disclosed the story of his Uncle Buck, a Buffalo Soldier who fought in the Philippines and Cuba. But when forced to build the roads in Northern California, he took off, declaring, paraphrased by Kambon: "I ain't no damn slave. I'm a fighting man. You going to teach a man how to kill and then you're going to work him like a slave?" Uncle Buck then joined a gang of outlaws and used his skills gained in the US military to survive out West. They stole cows and horses and robbed banks, stagecoaches, and trains. During his years as a Buffalo Soldier and an outlaw, he allegedly killed forty-six people. After the revenge killing of his wife and unborn child he fled to Canada with his brother-in-law, a Cherokee.[15]

As Kambon shared with his father his own knowledge about the famous slave rebellions of Gabriel Prosser, Nat Turner, and Denmark Vesey, his father dropped another knowledge bomb on him. He told him about the 1811 slave rebellion on the German Coast, near New Orleans, the largest slave revolt in US history. Inspired by the Haitian Revolution, some five hundred enslaved men wielding axes and guns, some dressed in military uniforms, carried out an armed revolt from January 8 to 11. They had a two-pronged military strategy—marching south down the River Road to New Orleans, while the enslaved Africans inside the city of New Orleans simultaneously revolted and captured an arsenal. The rebels, however, had mistakenly not anticipated a rear guard on their march south to New Orleans and were outmatched by the military might of the slaveholders. The militiamen found the escaping leader of the rebellion, Charles Deslondes, and killed him. They captured other rebels, including the Akan warriors Kook and Quamana. The planters held a tribunal, both to legitimize their violence as well as to reclaim their professed civility after engaging in such unconscionable acts of brutality. Whether killed in the initial battle, pursued and killed, or executed following the tribunal, the planters beheaded the rebels and stuck the severed heads on fence posts stretched across sixty miles along the River Road—as a display of their power and a warning to future insurrectionists. Kambon's father then revealed that his great-grandfather's was one of the heads on the posts.[16]

Kambon recounts stories of family members who were lynched in Texas, beheaded in retaliation for the 1811 slave rebellion, or a fugitive who countered white violence using the weapons of destruction taught to him as a Buffalo Soldier. What interests me most about these family stories is the social meanings derived by Kambon. Scholar Alessandro Portelli contends that narratives, whether factual or not, are valuable because "they allow us to recognize the interests of the tellers, and the dreams and desires beneath them."[17] Abiding by Frederick Douglass's charge to "tell the story of the slave," Kambon relays personal stories of African peoples to breathe life into the historical and structural apparatuses of anti-Black racism. He is a master storyteller and griot (or West African storyteller, historian, or cultural worker) in using the method of witnessing to testify to the experiences of Africans and the viciousness of power.[18] He also derives inspiration and pride in recounting the actions of rebellious Black people, stories too often missing from public memory and from the written records. These stories have captured his imagination and find form, to this day, in his drawings, paintings, watercolors, and sculptures. One of Kambon's watercolors, created in 2018, shows Black men, women, and children walking on a dirt road lined with trees, interspersed with heads on poles, referencing the German Coast slave rebellion of 1811. In another set of watercolor paintings (2017), a Black soldier is outfitted as a Buffalo Soldier; in another, the protagonist sits on horseback shooting back while being pursued. Curiously unusual for a nineteenth-century Buffalo Soldier, Kambon painted the soldier with long dreadlocks, perhaps as a way of seeing himself in the insurgency and fugitivity of his Uncle Buck. In a charcoal drawing (2015), Kambon created a moving scene of a girl teaching a grandmother to read exposing the racist policies and practices that prohibited teaching enslaved Africans to read and write. As I watched Kambon draw, it struck me that his artwork elicited greater emotionality and sensitivity than the original photograph from which it was drawn. Perhaps it was knowing the social meaning of this piece, with Kambon himself having struggled with functional illiteracy as a young adult. But there is also an affective power, a spirit and a truth captured in Kambon's work.

Kambon's selection of stories have one more important function. In a society that equates nonviolence with ethical behaviors, Kambon's life experiences and political philosophy challenge the easy narrative of the civil rights movement's alleged nonviolence and the discomfort for some with Black Power's focus on self-defense. Kambon is captivated with the German Coast slave rebellion. It is personal for him. But more than that, it is political. To him, the omnipotence and viciousness of white structural power and white violence intertwine with capitalist and colonial domination to render as reasonable the method of Black self-defense, up to and including the use of armed struggle, to defend oneself, one's family, and one's community. Kambon views the long history of the Black radical tradition—from Denmark

Vesey and Nat Turner, to the 1811 enslaved rebels and his Uncle Buck, to Robert F. Williams and the Black Liberation Army—as his political genealogy. He too was trained to kill as a US Marine in Vietnam and carries to this day the physical and psychological scars concomitant with that brutality.[19]

Kambon was nineteen years old when he was drafted. He had assumed that his earlier polio and his then functional illiteracy would safeguard him from the military, but when he reported for his physical, they were told to count off 1-2-1-2 to determine whether a recruit went into the army or the marines. He ended up in the marines. It was May 1966 and the Vietnam War was raging. He recalls being pumped up for 'Nam and feeling like he was the "baddest on earth," that is, until his older brother took him to a program at Sacramento High School, his high school, where he heard a dynamic presentation by Stokely Carmichael speaking against the war. This was December 1966, just before he was deployed to Vietnam. Kambon recalled, "I started tearing my uniform off right there." Carmichael's reasoning, along with his own experiences in Vietnam, turned Kambon from "military propaganda" to antiwar critique. As is his pedagogy, Kambon shows, rather than tells, through the use of story narratives or *testimonios*.

> In Vietnam we used to have what we called Soul Sessions. We'd meet every week—all the brothers [Black men] in our battalion, about thirty of us—and go through the newspaper, the *Stars and Stripes*. We go over letters from home and every week a brother was reading about one of his friends that got killed by the police. Then we got this one letter, the first Black Panther Party newspaper, "Why Was Denzil Dowell Killed?" That's where I first learned about the Black Panther Party. They were talking about doing to our people at home the same thing that they tell us to do to the "gooks." They tell us if you kill a woman or child, plant a grenade on the body and say that they tried to blow you up or they tried to reach for your weapon—you know, just like the police do. So that was something that really got me.
>
> We had this one brother who used to read to us. Detroit Blue was twenty-six, slightly older than the rest of us. He'd read this newspaper to us every week and explain stuff that we didn't understand. One week they had the rebellion in Detroit and about forty or fifty Blacks were killed. It was on the front page of the *Stars and Stripes*. Blue got to reading the paper and all of a sudden he stopped and tears welled up in his eyes and then started running down his face. He dropped the newspaper and he walked off. We all sat there looking, "What the hell is wrong with him?" So we picked up the paper and we started trying to figure out what was said; it talked about a Black woman who got shot in the face with a .50-caliber machine gun. She

ran a daycare center in her apartment. The National Guard said they saw a flash and they shot her in the face. Detroit Blue knew her. So we thought that's what had him break down. But a week later when we saw him again, he came over and apologized for breaking down. We said, "Aw, Man, we understand, you knew this sister." He said, "That ain't got nothing to do with it. What happened to me was, I felt betrayed by our own government using weapons that we can't use in war, but they can use them on our brothers and sisters and mothers and fathers at home."[20]

As a combat illustrator for the marines, Kambon's work was to document what he saw in the rice paddies, villages, and jungles. Years later, at his therapist's directive to draw the ten most stressful experiences he had in Vietnam, he created oil paintings that depicted soldiers raping a young village girl and a soldier trying to hold in the brains of a dying child. He also created an image from guerilla warfare school, which trained soldiers in the method of cutting open the bellies of pregnant women and then stomping on the fetuses' heads. These memories are forever embedded in his mind and body—and find expression in the stories he tells; in his paintings, watercolors, and drawings; and in his speeches against the wars in Vietnam, Afghanistan, Iraq and elsewhere at community programs, on college campuses, and at Veterans Day programs. In one particularly stirring painting, Kambon portrayed Detroit Blue reading the *Stars and Stripes* issue on the Detroit riots, with tears streaming down his face, and the words "Motown," "Black Is Beautiful," "Soul Power '67" written across his helmet.[21]

Kambon has had ongoing difficulties, in Vietnam and ever since, emerging from what he now understands as post-traumatic stress disorder (PTSD). He got into fights in Vietnam, including an incident in which he didn't remember a thing about how he tore up a movie theater and beat up fellow soldiers in defense of a Vietnamese boy who had been hospitalized with him. In Sacramento in 1973, a physical assault landed him in jail. After dropping off his seven-year-old stepdaughter to board a school bus, a motorist sped into the crosswalk and hit her, throwing her over the hood of the car. Kambon, then twenty-six, has no memory of what happened next, but was told he beat up the motorist, injuring the driver's eye, nose, and chin. During that incident, Kambon had fractures in both hands and said that he was beaten by the police. The all-white jury found him guilty of assault and the judge gave him a seventy-five-day jail term and a three-year probation—a sentence Kambon attributes to the numerous letters written on his behalf and the judge's recognition of his wartime traumas. For one suffering PTSD, Kambon reacted as if he was in a combat situation. At the moment of his daughter's scream, he had a flashback of the incident with the US soldier who used his bayonet to slit the vagina of a five-year-old Vietnamese girl and rape her. But it took another two decades before his fiancée and now wife helped him understand what he's suffering as signs of PTSD. After trying for thirty-four years, he was finally able to gain disability status and receive Veterans Affairs services. In 2010, after twenty-six years, he retired from his job teaching art at California State University Long Beach. He now spends his days researching and creating art.[22]

His focus on drawing and talking about what he witnessed in Vietnam is for self-healing, but it is also a political commitment to testify in opposition to what Kambon views as US imperialist wars at the expense of people in invaded lands and of the US working poor. To Kambon, the way the soldiers stomped the tiny bodies pulled from their mothers' wombs wasn't a strategic maneuver to ensure the baby's death, but more a reflection of the brutalizing and dehumanizing racist treatment of "Black" bodies that traces a lineage from slavery, to Emmett Till and Fannie Lou Hamer, to Ferguson, Baltimore, Minneapolis, Sacramento, Chicago, and Houston, and any number of US cities today.[23]

Joining the Black Panther Party

After several injuries and being discharged from the military on May 8, 1968, and airlifted out of Vietnam, Kambon returned to his Oak Park neighborhood of Sacramento. Two months later, he found himself caught in a chaotic racial disturbance.[24] Kambon heard a commotion and stepped across the street from his home on Sixth Avenue to McClatchy Park. He saw a man throw a brick at the police and then try to hide in some bushes. Kambon decided to throw the man the camouflage shirt he was wearing and continued on. As Kambon walked down Martin Luther King Jr. Blvd., as it's called today, he encountered a boy whose foot was stuck under a police car. As he tried to help, a police officer hit him on the back and shoulders with an axe handle. He then saw another police officer wield his axe handle to hit a girl on the head. As Kambon was yelling at the police to stop and about to get into an altercation, someone suddenly grabbed him from behind and carried him halfway down the block. He was surprised to see it was the brother who had thrown the brick, the recipient of Kambon's shirt. That brother was soon talking to Kambon about joining the Black Panther Party.[25]

Kambon was not interested. He had had enough of guns, enough of war, and enough of trouble. But the Association for Black Unity (ABU) asked Kambon to do a drawing for their newsletter of four Black men, representing the BPP, NAACP, Urban League, and the Nation of Islam. He obliged. Kambon found himself impressed by the discipline and fearlessness of the Panthers as they stood their ground before the police. He joined the Sacramento chapter of the BPP, recently formed in April 1968, headed by Charles Brunson and with women among the first members. The Panther office, at 2941 Thirty-Fifth Street, was on the other side of McClatchy Park, just a half mile from Kambon's home. As lieutenant of culture of the local BPP, Kambon worked to create revolutionary art and several of his drawings appeared in the *Black Panther* newspaper. As a veteran, he conducted weapons trainings. He spoke at Free Huey rallies, helped to implement the Sacramento Free Breakfast for Children programs, and like all Panthers, attended weekly political education study groups and sold the newspaper.[26] While the main focus of this chapter is on Kambon's post-Panther work, two topics warrant discussion—Kambon's creation of the *Black Panther Coloring Book* and his involvement in the Oak Park Four case.

For Kambon, the controversy surrounding the *Black Panther Coloring Book* still stings. It signals to him a betrayal by Panther leadership, but also represents a larger battle between the ideas of Black Power and the state's apparatus of repression. According to Kambon, shortly after he joined the BPP, he created the *Black Panther Coloring Book*, consisting of twenty-three pages of images depicting Black self-defense toward the white power structure, symbolized by Emory Douglas–inspired upright pigs in police uniforms. For Kambon, the coloring book was never intended for children. Instead, he deployed images to illuminate ideas about Black pride and resistance against power for adults like himself who had struggled with reading. He asserts that top BPP leadership asked him to change the words "African" to "Black," but otherwise approved the booklet. Apparently, twenty-five copies were run, but once the BPP said to end it—and Kambon obliged—it appears that someone else printed a thousand copies. According to Huey Newton, the FBI reproduced the numerous copies and, by contrast to Kambon's view, also added the captions. Newton wrote: "After its rejection by party leaders, however, an informant for the FBI stole one of the few drafts of this proposed publication and delivered it to the FBI. Thereupon the FBI added captions advocating violence, printed thousands of copies bearing the party's name, and circulated them throughout the country, particularly to merchants and businesses who contributed to the breakfast program" and subsequently withdrew their support.[27] Yet after the Sacramento BPP ended in 1970,

Kambon and other Panthers helped to sustain the free breakfast program continued through Sacramento City College Black Student Union.[28]

In June 1969, during the Senate Permanent Investigation subcommittee chaired by Senator John McClellan, the testimony of two former Los Angeles Panthers, Jean and Larry Powell, charged the BPP with violence and shakedowns of ghetto merchants and claimed that the coloring book was distributed at the BPP Breakfast Programs to turn children against the police (other Panthers deny that it was circulated at the breakfast programs). Vice President Spiro Agnew weighed in, saying that there should be "laws prohibiting the distribution of such inflammatory propaganda." BPP chief-of-staff David Hilliard also reportedly denounced the coloring book, "It was not geared to our party line because it was racist and nationalist."[29]

Scholar Ward Churchill contextualizes this controversy within the workings of the FBI's counterintelligence programs (COINTELPRO) directed most vehemently against the BPP. He contends that the FBI was concerned with the Free Breakfast for Children and other BPP "serve the people" programs because they made it impossible to characterize the BPP as only thuggish. When San Francisco FBI agent Charles Bates raised concerns that attacking the BPP programs would "convey the impression that . . . the FBI is working against the aspirations of the Negro people," the FBI domestic intelligence chief William Sullivan sharply rebuked that the BPP is "not engaged in the 'Breakfast for Children' program for humanitarian reasons . . . [but rather] to fill adolescent children with their insidious poison." Bates was then given two weeks to initiate COINTELPRO actions to eliminate the BPP's serve the people programs. Bates's agents found the coloring book, with its depictions of policemen as pigs and drawings of Black men, women, and children stabbing and shooting the police, as a tool for their means.[30]

According to Kambon, the Panther leadership initially supported and sanctioned his creation of the coloring book but then withdrew their support and asked him to denounce the book when things got hot for the Panthers and the finances were affected. This remains an unresolved issue for Kambon. But in 2016, he self-published the *Black Panther Coloring Book*, this time claiming his original authorship and authority to illustrate such provocative but important ideas.

The second major incident of his Panther days resulted in his imprisonment as one of the Oak Park Four. On the night of May 9, 1970, while driving north on Thirty-Fifth Street from Fifth Avenue, police officer Bernard Bennett, twenty-four, was hit in the back of the head when sniper shots were fired at his patrol car. He died four days later. The *Sacramento Bee* noted that "one of the city's most intensive" police investigations led to the arrests of seven young Black men on May 26, all held without bail.[31] Charges were dropped for three defendants. The "Oak Park Four" defendants (including Kambon, then Mark Teemer, twenty-three) were known to be "young black militants"; two were Black Panthers and all community activists.[32] The Black community feared that the Black youth accused of killing a white police officer would be railroaded into a conviction, especially after the police-instigated "riots" in Oak Park and the police raid on the BPP office, both on Father's Day, 1969. Community members charged the Sacramento police with creating "a military occupation in the heart of Oak Park" and "summer of police terror" so much so that "many Blacks abandoned 35th Street and James McClatchy Park as unsafe."[33]

The Black community responded with widespread support. Historian Clarence Caesar noted, "Not since the Archy Lee case in 1857 had a local criminal case involving blacks attracted the same kind of support the Oak Park Four case did within the community."[34] Shortly after the May 26 arrests, more than fifty students created the Oak Park Legal Defense Fund and sponsored dances, car washes, benefit fundraisers, sold the artwork of defendant Kambon, and had lawyers, law students, parents, and other volunteers investigating the case. The Black newspaper, the *Sacramento Observer*, ran a supplemental newspaper on the Oak Park Four case, published on October 1, 1970, featuring multiple articles that humanized the defendants and provided information on the trial to the community.[35]

The trial began on October 5, 1970, and was based primarily on the testimony of Lamont Rose, former "Oak Park 7" defendant-turned-state-witness, former Black Panther, and admitted drug user. Though the judge denied the motion to throw out Rose's testimony, the judge ruled that the testimony of two other key witnesses was "inadmissible as evidence" because they were coerced statements gained through police intimidation, harassment, and violence. One witness claimed that the police rousted him out of bed while pointing a shotgun at him.[36]

In the end, the unexpected happened. Based on the removal of coerced testimony, the district attorney asked the court to dismiss the murder and conspiracy to commit murder charges against the Oak Park Four; the judge complied. The *Observer* noted the case's racial meaning: "The ruling of Judge DeCristoforo marked the first time in the history of America that Blackmen [*sic*] accused and charged with the murder of a white policeman have been released."[37] While the court's ruling was of historical significance, Kambon issued a cautionary warning: "This isn't a victory. They are using us to make Blacks believe the system works for Blacks. In fact the system does not work for Blacks but against them. Any system which legally kills and maims Blacks cannot be considered just."[38] To Kambon, their case represented a pattern of police control and domination of Black communities. He told the *Sacramento Observer*, "Figures on Black deaths from various kinds of execution, between the years of 1930 and 1970 showed that out of 3,568 deaths by execution, over 2,066 victims were Black," representing more than 57 percent of those executed by the state. Kambon was referring to the structural oppression of the Black community, what some call Black genocide and what scholar Ruth Wilson Gilmore views as the defining characteristic of racism: "The state-sanctioned or extralegal production and exploitation of group-differentiated vulnerability to premature death."[39] Today police killings of Black people has reached a crisis situation. But for Kambon, the only new feature is the visibility of the killings and the mainstream opposition, whereas the systematic state-sanctioned killings of Black people date back to slavery, lynchings, chain gangs, and the violence of poverty. He himself knows this only too well.[40]

After the trial, he moved to Fresno, California, to escape the police harassment in Sacramento, and earned a bachelor's and then later master's degree in fine art at California State University, Fresno.[41] As he continued in his political education study, he began to embrace socialist Pan-Africanism. Even as Kambon has stated that he left the BPP because "they wanted reform, I wanted revolution," he also acknowledges that he learned about socialism in the BPP and believes that "all the Panther programs we were implementing were socialist programs."[42] He explained: "We started the Free Breakfast for Children programs to heighten the contradiction. Children shouldn't go to school hungry. This so embarrassed the government that the government started free breakfast and lunch programs." In the *Black Panther*, the BPP stated that "The Free Breakfast for Children program is a socialist program, designed to serve the people. All institutions in society should be designed to serve the masses, not just a 'chosen few.' . . . In capitalist America, any program that is absolutely free is considered bad business. . . . The Black Panther Party is educating the people to the fact they have a right to the best that modern technology and human knowledge can produce."[43] The Panthers' survival programs were indeed revealing contradictions of racial capitalism.[44] By showing how the Panthers could do so much with so few resources and how the government did so little with so much, the BPP argued that community needs could be met but only under a different organization of the political economy, one not designed for corporate profit-making and labor exploitation. The lessons Kambon learned in the BPP have become part of his political philosophy. He states: "You have to make people well when they're sick. You have to feed them when they're hungry. You have to educate them when they're not educated. This is something we have to do and something we have to figure out how to do. That's the bottom line."[45] What Kambon learned in the BPP enabled him to be ready for what was to come as he moved toward global Pan-Africanism.

Global Pan-African Politics and Art

Kwame Ture (née Stokely Carmichael) was the most ideologically influential figure in Kambon's life. Kambon had already been drawn to the power of Ture's ideas and compelling presentation when he first heard him speak against the Vietnam War in December 1966. When Kambon joined the marines in May 1966, he could not have predicted his conversion to Black Power and later to revolutionary Pan-Africanism. But the Black freedom struggle and the world itself was in a state of change. In January 1966, SNCC became the first "civil rights" organization to officially oppose the US war against Vietnam. In June 1966, Kwame Ture, as SNCC's newly elected chair, and SNCC member Mukasa Willie Ricks popularized the call for Black Power in Greenwood, Mississippi, during the March Against Fear. Ture himself was undergoing an ideological transformation. In 1967, as he traveled the world, he met with revolutionary leaders of Cuba, China, Vietnam, and Africa. Shirley Graham Du Bois introduced Ture to Kwame Nkrumah, the first democratically elected president of independent Ghana, who in February 1966 was overthrown in a CIA-instigated coup. At the time Nkrumah was developing his theoretical ideas for anticolonial struggle in the *Handbook of Revolutionary Warfare* and establishing an organizational formation to carry out the development of a democratic and socialist Africa, the All-African People's Revolutionary Party (AAPRP). In placing himself under the tutelage of Nkrumah and Guinea's Sékou Touré, Kwame Ture received Nkrumah's direction to organize the AAPRP in the diaspora.[46]

According to the AAPRP, Kwame Ture introduced the AAPRP to US audiences at Howard University in October 1972. As Ture spoke to an estimated 500,000 students in North America from 1970 to 1988, he consistently spoke about Nkrumah and the AAPRP.[47] Kambon was one of those who heard

Ture and joined the AAPRP in 1974, while living in Fresno. The heavy reading and theoretical study required of party members was difficult for one who by self-admission had only learned to read fluently after joining the BPP. Kambon recounts one incident when Ture asked him a question about the biweekly AAPRP readings only to discover that Kambon had not done his assignment. Ture became so angry that he stopped talking to Kambon for two straight days—and Ture was staying at Kambon's home. Kambon's shame motivated his serious study and reading of the books and ideas of Kwame Nkrumah, Sékou Touré, Amilcar Cabral, Walter Rodney, Eric Williams, and V. I. Lenin, among others. Now living in Long Beach, Kambon helped to organize the AAPRP's annual African Liberation Day programs, to use his artistic skills to create propaganda for the party, to educate about Pan-African socialism, and to build and participate in the biweekly study circles. The more he studied about global politics and history, especially about Third World struggles against colonialism, the more he embraced revolutionary Pan-Africanism.

Kambon first traveled to Africa in the mid-1970s. He visited several West African nations and insisted on traveling hundreds of miles by foot, interacting with the local villagers and townspeople. On his travels, he learned African techniques of sculpture and of bronze casting, a complicated, expensive, and time-consuming process requiring precision and constant vigilance to ensure the mold not crack and the melted metal turns into the envisioned sculpture. By the late 1970s, he was given the name Akinsanya Kambon, meaning "hero avenges" in the Yoruba language.[48]

While in Ghana in 1994, Kambon had a life-changing experience. He and Tamasha were visiting the widely known Elmina slave castle. In contrast to its grandeur as the largest European building in sub-Saharan Africa, built by the Portuguese in the 1480s, it came to serve as a dungeon holding hundreds of thousands of enslaved Africans in overcrowded, filthy conditions, their last stop in the journey across the Middle Passage into slavery in the Americas. When the tour guide was explaining how the overseer selected women in the courtyard and forced them to climb a ladder to be raped by the European master, Kambon experienced a fiery rage and stepped outside.[49] When the tour finished, the guide invited them back in to explore the building. During their self-guided tour, they briefly separated. Akinsanya went into the holding place for the enslaved Africans. He explained:

> I got on my knees and started meditating and got into deep meditation. All of a sudden I heard a female voice say, "We've been waiting for you." It scared the hell out of me. My heart almost skipped a beat. I looked up and

saw one of these, they didn't look like people, they looked like ghosts. They said, "We need you to teach our children who were stolen about our history, our cultures and our religions." And I thought to myself, I don't know much about that and she could hear what I was thinking. She said, "Don't worry. We've been guiding your hands." So I figured everything I've done they had guided my hands to do it.[50]

Kambon did not tell anyone about this experience for a long time, assuming people would think he had had a psychotic break. But he has since been able to embrace the experience as his calling from the ancestors—a point that seems contradictory with the materialist views of BPP, yet many former Panthers and Black radicals embrace a variety of spiritual practices.

For Kambon, knowledge already existed in Indigenous and African history, knowledge that has been appropriated, misused, distorted, and erased. Since visiting Africa in the 1970s, Kambon uses his distinctive style of sculpture to create hundreds of pieces of art. His magnificent sculptures are intricately crafted pot-shaped or cylindrical or tiered bases featuring three-dimensional images in bas relief, often busts from the shoulder or waist up, of African legends, warriors, gods, and ordinary people. He designs his sculptures based on the stories of Africa passed to Kambon in the oral tradition or through his research. Other faces appear in agony, symbolizing the anguish experienced by Africans witnessing yet another atrocity inflicted on their people. One story Kambon frequently tells is of the Yoruba *orishas* or spirits, Osanyin, the god of herbal healing and knowledge, and Shango, the god of justice, social responsibility, and thunder. These stories, carried on the slave ships, shape spiritual practices and philosophies throughout the Caribbean and the Americas. Kambon relays:

> I've been studying history and what our ancestors did. Because if you look at Indigenous and African history, we already figured shit out. This American system got rid of all that, the things we already knew. I studied about this cat named Osanyin. God gave him the ability to learn herbs and plants to use for healing. God said, now that you know this, when people get sick you go and make them well. Osanyin did that, but after a while he started thinking, when people are sick and going to die, they'll give me money for the medicine. So he starts selling medicine to these people. If people didn't have the money, he didn't give them the medicine. God knew what he was doing. He sent his enforcer down to tell Osanyin, you got to stop doing that. If I find out you're selling medicine to sick people, I'm going to jack your ass up. But Osanyin couldn't resist the money and kept doing it. So the enforcer caused an earthquake and made the palace that he built fall down on top of

him, put out one of his eyes, he became deaf in one of his ears, and had him hopping around. This cat is slick. He rebuilds his palace and starts selling out his back door.

Now there's another cat named Shango. He's over lightning and thunder. He's a bad cat. One day, Shango's wife Oya had twins. When one got sick, she brought him to Osanyin for medicine. (Shango was away at war; he's always away at war). So Osanyin looks at the baby and says, "Yeah, I have the medicine, but you have to have the money." She says, "I didn't bring any money. We didn't know we had to pay for it." But Osanyin wouldn't give the medicine. The baby died on the way home. When Shango found out, he was mad and goes looking for Osanyin. Osanyin was in his palace. He hears the thunder in the background and knows Shango's coming for him and tries to figure out what to do. He sees the lightning and thunder and heads out to hide behind this big baobab tree in the back. Shango saw him go there and throws a lightning bolt at the tree. The tree explodes. Osanyin took off running. Shango took that razor-sharp ax and took off after him and threw it at him. Chopped off one of his legs in full stride. Then Shango chopped off one of his arms. He looks at him. I'm going chop this fool's head off. Then the enforcer comes, "Now Shango, you can't do that. Because if you do that all the knowledge of medicine will be lost." So he took that razor and slit Osanyin's throat and took his voice box out. Now this fool hops around the forest on one leg, one eye, one ear, and can't talk. But he's giving out the medicine to the people.[51]

These two stories—of the ancestors in Elmina and of Osanyin—reveal personal messages to Kambon. Some say Kambon is unwise for not selling his art, with some of his sculptures appraised in the five-figure range. But he feels he cannot sell them, or more accurately, he does not create his art as commodities to be sold in the marketplace. If the ancestors gave their knowledge freely to him and are guiding his hands, then unlike Osanyin, he feels compelled to make the art not for his own financial aggrandizement but to "teach our children who were stolen about our history, our culture, and our religion." This has created a conundrum for Akinsanya and his business manager/wife, who have more than a thousand sculptures, paintings, and drawings in their studio.[52] After a 2018 extensive burglary of the studio and with Kambon aging, their desire to exhibit his art has become more urgent than ever. They recently established the Pan-African Art Museum to display the artwork, assure its care, and to teach the stories about African culture and history that Kambon has been learning over many years, passed to him from the elders and based on his own research.[53]

Art, Transformation, and the Gang Truce

By 1984, Kambon was living in Los Angeles, raising his preteen sons as a single father.[54] Professor Mary Hoover, then chair of Africana Studies at California State University, Long Beach (CSULB), rescued Kambon from homelessness (at the time, he was living in a van hustling Venice Beach by selling his artwork, while his sons performed Michael Jackson songs) and hired him to teach African and African American art at CSULB. Kambon initially opened the Pan African Art School in Long Beach in 1984, but had to close it in his period of fugitivity and while completing his jail sentence. He was able to reopen the school in 1991, where he has taught free drawing, ceramics, and other art classes to children and youth. Kambon observed the changes in his art. His art moved from "violent and ugly pig drawings" to "an art which portrays the lives and struggles of Africans from the days of slavery to the present. . . . [My] oils, charcoal sketches, and sculpture exude their own intensity and power. But they're now subtler—a slave's face that mixes sadness and fear, a black Moses whose face conveys defiance and wisdom; happy, shy African children whose innocent goodness personifies hope."[55] On the walls of the sizeable but modestly appointed building, Kambon displays paintings, watercolors, and drawings. The building housed table after table filled with sculptures and had works in progress and kilns in the back patio area.[56]

One day while teaching, a student recognized his professor as the former BPP artist Mark Teemer. That student, Danifu Kareem Bey (née Raymond Cook), was an original member of the Crips street gang. Bey was helping to organize the famed gang truce between the Bloods and the Crips and invited Kambon's involvement. Both Bey and Kambon contest the mainstream view that links Black gangs to theories of cultural deficiencies or pathologies and instead contend that the Black gangs that emerged in the late 1960s had roots in Black Power and Black nationalist politics. As young teens, the original Crips attended the BPP breakfast program and some like Bey sold the Panther newspaper. The youth were awed by the Black Panthers' militant style, leather jackets, and audacious confrontations with the Power structure. In Los Angeles, Bunchy Carter, former leader of the largest street organization in Los Angeles, the Slausons, recruited hundreds of gang members into the Los Angeles BPP chapter. Bey and friends wanted to join, but were told they were too young, so instead formed their own street organizations. Fifteen-year-old Raymond Washington is credited with founding the first new street gang, the Baby Avenues, or Avenue Cribs referring to their youthfulness, in 1969, which soon transformed into the Crips. Stanley "Tookie" Williams, executed by the state of California in 2005, was probably its most famous member. In forming the Cribs, Washington and others were influenced not only by the Panthers' guns and breakfast programs but also by the Watts rebellion that raised consciousness about the continuing conditions of poverty and racism. Danifu Bey describes "the spirit that the Crips were created [in] the climate of the Watts Riot. . . . Black people being awakened to freedom and tired of being treated like salves . . . the spirit of self-determination."[57]

By the early 1970s, core Crips decided to revive the original community-oriented principles of their founder and created CRIPS, the Community Revolutionary Inner Party Service. But in time, as the Crips increased their robbing, stealing, and illegal activities, a new verb was invented, *cripping*, to signify their aggressive criminal activities. One writer noted, "Because of immaturity and a lack of political leadership young Raymond Washington and his group never were able to develop an efficient political agenda for social change within the community."[58] By the time Kambon met Danifu Bey in the mid-1980s, intensified policing and the introduction of crack cocaine had resulted in a huge growth in gangs and in Black-on-Black violence. Kambon worked with Bey and others to implement a gang truce in the notoriously violent conflict between the Crips and Bloods. "They called this 'headquarters,'" Kambon told the *Los Angeles Times*, referring to the Pan African Art studio, where regular gang truce meetings took place. Gang members helped to build the canopy that covers the patio and to repair the house attached to the studio. One day, Kambon got to witness the work of Gangs for Positive Action, headed by Bey, when a woman and her daughter walked into the art studio looking for help to stop the domestic abuse taking place in her home. She didn't want to involve the police, the courts, or the prison system, so they held a people's tribunal to resolve the problem. It worked to end that case of domestic violence and others as well.[59]

Kambon has worked with Bey to organize or participate in at least six gang summits from the mid-1980s to 2005, held across Los Angeles, including at the Lakers former home, the Forum in Inglewood, and at St. Mary's Medical Center in Long Beach, as well as at Antioch Church in Kambon's hometown of Sacramento. Kambon had speakers such as Kwame Ture and Indigenous leader Ernie Longwalker address the gangs arriving from all over Southern California. About three hundred gang members participated in the first summit that Kambon attended. Bey had invited Kambon, recently returned from Africa, to show slides and talk about his trip, which inspired numerous gang members to want to go to Africa. Kambon told them: "It's good, but here's the thing. In Africa we don't need this gang banging and drugs and negative shit y'all doing."[60]

For Kambon, learning about the history and culture of Africa is part of the process for Africans in the diaspora to end the cycle of destructive activities and to decolonize their minds. In 1995, Akinsanya and Tamasha established Pan African Art, Inc., offering free art, culture, and leadership programs for youth. The art school held free art classes for children ages eight to eighteen to sculpt, paint, and draw every Wednesday and Saturday. "Any kid can come," stated Kambon. "You can come if you're red, green, blue, or brown. We will teach you free. That's what society should be about." At the studio, the young people were surrounded by African images including Kambon's paintings of Malcolm X, a Zulu king, and a collage of Angela Davis. Kambon has witnessed the change in children as they learn their own histories. He showed videos on Africa, taught lessons on African history and culture, and took the children on field trips, for example, to the Bowers Museum in Santa Ana to see a Nubian art exhibit. "You take a lot of kids with no hope, and they can identify with this work. They have more of a will to live and a will to succeed than they did before," he said.[61] For Kambon, education is a crucial pathway to escape the imprisonment of illiteracy, poverty, and prisons, as it was for him. He encourages going to college as well as learning through trips to the ancestral homeland. Among his fourteen trips to Africa, he has done continuous research, worked as a visiting professor, and taken groups of young people.[62]

As part of their work to use art to transform self and society and to link creativity with street life, Pan African Art sponsored a one-day expo in 1993 at Leimert Park in the heart of Little Africa in Los Angeles. "Graffiti, Tagger and Mural Expo," presented eight-by-four-foot murals that addressed the many forms of violence affecting US society and the world. Theirs was a participatory art project, involving more than fifty contributors, ages eight to twenty-seven, who created the art using a variety of media, including spray paint, acrylics, oils, and collage. In 1998, Kambon involved local youth and some gang members in painting tiles in a program with the City of Long Beach called, "Public Art in Private Places."[63] Kambon understands the power of participation and of art creation in generating new ideas, new political imaginaries, and new social relations. This kind of transformation through self-activity is also reflected in the work of Project Row Houses in Houston's Third Ward. Project Row Houses converted places of segregation into places of congregation, where single Black mothers live rent-free in small shotgun houses while completing college and where art is part of the process of re-creation to change lives shattered by poverty and gentrification into possibilities of hope and economic sustainability. Project Row Houses came into existence following the police killing of Carl Hampton, whose activist work in Houston was inspired by a visit to the Oakland BPP and whose killing by the police in 1970 was instigated by his defense of two Panthers harassed by the police for selling the *Black Panther* newspaper. Project Row Houses is taking the violence of poverty and the police and converting it into spaces of art-based community making.[64]

Kambon's work with gangs also involves presenting knowledge about the origins of their street organizations rooted in Black radicalism. In community venues and on college campuses, notably at California State University Sacramento, City College of Sacramento, California State University Long Beach, and Compton College, he talks about the inspiration of Malcolm X and the Black Panther Party as well as the Mau Mau in Kenya who in the 1960s liberated their country from colonialism. To Kambon, the devastation of Black communities and the rise of gangs is a legacy inherited from the FBI's counterintelligence program that was designed to eradicate the BPP Party and other Black radical organizations and individuals. Part of his success in working with gangs is that he draws from his own experience to show a different way forward, not of assimilationism, but of revolutionary transformation. "I can tell them this stuff because I've lived it," said Kambon, referring not just to poverty, inadequate schooling, incarceration, and warfare abroad and at home, but also to the power of knowledge, artistic creation, and liberation struggles.[65]

Always the Truth

In April 1997, as Kwame Ture was struggling with inoperable cancer and receiving medical treatment in Cuba, New York, and Guinea, Akinsanya and Tamasha hosted a fundraising dinner at the Pan African Art studio that also provided, at that time, a rare opportunity for guests to interact with Ture. The place was beautifully appointed, guests arrived in exquisite African clothing, revolutionary conversations abounded, and the local community contributed to Ture's health care needs.[66] Kambon lost his dear friend and greatest ideological mentor when Ture transitioned to the ancestors on November 15, 1998, in Conakry, Guinea. With the loss of his political anchor, Kambon began to drift away from the All-African People's Revolutionary Party, but not from its Pan African socialist politics. He had learned in the AAPRP that students were the spark of the revolution and continued his commitments to teaching African art, history, and politics to children, youth, and gang members.

In response to the widespread spotlight on police killings of young Black people, the recent growth of the movement (especially since the 2013 acquittal of George Zimmerman in the killing of Trayvon Martin) feels like coming full circle for Kambon. While most activists and media reports focus on the innocence of "unarmed" Black victims, Kambon wants to focus attention on the Micah Johnsons and Gavin Longs who responded to the police killings of Philando Castile and Alton Sterling with targeted shootings of police officers in Dallas and Baton Rouge, respectively. Unlike President Obama's remarks, "If you shoot people who pose no threat to you . . . you have a troubled mind," or the *Los Angeles Times'* headline, "A Study in Anger: How Gavin Long Went from Decorated Iraq Veteran to Cop Killer," Kambon's theorizing does not dwell on personal responsibility or individual psychology.[67] Instead, he places such actions within the social structure of race and oppression, examining the why of Long and Johnson's actions against the police in the wake of massive police violence against Black communities. Unlike the mainstream protest communities, Kambon wants the names of Micah Johnson and Gavin Long to be remembered within a tradition of Black militant resistance to white supremacy and racial capitalism that traces a line from not only the famous like Nat Turner and the Black Panther Party but also to the innumerable unknown resisters, including his great-great-grandfather who was beheaded in the aftermath of the 1811 slave revolt and his own trials and tribulations as a US Marine destroying Vietnamese people and land, as an Oak Park Four defendant, and as a fugitive. He embodies a legacy of marronage that flows from the runaway slaves, to his Uncle Buck who dared to kill fifteen white men, avenging the rape and murder of his Indigenous wife, to the underground work of his Panther comrades.

Kambon's life teaches us not only about the use of creativity and art to transform society, but also of a need to examine the hard truths of violence and structural oppression and to raise difficult questions about methods of resistance. For Akinsanya Kambon, we can say, always the art, always the youth, and always the truth.

A collaboration between Emory Douglas and Richard Bell, one of Australia's most renowned Indigenous artists, *We Can Be Heroes* depicts the Australian sprinter, Peter Norman, in solidarity with the Black Power protests of US runners Tommie Smith and John Carlos at the 1968 Mexico City Olympics. © 2019 Emory Douglas / Artists Rights Society, New York

IV.
ART, REVOLUTION, AND A SOCIAL IMAGINARY

Emory Douglas, former BPP minister of culture, center, with Panther comrades Charlotte and Pete O'Neal in Arusha, Tanzania, 2018. Douglas's art continues to influence artists and activists worldwide. Photo courtesy of Emory Douglas

Opposite page: As one of nine panels of the Oakland Palestine Solidarity Mural, created in 2014 as bombs fell on Gaza, Emory Douglas's painting, *If the Tree Knew*, reflects the anguish of the people, yet the abundant foliage on the tree offers hope and liberation through the connection of a people to their history and land. © 2019 Emory Douglas / Artists Rights Society, New York

For the Zapantera Negra art exhibit in Chiapas, Mexico, Mayan women created beautiful embroidery pieces integrating the iconic Black Panther Party artwork of Emory Douglas with Mayan designs and symbolism. © 2019 Emory Douglas / Artists Rights Society, New York. Photo by Rosika Desnoyers

CHAPTER NINE

Art That Flows from the People: Emory Douglas, International Solidarity, and the Practice of Cocreation

Diane C. Fujino

In regard to my work with the Black Panther Party, it wasn't that the art came through me or by me, but it was a collective interpretation and expression from our community.

—Emory Douglas[1]

What critics and curators often describe as community-based art making is better described as art-based community making—a form of democratic interaction that enacts the just social relations that social movements often only envision.

—George Lipsitz[2]

The iconic images associated with the Black Panther Party—of police as pigs in human form; of audacious and armed resistance; and of ordinary Black folks struggling to survive, infused with dignity—inform how generations of people came to understand and remember the Panthers. Against the amplified power of his instantly recognizable drawings, Emory

Douglas as the artist behind these images is much lesser known. One could argue that he is the most prominent little-known Black Panther. That is changing in some ways for Douglas since the publication of his book, *Black Panther: The Revolutionary Art of Emory Douglas*, in 2007. That book, published at the thirtieth anniversary of the BPP, has sparked a renewed interest in Panther art and invitations to Douglas to speak and exhibit his work in local, national, and international venues. His art continues to influence and impact the radical imaginations and liberation struggles of generations of activists and artists following the demise of the party. His global reach might be best represented by the coining of a new term, "Zapantera," to signify the creation of blended imagery and blended struggles of the Black Panthers ("las Panteras Negras" in Spanish) and the Zapatista movement in Southern Mexico. Emory Douglas's images are unmistakably the primary Panther influence present and reworked in Zapantera paintings, Mayan women's embroidery, and other art pieces.[3]

Douglas's commitment to a collaborative process of art-making is a major feature of his art practice from his time in the Black Panther Party (BPP) to the present. Even as he created most of the Panther images as a solo artist, his drawings reflected the themes and work of the BPP and the Black Power and global Third World movements more generally. In creating his art, he was consistently open to ideas and critiques from others. Douglas refers to his work as "not me art, but we art" and in an art exhibit in Chiapas, Mexico, Douglas proclaimed the slogan, "I Am We."[4] His values and practice reflect what Daniel Fischlin, Ajay Heble, and George Lipsitz call "the ethics of co-creation." The work of improvisation, so central to certain types of music, theater, and art-making, is not simply about doing your own thing, but rather requires actively listening to the other musicians and artists, the heightened skills and self-discipline to know when to play solo and when to be collective, how to riff off others, and the ability to look for openings and to hear the unexpected. Their book, *The Fierce Urgency of Now*, examines how within forms of Afro-diasporic expressive culture, social transformation requires the democratic participation of the many. Moreover, the political and cultural are intertwined. Lipsitz notes that "what critics and curators often describe as community-based art making is better described as art-based community making—a form of democratic interaction that enacts the just social relations that social movements often only envision." This art-based community making can offer us hope. The ethics of cocreation, write Fischlin, Heble, and Lipsitz, "teaches us to make 'a way' out of 'no way' by cultivating the capacity to discern hidden elements of possibility, hope, and promise in even the most discouraging circumstances."[5]

The art of cocreation envisioned by Douglas is used not only to "educate, inform, and enlighten," as he explains but also to inspire active innovation, turning spectators into participants and consumers into producers. His is the work of improvisation as social practice, one that prefigures the kinds of liberatory social relations that activists advocate but too often fail to enact. Douglas's humanistic instincts and collective habits developed in the BPP are reflected in a cooperative and self-consciously anticapitalist art practice. When another artist, Akinsanya Kambon (then Mark Teemer) joined the Sacramento BPP, another comrade chided, "Emory, you've got some competition now, don't you?" Douglas, in his ever humble and quiet ways, responded, "Nah, this not competition. We work together collectively for the same cause." Douglas's generosity of spirit made an impact on Kambon, who recalled the story fifty years later.[6] Similarly, when Douglas discovered that the Cuban-based Organization of Solidarity with the People of Asia, Africa, and Latin America (OSPAAAL) used a drawing of his on one of its 1968 posters—without permission or credit—far from being outraged, he was delighted and honored.[7] At that time, and today, he rejects capitalist-based ideas about intellectual and artistic copyright. Beyond an individual practice of sharing, he believed the images were not strictly his creation, but rather emerged out of the anticolonial struggles occurring worldwide in the 1960s and '70s. It is noteworthy that Douglas's artwork contained the presence of strong Black women, unusual for the time, but that, to him, reflected the influence of the women in the party and in national liberation struggles in Vietnam and elsewhere.[8]

Douglas's collective process of art-making became even more overtly collaborative in the early twenty-first century. His Panther art and ongoing creations continue to influence current generations of artists and activists throughout the world. While this chapter's main objective is to examine the afterlife of Douglas's Panther art, a brief biography of his early life and his work in the BPP is in order before attending to his post-BPP activism and artistry. The themes of art cocreation and global solidarity emerge strongly in his work.

A "Bad Little Kid" in a Family of Women

Emory Douglas, born on May 24, 1943, in Grand Rapids, Michigan, grew up in a family of women. After leaving an abusive marriage his mother raised him as a single mother. Later, in 1951, they moved to San Francisco, to ease

Emory's asthma, and found support in being surrounded by extended family. They initially lived in the Double Rock area, where his mother's sister lived and where "the military barracks used to be, where the 49ers football stadium stands, and where the shipyards were." His mother had another sister who lived in the predominantly Black neighborhood of the Fillmore District, adjacent to the primarily Japanese American Western Addition, and Emory caught the bus back and forth between Double Rock and the Fillmore. In Grand Rapids and in San Francisco, Emory was, as he states with a light laugh, "a bad little kid." Emory recounted, "I used to get into mischief. They tell me not to throw rocks and I throw rocks and broke a woman's window. You know, those kinds of things."[9] Emory was the only child of Lorraine Douglas, born Luren Crawford on a riverboat in Tulsa, Oklahoma, as Emory recounted. His mother was among the poor Blacks who entered the world outside the structures of establishment society.[10]

After working in a box factory, his mother, who was legally blind, gained an opportunity to manage a concession stand in one of the government buildings; hers was at the juvenile hall. She first worked with a white woman, who was also blind, and when that woman died, his mother ran her own concession stand selling donuts, candy, and cookies (and unauthorized home-cooked dinners as part of the informal economy) for more than thirty-five years into the 1990s. So, while Emory was in and out of the youth incarceration system for "being bad as a youngster"—for truancy, playing dice with the older kids, "throwing bottles and turning and running right into the police," according to Emory—his mother knew many of the people at juvenile hall. Emory recalls his mother being fiercely independent, never wanting any help, despite being blind. She was also a "partier," not a "church goer," and "everybody in the neighborhood knew her." Around the time Emory was a young teenager, his mother set up residence with and later married Douglas Morris. In their later years, Emory became the main caregiver for his mother and the man he refers to, with affection, as his stepfather.[11]

Douglas recalls that the brothers from the hood in the Fillmore knew his mother and would try to watch out for him to keep him out of trouble. Community and cultural centers were also vital spaces providing him with safe and productive outlets. He was part of the young people participating regularly in the programs and summer camps of the Booker T. Washington Center and the YMCA in the Fillmore District. "I grew up there like everybody else," Douglas said. He recalled two counselors as outstanding, a brother named Mr. Payne, and his first counselor, a Japanese American named Yori

Wada, whom Douglas dubbed "a miracle worker" because he managed to get so many kids out of prison. He also got schooled in the events of the day, aware of the jazz scene in the Fillmore and attending school with the daughter of Charles Sullivan, who brought renowned Black musicians to the Fillmore Auditorium. Douglas also recalled when two Black men, whom he frequently saw on television news, came to San Francisco. Only later would he understand the historical, political, and cultural significance of W. E. B. Du Bois and Paul Robeson, but he already understood that they were powerful Black men. In the 1950s, the television would have also brought scenes of dogs, water cannons, and the police attacking peaceful civil rights activists. When Emory was around nine, he traveled with his aunt to Tulsa, Oklahoma, and witnessed firsthand the Jim Crow segregation of public facilities. As Douglas insightfully observed, "You can also understand that consciousness comes from when you grow up."[12] He was speaking to the blues epistemology, or the knowledge and culture already present and emerging from the conditions of working-class Black communities.[13] This knowledge and these experiences form the basis of his art-making, with its focus on everyday Black experiences and the honoring of Black resistance.

Life in the Party

Emory's political consciousness developed alongside his formal art training. For him, the cultural and political were closely intertwined. He had dabbled in art as a child, drawing, painting, and copying images out of magazines. At the advice of a probation officer who encouraged him to pursue art, he took his first art class at City College of San Francisco, where he ended up majoring in commercial art. He was at City College in the mid-1960s, as Black Power emerged in the San Francisco Bay Area. Across the bay in Berkeley and Oakland, inspired by local visits by Robert F. Williams and Malcolm X, Don Warden started the Afro-American Association (AAA) in 1962 as one of the earliest Black nationalist organizations on the West Coast. With a couple of hundred active members at its peak, AAA grew into one of the largest Black nationalist groups in the East Bay since the demise of the Civil Rights Congress in the early Cold War period.[14] Merritt College in Oakland was a pivotal foundation for Black studies. Merritt began offering Black studies courses as early as September 1964, was the first junior college to offer an Associated Arts degree in Afro-American studies by 1967, and was among the first Black studies departments in the nation after the Faculty Senate approved department status in November 1968. In the mid-1960s, Huey Newton and Bobby Seale, soon to be BPP cofounders, worked with the Soul Student Advisory Council at Merritt College, where they honed their political ideas and organizing skills. Merritt College was, in fact, a hotbed of Black militancy, so much so that the *Wall Street Journal* issued a warning, dubbing it, "A Campus Where Black Power Won."[15]

In this tense and shifting milieu, Douglas became an early participant in the political and cultural struggles that transformed the San Francisco Bay Area into one of the most important sites of the Black Power and Black Arts movements. As a student at City College in the mid-1960s, he became involved with the efforts to rename the Negro Student Association as the Black Student Union, reflecting the new political consciousness of the time. He was also active at the Black House in the Fillmore District. In 1966, Marvin X and Ed Bullins, two of the most significant playwrights and poets of the Bay Area, started Black Arts West and soon thereafter convinced future BPP leader Eldridge Cleaver to contribute his advance from *Soul on Ice* to convert a large, two-story Victorian house at 1711 Broderick Street into the Black House as a cultural, work, and residential space for weekly poetry readings, performances, and organizing meetings. Bullins and Marvin X were inspired by Amiri Baraka (then LeRoi Jones), the renowned Greenwich Village Beat poet whose sudden transformation into a Black nationalist in the wake of Malcolm X's death impelled Baraka to found the Black Arts Repertory Theater/School (BART/S) in 1965 in Harlem. The Black Arts Movement, considered to officially start with BART/S, is what Larry Neal described as the "aesthetic and spiritual sister of the Black Power concept" that required "a radical reordering of the western cultural aesthetic" based on "the Afro-American's desire for self-determination and nationhood."[16]

This emerging new consciousness and new network of artists and activists formed the context in which Douglas learned to intertwine the politics of art and the art of politics. In a move that would transform the nascent Black Arts Movement on the West Coast, the Black students at San Francisco State College brought three important New York/Newark–based Black Arts poets to their campus as visiting professors, beginning with Sonia Sanchez in the fall 1966, followed by Amiri Baraka and then Askia Touré. Baraka proposed that his residency be used to establish a "Black communications project" (BCP), sponsored by SF State but headquartered at the Black House, to produce plays featuring Black playwrights and Black actors and to host poetry readings and African dancers and singers. A budding young artist named Emory Douglas worked as the resident set designer for the BCP productions and not only got schooled by Baraka but forged a lifelong relationship that endured through turbulent internal conflicts within the Black Power/Black Arts movements.[17]

Douglas connected with the Black Panther Party for Self-Defense (BPPSD), newly formed in October 1966, in the organizing leading up to the San Francisco visit of Sister Betty Shabazz, Malcolm X's widow. Shabazz spoke at a program on February 21, 1967, the second anniversary of Malcolm's assassination, organized by a different Black Panther organization, the Black Panther Party of Northern California (BPPNC)—the brainchild of Eldridge Cleaver, according to Joshua Bloom and Waldo Martin. Douglas recalls that it was Hank Jones, then with the BPPNC and later with the BPPSD, who informed him about the program being organized. Douglas was asked to create a poster for the event and readily obliged. At the same meeting, he learned that Shabazz had not yet responded to the BPPNC's letter of invite and accompanied the group to ask Cleaver to appeal to Shabazz on their behalf. Despite the organizing work of the BPPNC, it was the discipline and audacity of Huey Newton and Bobby Seale's BPPSD's security delegation, which arrived at the airport with guns displayed and walked straight up to the gate to escort Sister Betty, that most impressed Douglas—as well as Cleaver and Jones—all of whom soon joined the BPPSD.[18]

As Douglas recalls, Newton and Seale would come by the Black House, where Cleaver lived upstairs and cultural programs took place downstairs, to try to recruit Cleaver for the BPPSD newspaper. At one point, Seale was at the Black House trying to create with a pencil the headlines for the first issue of the *Black Panther* newspaper, published April 25, 1967. Douglas told him that he could improve the quality of the graphic design. Douglas hurried to his home on the other side of town to get some art tools, but when he returned, they had already finished the layout. From the second issue on, however, Douglas worked on the *Black Panther* and created its more professional layout and design.[19] Bobby Seale recalls, "Huey, Eldridge, Bobby Hutton, Kathleen Cleaver, and I . . . were flabbergasted by Emory's artistic abilities." Mumia Abu-Jamal, who was the Philadelphia BPP's lieutenant of information and later became a journalist (and the most renowned US political prisoner), stated: "Emory didn't just do the front and back pages of the paper. He did layouts for almost the entire paper, every week. He isn't just an artist but a gifted graphic artist who used his eye to place and block-in texts and graphics." Douglas views his training in art at City College, where he learned graphic design and commercial art and participated in a healthy process of critique, as indispensable to his work in the party. The BPP gave Douglas the title of "Revolutionary Artist," and then during the reorganization of the party following Newton's arrest in October 1967, appointed him minister of culture.[20]

There is much to say about the significance of Douglas's art and his brilliance as a revolutionary artist. His book, *Black Panther: The Revolutionary Art of Emory Douglas*, with numerous reproductions of his artwork and eight essays illuminating his contributions, is an excellent place to start. Given this essay's focus on the afterlife of the BPP, suffice it to briefly discuss two aspects of Douglas's work in the BPP. First, the images he created were indispensable to the development of the BPP. Douglas himself recognized the importance of translating the complex ideology and practices of the party into readily comprehensible images. A goal of his is to create art "that even a child can understand."[21] But his art did much more than is conveyed by Douglas's humble words. Artist and art scholar Colette Gaiter posits, "Radical change starts with pointing out plainly and clearly what no one else will dare talk about or represent, and Douglas' work shouted the Panthers' mission through images." What made his images so compelling were the ways they reflected and gave meaning to everyday Black life—what Amiri Baraka dubbed his "homeboy familiarity" combined with "expressionist agitprop." Significantly, his images moved beyond reflecting life to "construct[ing] a visual mythology of power for people who felt powerless and victimized," Gaiter observes. As Laura Mulvey argues, "moving from oppression and its mythologies to a stance of self-definition is a difficult process and requires people with social grievances to construct a long chain of countermyths and symbols." Douglas's images—of strong African women, often holding a baby and a gun; of older Black men and women looking downtrodden but dignified; of proud brothers working for radical change; and of the vulnerability of power, symbolized by the pig—did the work of creating the kinds of countermyths and symbols that function as a "cleansing force," in the words of Frantz Fanon, to advance the process of decolonizing the mind. Douglas's images provided an alternative vision, gave people hope and courage, and made revolution look like a reasonable response. His were images created for ordinary Black folk and other oppressed peoples—and not to comfort those in power.[22]

Second, Douglas somehow managed to bypass major internal conflicts in the Black House and the BPP. Douglas himself attributes this to focusing on the art and on producing the newspaper, which were valued by all sides. But how he averted getting trapped in the chaos of the internecine fighting is a subject worthy of further investigation. The Black House provided a space that brought together Black artists and Black revolutionaries, but ironically conflicts between the two groups also led to its demise. As James Smethurst discusses in *The Black Arts Movement*, Black House cofounders Ed Bullins and Marvin X connected Eldridge Cleaver with the Black House. But in less than a year, Cleaver was charging Black House leaders with being "cultural nationalists" who were "more interested in making symbolic gestures than in doing the hard work of seizing real power, and the artists feeling that Cleaver was far too deferential toward the 'white Left.'"[23] Cleaver and the BPP evicted Marvin X, Bullins, and most of the other artists from the Black House in 1967. These same aesthetic and ideological conflicts, ostensibly a divide between cultural nationalists and revolutionary nationalists/internationalists (with some of the latter already or soon-to-be Marxist-Leninists), also led to the demise of BART/S in Harlem and Black Arts West in San Francisco in the mid-1960s—all within a year of their formation. Somehow Douglas managed to transcend the intense and inflated conflicts between cultural workers and revolutionary political activists. He was an artist clearly aligned with the BPP—and a growing leader within the party—who made his artwork relevant and necessary to illustrating the ideas of the BPP. Against the pressures of the times, in the early formation of Black Power, his graphic images built a bridge between the cultural and the political, helping to develop the ideas about the necessity of revolutionary art to political struggle. This intertwining of cultural and political work built on the tradition of ideas advocated by Paul Robeson, Mao Zedong, Amilcar Cabral, and many others.

Douglas also averted being trapped by what is arguably the most visible and deadliest internecine conflict within the BPP, the split between Huey Newton and Eldridge Cleaver. On a live television program in San Francisco in February 1971, Cleaver called in by phone from Algeria to denounce Newton for purging Geronimo ji Jaga Pratt and the New York Panther 21, and, in a phone call immediately after, Newton expelled Cleaver from the BPP. Shortly thereafter two Panthers, Robert Webb and then Sam Napier, were killed, allegedly as retaliation on both sides.[24] How was Douglas, who was close to Panther leaders on both sides, able to seemingly transcend the split? First, the strong relationships he had developed with Newton, Seale, *and* Cleaver, rather than creating mistrust, worked to heighten Douglas's integrity in the eyes of Panther leaders. Douglas was very close with Cleaver, working daily with him on the *Black Panther* newspaper, as housemates in a home that also served as a center of San Francisco BPP activity, and as the travel companion to Kathleen Cleaver, eight months pregnant, en route to Algeria in spring 1969 to meet her husband in political exile. Douglas had also developed strong relationships with Newton and Seale, who "used to come over every day after they'd been organizing in the evening, and we'd cut it up, talking and all." Douglas also caught the bus to Oakland, where they would regularly meet at Bobby's house to "hang out" or to go on police patrols. Contrary to the public understanding of the Newton-Cleaver split, Douglas asserts that Huey himself made it possible to support Eldridge's people and not be seen as Huey's enemy. Douglas explained: "Huey always said it wasn't about DC. It wasn't about Kathleen. It was about none of that. It was about what Eldridge did in that context." DC or Donald Cox, the premiere BPP field marshal, traveled to Algeria (with Douglas) in 1970 and made the decision to stay in exile there. The Cleavers also urged Douglas to remain in Algeria, but he viewed the Bay Area as the place he needed to be. After the split, Panthers in the Bay Area, including Douglas, had no further communication with the Cleavers in Algeria, but Douglas continued to work well with Newton and Seale in the BPP and on the newspaper, and in fact outlasted both as an active member of the party.[25]

The second factor that mediated Douglas's ability to avert the problems within the party was, as he observed, "The paper was something that transcended all the personalities and conflicts." He noted that "some of the people on the other side used to take some of the Panther cartoons and publish them in the [East Coast BPP's] *Right On!* paper and what have you. You had other activists using them in flyers and other stuff. So you knew that it was bigger than just the Panthers."[26] Douglas makes an important point about the significance of art and of the newspaper to exceed internal conflicts. Still, the issue remains complex. Others viewed the newspaper as being used "against any that fell from their favor—the slander against Geronimo at the time of his expulsion being an eloquent example," as DC asserts.[27] Then too Sam Napier was the distribution manager of the *Black Panther* newspaper and was killed in the internecine fighting. Douglas likewise was never free from risk and vulnerability as a leader of the BPP, from the police and FBI as well as from the internal fighting.[28]

Douglas was one of the few members in the BPP from nearly the beginning to nearly the end, staying until about, as Douglas recounted, three to six months before its demise. The BPP is said to have officially ended in 1982, when the last Panther program, the Oakland Community School, closed its doors. By then, the party was a shell of its former self, with about a dozen members, all in Oakland.[29] After a short stint as a screen printer, Douglas went to work with Dr. Carlton Goodlett at the *Sun-Reporter* doing production and illustration for more than twenty years until Douglas's retirement in 2004. The *Sun-Reporter* was San Francisco's first major Black newspaper and was said to have a circulation of over one hundred thousand. Dr. Goodlett, or "Doc" as Douglas called him, had strong ties with the communist left from at least the early Cold War, especially with Paul Robeson and William Patterson. Goodlett didn't always agree with the BPP (his paper had called the BPP's Sacramento protest "a bit too audacious," saying it "probably did more harm than good for the Negro's cause"), but, unlike the mainstream press's alarmist reporting of Black men with guns, he covered the Panther's political views and the conditions in the Black community that gave rise to such protest. Douglas talks about Doc with great respect and admiration: "When Malcolm [X] would come to town . . . first place he'd go was the *Sun-Reporter*," the BPP "bought our first printing operation from [the *Sun-Reporter*] when they were upgrading back in the day," and "when a confrontation with the police almost led to a shootout, Dr. Carlton Goodlett and Mr. Thomas Fleming came and stood in front of the [BPP] office and calmed things down."[30]

After he left the party, Douglas continued his social justice and art work, even as his direct activism declined. "I was doing a part of the revolution that is solidarity with the people, with the community," he stated. In the 1990s, for example, he regularly visited former Panther Geronimo ji Jaga in prison and worked with many others to gain his release.[31] He also supported the political prisoner and former Panther Mumia Abu-Jamal after Pennsylvania governor Tom Ridge reinstated the death penalty in 1995. Douglas initially hadn't realized that Mumia was the same person he knew as Wesley Cook, whom he had shown around the Panther newspaper operations in California and with whom he interacted in Philadelphia shortly after the police raid on the Philly Panther office in August 1970. Douglas also continued to provide graphic and printing services, at low or no cost, to community and activist groups. He had started this work while in the BPP, working at Emory's Printing and Graphic Service, after taking over Ben's Community Printing and Graphic Service from Benny Harris. During this period, he had heavy elder care responsibilities for thirteen years from the early 1990s until about 2004, when his stepfather and then his mother passed. His familial obligations meant that he could not travel, but he was able to participate in local activism, as the freedom struggles intensified in California in the 1990s.[32]

The Enduring Significance of Black Panther Art

"We Were One": Zapatista-Panther Encounters

The development of a new project and a new phrase, "Zapantera Negra," is symbolic of the continuing influence of Emory Douglas's art in the post-Panther period. The new work displays a direct lineage to the BPP. It shows how the BPP transcended Black experiences to connect with communities through antiracial and anticolonial theorizing. It reveals the internationalization of the BPP and of Douglas's work—processes that are not new but rather a continuation of Panther's global relations and networks. It demonstrates that the BPP's images and ideas were never static but open to different interpretations and to different creations. It challenges further discussions about similarities and differences of approaches between the Panthers and Zapatistas. The Zapatistas are famously known for their daring armed uprising on January 1, 1994, in the southernmost state of Mexico, in protest of the implementation of the North American Free Trade Agreement (NAFTA) that, as expected, promoted neoliberal austerity, benefited multinational corporations, and devastated local economies and communities. Former Panthers—and most around the world—would benefit from paying attention to the Zapatistas' intensively democratic processes. Zapatistismo depends on the active listening to local Indigenous peoples (*preguntando caminamos*), those too often deemed disposable as neither consumers nor producers in the global capitalist economy and as such are considered to be part of the "Fourth World."[33] By listening and learning from Indigenous peoples, Zapatista leaders transformed their (neo)Marxist ideology to a new epistemology and practice centering on Indigenous ways of knowing combined with efforts to build democratic communities and to loosen the power of the Mexican state and paramilitary violence as the Zapatistas create their own "autonomous municipalities" and "good government" structures. Douglas not only participated in the art projects but also learned about the Zapatista movement in the making.

In November 2012, Douglas participated in a two-week artist residency in San Cristóbal de las Casas, Chiapas. The invitation came from EDELO, founded by Caleb Duarte Piñon and Mia Eve Rollow in 2009 as a community art center and experimental artist residency. The space that EDELO inhabits had been the offices of the United Nations, until fall 2009, when a hundred Indigenous peoples occupied it to bring international attention to their plight. Surely it would take an artist to name their project, EDELO, meaning En Donde Era la ONU (Where the United Nations Used to Be). Upon learning the meaning of EDELO, artist Rigo 23 thought it to be "genius" in the way it "announces, and immediately occupies, the void left behind by that grandiose twentieth-century global organization . . . where a handful of the world's biggest arms manufacturers get to veto while all the other nations get to vote." By contrast, EDELO was localized but with global visions, democratic, innovative, and challenging (as in the indeterminacy of "a wordless place . . . so that the public became confused, obstructed with questions, with impossibilities that spur possibilities," stated Rollow). Duarte, Rollow, and Rigo 23 conceived the idea to develop an art exhibit titled *The Encounter: Black Panthers-Zapatistas*, where local Zapatista artists explore linkages between the BPP and Zapatista movement. They also produced a single-issue newsletter that presented Douglas's art and new articles and artwork on Zapatista-Panther interconnections. Rigo 23 coined the term "Zapantera Negra," to join Zapatista with *pantera negra* (meaning "black panther" in Spanish) and Mexico City artist Omar Perez designed the Zapantera Negra poster for the exhibit.[34]

The Zapantera Negra project turned out to be incredibly generative. It inspired embroideries created by a Zapatista Mayan women's collective that emphasized Mayan decorative designs and symbolism that merged with seven of Douglas's images. The project, funded as a Kickstarter dependent on grassroots contributions, was originally conceived as a global project, rooted in Chiapas and intended to travel to at least five different countries. Zapantera Negra was exhibited in San Francisco in February 2013, Montreal in June 2014, Australia in March–April 2015 and elsewhere. Douglas, often with Duarte, Rigo 23, or Rollow, participated in and spoke at each of these venues. The Montreal exhibit at Concordia University resulted in the publication of *Zapantera Negra: An Artistic Encounter between Black Panthers and Zapatistas*, edited by Marc James Léger and David Tomas. The book includes transcripts of the public talk and discussion with Douglas, Rollow, and Indigenous Zoque artist Saúl Kak as well as a lively essay by Rigo 23, an interview with Duarte, and BPP and Zapatista documents. Douglas continues to speak about the Zapantera Negra project in multiple venues, including at the Chinese Progressive Association in San Francisco in August 2013 where this author first learned about the project.[35]

As Douglas was leaving Chiapas in mid-November 2012—in fact, to Argentina to give a "Las Panteras Negras" presentation—he was invited to return to Chiapas for an international Indigenous conference. They had been wanting to invite a former Black Panther to give a presentation on the party as well as the case of Mumia Abu-Jamal. So on December 25, 2012, Douglas found himself back in Chiapas for the conference, accompanied by his daughter, Meres-Sia Gabriel, who introduced her father with this powerful statement:

> I speak these words in solidarity with the Zapatista community—may they please the ancestors. Long before Spain invaded the Americas, with ship-loads of enslaved Africans, before America was called "America" and Africa was called "Africa," when a snail was just a snail and a panther was just an animal, historians write of an ancient Mayan-African relationship, of trading and exchanging ideas, cultures, goods, and more. Some archeologists go further. They write that before Mayans and Africans traded, before they were two distinct people, they were one. When I heard that my father would present on the legacy of the Black Panther Party for this symposium, I felt an impulsive reaction to attend, an ancient calling urging me: "Be there! Let your presence be testimony to the ancestors, that your spirit remembers a time before colonization, subjugation, and plantations." Before Zapatistas took to the mountains in Chiapas, and the Panthers to the streets in the US, before we were revolutionaries, fighting our own distinct battles in different countries, before there was you and I there was we, and we were one.[36]

Gabriel's words signal not only her knowledge of African and Indigenous histories and interactions but also the ways she derives knowledge from the ancestors and locates herself within this genealogy.[37] Her statement, "We were one," speaks to the collectivity that guides the Zapatistas, the Black Panthers, and Douglas's own art, activism, and way of being in the world. The daughter, like the father, draws on epistemological and ontological frameworks rooted in African culture and history and extended to US Black communities as mixtures of, as Cedric Robinson relays, African, Indigenous, and European contexts.[38]

On the twentieth anniversary of the Zapatista uprising, Douglas returned to Chiapas for a third time. He was there to ring in the New Year with local families and to celebrate "twenty years of dreams and struggle" (or "VIENTE ANOS DE SUENOS LUCHA," as Santiago Mazatl and Roger Peet painted on a mural in La Union's small Zapatista community). In January 2014, Douglas worked on a collaborative mural project with other activist-artists, including Favianna Rodriguez, Roger Peet, and Santiago Mazatl of Justseeds, Moises Gandhi, and Zanpantera Negras comrade Caleb Duarte. They painted the mural on a Zapatista store in the village of Comandanta Ramona on land reclaimed in the January 1, 1994, Zapatista rebellion and defended ever since.

The artists painted bold red sun rays emanating from the main archway, clearly borrowing from Douglas's artwork that utilized thick sun rays to frame people's portraits. Douglas himself, even at age seventy, scaled a rickety scaffold to paint the iconic Zapatista snail, stylized with a Zapatista mask, Black Power fists, and the light blue and black of the BPP's uniforms. Altogether, the mural reflected the themes of production, culture, education, and health.[39]

Douglas's participation in Chiapas extended far beyond creating art or speaking as the most iconic Panther artist. The mural painting came at the end of a working trip in December 2013 where, as Douglas recalled, "I was accepted" as one of about fifteen hundred people invited to live and work with a Zapatista family for a week as part of their *escuelita* (little school) program. This also took place in the village of Comandanta Ramona, named after the most visible woman leader of the Zapatista insurgency in 1994. Douglas soon found out why they call it "school of the dirt." Like everyone else, Douglas traveled the approximately five-hour ride to get to his host family. They slept on cots made of wood planks with a single blanket to keep them warm and stayed in a wooden house with dirt floors, tin roof, an outhouse bathroom, and no electricity. These were "the same types of houses that the (Black) sharecroppers had in the United States," Douglas observed. They ate simple foods of tortillas and beans, which worked for Douglas, who had been a vegan for several years. They also had to travel through difficult terrain to get to the different areas to plant corn and banana bulbs and to pick coffee beans. Douglas recalled, "You start walking in the mud and your foot sticks down into it almost up to your ankles and you try to pull your foot out and your boot is about ready to come off. And you're used to city walking and the next thing you know you're flipping over into the mud. It was rough, but I stuck with it all the way through! One time I had to use this ledge where you can almost fall off, and I fell about five times that first day. The last time I fell they got worried, so they chopped up two sticks for me so that I was walking with the two sticks." Douglas was certainly humbled by this experience and in awe of the local people's agility and knowledge of the terrain.

On another trip, a man was carrying a baby in his arms across the rugged terrain and little girls went running and jumping from rock to rock across a creek. Douglas relayed laughing, "I was trying to figure out how I'm going to get down off of this and get over to the other side. So I just slide down into it." Rough as it was, Douglas was honored to travel, not as a tourist, but as part of a work trip, akin to the brigades people took to Cuba to provide labor for the country as well as to see what everyday life was like for the people after the revolution. Back in Oakland, Douglas is a regular member of the Chiapas Support Committee that works to educate locally and to accompany the process of building autonomous self-governing institutions in Chiapas.[40]

Renewal and Resurgency

In 2007, two interrelated projects signaled a renewed public spotlight on Emory Douglas's art and activism and the intensified internationalization of his political and cultural work. Artist Sam Durant had been working with Douglas and others, especially Kathleen Cleaver, to compile Douglas's artwork and eight essays into book form. The idea first emerged when Douglas spoke at Durant's art show at the Museum of Contemporary Art (MOCA) in Los Angeles in 2002 and Durant wondered aloud why there wasn't a book on Douglas's art. That book, *Black Panther: The Revolutionary Art of Emory Douglas* (2007), is a coffee table–style book, half the pages filled with images, in color, and the other half with essays by activists, artists, and scholars, including Danny Glover, Bobby Seale, Sam Durant, Kathleen Cleaver, Colette Gaiter, Greg Jung Morozumi, Amiri Baraka, and St. Clair Bourne. As a concurrent project, Durant curated an exhibit of Douglas's art at MOCA that ran from October 2007 to February 2008. Since his Panther days and beyond, Douglas has been speaking about and showcasing his work. In 1997 and again in 2004, for example, Greg Morozumi, a Japanese American radical activist and staff member of the Eastside Arts Alliance in Oakland, had helped to organize exhibits on Douglas's art. Still, the book and MOCA exhibit in 2007 marked a transition to an amplified period of speaking, exhibiting his work, and traveling for Douglas, in a period of increased social movement activities in the nation and in the world and at a time when Douglas had lesser family responsibilities.[41]

Douglas's powerful and distinctive images are instantly recognizable, yet he as a person remains, to this day, relatively little known outside of activist circles. A 2014 article in *Dazed and Confused* noted: "Until recently the work of Douglas has been largely forgotten. Emory's work has never been taught in art schools or displayed, framed, and catalogued in galleries. But then the art gallery was never Emory's domain, even when his creativity was at its peak." As Douglas himself articulated in 1970, "The ghetto itself is the gallery for the revolutionary artist's drawings. His work is pasted on the walls of the ghetto; in storefront windows, fences, doorways, telephone poles and booths, passing buses, alleyways."[42] Indeed, this is the impact Douglas seeks—not mainstream recognition and standards of success but an ability to connect with everyday people, transform ideas and visions, and to move people to action in service to justice and liberation. By this standard, one can state, without hyperbole, that through his art Douglas has become one of the former Black Panthers who has had the greatest impact on post-BPP social movements.

As would not be surprising to anyone who knows BPP history, Douglas already had an international outlook from the time of his Panther days. The politics of the party were intertwined with world history, especially Third World colonial history and decolonial resistance. Globally, the International Section of the BPP was established in Algeria; Panther formations emerged in Bermuda, India (Dalit Panthers), England, Palestine, Israel, Australia, New Zealand (Polynesian Panthers); and the Panthers influenced struggles in Cuba, Vietnam, and beyond. Panthers traveled to Japan and Asia (including the widely known BPP-led multi-organizational delegation to China, North Korea, and North Vietnam in summer 1970), Sweden, Denmark, Germany, France, and elsewhere, while former Panther Assata Shakur remains in exile in Cuba.[43] Douglas himself had traveled twice to Algeria, once to accompany Kathleen Cleaver to meet her husband in exile and attend the Pan-African Cultural Festival and a separate time with Donald Cox, who stayed in Algeria in exile and then moved to France. Douglas was also part of the month-long BPP delegation to China. Nevertheless, the post-2007 years represent the most intensive period of international travel in Douglas's life. He traveled to Manchester, England in 2008; Sydney, Australia, in 2008 and 2011; Brisbane, Australia, in 2009, 2011, and 2015; Beirut, Lebanon, in 2010; Rotterdam, the Netherlands, in 2010 and 2011; Lisbon, Portugal, in 2011; London in 2011; Nottingham in 2011; Chiapas, Mexico in 2012, 2013, and 2014; Mar del Plata, Argentina, in 2012; New Zealand in 2013 and again in 2015; Mexico City in 2013; Montreal, Canada, in 2014; Rio de Janeiro, Brazil, in 2014; Madrid, Spain, in 2014; Bogota, Colombia, in 2015 or 2016; Amsterdam in 2016; Palestine in 2016; Cuba in 2016; and London in 2017.[44] The point is not to provide an exhaustive listing of Douglas's travels, presentations, or art shows, but rather to make the argument for the global impact of the BPP on generations of activists and artists.

Aboriginal-Black Collaborations

Another major collaboration of Douglas's took place with Aboriginal artist Richard Bell of Australia. Douglas met Bell in 2008 when their artwork was displayed side by side at the Sixteenth Biennale of Sydney, "Revolutions–Forms That Turn," an ambitious showing of 180 artists from more than forty-two countries in spaces throughout Sydney. Bell, ten years Douglas's junior, was born into the Kamilaroi tribe in Charleville, Queensland, and faced the daily hardships that poverty and life as an Aboriginal person virtually guarantees. In Bell's community, the men were gone for months doing seasonal work and the women raised the children essentially as single mothers on scarce financial resources. They had to live off the land, hunting for food and living in tin huts. Before and after Bell won the Australian National Indigenous Arts Award, considered to be the highest arts honor bestowed on an Indigenous artist, he relied on Indigenous life experiences and activist work in the Native and Black consciousness movements that spurred his controversial artwork. Douglas discovered a profound personal, political and artistic synergy with Bell, rooted in a common life of oppression and radical resistance, even as Bell, described as having a "strong presence and loud personality" seems at odds with the quiet and humble Douglas. The next year, Douglas and Bell cocreated the exhibit, "All Power to the People," held at the Milani Gallery in Brisbane, Australia, which featured framed prints of Douglas's Panther art as well as a floor-to-ceiling painting of his 1969 image of a Black woman with spear and gun and pink "sun rays" emanating from behind her.[45]

Douglas found himself back in Australia in 2011, this time for a project that depended on greater collaboration with Bell and greater community participation. The two artists cocreated a mural for the exhibit "Edge of Elsewhere" at the Campbelltown Arts Centre in Sydney that involved children from the local community. Theirs was a provocative piece titled, "Peace Heals, War Kills (Big Ass Mutha Fuckin Mural)," displayed along a long rectangular wall (fifty feet long and sixteen feet high) that features bombs hitting the words "peace;" dismembered, artistically rendered stick-like figures; a graphic rendition of a child with artificial limbs; and the earth as the flame of a Statue of Liberty–like torch featuring the word "peace."[46]

That same year, Bell, working with Douglas, created a powerful painting, titled *We Can Be Heroes*, of the iconic image of US Black athletes Tommy Smith and John Carlos raising their fists in the Black Power salute at the 1968 Olympics in Mexico City. The second-place medalist on stage in 1968 was a white Australian, Peter Norman, prompting Bell's interest in a joint Aboriginal-Black project. Norman appears to be indifferent, unaware even, about the Black Power protest taking place behind him, but on that stage he wore an Olympic Project for Human Rights (OPHR) badge in solidarity with the two Black athletes. Norman was ostracized when he returned home, overlooked for the 1972 Munich games, and despite holding the Australian record for the 200 meter to this day, virtually ignored even in the 2000 Olympic games held in his native country.[47] Bell acknowledges that Norman's stand "did give me a lot of hope in all the despair." He provocatively calls this painting his "peace offering to White Australia."[48]

The OPHR, founded in fall 1967 by Harry Edwards, was influenced by Black Power struggles to expose how Black athletes were used to project an image of racial equality. To protest US and global racism, the OPHR sought to organize a Black boycott of the 1968 Olympic games, demand that fascist apartheid South Africa and Southern Rhodesia be banned from the Olympics, and protest the treatment of Muhammad Ali for his Vietnam War draft resistance. Forty-four years after the famous Mexico City Olympics, UC Berkeley professor Harry Edwards, along with UC Berkeley doctoral student Ameer Hasan Loggins, found himself recommending books on Black history and Black Power politics and engaging intellectual discussions with another Black athlete soon-to-be famous for his political stance. In 2016, San Francisco 49ers professional football player Colin Kaepernick ignited a national controversy by "taking a knee" or kneeling during the national anthem at NFL games to protest anti-Black police violence.[49]

The same year Kaepernick began his public protest, Douglas found himself in another collaboration with Bell, this time in Amsterdam at the invitation of Bell to participate on his project, "Bell Invites." Bell's provocation turned art-making, often isolating and product-focused, into a communal space through a collective mural project with local artists, dance performances, and a partnership with the University of Colour, a student collective dedicated to "decolonizing the University."[50] Then in 2017, Douglas engaged a public conversation with the 1968 Olympic medalist John Carlos in a program at Yale University titled, "Game Realizing Game," following by a collective project with Yale art students focusing on Douglas's artwork. For Douglas, the linkages among Black Power and global decolonization, art and athletes continue to form webs of interconnections.

Solidarity with Palestine

As Israeli bombs fell on Gaza in the summer of 2014, Douglas participated in a collective art project in Oakland, California, that "interlinked histories of colonization, environmental exploitation, and international solidarity" in the struggle for Palestine. The Oakland Palestine Solidarity Mural brought together ten artists from diverse backgrounds to cover the entirety of a 157-foot-long building in downtown Oakland. Inspired by Sameeh Shqeir's song lyrics, "We die like trees standing up," the artists—Palestinian, Indigenous, African, Asian, Chicana/o/x, and Jewish—created their interpretation of dying like trees in each of the nine panels comprising the large-scale mural. An Indigenous artist depicted the interconnectedness of all Native people rooted in their relationship to the land. A Japanese American artist drew a line from Amache (US concentration camp) to Palestine through forced captivity and "unspeakable" human rights violations. Douglas painted an anguished Palestinian tightly embracing a tree abundant with green foliage, with the words "Free the Land" etched into the trunk. His panel speaks to the suffering of the people but also gives hope for a liberatory future, represented, not by a dying tree, but by one full of life and new growth. The "Free the Land" inscription announces the source of oppression, not as civil rights violations per se, but as land theft and colonial occupation, which then demands an anticolonial solution. That the person's lower half morphs into tree roots flowing into the earth suggests that the foundation of a people and their liberation is connected to their history and to the land.[51]

The Oakland mural was unveiled in a program on Sunday, August 10, 2014, in the midst of what would become seven weeks of devastating Israeli airstrikes and Hamas "rockets" that resulted in the killing of more than two thousand Palestinians, all or nearly all civilians, including 490 children, compared to deaths of sixty-four Israeli soldiers, six Israeli civilians and one Israeli child. Up to half a million Palestinians were displaced and twenty thousand homes destroyed. Six days after the mural unveiling, Bay Area activists organized a Block the Boat action, gathering at the Port of Oakland to prevent the loading and unloading of an Israeli freighter, in solidarity with actions at ports in Los Angeles, Tacoma, and Seattle, and rallies nationwide.[52]

Douglas's solidarity with Palestine first developed in the BPP beginning in the late 1960s. The Student Nonviolent Coordinating Committee (SNCC) was the first US Black organization to support Palestine. They printed a two-page centerfold in the *SNCC Newsletter*, framing Israeli aggression as occupation and colonialism, in response to the Six-Day War in June 1967 in which Israel seized Gaza from Egypt, the West Bank from Jordan, and the Golan Heights from Syria. The BPP soon directed its anti-imperialist politics in support of Palestine. As Alex Lubin observes, the *Black Panther* newspaper became one of the most reliable sources for US-based news on the Israeli occupation of the West Bank and also featured editorials by Yasser Arafat of the Palestinian Liberation Organization (PLO) and George Habash of the Popular Front for the Liberation of Palestine (PFLP). In October 1968, the *Black Panther*'s first article on Palestine connected Palestinian and Black liberation through the intertwined relationship between Zionism and US imperialism. In September 1970, the BPP called a press conference (to deny the allegation that the BPP had a delegation in Jordan led by Stokely Carmichael) and asserted its support for the "Palestinian's just struggle for liberation." They also provocatively claimed that the BPP international section in Algeria, led by Eldridge and Kathleen Cleaver, was in "daily contact" with the PLO. The Panthers framed their theoretical position of Black and global liberation not merely around antiracism but also "the need to transform the structure into a socialist society," even as they recognized that "socialism will not wipe out racism completely." The Panthers warned against the kind of "reactionary nationalism" that aligns itself with US imperialism and instead called for "the Jewish people and the Palestinian people to live in harmony together." The BPP published two position papers on the Middle East conflict, in 1974 and in 1980, the latter following Huey Newton's trip to Lebanon, Syria, and the occupied West Bank. The Panthers continued to see connections between US Blacks and Palestinians as communities trying to survive under US imperialism and racial capitalism.[53]

Twenty-six years after Huey Newton's visit, Emory Douglas made his first trip to Palestine with a prisoner, labor, and academic solidarity delegation, headed by Professor Rabab Abdulhadi. The nineteen-member delegation spent ten days in March and April 2016 in the occupied West Bank and Israel meeting with dozens of former political prisoners, human rights and prisoner support organizations, scholars, trade unionists, political leaders, women leaders, and cultural workers. In an intensive, nonstop trip, the then seventy-two-year-old Douglas, disciplined from years in the BPP, global solidarity travels, and a collective politic, was always on time and at the front of the group. One particularly moving encounter for Douglas took place in the backyard of a former political prisoner, imprisoned at age twenty for twenty-six years for organizing resistance against the Israeli occupation and colonialism. His father had been a freedom fighter against the 1948 colonization of Palestine and he himself became conscientized at age thirteen, when his older brother was arrested and imprisoned for resistance to occupation. This former prisoner sat in a circle among the US activists, his young son on his lap representing a new life, and asserted his continued commitment to the struggle for Palestinian liberation. He expressed that he could survive fifty-seven days of "extreme interrogation" because he felt much stronger as part of a collective and that even in the midst of the harshest torture and interrogation, he was thinking of what he would do next, mentally preparing himself for the next stage in the struggle. The entire experience in Palestine, and this former political prisoner in particular, inspired Douglas to create new graphic designs in support of the Boycott, Divestment, and Sanctions campaign (BDS), initiated by Palestinian civil society in 2005. Douglas's designs prominently announced "Free the Land" and "Down with Apartheid," slogans that called forth issues of settler colonialism, occupation, and linkages with the racism of South African apartheid. His designs also called out corporations such as G4 and Airbnb to divest and governments and movements worldwide to support the BDS movement. Following his return, Douglas participated in several delegation report backs and radio interviews, particularly in the Bay Area.[54]

That Douglas's art for Palestinian liberation preceded his involvement with the 2014 Oakland mural project reflects his ongoing involvement with grassroots political struggles. His art didn't emerge in response to the specter of bombings in Gaza, but rather was connected with local support for Palestine, especially in the aftermath of the BDS call for international solidarity. In 2010, for example, Douglas created a design showing two missiles, one labeled USA and the other bearing an Israeli flag, attacking an image of the world with the word "peace" breaking apart. Another design depicted two youth throwing rocks against the clearly outsized power of two rockets. That Douglas chose to use photographic representations of the boys marked the situation as tangible and urgent.[55]

These projects represent significant art-activist works since Douglas's intensification of his activism around 2007. Still, they are but a subset of his artwork and organizing that focuses heavily on police violence, prisons, Third World struggles, tributes to Black and other revolutionaries, and BPP commemorations. To Emory, the social and political are intertwined, so on his Facebook page he also posts his designs of mother and child or father and child to extend "Happy Mother's Day" or "Happy Father's Day" greetings, while creating images of Black pride. Douglas's artwork continues to deploy the form and content that characterize the iconic Emory-esque designs—bold graphics and strong lines, transparent political messages, and emphasis on Black life.

Even as his drawings tend to be less polemical than in his early Panther days, he also reproduces, at times, his BPP representations of the "pig" to signify US military, police, and state apparatuses of power. Like the ideas and the images of the BPP, Douglas's artwork has staying power. It has been resurrected by multiple generations of activists and is particularly meaningful today when we are witnessing the most widespread and powerful social movements and expressions of political imaginations that the world has seen since the 1960s.

Conclusion: "Art That Flows from the People"

Across more than fifty years, Emory Douglas's art retains its political provocation, commanding our attention to think, feel, and act differently. While bypassing the more nuanced theoretical discussions of the BPP, his artwork focused on exposing conditions and contradictions of widespread Black poverty in the richest country in the world and of US and global Third World resistance to US imperialism. In October 2018, as I was making the revisions to this chapter, Douglas found himself embroiled in a public controversy arising from his artwork's ability to reveal just such contradictions. In an hour-long presentation at the University of Michigan, which included nearly two hundred slides, Douglas showed a collage he had made of Hitler and Netanyahu with the words "Guilty of Genocide" running across their foreheads, below which genocide was defined as "the deliberate killing of a large group of people, especially those of a particular ethnic group or nation." This took place at a time when Israeli army gunfire had killed at least 195 Palestinians since the Gaza border protests began in March 2018; the World Bank issued a report that the economy in Gaza is "collapsing" under the eleven-year Israeli blockade, with over 70 percent unemployment, half the people living in poverty, and lack of clean water and sanitation; and the Israeli Knesset, at Prime Minister Benjamin Netanyahu's urging, passed a law that made Israel a "nation-state of the Jewish people," circumventing the democratic rights of Palestinians living inside Israel, including removing Arabic as an official national language.[56] In response to this one image, a student raised the charge of anti-Semitism—a charge that was widely circulated in pro-Israeli media outlets. Yet for Douglas, his collage is neither anti-Semitic nor anti-German; to the contrary, it extends camaraderie with the Jewish people as a people persecuted by the Nazis. As artist Rigo 23 expressed: "In this artwork Emory Douglas depicts solidarity with the Jewish people who, along with the Roma, communists and homosexuals (as they were then defined) were taken en masse to concentration camps by Adolf Hitler's regime. . . . In this artwork Emory Douglas also depicts solidarity with the Palestinian people, who have been shot at indiscriminately, deprived of land and nationhood, and legislated as second-class citizens by the regime led by Benjamin Netanyahu."[57] This is part of the courage to speak truth to power displayed by Emory Douglas. He does not rest on the nostalgia of the Panthers, but instead continually engages in today's struggles, while showing a willingness to take the risks necessary to demonstrate deep solidarity with oppressed people around the world.

If Douglas's artwork is to be evaluated by a statement he wrote and published in the *Black Panther* newspaper in 1970, then his art and activism have been well served. In Position Paper No. 1, "On Revolutionary Art," he wrote:

> Revolutionary Art, like the [Black Panther] Party, is for the whole community and its total problems. It gives the people the correct picture of our struggle, whereas the Revolutionary Ideology gives the people the correct political understanding of our struggle. Before a correct visual interpretation of the struggle can be given, we must recognize that Revolutionary Art is *an art that flows from the people.*[58]

Douglas's articulation of knowledge and analysis as emerging from the everyday experiences of Black communities (and from the ancestors, as in his daughter's statement to the Zapatistas) is synergistic with a longer tradition of Black ways of being and knowing that includes Clyde Woods's concept of the blues epistemology, the story circle learning of the Students at the Center in New Orleans, and the Transformative Pedagogy Project of the UCSB's Center for Black Studies Research.[59] Douglas's art reflects the ethics of cocreation and the collective process of knowledge development, whether the art is actually created together with others or in solo but with ideas drawn from the political struggles and daily lived experiences of Black and other communities in resistance. Douglas wrote in the *Black Scholar* in 1977, "By participating in the survival of our community we become aware of the needs of the people, of their desires and wants; therefore we can more accurately create positive images in our art that reflect the bright side and dark side of life and draw nearer to the ideal of what life should be." For Douglas, creating art that flows from the people enables his artwork to challenge conventional ideas and to provide the kind of clarity and analysis needed to produce alternative ways of thinking: "By making these strong roots among the masses of the Black People, the Revolutionary Artist rises above the confusion that the oppressor has brought on the colonized people." His ways of being and thinking and his art-making insist on living among the people, experiencing the same struggles they experience, and accompanying the people in daily life and in resistance.[60] When he relayed the story of walking through mud—and falling—in Chiapas, he was honoring the local people's knowledge of the land, while also revealing a blues epistemology that derives knowledge (and for Douglas, art-making) only by walking among the people and learning from them. Douglas's way of being—whether in Chiapas, the West Bank, or Oakland—rejects celebrity treatment and instead humbly embodies the Zapatista concept of *preguntando caminamos*, interpreted as "make our way by asking" or "asking we walk."[61]

His art further aligns with the blues epistemology's critique of "the plantation bloc, its political economy, and its tradition of social explanation."[62] Douglas's political art enables a social explanation for everyday conditions of poverty, racism, and colonialism that rejects blaming the poor and instead exposes and critiques contradictions of US capitalism, racism, imperialism, and other apparatuses of power. But during his Panther days and continuing to the present, his work was not only intertwined with, but more so, derived its power from the organizational and ideological work of the BPP. Douglas's statement, "Without the party, the paper wouldn't have had the same impact," could have easily been applied to the relationship between the BPP and his art.[63] He viewed his artwork as being shaped by the ideology, program, and activities of the BPP, while simultaneously functioning as a visual translation *and interpretation* of that message. In other words, his artwork was not incidental to the political movement nor was it a mere reflection of its politics. Instead, his art was crucial to building the BPP, Black Power, and the Black Arts Movement. To Douglas, his art was intended to bring the Panther program and analysis to those who couldn't read—"Create art of social concerns that even a child can understand"—yet, it also powerfully illuminated Panther ideology and activities for those who could and did read the BPP newspapers and theoretical ideas.[64] His art provokes discomfort, challenges one's consciousness, and sparks the imagination. In doing so it plants seeds of struggles that have the potential, when connected to a serious political study and movement building, to transform oppressive systems into democratically based institutions and communities. His conceptualization of revolutionary art challenges the alleged divisions between the cultural and the political and instead insisted on their intertwining, as was the work of the Black Arts Movement.

Throughout his life, Douglas emphasized in his art and activism the BPP's focus on international solidarity as well as what Martin Luther King

Jr. called "the inescapable network of mutuality."[65] Douglas expressed, "It is our duty as the makers of The Arts of Resistance to always recognize the oppression of others."[66] His belief in the necessity of solidarity struggles is made even clearer in his statement "On Revolutionary Culture": "[O]ut of the struggle for liberation comes a new literature and art. . . . This newborn culture is not peculiar to the oppressed Black masses but transcends communities and racial lines because all oppressed people can relate to revolutionary change which is the starting point for developing a revolutionary culture."[67] Just as the struggles and visual revolutionary art emerging in Vietnam and Cuba shaped Douglas's BPP art, current-day struggles in Chiapas, Palestine, Australia, Haiti, the United States, and beyond inspire Douglas's art today. His artwork continues to be relevant in part because the social, political, economic, and cultural contexts that produced the BPP remain, albeit with differences in political economies and racial structures, but nonetheless with similar forms of police violence directed against Black people from slavery, convict leasing, and sharecropping, to today's police killings, mass incarceration, and practice of Black disposability under an economy of racial neoliberalism. When Douglas posts his artwork created in the BPP on Facebook he is, with intentionality, showing the continuities across time and space. In one such art piece, "The Black Code" is written across the hand of a judge, with the following words, paraphrased from Chief Justice Roger Taney's ruling in the 1857 Dred Scott case, printed across the face of Sandra Bland: "A black person has no rights which an institutional racist judicial system is bound to respect. It gives the appearance of being fair and just when the biased decisions have already been decided." In another image, Douglas depicts a missile, with the words "police terror" and "USA," targeting the back of a present-day handcuffed Black youth. So that even a child could understand, he accompanied the image with this text, "As much as things change, some things stay the same," and "Why do they get to brutalize and murder us and we get the blame?"[68]

In the transformative pedagogy expressed by Douglas's art, it is fitting to conclude with his words. Douglas wrote:

> The battle cry, "Culture Is a Weapon" is a powerful tool of its expressions and forms. It has the power to transform the colonization of the imagination. . . . It is not absolute but a continuation of expression and interpretations, compassion, love, beauty, pain and suffering that one feels and observes that penetrate the souls of the resistance via the resistors (We the People) against all forms of cruel and unjust authority.

Ultimately, this is the impact of Emory's artwork and its staying power. Emory Douglas's art, from the 1960s to today, illuminates the joy and love, pain and suffering of Black and other vulnerable communities, infused with dignity and resistance, and gives us hope, in the face of unbearable hardships, that through a process of cocreation we might actually build the kinds of democratic institutions and just social relations that form the basis of a liberatory society.

Fred Ho, avant-garde musician and political revolutionary, center, with vocalist Iyanna Jones, left, and musician-scholar-activist Ben Barson. Ho's politics and art were heavily shaped by and contribute to the building of Asian American and Black radicalism. Photograph by Ana Perero, 2013

CHAPTER TEN

Poetic Justice: The Dialectic Between Black Power Politics and Fred Ho's Revolutionary Music

Ben Barson

When baritone saxophonist and composer Fred Ho organized sixteen musicians to tour New York City and Vermont in February 2014, NPR reported that the "band wants to introduce a new audience to the voice of Fred Ho."[1] The tour, the "Red, Black, and Green Revolutionary Eco-Music Tour!" however, did not focus on Ho's own compositions, but rather on the work of the Black Panther–affiliated trumpet player and composer Cal Massey. Massey, active in the 1950s and '60s, was an overlooked iconoclast with close links to the core of the post-bop New York scene. This included musicians such as McCoy Tyner and John Coltrane, the latter having recorded one of Massey's songs, "The Damned Don't Cry," during his 1961 *Africa Brass* sessions (and according to Fred Ho, McCoy Tyner's first professional date was with Cal Massey). Ho's ensemble performed Massey's 1969 opus, *The Black Liberation Movement Suite,* which was interspersed with spoken word performances, rousing discourses from veterans of the Black Panther Party, and visual art that celebrated Black liberation activist and long-held prisoner Russell Maroon Shoatz. On this, Ho's final tour before his passing—Ho transitioned after a grueling cancer battle just two months later—he decided to highlight the work of Massey and activists affiliated with the Black Panther Party instead of his own compositions. In other words, Ho placed the Black liberation movement at the front and center of his legacy as he presented his final performances. Instead of boasting of his compositional brilliance or foregrounding his mind-bending virtuosity on the baritone saxophone, Ho looked to other goals auxiliary to cementing his place in the jazz or new music canon. He located himself, his imaginations, and the music he loved to play and compose as among the ranks of forgotten and erased cultural workers of an as-of-yet unfinished revolutionary process. It was as if to say that, in his final hours, history should only judge his significance insofar as it was embedded within a movement to liberate an oppressed Black nation—indeed, oppressed Brown, Yellow, and Red nations—from American imperialism and the toxic capitalist modernity that now threatens the world.

This strategy portended a wonderful and historic event. After four days of touring through grueling blizzards, in the middle of a concert at the University of Vermont before more than three hundred students, musicians, and organizers received a joyous phone call. Former Panther Russell Maroon Shoatz, held in solitary confinement for twenty-three years, had been released from his cell (which measured only seven feet wide and twelve feet long) into the general prison population. Shoatz was widely speculated to have been given this cruel treatment and exceedingly long sentence because of his provocative political beliefs, which he continued to publish while serving his life sentence.[2] Ho decided to publish these writings, which ranged from histories of maroons in Haiti to appeals for women's leadership in social movements within an ideological framework that Shoatz termed revolutionary matriarchy. The resulting volume, *Maroon the Implacable*, generated intense interest among the university and community audiences for whom the band performed—indeed, Shoatz's words were an essential part of the performance. Many not only purchased the book but also participated in a letter-writing and mass call campaign to Pennsylvania's Department of Corrections (who were administering Shoatz's state-sponsored torture). Ho and the musicians employed the power of cultural activism to engage youth and elders alike in a political process, teaching them both about the history of the Black Power movement, and motivating audiences to challenge Pennsylvania's attempt to silence and virtually erase this revolutionary.

Many aspects of the Red, Black, and Green Revolutionary Eco-Music Tour—its invocation of the revolutionary artist Cal Massey, the fundraising and publicity generated for the campaign to free Shoatz, the interdisciplinary aspects of the performance—brought to mind some of the most salient influences of the Black Panthers' on Fred Ho. This connection is important because Fred Ho was perhaps *the* consummate revolutionary organizer-musician of the early 21st century. Despite the immense discipline required to become an incredible baritone saxophonist with a six-octave range, Ho also published ten books, released twenty-five recordings, and composed twelve anticolonial operas. But his revolutionary organizing was always first. He was also the self-described "professor emeritus of revolutionary imagination" for the organization Scientific Soul Sessions, which I helped to found with Ho and others, and whose members were "united by the drive to prefigure a new society free of imperialism, colonization, racism, heteropatriarchy and capitalist exploitation."[3] Scientific Soul Sessions was unique in its ability to attract a range of participants, including veterans of sixties revolutionary movements, creative jazz musicians, and a newer generation of younger activists.[4]

This essay is about how the inspiration and influence of the Black Panther Party (BPP) fueled Fred Ho's uniquely productive, relentlessly provocative life in the world of avant-garde jazz and radical politics. Some may find it puzzling that the BPP would be so formative to a leading Chinese American artist who is widely recognized as a foundational figure in the construction of an Asian American musical aesthetic. Weihua Zhang considers Fred Ho to have been both "one of the leading figures in the Asian American jazz movement" and someone who succeeded in "develop[ing] an Asian American musical content and form that is transformative of American music . . . [which] cannot be subsumed into one or another American musical genre such as 'jazz.'"[5] This essay argues that Ho's ability to defy the expectations of genre occurred precisely because he was driven by a vision of communally centered work inspired by the BPP, the Black Arts Movement, and the Asian American movement, which helped him build alternative spaces to the music industry. A communal and DIY ethos, embodied in his interdisciplinary work and his understanding of music as a political expression, were all the practical legacies of his education within the Black Power and Black Arts movements—the latter being what Ho understood as "the cultural and artistic wing of the Black Liberation Movement."[6]

As a first-generation Chinese American who came of age in the turbulent sixties, Ho's work embodied the politics of the "US Third World Left," a multinational political project that linked its vision of social transformation to the anticolonial movements sweeping Africa, Asia and Latin America.[7] However, Ho's work was unique in this tradition for a number of reasons.

One was his endurance. Unlike several other activist-musicians who inherited the models and spirit of sixties collectives, Ho's work never became depoliticized with the ascent of neoliberalism and the decline of revolutionary anticapitalistic movements. Through thirty-five years, his song titles constantly incorporated debates around patriarchy ("Yes Means Yes, No Means No, Whatever She Wears, Wherever She Goes!"), racism ("We Refuse to Be Used and Abused!"), liberation movements ("The Underground Railroad to My Heart"), colonial violence ("Beyond Columbus and Capitalism"), and global geopolitics (*Deadly She-Wolf at Armageddon!*).[8] Such titles and didactic messages were not a passing phase; Ho consistently performed work dedicated to political causes until the end of his life. Despite this, he was a commercially successful artist with significant accolades from mainstream institutions. Poet and collaborator Magdalena Gómez colorfully describes this contradiction:

> Fred has been favorably reviewed by the *New York Times*, has been written about in most major jazz magazines, the Harvard alumni magazine, referenced in countless periodicals, journals, articles, papers, and books, and is known in radical circles as someone who has never sold out, a fact espoused even among his detractors. Fred's anticapitalist stance and outspoken radical politics have kept his work off the main stages of a dummified, Disney-fied, sanitized, pull-plays-out-of-your-ass-in-a-day-and stage them, acultural, procommodity North America that has committed genre-cide.[9]

In this aspect as well as many others, Ho's success—as well as his premature death—mirrors the trajectory of the BPP, a movement that still strongly captures the political imagination of both activists of color (or "oppressed nationalities," in Ho's vocabulary) and mainstream audiences, a fact demonstrated by the countless museum shows, academic panels, art exhibits and political work done to examine the legacy of the BPP. Ho was composing work such as *The Black Panther Suite* as early as 1999.

This essay will connect these aspects of Ho's life and work to his engagement with the BPP and Black Arts Movement (BAM). But rather than consider Ho's alliance of radical Chinese American and African American radicals as an aberration, I want to argue for the continuities between Black and Asian American arts and activism. And so I begin with a review of Afro-Asian studies literature that has highlighted the historical exchanges and alliances between the Black Power and Yellow Power movements, contending that these alliances were shaped by, and part of, a global moment of Third World solidarity framed by decolonization and visions of a new economic order, in which Ho self-consciously positioned himself and his work. I then analyze the concrete relationships Ho developed with a coterie of Black Panther activists and BAM luminaries such as Sonia Sanchez, Jayne Cortez, Amiri Baraka, and Archie Shepp, and how their praxis deeply infused his work. I conclude with a summary of Ho's work with political and cultural activist collectives as embodied in the organization Scientific Soul Sessions, culminating with their aforementioned engagement with the music of Cal Massey and former Panther Russell Maroon Shoatz. This essay thus hopes to illustrate the complex rivers of influence stemming from the BPP and BAM into Ho's own work as well as his organizing with New York City radical activists. These influences were central to what Tamara Roberts describes as "[t]he progressive potency of [Ho's] work," which "lies in the ways in which multiple traditions work together to shift the shared context in which they reside, an intervention into the de-radicalization of hegemonic multiculturalism."[10] Ho's ability to "re-radicalize" multiculturalism lay in his ability to reapply his work from his affiliation with the Black liberation movement (BLM) into his cultural productions, and to use the latter as a tool for organizing. The lessons he drew from the BLM were both organizational and ideological, as Ho emphasized the freedom of land and called for political and cultural self-determination of oppressed communities, both viewed through the lenses of communities in struggle. Yet even these evolved with his continued engagement with the BLM. As we will see, Ho's relationship with Maroon resulted in his embrace of matriarchy.

Between Yellow Soul and Black Power:
Afro-Asianisms in Dialogue

Newly independent nations in Africa, Asia, and Latin America framed the political awakenings of many African Americans in the 1960s.[11] Two prominent activists—Black Power advocate Robert F. Williams and poet and organizer Amiri Baraka—were transformed by their experiences in Cuba, while W. E. B. Du Bois (and again Robert Williams) met with governmental delegates in China. Richard Wright recalls, as an enthralled journalist at the Bandung Afro-Asian Unity Conference in Indonesia, 1954, "This is the human race speaking."[12]

The Bandung Afro-Asian Unity Conference had reverberations far beyond the nation of Indonesia and the year 1954. Historian Bill Mullen has described the gathering of some twenty-nine decolonizing heads of state as "the watershed and high mark of black-Asian affiliation,"[13] while Prashad has noted that "[t]he Idea of the Third World moved millions and created heroes . . . provid[ing] the elements of a new imagination for its cultural workers—people such as the poet Pablo Neruda, the singer Umm Kulthum, and the painter Sudjana Kerton."[14]

The Black Panther Party responded directly to this new global movement; the inspiration for their unique political organizing lay as much in the work of Robert Williams' insistence on self-defense as in the Chinese Cultural Revolution. Along with Frantz Fanon, Mao Zedong was among the most important Third World decolonial theorists influencing the BPP. BPP cofounder Huey Newton wrote, "My conversion was complete when I read the four volumes of Mao Tse-Tung to learn more about the Chinese Revolution."[15] As Robin Kelley argues, "For Huey Newton . . . the African revolution seemed even less crucial than events in Cuba and China . . . well before the founding of the BPP, Newton was steeped in Mao Zedong thought as well as in the writings of Che."[16] According to a July 18, 1973, internal BPP memorandum, 50 percent of the morning political education classes concentrated on the "little red book."[17] Afro-Asian solidarity animated the zeitgeist of the sixties and the BPP was no exception.

African American artists also tapped into the new possibilities the Bandung era unleashed. The writings of the avant-garde jazz musician Wadada Leo Smith, based in Chicago with the Association for the Advancement of Creative Musicians, argued that embracing the culture of the decolonizing world was essential to build a new political order beyond white supremacy: "i feel that the creative music of afro-america, india, bali and pan-islam . . . is also creating a balance in the arena of world music . . . and that this music will eventually eliminate the political dominance of euro-america in this world."[18] As an artist, Smith felt that embracing these improvisational traditions was his ethical duty as an artist and activist—a foundational act in learning how to build a new society based on mutual respect and solidarity. Smith declares that we must seek out other cultures that "have improvisation as their classical art music (india, pan-islam, the orient, bali, and africa) and make lasting cultural commitments with them."[19] These "lasting cultural commitments" may have been prefigured by early African American cultural nationalist fairs in the US, including those organized by the Nation of Islam, which were often advertised as "African Asian Unity Bazaars."[20]

Smith's declaration is an example of what Christopher Lee has called a "Bandung moment"[21] in which African Americans self-identified with an imagined community that spanned the decolonizing "darker nations." In such spaces, participants construct an Afro-Asian culture that "tries hard to cultivate the epistemological and historical archive of solidarity."[22] As Loren Kajikawa has shown, those who tried hard included not only artists associated with jazz's left-wing avant-garde but also more mainstream musicians. The cover of McCoy Tyner's *Sahara* (1972) features an image of Tyner sitting with a koto in the Saharan desert. Gary Bartz's performance on the song "Viet Cong" celebrates Vietnamese resistance against American armed forces, as does violinist Billy Bang's "Yo! Ho Chi Minh Is in the House" on his 2001 release *Aftermath*. Afro-Asian soundscapes were also invoked by Thelonious Monk in "Japanese Folk Song," and Coltrane in his composition "India." Kajikawa refers to these Bandung moments as a type of "musical cosmopolitanism" on the part of African American artists, who "turned away from European influences and embraced other cultures in an era of heightened global consciousness and anticolonial struggles."[23]

Saxophonist John Coltrane deserves special mention in this regard, in part because his inclinations toward a non-Western aesthetic have been often overlooked. Coltrane had a deep interest in Third World cultures and soundscapes, although the politics of these invocations has been debated. [24] Trane linked his music to Third World imaginaries, as did Malcolm X.[25] His work continuously reinvented itself through his career, and his inclusion of non-Western scales and aesthetics was an important part of this. (Coltrane developed a relationship with Ravi Shankar and named his son, Ravi, after him.[26]) Coltrane weighed in on this matter in a remarkable letter addressed to critic Nat Hentoff, who had given him the Aaron Copland book *Music and Imagination*. As Trane opines, "The 'jazz' musician (you can have this term along with several others that have been hoisted upon us) does not have to worry about a lack of positive and affirmative philosophy. It's built in us. The phrasing, the sound of the music attests this fact. We are naturally endowed with it. You can believe all of us would have perished long ago if it were not so. As to community, the whole face of the globe is our community. You see, it is really easy for us to create. We are born with this feeling that just comes out no matter what conditions exist."[27]

Here Coltrane takes a very politicized stance: he rejects the term "jazz" as a meaningful descriptor of the music, a position shared by many musicians ranging from Charles Mingus to Archie Shepp. He implies that the Western art canon suffers a chronic alienation and suggests that Black music has been a means of preventing Black genocidal and cultural erasure. In general, Coltrane's position prefigures Creolization doctrine, as theorized by Edward

Brathwaite and others.[28] For Coltrane, the music acts as an expression of a self that is linked to and intertwined with the Other. "The whole face of our globe is our community," Coltrane noted. Coltrane's words and music speak to the "common sense" of a polycultural space that jazz musicians so adeptly constructed.[29] These African American jazz musicians shared much with the BPP and the BAM's aesthetics, which were looking toward building meaningful connections with the Third World. It was this political and sonic imaginary that touched every aspect of Fred Ho's cultural and political work, turning his life into almost a "back to African-America" movement that crossed the bridge erected by prior generations.

Yet jazz musicians rarely become central figures in the scholarship related to BAM. James Smethurst, in his influential book on the Black arts literary movement, acknowledges this omission. He explains, "[S]uch a roll of poets and playwrights fails to delineate the full dimensions of the black avant-garde in New York during this period because it leaves out such musicians as Ornette Coleman, John Coltrane, Archie Shepp, Marion Brown, Sam Rivers, Cecil Taylor, [and] Sun Ra and His Arkestra . . . . Many were [also] serious writers or dramatists."[30] The overlooking of musicians as serious figures in political and intellectual movements fits a wider trend in scholarship on social movements and Black political and cultural formations in the Sixties.

Baraka wrote extensively on this new Black music, perhaps more than any other subject.

He extended his analysis to the jazz avant-garde of the 1960s, which he called the New Black music, emphasizing the music's pedagogical potential, "But at its best and its most expressive, the New Black music is expression, and expression of reflection as well. What is presented is a consciously proposed learning experience."[31] Fred Ho was deeply invested in this type of learning and self-discovery.

Baraka also lauded the new music for resisting the aesthetic hegemony of European forms, and suggested that its innovations derived their expressive power from their confrontation with Western reason. "[N]o matter the 'precision' the Europeans claim with their 'reasonable' scale which will get only the sounds of an order and reason that patently deny most colored peoples the right to exist."[32] He locates Coltrane as the avatar of a revitalized Black consciousness through this decolonized music: "[Coltrane] showed us how to murder the popular song. To do away with weak Western forms. He is a beautiful philosopher." Baraka's reading of Coltrane even took on Fanonian proportions, when he described the ways in which "murder" helped decolonize the Black self, "New Black Music is this: Find the self, then kill it."[33] As Scott Saul contends, "Baraka heard something earthshaking: a black consciousness so in touch with itself that it could begin to transcend its past."[34] One cannot overstate the effect Coltrane and the New Black Music had for Baraka and his project of cultural revolution. Except for his visit to Cuba in 1959, this may have been the single most important influence of Baraka's trajectory as a political activist and self-styled cultural revolutionary.

Commentary written by Fred Ho can also serve as a corrective. He writes that "a dynamic and dialectical interplay existed between both political and artistic energies" in the 1960s African American community. Comparing the vanguard positions of Malcolm X and Coltrane in politics and culture, respectively, Ho argues that "it is clear that both enormously effected and were affected by the weltanschauung of the era and considerably contributed to and were shaped by the zeitgeist of the 1960s. . . . Both personified and embodied the apex of black American political and artistic creativity and commitment: gloriously un-co-optable and unquenchable."[35]

While Kajikawa and Susan Asai have written on the circles of influence between Asian American and African American artists, little has been written on how Asian American musicians related to African American political activists.[36] While historians of poetry and the visual arts have overlooked musical links of the sixties' new social movements, scholars of the music have paid less attention to the moments when poetry, ideology, and revolutionary Black nationalism intersected with avant-garde music. Fred Ho's political and artistic history opens up a window into this interdisciplinary and intercultural world where jazz musicians, dramaturgs, chorographers, poetic playwrights, educators, and activists moved in and out of the same spaces. Sometimes, in the case of Archie Shepp, participants wore all these hats at the same time.

Poetry and Interdisciplinary Arts: Fred Ho and the Black Arts Movement

Fred Ho's work is difficult to put into a box: it spans genres, media, subject matters—and sometimes has little to do with music at all. Magdalena Gómez describes it as

> Combining elements of "jazz" (a term Ho qualifies by instructing us on its racist origins), Chinese opera, experimental, global working-class and oppressed-class musical traditions, various dance and martial-arts traditions, comic book . . . aesthetic[s], science fiction and poetry, Fred's theatrical

works cannot be classified; no one box can be checked. This inability to fit in the crayon box and his revolutionary politics (rooted in self-defense, not violence) render Fred's work a threat to the unimaginative and the purveyors of bottom-line, crowd-pleasing mediocrity.[37]

Ho's constant collaboration with radical poets was especially deep. He was not alone in pursuing such collaborations; jazz-poetry syntheses were an important form and aesthetic of the BAM. This was a legacy Fred directly credits to the movement: "[The] generation of [Black Arts Movement] poets could virtually be called 'jazz poets' both from their deep and profound appreciation of and usage of 'the music' as well as their close collaborations and social connections with the musicians."[38]

One such poet was Jayne Cortez, a seminal figure in the BAM who has been described as having revolutionized the distinct poetic invocation known as the "Coltrane Poem."[39] As Ho recalls,

> [d]uring the 1970s and 1980s, I made contact with Jayne as a cultural correspondent with the League of Revolutionary Struggle newspaper, *Unity/ La Unidad*, with a full-page feature on her writing and excerpting her magnificent poem "If a Drum Is a Woman, Why Do You Beat Your Drum?" an incendiary indictment of relationship violence against women, employing a sardonic motif from the title of a Duke Ellington composition, "A Drum Is a Woman."[40]

Influenced by this eloquent critique of patriarchy, Ho goes on to elaborate the lifelong relationship he developed with Cortez. In fact, Ho composed a percussion suite at her request, and later Cortez would return the favor by writing a libretto for Ho's opera *Every Time I Open My Mouth to Sing* (2008), which contains a piece titled "Start with Yourself." This piece expressed BAM's philosophy that self-realization was an essential component of decolonization.

> *Start with yourself*
> *start in the middle of the voyage . . .*
> *A blue whale is wailing your name my love*
> *you already know who's in the business of*
> *land grabbing from natives*
> *because you have been mixed in the scorched*
> *earth policy of the land act*
> *& the leaves are smoking on both sides of the*
> *equator*
> *So start with yourself*[41]

If Ho's gender politics and ideas of self-reliance deepened through his work with Cortez, Sonia Sanchez had a particular influence on his pedagogical approach. Ho began working with Sanchez when he was still a high school student in Massachusetts, initially by sneaking into her classes at nearby Amherst College. In Ho's retelling,

> Another influential figure for me, and a towering figure in her own right in the Black Arts Movement, was Sonia Sanchez. I remember Sonia for her warmth and accessibility to students. . . . Her own poetry reflected both the vernacular language of urban black America and the poetical avant-garde. Written words would be spelled differently, almost phonetically, and have a musical quality when she read them . . . she used what I now appreciate and recognize as a "dialectical" method of teaching.[42]

Ho's interest in Sanchez's "dialectic" model is resonant with the larger themes of BAM cultural democracy initiatives. Ho credits Sanchez's dialectical method for helping make the connections between American anti-Blackness and his unconscious hatred of his Chinese culture, an internalized racism which Sanchez helped him overcome in order to transition from "Banana to Third World Marxist."

Ho's lifelong association with Amiri Baraka deepened his understanding of cultural democracy that was antiracist, antiimperialist, and a force for liberation. He frequently performed with Baraka, and the poet wrote the liner notes for Ho's first album, *Tomorrow Is Now!* Outside of music, the two were in the League of Revolutionary Struggle (LRS) together, a Marxist-Leninist organization with representation from Latino, Asian American, Native American, white American and African American activist communities, and included veterans of the Black Panther Party. Toward the end of both their lives, Baraka participated in a Russell Maroon Shoatz event with a saxophone quartet that included Ho, James Carter, Darius Jones, and Bhinda Keidel.

Baraka was deeply involved with the heart and soul of the Black liberation movement, and especially its insistence on communal economics. An important legacy of the BPP, which promoted cooperative housing for the community, established cooperative bakeries and free breakfast programs for children. Indeed, cooperative economic development was a "major objective" in Black urban communities—providing an alternative to capitalist economic development or state-sponsored welfare.[43]

According to Ellison (1980), the key inheritor of this economic-cooperative legacy was the Congress of African Peoples (CAP) led by Amiri Baraka. CAP helped install consumer cooperative and low-income credit unions, and later evolved into the League of Revolutionary Struggle, with its explicit goal of liberating the Black working class.[44]

Ho loved Baraka's multigene jazz operas, writing of them often in LRS's *Unity/La Unidad*. As Ho matured as an artist, he began moving in adventurous multigenre and multimedia directions, such as in *The Black Panther Suite*. Conceived of as a "revolutionary visionquest," the work was a one-hour performance that combined the video artwork of Paul Chan and martial arts choreography of Jose Figuero. The work provides images of Black Panther Party luminaries, and also connects several pertinent themes, such as a critique of the commodification of the Black Power movement and Black life under capitalism. The music is intense and syncretic, moving between free jazz, horn voicings that are very "fourth-centric"—reminiscent of East Asian harmonic motifs—and rhythmically robust underpinnings evoking West African and Ewe drumming traditions. The collage of images of Chan's "visionquest" was superimposed and magnified behind the band, in a panorama of resistance and oppression, and a single minute might situate photos of anti-black police violence with portraits of Sojourner Truth. In one scene, images of Panther chic, such as berets and sunglasses, are marketed at $19.99, with large colored font parodying a marketing campaign. Thus, Chan and Ho's engagement with the Black Panther Party was also a critique of the ways in which their revolutionary symbols were in the process of being coopted by the marketplace and mainstream institutions—a somewhat prophetic foreshadowing of the recent blockbuster release *Black Panther*.

The critique of capitalist-based empowerment welding into Ho's homage to the BPP is no coincidence. It is Ho's nod to the ideological tradition that connected the Panthers and their Black Arts Movement successors: their emphasis on noncapitalist communal economic development, and its successors, such as the Congress of African People and Amiri Baraka. Furthermore, the piece artistically reflects Baraka's influence as a director and a theoretician: not only is a multimedia aesthetic employed but the critique of commodification was a central theme in Baraka's own *Money: A Jazz Opera*.

The publicity materials for *The Black Panther Suite* offer a rare glimpse of Ho directly addressing the influence of the BPP on his political vision of cultural democracy and revolutionary organizing:

> The energy of this movement and the music of that time set the direction for both my life and my music. I even joined an Asian American counterpart to the Black Panthers. . . . I believe that the same issues of thirty years ago continue today with even more urgency and intensity. That is why I

envision *The Black Panther Suite* not as a docu-drama looking back to the late 1960s / early 1970s, but as an occasion to continue the energy, spirit and vision of that period and link it to today. This, I feel, would be the real and sincere way to commemorate the Panthers.[45]

Put differently, Ho had ambitions to further their revolutionary project, and that was what this aesthetic was all about. In fact, by employing martial arts in the work, especially the Chinese kung fu and wushu components, Ho wrote that he meant to "pay homage to the inspiration of the Chinese Revolution and Mao on the Black Panthers."

What is striking here is Ho's refusal to create a "docu-drama." As a committed revolutionary activist, Ho saw that it was more important to connect the Panthers' critique of colonialism, police brutality, and capitalism within the present-day context. He also uses the multidisciplinary and multinational aspects of the work—West African drumming, African American improvised music, and Chinese marital arts—to evoke both the culture and spirit of multinational solidarity.

Kalamu ya Salaam was another important poet and force in Ho's life. At the height of the BAM, Salaam was a member of John O'Neal's Free Southern Theater for five years and was a founder of BLACKARTSOUTH. Ho and Salaam developed a personal and professional friendship and several of Salaam's historical and theoretical writings directly influenced the saxophonist. One of Salaam's ideas that particularly changed Ho's vocabulary was the former's description of the main principles of the BAM in his book *Magic of Juju*.[46] "In an excellent manuscript," Ho writes, "Salaam summarizes . . . the BAM was multidisciplinary and innovative, and promoted a 'popular avant-garde.'"[47] Ho has written extensively about revolutionary art and its necessary relation to popular culture. Here he demands a clear set of four attributes: revolutionary art must speak to the people, go to the people, involve the people, and change the people.[48]

These ideas were as much a legacy of the BPP as the BAM. That is because, again, these movements were so interconnected that it is difficult to determine where one begins and the other ends—a point Ho acknowledged when he described their "dynamic and dialectical interplay." Kevin Fellezs has suggested that in this regard:

Ho's views echo those of Angela Davis, who has argued that "as Marx and Engels long ago observed, art is a form of social consciousness—a special form of social consciousness that can potentially awaken an urge in those affected by it to creatively transform their oppressive environments. Art can function as a sensitizer and a catalyst, propelling people toward involvement in organized movements seeking to effect radical social change.[49]

Ho was no stranger to Marxists or Angela Davis and was grounded in their writing as much as in the activists and legacies of the BAM. Ho cited Salaam's reference of a "popular avant-garde" to inform his own work, and it was a phrase he used continually to describe his own musical productions. When Ho's focus was Chinese American traditions, he often foregrounded the political legacies of Cantonese opera, which he explains in "Revolutionary Asian American Art" was a rebellious art form connected to the insurgency against the imperial government. He invokes the example of Cantonese opera actor Li Wenmao who led an armed uprising against the Chinese imperial government in 1854 during the Taiping Rebellion. All performances of Cantonese opera were subsequently banned and went underground."[50]

Thus, Ho's *Journey beyond the West: The New Adventures of Monkey* (1996), which combines Cantonese opera with jazz and Afrodiasporic musical forms, both draws attention to and is an expression of "the revolutionary roots of Asian American cultural tradition."[51] And like Baraka's credo—Find the Self, and Kill It[52]—Ho's work is also a consciously proposed learning experience—refusing to simply replicate tradition and instead reinventing the meaning of the archetypal tale. Susan Asai notes, "Within the socialist framework of Ho's politics, the Monkey King can be thought of as the equivalent of a working-class hero defying the capitalist, bourgeois forces that oppress the masses."[53]

All of this is to say that Ho's vision of a "popular avant-garde" is deeply embedded in the lessons and experience he drew from BAM poet-theorists, as well as Black Panther–affiliated artists such as Emory Douglas and Cal Massey. Yet perhaps the most important legacy of the Black Power/BAM that influenced Ho was their emphasis on community-driven initiatives that blurred hierarchies and created truly egalitarian structures. In a lengthy interview with Salim Washington, Ho explained what appeals to him about the idea of "cultural democracy" and the need for a truly participatory dialectic between performer, community, and audience:

> That was the greatness of the Black Arts Movement; it allowed that proliferation . . .
>
> Cal Massey being one example. The explosion of cultural democracy . . . allow[s] the determination of what happens much more on a popular level—not by anointers. Not by the establishment. And that's why the Black Arts Movement was such a threat. It continues to be a threat to the

establishment because it's set its own criteria. It set its own determination of who was legitimate and qualified, and not institutional arbiters. . . . So, that's why it was revolutionary. The most revolutionary thing is to exert independence.[54]

Here Ho describes the communalistic and collectivistic ethos of the BAM—an ethos that was shared, albeit less systematically, among the avant-garde jazz musicians of the sixties and seventies. Michael Heller discusses this idea in terms of both "freedom to" and "freedom from" in his description of the cultures that undergirded New York's seventies loft jazz scene: "Collectivism desired the *freedom to* achieve respect and professional opportunities by building support and advocacy networks within a cultural milieu. . . . Communalism sought *freedom from* that [potentially hostile] milieu by building alternative social and artistic domains that were self-cultivated, meaningful, and did not rely on outside support."[55]

One musician from the loft scene who had significant crossover with the BAM is Archie Shepp. "More than any artist," Ho wrote, "[Shepp's] work and persona has had the biggest impact upon mine. Even before meeting him, he was larger than life to me." Shepp's fusion of politics with his bombastic tenor playing helped provide Ho a blueprint for his own work, "What fascinated me about Archie was the combination of his outspoken militant political views fused with Marxist influences."[56]

Shepp's influence on Ho can be heard not only in Ho's tone and improvisational approach but also in his choice of repertoire. Shepp included poetry and spoken word in a significant amount of his work, reflecting his own involvement with BAM literature."[57]

As Ho explains, Shepp's poem "Mama Rose" was a major influence upon his own work. He refers to it as a "tour-de-force poem by Shepp . . . written in the early 1960s upon the death of his grandmother, but a searing indictment of colonialism. Ho recorded a poem orated in a very similar structure and cadence that paid tribute to Vincent Chin, who was viciously pursued and killed in a widely known case of anti-Asian violence. On the 2011 album *Big Red!* (Innova 794), Ho riffs on Shepp's reference to the United States' assassination of Patrice Lumumba ("your corpse turned up to the sky/a putrefying Congolese after the Americans have come to help") description of the murder of Vincent Chin ("Turned up to the murdering sky like a mutilated Vietnamese after the Americans have come/To set them free/Buy Democracy.") The poem is orated dramatically and sardonically, mimicking Shepp's own cadence.

The poem connects, in a single gesture, the assassination of Vincent Chin to the American invasion of Vietnam as well as the US's Cold War interventions in the Congo. This three-way movement links the oppression of Asian Americans in the United States to geopolitical histories of imperialism and argues for the shared oppression of African and East Asian peoples. The entire poem signifies, in a way, on the interconnectedness of African and Asian oppression and shared destinies, and through performance creates a space of solidarity.

While certainly Shepp's sound in the "energy music" school also deeply influenced Ho's improvisational concept, his oratorical skills and ability to combine political critique with a bombastic sound also left an enduring impact upon Ho.[58]

Scientific Soul Sessions

In 2010, Ho's lifelong inspiration from the BPP and BAM led to the creation of an organization in Harlem known as Scientific Soul Sessions (SSS). Meeting in Harlem, the group brought together an eclectic, diverse, and committed group of cultural workers and self-identified revolutionary intellectuals, including Salim Washington and Melanie Dyer, as well as filmmaker and Young Lords cofounder Iris Morales. While this was a collective space, Ho's experience and politics had an outsized influence on the group. Yet his views were certainly not left unchallenged when aspects of them became too dogmatic or didactic for those in room.

In four years of activity, the organization produced more than thirty-five events highlighting activists, artists, and revolutionaries. It released a book, *Maroon the Implacable: The Collected Writings of Russell Maroon Shoatz*, and petitioned Pennsylvania's department of corrections to free Shoatz from solitary confinement. SSS also produced the inaugural concert of Cal Massey's *The Black Liberation Movement Suite* at the Red Rooster restaurant, a vital new venue in the contemporary music scene in Harlem, in 2012. This was the first time in several decades that Massey's suite had been performed. *Wall Street Journal* jazz critic Will Friedwald commented on the significance of the concert:

> Although Massey's music is hardly unplayed, the man himself has been largely unsung since his death at 44 in 1972. Thankfully, the saxophonist, composer and bandleader Fred Ho has taken up Massey's gauntlet: After compiling enough information for an extended biographical essay (in his 2009 book,

Wicked Theory, Naked Practice), Mr. Ho has, even more importantly, exhumed and recorded Massey's most ambitious work, *The Black Liberation Movement Suite*. Over the years, the suite was re-orchestrated by Massey collaborator Romulus Franceschini. But it is only now being heard in its totality on [the] new album, *The Music of Cal Massey*, and this week at Red Rooster.

In introducing the suite, Mr. Ho states, correctly, that it ranks with the masterpieces of extended jazz composition, most of which were the work of Duke Ellington. Massey's roots are evident, but what's more amazing is the music that it anticipated: on a blindfold test, I would have pegged some of these tracks for David Murray's "avant-gutbucket" ensembles, Butch Morris' conduction pieces, and some of the multifaceted compositions of Maria Schneider.[59]

That SSS would highlight this work was no coincidence: it actively embodied the principles embedded in the BAM of self-sufficiency, cultural democracy, aesthetic innovation, and the ethos of the Black liberation movement. In his essay "The Damned Don't Cry," Ho notes that his relationship to Massey's music was an outgrowth of his work with Shepp: "I was introduced to Mr. Massey's music through his compositions performed and recorded primarily by Archie Shepp. Titles such as 'Hey, Goddamn It, Things Have Got to Change!,' 'The Damned Don't Cry,' and 'The Cry of My People' spoke directly to a consciousness of oppression and a politics of liberation."[60] Ho was moved by the "soulful and searing melodies" and "sophisticated and glorious harmonies" he heard in Massey's work; he also found Massey to be the consummate example of the activist-musician that Ho himself aspired to be.

Ho had researched Massey's life extensively while living in New York in the 1980s. In *The Black Liberation Movement Suite* he found a story that reflected some of the most powerful examples of jazz musicians contributing to a Black Arts political impulse. Although the work was only performed three times originally, all were at benefits for the BPP. The first concert, held in 1972 in Brooklyn, featured a jaw-dropping group of avant-garde and mainstream luminaries, including Alice Coltrane, Freddie Hubbard, Lee Morgan, Archie Shepp, Leon Thomas, Pharoah Sanders, Leroy Jenkins, James Spaulding, Carlos Ward, Roland Alexander, Dan Jones, Charles McGhee, Michael Ridley, Curtis Fuller, Charles Stephens, Kiane Zawadi, Lonnie Liston Smith, Reggie Workman, Rashied Ali, and Joe Lee Wilson, among others. The concert raised funds for the party's legal defense fund and its political prisoners. Ho was attracted to this exciting bricolage of jazz artists bringing revolutionary music to people in the community, seeing Massey's work as connected to the BAM's insistence on building independent institutions:

"Cal Massey's self-produced concerts were also part of the thrust for artistic self-control and the Black Liberation Movement's goal for self-determination through creating alternative cultural institutions and forms of cultural production for the benefit of the black community."[61]

Scientific Soul Sessions did not survive Fred Ho's passing on April 12, 2014. But its influence is still felt among significant elements of the New York City young multinational left. One formation that has significant overlap with SSS is a new Black Arts Movement that continues to produce communally driven events with political themes linking decolonization and self-transformation, often with former Panthers in attendance. Others who participated in SSS continued their work by international examples of revolutionary social change in the global South, such as when several alumni facilitated the emergence of the Ecosocialist International in the maroon-descendent community of Veroes, Venezuela, in 2017. And the Afro-Yaqui Music Collective, an ensemble (cofounded by this writer) that performs Ho's Afro-Asian repertoire with new orchestrations that reflect indigenous influences from nations such as the Yaquis and Mayans, and seeks to continue the political project of revolutionary matriarchy within a contemporary musical practice.[62]

In sum, the BPP and BAM were inspiring and educating forces in Ho's praxis, bringing a new dimension to the BAM scholarship. Moreover, it can be argued that the BPP was not a movement that was restricted to the 1960s, but rather a foundational moment that generated new social movements and generations of innovative cross-disciplinary artists and revolutionary activists. Its connection to the jazz world was one of mutual influence, as the examples of Massey, Shepp, and Ho have demonstrated.

It would be overly romantic to suggest that the influences Ho inherited were uniformly positive. In some of the same essays in which Ho expresses admiration and acknowledgment of Baraka and Shepp, he also maintained a critical distance.[63] Similarly, in an internal position paper circulated within Scientific Soul Sessions, Ho celebrated the party's initial "revolutionary nationalist" position but noted that "it quickly, via the leadership of Huey P. Newton after released from prison and with Elaine Brown, took the BPP into national and local electoral politics, with a rapid downfall into NGO-ism." NGOism, for Ho, was a dirty term that connoted grant hustling and dependence on the system, limiting revolutionary initiatives and forcing organizations to take reactionary and self-defeating positions. Perhaps it was this critique that led Ho to identify more practically with the BAM and the Black Liberation Army (BLA) of which Russell Maroon Shoatz was a part.

Ho identified with how Assata Shakur distinguished the BLA from the BPP: "The Black Liberation Army was not a centralized, organized group with a common leadership and chain of command. Instead, there were various organizations and collectives working together out of various cities, and in some larger cities there were often several groups operating independently of each other."[64] Ho often critiqued such centralism and embraced the model Shakur describes, and which Russell Maroon Shoatz conceptualized as the "hydra" as a decentralized formation, which provides more collective agency and self-realization than a stifling bureaucracy present in top-down movements. Ho celebrated this approach as "Maroon's latent indigenous-centrism."[65]

As Ho himself once wrote, "Revolutionaries are not saints. Revolutionaries, as with all humans, display behavior and traits that span the range from excrement to the angelic."[66] And so the intent of this essay is not to flatten complex coalitions into monolithic narratives or singular qualities. It is rather to demonstrate that there is rich ground to uncover when we explore arts, activism, and transnational communities as an integrated whole, sharing both influence and creating new social worlds through collaborative efforts in sound and performance. When historians undertake this challenge, one can agree that the damned don't cry—they sing, poeticize, philosophize, strategize, and challenge the conditions of their damnation in unpredictable and fascinating ways. Ho's inspiration from the Black Panther Party, and its myriad cultural workers, opened a door for him to carry both his cultural work and the struggle for liberation forward.

V.
THE REAL DRAGONS TAKE FLIGHT:
ON PRISONS AND POLICING

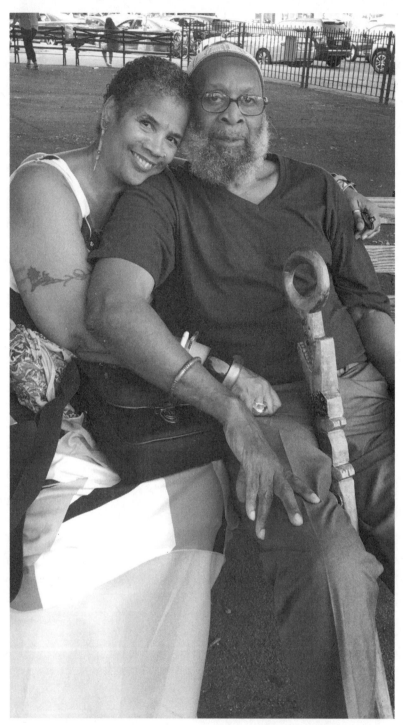

Sekou Odinga, former Panther and Black Liberation Army activist, after his release from thirty-three years in prison, right, and déqui kioni-sadiki, journalist, political prisoner supporter, and former member of the Black Panther Collective. Photo courtesy of authors

CHAPTER ELEVEN

Legacy: Where We Were, Where We Are, Where We Are Going

Sekou Odinga and déqui kioni-sadiki

The great force of history comes from the fact that we carry it within us, are unconsciously controlled by it in many ways, and history is literally present in all we do.

—James Baldwin

As Langston Hughes wrote in his seminal "Mother to Son" poem for Afrikans born in amerikkka, "Life ain't been no crystal stair."[1] But more than tacks, splinters, and boards torn up, life for Black people on this stolen land of genocide and enslavement has been filled with centuries of grinding cradle-to-grave oppression, repression, and suppression; the violence of white supremacy, capitalism, imperialism, and colonialism; and the tyranny and terror of lynching, post-Reconstruction Jim Crow apartheid, political and mass imprisonment. Within these historical realities live the histories and herstories of resistance that began in those slave dungeons, slave ships, and plantations and continued into the so-called "nonviolent" civil rights movement, the Black Panther Party for Self-Defense (BPP), Black Liberation Army (BLA), and Black Power movement (BPM) of the 1960s. This essay offers perspectives and an examination of the BPP and BPM legacy and impact on the struggle for land and independence, Black self-determination, justice, and the work to free US-held political prisoners and prisoners of war (PPOWs)—both inside and out the prison walls.

Fifty years after its founding, the BPP and BPM continue to represent one of the most significant movements for Black liberation in the twentieth and even twenty-first century. It was an overwhelmingly grassroots and youth-led global social, political, and cultural phenomenon. It made revolutionary struggle irresistible to a nation of young people by putting forth visions and programs that inspired youth to join the struggle. It was a movement that was of the people, for the people, and by the people. It was a socio-political mandate for Black self-determination, Black radical politics, and Black liberation that was unapologetically radical. It was a movement that connected the struggles of oppressed Black people in the united states with the struggles of oppressed people in Africa, Vietnam, the Middle East, and South America.[2] It threatened the united states government and capitalist power structure so much so that J. Edgar Hoover waged a covert and illegal FBI counterintelligence—COINTELPRO—campaign "to expose, disrupt, misdirect, discredit, or otherwise neutralize the activities of black nationalist, hate-type organizations and groupings, their leadership, spokesmen, membership, and supporters." That COINTELPRO legacy continues with the thirty-to-fifty-years-and-counting political imprisonment of Sundiata Acoli, Imam Jamil Al-Amin, Veronza Bowers, Romaine "Chip" Fitzgerald, Ruchell Cinque Magee, Jalil Muntaqim, Ed Poindexter, Kamau Sadiki, Mutulu Shakur, Russell "Maroon" Shoatz, Kenny "Zulu" Whitmore, and those from other radical formations of the 1960s; the state-sanctioned medical neglect and murder of Albert "Nuh" Washington, Richard Wells, Teddy "Jah" Heath, Kuwasi Balagoon, Bashir Hameed, Abdullah Majid, and Mondo we Langa behind the wall; the exile of Assata Shakur, Nehanda Abiodun, Pete O'Neal, and others; and the fractured sectarian state of a weakened movement—or lack thereof—that exists today.

Sekou Odinga

I was a member of the Black Panther Party for Self-Defense, a Black Liberation Army soldier, and for thirty-three years a US-held political prisoner of war. Most of my adult life has been spent in the struggle for Black self-determination, Black revolutionary politics, and Black liberation. As such, my life speaks to the oft-heard expression, "Oppression breeds resistance and resistance breeds repression."

My political consciousness began when I was a youthful offender at Comstock Correctional Facility in upstate New York with a good friend and close comrade, Lumumba Shakur. Lumumba's father, Hajji Salahuddin Shakur, would send his son reading materials on Malcolm X, his teachings, nationalist politics, the struggle for land and independence, and most pointedly, the human right Black people must exercise to arm and defend themselves against violence, state or private. Lumumba would share those materials with me, and after serving a three-year sentence, I was back on the streets and seeking the Malcolm that had inspired me in prison. I joined Malcolm's Organization of Afro-American Unity (OAAU). That membership was short-lived when Malcolm was assassinated soon after I joined. Because the OAAU was not headed in a direction that I felt Malcolm wanted it to go, I no longer wanted to be a part, so I left. Two years after the founding of the Oakland, California, BPP, the central committee sent a delegation to the East Coast to establish a New York City BPP chapter. It was early 1968, and initially, the party sought out the Student Non-Violent Coordinating Committee (SNCC). Lumumba and I were not members of SNCC. However, we liked what we saw and what the BPP represented as we watched on television members of the BPP storm the California state capitol with arms. Right then and there, I wanted to be part of that level of resistance. Lumumba and I joined the BPP. We held our first weekly meetings at the Brooklyn campus of Long Island University. Those meetings drew hundreds of Black youth wanting to connect with the BPP, and we quickly outgrew that space. We opened our first BPP office in Bedford-Stuyvesant. Brooklyn followed with an office in Brownsville. People traveled from across the five boroughs to visit those offices. This led Lumumba, the Harlem section leader, and me, the Bronx section leader, to combine our chapters into one. And the Harlem-Bronx section opened with an office on Seventh Avenue and West 123rd St. in Harlem.

During the same year, the Republic of New Afrika (RNA) was forming in Detroit, Michigan, in a push for land and independence. Mississippi, South Carolina, Louisiana, Georgia, and Alabama were the five states the RNA declared as territories owed to the formerly enslaved and colonized Black nation. As a believer in the principles Malcolm spoke of, I too believed that land and independence are the basis for Black self-determination and became a conscious citizen of the RNA. My citizenship in the RNA was separate from my membership in the BPP.

Around this time, the FBI's COINTELPRO was waging a vicious and unrelenting war on the BPP and the Black Power movement in general.

COINTELPRO forced many of us underground, into exile; some of us were jailed or assassinated. On April 3, 1969, an early morning police raid led to the indictment, trial, and subsequent acquittal of members of what became known as the New York Panther 21. I escaped arrest and a trial that levied an incredulous 156-count conspiracy charge against the thirteen defendants.[3] That trial was nothing more than a COINTELPRO attempt to remove the New York City Panther leadership from the streets. And it worked. For two years, instead of serving and defending the material needs of poor and working-class Black people our membership focused on fundraisers, protest demonstrations, and speaking engagements to raise the people's consciousness and understanding about this criminal injustice. These were some of the BPP's first political prisoners. By this time, I had left the united states for Algeria where the party sent me to help establish its international section. Eventually, there was a contingent of Panthers in Algeria that included my wife at the time, Awode, Eldridge and Kathleen Cleaver, Donald "DC" and Barbara "BC" Cox, Michael "Cetewayo" Tabor, Connie Matthews and Larry Mack. There we worked to establish solidarity relationships with the anticolonial struggles, among them the African National Congress, People's Movement for the Liberation of Angola, Zimbabwe African National Union, and Palestinian Liberation Organization, along with other liberation movements and progressive governments of Algeria, Cuba, China, North Korea, and others.

After the destruction of the Black Panther Party by COINTELPRO and forces within the party itself, some of us continued to struggle both above and underground. I chose to continue to struggle underground as I had been doing since early 1969. We were very involved in health care and political prisoner support. We were able to assist in establishing a great health clinic in Harlem. We also helped free several political prisoners—probably the best known was Assata Shakur who is still living free in Cuba.

In October 1981, I was captured and charged with multiple "crimes" for resisting our oppression in the manner that I did. The New York City police and the FBI joint task force tortured me for seven hours. They beat me continuously, burned me with a cigar, ground off my toenail and waterboarded me by holding my head in a toilet while flushing it. The result of the torture left me hospitalized for more than three months trying to heal. Immediately afterwards, I was snatched out of the hospital and rushed into two trials, first by the federal government and then the New York state courts. The federal government found me guilty of helping to liberate Assata Shakur and the expropriation of an armored truck. Without any time to prepare New York forced me into its state trial, and found me guilty of the attempted murder of New York City police officers. I received a sentence of twenty-five years to life for that conviction and forty years for the federal conviction. After thirty-one years, I was paroled to New York to begin serving the state sentence. I was then able to get back into court on a technicality. I won. The court forced New York to give me a parole hearing. After serving thirty-three years, I left prison on parole in November 2014.

Since coming home, I helped cofound and organize the Northeast Political Prisoner Coalition (NEPPC). NEPPC's purpose is to heighten the awareness about the existence of political prisoners (the US government claims that there are no PPOWs in this country), support them, and work for their release. We protest, work with, and support other PPOW organizations. We also organize fundraising programs, send commissary funds and packages to PPOWs, visit them, and help their families visit them. I along with others have also taken our message and support of PPOWs to schools, community, and legal and religious organizations around the country. Although we still have many political prisoners locked down in federal and state prisons across the country, we have also had a few victories. In the last few years, we have welcomed home several PPOWs. In 2018 alone Herman Bell, Robert Seth Hayes, Debbie and Mike Africa have come home.

Of course, we still have much to do and face many challenges. Even if every PPOW in the United States left prison today, we would still be living in a corporate capitalist, imperialist, white supremacist nation with all the ills it brings to millions of people. Those of us that the united states claims to represent have a responsibility to stand up, speak out, and struggle to bring about a more humane society.

Those who are considered to be leading the movement today don't seem to be committed to struggling for revolutionary change. They seem to believe that they can reform this system to make it equitable for everyone. They do not seem to understand that this system was created to be inequitable. This system began and still is a racist, white supremacist, male-dominated, capitalist system. Unfortunately, many of the younger comrades today do not seem to make political education a priority in their movement organizing. That may be why we do not hear them talk about struggles against colonialism, imperialism, and white supremacy. They do not seem to recognize that these are the engines that make this system of government run. PPOWs stood against colonialism, imperialism, and racist white supremacy, which is why they have been separated from their families and locked away in prison dungeons for decades.

As the BPP clearly demonstrated with its Ten-Point Platform and Program, resistance does not happen in a vacuum. When the BPP implemented survival programs—free breakfast for children, health clinics, food pantries, clothing drives, sickle cell anemia testing—they were instituting a radical response to the social injustices endured by poor and working-class Black families/communities in this country. Their purpose was to politicize the people as to the ways in which capitalism, imperialism, and colonialism are functions of a state apparatus that is responsible for hunger, poverty, and oppression. It was to nurture a culture of self-determination while building a movement of resistance. It worked. Young people joined the BPP and other left movements in droves. This put the state on the offensive and was manifested by the violent repression and political imprisonment of those I speak of here today. We ought to ask ourselves if what exists today as a left movement here in the united states is consistent in any way with the left movements of the 1960s. If so, what are we resisting? Is it a person, a political party, the police, the military, an economic system? How are we resisting? Is the US left working in solidarity with left movements around the world? The left movements of the 1960s made clear to millions of poor and working-class Black/ Brown, Asian, Indigenous, and white people that US imperialism, capitalism, and colonialism are the enemy of oppressed people—both nationally and internationally. They held political education classes to politicize people with the understanding that police were the domestic occupying military force in their communities; that prisons, poverty, lack of decent health care, housing, education, and unemployment were a function of the capitalist system; and that a revolution to dismantle these systems is possible.

For the US to acknowledge the existence of PPOWs would be an admission that there are fundamental injustices that stem from the settler colonialism that built this nation; that those internally oppressed nations have the right to self-determination, self-defense, and liberation; as well as the right to struggle by whatever tactics and strategies—armed and otherwise— as guaranteed by the US's own Declaration of Independence. From slave ships to plantations to Harriet Tubman, the Deacons for Self-Defense, the African Blood Brotherhood, and many others, the use of arms was a strategy of self-defense against the terror of white on Black violence—state as well as private. The whole while we also had to suffer the criminalization of resistance, especially Black resistance. And forty-five years later, while PPOWs from other movements have returned home to their families and communities, those from the Black liberation movement remain the longest held.

For millions of poor and working-class people enduring the displacement in gentrified communities; the lack of a livable wage; lack of access to decent education, housing, and food; environmental racism, police terror and murder, mass imprisonment, deportation, anti-immigrant policies; and a myriad of other social injustices, resistance looks qualitatively different than it does for those in the middle class. Is there a left movement in the United States that is challenging this oppression as it relates to millions of poor and working-class people in this country?

Throughout much of the discourse on the "failed policy" of mass incarceration, the roots of mass incarceration are rarely examined. Historically, from Black Reconstruction to the Black Power movement, mass incarceration is a tool to control and destroy Black self-determination in the same way that the "war on drugs," "war on terror," and the xenophobic attacks on immigrants are weapons to repress nonwhite youth, Arab, Muslim, and immigrant communities. These are strategies of war meant to dismantle, disrupt, and otherwise, neutralize poor and working-class families' and communities' self-determination and the potential for militant resistance.

déqui kioni-sadiki

In the summer of 1992, I became a single mother of two young children and left the New Jersey suburbs to return to the borough in which I was born and raised. Moving back to the People's Republic of Brooklyn, as it's known in movement circles, led me to learn and live in the legacy of the Black Panther Party for Self-Defense and the Black Power movement, first as a student at the historically Black Medgar Evers College of the City University of New York (CUNY) and then as a member of the Black Panther Collective. And the rest, as is so often said, is herstory.

Medgar Evers College (MEC) was founded in 1970 and served as an incubator for my Black radical, Black feminist politics and activism. MEC was born out of a struggle between grassroots activists, scholars, community residents, and elected officials in the Flatbush, Crown Heights, and other central Brooklyn communities and the CUNY Board of Trustees. It began as an institution meant to serve and address the educational needs of the marginalized, underrepresented, and underserved Afrikan and Caribbean diasporic communities. It did. When I arrived on campus, a good many people that had participated in the struggle to create the institution, and those who contributed to the BPM and Black Arts Movement of the 1960s, were still there. I was surrounded, nurtured, supported, encouraged and mentored by a bevy of Black radical thinkers, activists, and scholars. This helped pave the way for my outspoken student advocacy and leadership on campus, as well as with the citywide CUNY United Student Senate organization and as chair of the People of African Descent caucus for the national United Students Senate Association.

I graduated MEC in 1998 with a bachelor's degree in public administration and a decade later earned a master's degree in urban affairs at Queens College – CUNY. Time and circumstance have shifted MEC from being a hotbed environment of radical politics, activism, and struggle. Nevertheless, MEC will forever hold significance for me as opening a groundswell of knowledge, appreciation, and understanding about centuries of Afrikan/New Afrikan histories and herstories, inventions, contributions, Black Power politics, resistance—armed and otherwise—and Black feminist theory.

It was at MEC that I became associated with the Black Panther Collective (BPC), an organization created by former members of the BPP/BLA—the late Safiya Bukhari and Oscar Washington, Ashanti Alston, Thomas "Blood" McCreary, Jamal Joseph, Shep McDaniels—and others who wanted to build an intergenerational dialogue, solidarity, and grassroots organizing that joined former BPP members with the next generation of radical activists and would-be revolutionaries to carry forward the principles, programs, and legacy of the BPP. Just like in the BPP, BPC members were required to attend weekly meetings, political education classes, conferences, symposiums, table at political and cultural events, assist in the distribution of an updated *Black Panther News Service*, participate in the "Feed the People" programs, do cop-watch patrols, and work in solidarity with the Malcolm X Grassroots Movement, Black United Front, and other organizations. Most particular to the work I am engaged in today, I received an introduction to and an education about the existence of US-held PPOWs.

It was through the BPC that I first met the late Baba Herman Ferguson, chair emeritus and co-founder of the Malcolm X Commemoration Committee (MXCC) and the National Jericho Movement for Amnesty and Recognition of US-held political prisoners and prisoners of war; former BPP/BLA members Safiya Bukhari and Jalil Muntaqim (aka Anthony Bottom), still imprisoned. Baba Herman was for me a surrogate father, teacher, fierce leader, and legendary example of Black resistance, and I now proudly serve as chair of the MXCC and am a member of the National Jericho Movement.

The BPC also led to my meeting the brilliant and late Pan-Afrikanist Elombe Brathe. Elombe opened his 125th Street Patrice Lumumba Coalition offices for the BPC to meet regularly. Elombe's encyclopedic knowledge of Afrikan history deepened our knowledge, understanding, and embracing of Pan-Afrikan politics.

The BPC instilled in me the principles of education for liberation, our need to struggle for Black self-determination, justice, and liberation, and of being in the service and defense of the Black nation. In the years since, I have developed a global worldview, radical politics, race and class analyses, critical thinking, and public speaking skills and solidarity with other oppressed communities that I can only attribute to the legacy of the BPC, and by extension, the BPP and BPM. It has been through the combination of the three that I discovered the identity of this settler-colony that is founded on the genocide of Indigenous nations and the enslavement of Afrikan peoples, along with US global domination, tyranny, terrorism, violence of white supremacy, racism, and capitalism, imperialism, and colonialism. The lasting influence of these organizations/movements showed me how these socio-political structures exist to dispose people to lose their language, culture, spirituality, and religion, exploit their labor, and conquer and extract the natural resources of their land. I learned that from 1619 to the present, this is how a nation of Black folk have suffered the pernicious denial of their freedom dreams, humanity, human rights, and justice. All of my newfound knowledge helped me to see how little difference there is that separates the state-sanctioned violence of seventeenth-century slave dungeons, slave ships, auction blocks, and plantation life from the state-sanctioned violence of twenty-first-century poverty, hunger, unemployment, criminalization, political and mass imprisonment, and lack of decent housing, health care, and education, plus the now occurring every twenty-three-hour unpunished murder of an unarmed Black person by a white male—in or out of uniform.

Clinton like Attica like Comstock like Greenhaven and every other prison I've visited is a chilling, stark, and foreboding reminder that amerikka's "peculiar institution" of white overseers lording over the movements of an enslaved Afrikan population is alive and functioning well with white prison guards overseeing the Black and Brown prison population.

These historical realities are what I learned as a legacy of the BPC, and it informs the practice of my life and work around PPOWs. This is not something I do, but rather someone I've become. The political understanding and kinship bonds I've developed over the years have transformed and enriched my life immeasurably. Today, I have an extended revolutionary family that consists of sistas and brothers who journeyed with me through the BPC.

In the years that I have engaged in the work of visiting and supporting PPOWs, there are two who stand out as having made the most indelible imprints on my life and development, Albert "Nuh" Washington and Abdullah Majid. I met Nuh in the early 1990s on a BPC visit to Clinton Correctional Facility in Dannemora, New York. Clinton is about an hour's drive from the Canadian border and a six- to seven-hour drive from New York City. It was my first prison visit and the last prison halls my husband walked before his semi-freedom release on parole in November 2014. That morning of Sekou's release felt like I'd come full circle.

Nuh was calm, soft-spoken, and patient, a steady listener with a gentle smile and easy laughter. I was constantly juxtaposing this man I had come to know as my brother, mentor, and friend with the Black liberation freedom fighter who so terrified the power structure that whenever he was moved or appeared in court, was shackled from neck, waist, wrists, and ankles and surrounded by law enforcement. Our bond of kinship grew over years of monthly telephone conversations, letters, and postcards from my travels and visits. Nuh would often counsel and encourage me when I became frustrated by the lack of a movement on his and other PPOWs' behalf. When I learned that he had terminal liver cancer, I was devastated. On April 28, 2000, Nuh made his transition. Eighteen years later, I sometimes think of him alone in that prison hospital bed with no family, comrades, or friends to comfort him as he made his way to the other side and I want to smash the insanities, injustices, and cruelties of state-sanctioned prison murder. Other times, I think of him and cherish the wonderful memories I have of Sheik Nuh, grateful for our revolutionary love, political discussions, and the important life lessons he gifted me.

I feel the same for Abdullah Majid, another former BPP/BLA soldier who served thirty-plus years of unjust political imprisonment in upstate New York prisons. Throughout his incarceration Majid remained in the service of oppressed people and had his fingers on the pulse on everything happening nationally and internationally. Majid was unwavering in making clear that no injustice happened in a vacuum. He often shared his ideas and action plans for grassroots organizing with us fully expecting us to undertake his "marching orders." Majid critiqued and challenged the horrors of mass imprisonment and political imprisonment long before the former became a politically correct social injustice issue. His mantra that we use today, "Freedom ain't free and it don't come cheap," was unfailingly delivered with his one-two-punch sense of humor, sarcasm, wit, resolve, and self-determination of a man who refused to be defeated by the system or cooperate with its unjust laws. Majid was also my friend, mentor, and brother in struggle. He was funny, intelligent, principled with an indomitable spirit that made him seem almost invincible. But he was not. On April 3, 2016, Majid succumbed to state-sanctioned medical neglect and murder from a ruptured gall bladder. His death is as painful and devastating a loss as Nuh's. His life and sacrifice remind every day that each of us must deepen our resolve to free the rest of our BPP/BLA soldiers behind the wall.

In the years between Nuh and Majid, I have also come to know and love Sundiata Acoli, the octogenarian codefendant of Assata Shakur. I've visited Sundiata across decades in federal and New Jersey prisons. The same is true of Jalil Muntaqim, Herman Bell, and Robert Seth Hayes prior to their respective April and July 2018 releases in New York. I have visited Ed Poindexter and his codefendant Mondo we Langa, now deceased, in an Omaha, Nebraska, prison. After many years of corresponding via mail, I had the great opportunity of visiting Russell "Maroon" Shoatz in Pennsylvania with his daughter, Sharon, and another of our sistas in struggle, Valerie Haynes.

The only PPOW whom I knew prior to his imprisonment is Kamau Sadiki (aka Freddie Hilton), currently in prison again because he refuses to collaborate with the government and accept the $1 million bounty to help capture Assata, the mother of one of his daughters, or be coerced by government threats that he will spend the rest of his life in prison if he doesn't aid and abet bringing Assata back from exile in Cuba.

In the early 1990s, I was a committee coordinator for the New York–based Free Mumia Abu-Jamal Coalition. Mumia is a former BPP and death-row journalist whose name and case had not yet become a cause célèbre. Under the leadership of Sista Safiya Bukhari, with Sally O'Brien and other BPC members, I traveled across the tristate area doing public speaking engagements at churches, conferences, community events, and colleges that advocated on Mumia's behalf and also for our other PPOWs. Initially, I felt inexperienced to speak effectively on so urgent an issue as the unjust political imprisonment of our freedom fighters. As my BPC and former BPP members advised, I simply spoke from the heart and prayed that people would respond accordingly. That was great advice then and it still is now. In 2009, we experienced the victory of Mumia leaving death row and moving into general prison population. However, close to a decade later, he remains one of thirteen members of the BPP/BLA still held in unjust political imprisonment.

Today, I am chair of MXCC, an organization cofounded by Baba Herman, the late Yuri Kochiyama, Jean Reynolds, Walter Bowe and others who, as members of the Organization of Afro-American Unity (OAAU), sought to challenge the distortions and commodification of Malcolm's legacy following the 1993 release of filmmaker Spike Lee's fictionalized representation of Malcolm's life.

MXCC holds an annual dinner tribute to the families of our PPOWs that was started by Baba Herman's wife and comrade in struggle, Mama Iyaluua Ferguson, who recognized the tribute as a way for us to pay respect to our PPOWs and their families for their decades of endurance and sacrifice to the Black liberation movement and raise funds for the commissary accounts of the PPOWs represented at the dinner. In 2018 we marked twenty-two years of this dinner tradition. We also continue cosponsoring, with the Sons of Afrika, the annual May 19 pilgrimage to the Ferncliff Cemetery to celebrate Malcolm's birthday.

I also cohost and coproduce a weekly public affairs show, *Where We Live* (*WWL*), on New York City's listener-sponsored WBAI radio. Journalist Sally O'Brien created *WWL* in 1988 to give voice to those individuals Coretta Scott King spoke of who refuse to cooperate with unjust laws. It is a grassroots format with a focus on US-held PPOWs and their families, the family members and survivors of police terror, Puerto Rican issues, the fight to stop repressive legislation, and other grassroots organizing efforts. Sally and I begin each show with a commentary by Mumia. For decades *WWL* has provided space for dozens of current and former political prisoners and their supporters to have their voices heard. My work on the show is an extension of my revolutionary love for our PPOWs and their families, the legacy of the BPP, the BPM, and those who dare to struggle.

I have also come to know that the road to freedom, whether inside or outside the prison walls, is often complicated by the disappointments of revisionism, betrayal, opportunism, and "cult of personality" that derail the true retelling of the history and herstory of movements. Despite this understanding this is still a beautiful struggle made richer by the love and commitment our revolutionaries—our PPOWs—continue to have for the people. It is that love that has held our PPOWs firm in their commitment to the principles of their politics over these many decades of unjust imprisonment. These are the individuals that radical activist and author James Baldwin spoke of when he said: "The obligation of anyone who thinks of himself as responsible is to examine society and try to change it and to fight it—at no matter what risk. This is the only hope society has. This is the only way societies change."[4]

Where Do We Go from Here?

There are many valuable lessons that can and should be learned from the legacy of the BPP and BPM. This is part of the BPP/BPM legacy: leading, serving, politicizing, and helping a Black nation move closer to revolution than people think is possible today. One of the greatest legacies must be the understanding that the histories and herstories of Black lives are not just timelines in a series of past events. Our resilient past carries on in the everyday moments that Black folk live fully, love against all odds, and resist injustice. And if we are to continue moving forward in the tradition of Black resistance, we must study where we were, where we are, and where we are going. This means today's activists ought to understand what white supremacy, colonialism, corporate capitalism, imperialism, and racism are.

The task that lies ahead for a younger generation of activists is to study what worked and what didn't work about the BPP and BPM. Some of what worked was a Ten-Point Platform and Program, along with other survival programs, that addressed the material needs of poor and working-class Black people. These programs ended the reality of millions of children going to school hungry. The police patrols and other community actions imposed consequences upon the state that decreased the number of unarmed Black people being shot down by killer police. The establishment of free health clinics, food pantries, sickle cell anemia testing, voter registration and other community-control programs was so important to our communities, yet so dangerous to the status quo that the US government destroyed these programs, coopted them, and continue them today.

When considering joining or creating an organization for Black liberation be mindful of each volunteer's and recruit's motivations. Perhaps even devising a line of questions or processes for getting to know activists or members within an organizational structure or group may be essential for the safety of the collective. Perhaps having a protracted "initiation" or feeling-out period that includes mandatory study and community assignments for an extended period of time before trusting newer members with deeper organizational responsibilities can be another protective measure.

Some of what didn't work: We now know that allowing any person who wanted to join the BPP was not a good idea. In fact, it turned out to be disastrous as several chapters are now known to have been heavily infiltrated and/or started by agents provocateurs. We also know what didn't work was the development and spread of the cult of personality and how it allowed elements within BPP leadership to operate with impunity. Or that when contradictions arose, and were not resolved, it ultimately gave way to liberalism and the loyalty of relationships versus the principles of a revolutionary organizational structure. We know that inflated ego-tripping and contradictions between the Afrikan-centered cultural identity and the American Negro cultural identity exposed some major differences, as did the factions within the organizational structure that embraced armed struggled and/or electoral politics. As these differences went unresolved, it enabled the BPP to be destroyed both internally and externally, with aid of course, from the machinations of COINTELPRO.

It also didn't work that the BLA was outgunned and out-weaponized, but the BLA stepped out ahead of the people to engage the power structure militarily without the people's understanding. In hindsight, some feel it was a mistake to do so without the people's support. Also, some say the people are not prepared for that level of armed struggle. Before armed struggle is considered as a necessary step in the people's resistance, we must study the history of armed struggle. What does it take for a people to prepare for armed struggle and how do we know the people being defended are ready to support it?

International Cooperation

The BPP and BPM connected the struggles of Black folk in the united states with the struggles of Black folk in Africa, Asia, the Middle East, and South America. It was a movement that engaged proactively in international solidarity with oppressed people and nations around the world in their struggles for land and independence from US and European imperialism, colonialism, and capitalism.

Need for Youth Leadership

There needs to be a push for the education and training of Black children, as young as five, six, and seven years old, to participate in and one day lead the struggle for Black self-determination. We need an army of New Afrikan Scouts to help Black children understand what it means to be Black in amerikkka, and what it means to have self-worth, to know their ancestors' history/herstory and contributions to this settler-nation. Too often Black children go to public schools that teach them nothing about their true history. What they learn is the indoctrination of white supremacy. Black children do not learn about Black resistance and community control of the institutions where they live. We must teach our children that they are the solution to the problems we face by having more elders engage with our youth. Each one must teach one to honor, respect, value, and not be afraid of one another.

Survival Programs

With massive unemployment, rampant homelessness because of the ethnic cleansing happening in communities across the country, and thousands of formerly incarcerated men and womyn returning to fractured homes and communities, now more than ever before, the people need programs like those the BPP provided. Black people need grassroots community resources that address their material needs. **All power to the people!**

Stark graphic image by MICAL commemorating forty years of Black August organizing featuring silhouette of Shaka At-Thinnin, who was part of the first group to originate, organize, and observe Black August while still inside prison

CHAPTER TWELVE

Black August: Organizing to Uplift the Fallen and Release the Captive

Matef Harmachis

*O*n *August 5, 1968, Los Angeles Black Panther Party members Steve Bartholomew and his brother Tony, Tommy Lewis, and Robert Lawrence were riding in a little Volkswagen doing party work to serve the community. The police had been following them off and on all day. They stopped at a service station at the corner of Adams and Montclair. Steve got out and opened the hood. Two policemen in a patrol car pulled in behind them. The driver approached Steve ordering him to open the trunk. The other cop ordered everyone else out of the car. When Robert came out the second officer shot him without warning. When the shooting stopped two Panthers were dead, another would die on the way to the hospital. Somehow Tony fled the scene avoiding physical harm.[1]*

On August 25, 2018, some thirty of us boarded a chartered bus in front of the Afiba Center on Crenshaw Boulevard just south of Little Africa. We were on the annual Black August Martyr's Tour to commemorate lives lost in the struggle for African liberation. Organized by former Los Angeles Black Panther Party members and their supporters we visited important sites related to our movement's fallen s/heroes.

September 10, 1971, Panthers Harold Taylor, John Bowman, and Ray Boudreaux stopped in their car at the intersection of 65th and Hooper. The police attacked them, firing more than 300 rounds into the car. All three were hit but survived because gathering witnesses frightened the police to cease fire.

We got off the bus at cemeteries where Black Panther Party leaders

Bunchy Carter and Melvin X are buried. Carter, killed along with John Huggins on January 17, 1969, at UCLA, died at the hands of agents of COINTELPRO. Melvin X, a cofounder of the Black Student Alliance, was assassinated execution-style at 45th and Western. We viewed the vacant lot at Imperial Highway and Fernwood where a city worker discovered on November 19, 1971, Party member Sandra Pratt's eight-month-pregnant body in a trash bag. Witnesses to the December 8, 1969, Los Angeles Police Department's attack on the Panther offices at 41st and Central explained how thirteen wounded Panthers withstood a militarized assault of 300 police for four and a half hours—the exact amount of time the police allowed Mike Brown to lie dead on a street in Ferguson, Missouri, on August 9, 2014. Harold Taylor of the San Francisco 8 testified about his jailhouse torture and coerced confessions. Our guides showed us the house where family and friends of prisoners in Soledad State Prison formed the Soledad Defense Committee in 1970. Others praised the lives and sacrifices of George and Jonathan Jackson or heralded the philosophical originator of Black August, Khatari Gaulden.

"*On August 1, 1978, while playing a game of football on the asphalt and brick yard in the San Quentin Adjustment Center Khatari fell and struck his head. The severe blow left him comatose. Even after several hours lying on a cot in the infirmary with untrained personnel who could do nothing for him, the administration refused to transfer him to a nearby hospital. Khatari lay bleeding internally until he died. We were devastated to say the least. Once again a beloved soldier, leader, teacher, friend and brother lay dead at the hands of those with the keys to our chains.*"[2]

Every August since 1979, Black August events take place in numerous cities across the United States to commemorate the deaths of African prisoners and activists. The killing of Africans inside, including Khatari Gaulden and George Jackson, provided the initial impetus for Black August. Black August has since developed into a commemorative for the martyrs of the Black Power movement. In honoring those who gave their lives, Black August asks us to recall the history of the Black radical tradition and to call into being the present work of African liberation and prison abolition. These are intergenerational events that rely on African oral traditions with former Black Panther Party (BPP) Elders telling their collective narratives and younger cohorts of activists not only listening and learning but also transforming that history into what needs to be done in today's urgent struggles to prefigure the society of tomorrow.

Black August is a response to the brutality inside California prisons. Prisoners who knew George Jackson and Khatari Gaulden wanted the legacy of their mentors kept alive. These prisoners used the month of August as a time to spread the word of what was really going on behind the walls of California's prisons. To them what was really going on was the California Department of Corrections' overt attempt to silence all prisoner resistance to the daily torture of prison life.

First on the hit list was Hugo "Yogi" Pinell, a good friend and comrade of George Jackson.[3] On that day Yogi was out to court and not on the yard. W. L. Nolen—widely known for his many successful legal filings against prison torture—Cleveland Edwards and Alvin Miller were the three Africans selected for assassination. The tower guard was chosen for his marksmanship and racist philosophies. "The guards allowed both black and white prisoners on the O wing yard at the same time," said our Martyr's Tour guide, Jitu Sadiki. "That's a no-no." Once on the yard white convicts initiated an altercation at the water fountain.[4] Shaka At-Thinnin, chair, Black August Organizing Committee, remembers January 13, 1970: "Three shots fired. Three Africans died. The guard received exoneration and the prisoners who started it received rewards and privileges."[5]

There was an unquestionable influence of the BPP via George Jackson and other Panthers inside. Through Jackson's call for unity At-Thinnin and others accepted progressive individuals from the BPP, the US Organization, the Republic of New Africa, and other formations. "We were not Panthers even though our leader, George Jackson, was field marshal of the Black Panther Party," said At-Thinnin. "Our common bond was belief in what we were doing for Africans. We taught reading and writing, African history and political science. We taught world history and world governmental formations. It was within our response to brutality that the seeds of Black August began to manifest."

For Black August, study was supported by fasting, in part to build self-discipline, in part "as a constant reminder of the sacrifices of our fallen Freedom Fighters and the ongoing oppression of our people," said Mama Ayanna Mashama, cofounder of the Black August Organizing Committee.[6] Prisoners and their families also fasted from media and entertainment in order to spend more time to study (mental) and train (physical).

The state charged Jackson along with Fleeta Drumgo and John Clutchette with a retaliation killing of a guard for the murder of the three Africans on the O wing yard. These three defendants became the Soledad Brothers.[7]

Jackson's younger brother Jonathan would be the next to die in the well-publicized Marin County Courthouse shootings on August 7, 1970, attempting to free his older brother. San Quentin prison sharpshooters at the courthouse opened fire, killing everyone in the escape vehicle except Ruchell Magee, who was gravely injured; the prosecutor and a juror, who were also wounded, survived.[8] On August 21, 1971, one year and two weeks after his brother died in the parking lot of the Marin County Courthouse, guards shot George Jackson to death in the Adjustment Center courtyard behind the chapel in San Quentin.[9]

It was in this pit of violence that the resistance inside prisons gave birth to Black August. To make sure these many deaths and the contributions of the martyred were memorialized, a collective formed in the San Quentin Adjustment Center. The members based their coming together on Khatari's ideas and called themselves Black August. In Oakland a corresponding organization, the Black August Organizing Committee (BAOC), surfaced in August 1979.

BAOC began to enlighten the public about the atrocities of the lockup units. BAOC cofounder At-Thinnin said, "In the beginning we went door to door talking to people about what it was really like for their loved ones after the courts disappeared family and friends into prison." Through community interaction they learned the everyday needs of families and did work that paralleled the BPP community survival programs. "The community called on us to provide transportation for elders, help people move, repair cars and houses, protect women from abuse. Sometimes we planted gardens in people's yards to help with sustainable foods because it was very hard on families supporting someone inside and keeping families together outside," said At-Thinnin. "Educating the public about prison conditions and political prisoners while working on community issues helped people know our stand." Drawing from the internationalism of the BPP, the BAOC worked to build solidarity with the Native American movement, the popular struggles in El Salvador and Iran, liberation struggles throughout Africa, and other Third World and progressive movements.[10]

BAOC's service drew unwanted attention. The Special Service Unit, a little-publicized and highly trained investigation and apprehension unit recruited from prison guards, along with the Oakland and Berkeley police departments, began arresting Black August members on a multiplicity of charges, which disrupted BAOC's organizing work.[11]

In 1981 the California Department of Corrections (CDC) actions against Black August increased both inside and out of prisons. "The effort was intended to completely dismantle the positive growth and good will generated by Black August's hard work, determination, and principled behavior,"

At-Thinnin said. "On April 17 and April 20 guards beat and gassed prisoners in San Quentin Adjustment Center in unprovoked attacks. More than forty men needed medical attention. BAOC helped to form the Prison Crisis Committee, a coalition of former prisoners, lawyers, legal workers, and community support people. Through talk shows, protest letters, and a class action lawsuit, Black August helped to bring about significant change in the prison administration."[12] The organizing was effective enough to force the warden and an assistant warden to resign. Consequently the state's attacks on BAOC intensified. Several organizers went back inside on supposed parole violations regardless of whether the charges seemed plausible.

The blow to BAOC was severe. It seemed all those having anything to do with Black August were the targets of a coordinated agenda to stop them. The effect was fewer persons becoming or remaining active in anything initiated by BAOC.[13] At-Thinnin said, "Everyone we talked to received visits from the CDC. Fewer people attended our events, and our effectiveness in the community tapered off."

Nevertheless, by the end of the '90s Black August commemoratives were taking place across the United States. Mama Ayanna writes: "In alliance with the BAOC, members of the New Afrikan Independence Movement (NAIM) began practicing and spreading Black August during this period. The Malcolm X Grassroots Movement (MXGM) inherited knowledge and practice of Black August from its parent organization, the New Afrikan People's Organization (NAPO)."

In Philadelphia Black August events include an August 30 "Pack the Court" for political prisoner Mumia Abu-Jamal.

In Jackson, Mississippi, Cooperation Jackson holds Black August events including "Binge Series Watching Underground," where they have free screenings of revolutionary documentaries and movies with discussions of the films shown afterwards.

In Durham, North Carolina, a coalition of MXGM, Critical Resistance, *4Struggle Magazine*, and other supporters of political prisoners have Black August in the Park, a family reunion–style event that connects social justice groups with the larger African population.

In Atlanta Black August commemorations promote wellness with a Happily Natural Day, a summer festival dedicated to holistic health, cultural awareness, and social change. All Natural ATL holds an Annual Black August 5K Run for Freedom, with the RBG Fit Club, Helping Africa by Establishing Schools at Home, FTP Movement, Community Movement

Builders, and Afrikan Martial Arts Institute to promote health and fitness with a cause. After the run there's Kemetic yoga, martial arts, archery, and fitness training along with a Black August Block Party gathering.

In Oakland more organizations, including the Eastside Arts Alliance and the Freedom Archives, organize events showcasing the history of Black August in relation to contemporary racial justice organizing.

In Cuba New Afrikan political exile Nehanda Abiodun conceived "Black August Hip Hop" benefit concerts to raise awareness about political prisoners, prisoners of war, and political exiles, which inspired the MXGM's work to extend Black August to the hip hop generation. This brought awareness to a new coterie of activists.[14]

In Venezuela online articles by Ajamu Nangwaya and the Upstate Chapter of Northeast Political Prisoner Coalition promoting the institutionalizing of Black August appeared in English and Spanish.[15]

Globally the Black August Hip Hop Project organized annual events between 1998 and 2010, including international delegations of artists and activists to Cuba, South Africa, Tanzania, Brazil, and Venezuela.

The organizing work on behalf of political prisoners and prisoners of war (PP/POWs) by a multiplicity of groups like Jericho, Release Aging People in Prison, the Family Africa (MOVE), Family and Friends of Mumia Abu-Jamal, Anarchist Black Cross, Interfaith Prisoners of Conscience Project, Critical Resistance, and many other support and abolitionist groups plus BAOC have been instrumental in the release of former members of the BPP from prison and generated strong backing for former Panthers still inside. However, many organizers would say there is still scant consciousness of the existence or the plight of PP/POWs still incarcerated because of their work in the BPP and for the liberation of African people. It will take broader community demands to get PP/POWs released.

In 2004, because of the unevenness of content at the events, BAOC reestablished guidelines and called for a broad coalition of organizations to work together for PP/POWs worldwide. This rededication to the international struggle for prisoners grew into one of the most powerful Black August commemorations ever. BAOC pulled together a broad spectrum of nationalities and organizational groups for a Black August in Oakland that participants still talk about today.

But state repression continues unabated. In 2016 the CDC accused BAOC of planning criminal activities for the month of August involving intended murders of correctional personnel and other despicable crimes. The

CDC ran a negative campaign against Black August on radio, TV, and in newspaper ads. The CDC also fed disinformation to hospitals, clinics, law offices, and places frequented by former prisoners.[16]

On August 1, 2018, it had been forty years since the CDC allowed Khatari Gaulden, the intellectual founder of Black August, to lie injured, unattended, and die. On that day in Oakland the BAOC commemorated Khatari and recommitted to the struggle for those gone and all those still held captive.

BAOC organized the First Black August National Conference that will reconvene the type of international broad-based coalition of prisoner support that the BAOC built in 2004. The daylong event at the East Oakland Youth Center included a strategizing session for the way forward, not only for Black August but also for prison abolition work in general.

As we exited our tour bus back at the Afiba Center the sons and daughters of Africa, Asia, Europe, Oceania, and Turtle Island hugged our goodbyes. Through the testimonies we heard and the sites we saw, we are now called to participate as witnesses to remember the sacrifices required of those in resistance and to build forward the unfinished work of African liberation.

Jalil Muntaqim, New York 3 and San Francisco 8 political prisoner, former Panther and Black Liberation Army member, initiated the call for the Jericho campaign and rally in Washington, DC, in 1998 to free US-held political prisoners. Photograph by Bryan Shih, 2018

CHAPTER THIRTEEN

The Making of a Movement: Jericho and Political Prisoners

Jalil A. Muntaqim

I was captured on August 28, 1971, in San Francisco after a car chase and gun battle with San Francisco Police. It was alleged that my codefendant Albert Nuh Washington and I were attempting to avenge the assassination of George L. Jackson, which occurred on August 21, 1971. I was convicted for the San Francisco shootout, a federal bank robbery, and in 1975 convicted of the killing of two police officers in New York that occurred on May 21, 1971. Having been a member of the Black Panther Party and the Black Liberation Army, my imprisonment made me a political prisoner of war. Unfortunately, the United States does not recognize the existence of US political prisoners. Because those captured for revolutionary political-military actions are charged in a criminal proceeding, the US criminalizes political rebellion.

After my conviction in New York City, I was returned to California to complete the San Francisco conviction and sentence. I was placed in San Quentin Adjustment Center, locked on the first floor in a cell between Ruchell Cinque Magee and Charles Manson. The San Quentin Six were locked a few cells away on the same tier. In 1975, I received a newsletter from Yuri Kochiyama, representing the New York chapter of the National Committee for the Defense of Political Prisoners (NCDPP). The newsletter highlighted a call for the United Nations to consider the existence of US political prisoners. After reading that newsletter, I drafted a proposal for progressives

229

and activists to assist political prisoners to petition the United Nations in our behalf to call for a formal investigation into our existence and the conditions we suffered in prisons across the country. I showed the draft to Ruchell, who thought it was very good but suggested that I let Geronimo ji Jaga (formerly Elmer Pratt) review it. I had the proposal smuggled to the second floor of the Adjustment Center for Geronimo's critique. He tweaked the proposal and sent it back to me, I rewrote it and sent it to Yuri and NCDPP to implement.

Unfortunately, after several weeks there was no response from Yuri or NCDPP, so the proposal was abandoned until 1977. At that time I met a white guy in San Quentin nicknamed Commie Mike, and I shared the proposal with him. He put me in contact with the United Prison Union, a prison reform advocacy group in San Francisco. After meeting with Pat Singer, a leader of UPU, it was agreed to assist with the development of the now National Prisoners Petition Campaign to the United Nations. Soon thereafter, the Prairie Fire Organizing Committee joined in support of UPU in building the petition campaign to the UN. We were able to obtain assistance from former Amnesty International attorney Kathryn Burke with the development of the petition to be presented to the United Nations.

By 1978, the campaign had prisoners in twenty-five states, including Hawaii, supporting the petition. The petition was submitted to UN Subcommission on Prevention of Discrimination and Protection of Minorities and recorded as UN document E/CN.4/Sub.2/NGO/75. This was the first time a document concerning the existence of US political prisoners and racist prison conditions had been filed, recorded, and heard at the UN. In 1979, out of this initiative, an effort was made to have the International Jurist tour the US and interview political prisoners. After those interviews, the International Jurist filed a report to the United Nations affirming that political prisoners existed in the United States. Also, in 1979, our campaign knew a journalist in Paris who would be attending a news conference by US Ambassador Andrew Young to the United Nations. I was asked were there any specific questions I wanted asked, and I said, "Only one: do political prisoners exist in the US?" Ambassador Young answered truthfully, stating, "Perhaps thousands." For his truthfulness then-president Jimmy Carter fired Andrew Young from his post. It should be noted that also as a part of this overall campaign, Cuba's president Fidel Castro offered to trade US political prisoners with prisoners in Cuba the US wanted. Unfortunately, that trade did not happen.

Many years later the Provisional Government for the Republic of New Afrika organized an annual march around the White House and demonstration calling for the release of US political prisoners. In 1995, the RNA stopped these Jericho marches, which I thought should continue. So, in 1996, I distributed a call for action for the reestablishing of the Jericho march. Comrades Safiya Asya Bukhari and Herman Ferguson came to visit me, decrying that they were unable to organize a national Jericho march in a year's time. In our meeting in the visiting room at Eastern Correctional Facility in New York State, we agreed that a concerted effort would be made to organize the Jericho march for 1998.

Sista Safiya Bukhari and Herman Ferguson's organizing ability was incomparable; their indomitable spirit and revolutionary determination successfully brought six thousand activists from across the country for the Jericho march and rally.

After the march and rally in Washington, DC, it was decided that the momentum from that effort should continue, and the Jericho Amnesty Movement was born to provide continued support for US political prisoners, calling for amnesty and their release, especially those of COINTELPRO convictions. In 2018, the Jericho Amnesty Movement reached a milestone of twenty years of actively fighting in behalf of US political prisoners. In these twenty years, Jericho has established a medical committee to assist political prisoners in their health needs, legal defense to assist in political prisoners' legal challenges, and assistance for families of political prisoners to visit, and has continued to fight for political prisoners' release. There have been initiatives to raise the profile of US political prisoners at the United Nations. The most recent trip was in 2016, when Jericho's chairman, Jihad Abdulmumit, made a presentation in Geneva, Switzerland, in behalf of US political prisoners. Jihad was a member of the Black Panther Party and former political prisoner who understands this struggle to forge a determination to free US political prisoners.

When we consider that many of those who were COINTELPRO targets are still in prison, we can agree that Jericho is an important bridging of the generations from the struggles of the '60s and '70s to the millennium. Obviously, for any movement to be sustained, grow, and evolve, activists must support their political prisoners. The Black Panther Party was instrumental in forging community organizing and political objectives to be achieved. The party made people understand the process of fighting examples of power, to empower the community. That is the primary reason the FBI's COINTELPRO launched more than three hundred attacks against the BPP. In fact, the FBI employed every tactic used to destabilize a country in order to destroy the

Black Panther Party. However, it was the indomitable spirit of the thousands of young people who joined the party, dedicating themselves to empowering the community, that served to preserve the continuum of struggle that began from the time New Afrikans were brought to the country as slaves. When Willie Ricks and Stokely Carmichael proclaimed our struggle was one for Black Power, it ignited a political cataclysmic storm of youthful energy for freedom. However, the Black Panther Party manifested that declaration in the pragmatic development of progress in behalf of our people.

I was one of those young people when at sixteen years of age I first signed up to become a Panther and at eighteen years old when I was recruited into the Black underground. A little more than a month before my twentieth birthday I was captured, and I am now one of the longest-held political prisoners in the world. With forty-five years in prison, I continue to seek ways in which I can contribute to the overall struggle. The writing of my books, *We Are Our Own Liberators* and *Escaping the Prism—Fade to Black*, is part of giving back to the next generation. It is necessary to ensure the continuum, from one generation to the next, and it is incumbent on each generation to support political prisoners who paved the way, passing the torch of revolution.

In this regard, recently the Jericho Amnesty Movement has embarked on a national and international campaign to persuade the International Jurist to initiate a formal investigation on human rights abuses of US political prisoners, and the failure of the US corporate government to implement the UN Minimum Standards on the Treatment of Prisoners. The Jericho campaign motto is "In the Spirit of Nelson Mandela," and activists across the country are urged to join and support in whatever way they are able in political solidarity, toward the building of a National Coalition for the Human Rights of Political Prisoners. For more information on this campaign or on the existence of US political prisoners, contact www.thejerichomovement.com.

About the writer: Jalil Abdul Muntaqim (Anthony Bottom) is one of the longest-held political prisoners in the world. He is the author of *We Are Our Own Liberators*, a compilation of prison writings. Many of his essays have been published in anthologies such as *The New Abolitionist: (Neo) Slave Narratives and Contemporary Prison Writings*, edited by Joy James (2005); *Schooling a Generation*, edited by Chinosole (2002); and *This Country Must Change*, edited by Craig Rosebraugh (2009). Jalil's articles have appeared in New York City *Amsterdam News* and San Francisco *BayView*, and many progressive publications. He has completed an unpublished novel and teleplay.

His most recent book, *Escaping the Prism—Fade to Black*, a compilation of poems and essays with extensive afterword by professor Ward Churchill, was published by Kersplebed Publishers and Distributors in Canada and can be purchased on Amazon and from AK Press. For more information on Jalil's case and fight for parole, check www.freejalil.com.

Michael Zinzun featured in the "They Claim I'm a . . . Criminal" mural commissioned by the Southern California Library, Los Angeles, California. Zinzun, former Panther, was cofounder of the Coalition Against Police Abuse and a founding member of Community in Support of the Gang Truce. Mural artist Man One said, "The first thing I noticed when I saw the wall were the street poles located directly in front of the mural. They cast an awful set of moving shadows across the wall throughout the day. So rather than fight it, I embraced it . . . it all came together and made perfect sense. Depending on what time of the day you view the mural, the figures are either locked up or free!" Photograph by Man One, 2010

CHAPTER FOURTEEN

Dialogical Autonomy: Michael Zinzun, the Coalition Against Police Abuse, and Genocide

joão costa vargas

This essay honors Michael Zinzun's lifelong work of collective organizing. By focusing on contradictions within some of the political formations in which he participated, it aims at providing a reflection that may be effective for grasping and evaluating contemporary progressive Black collective fronts. How does an analysis of Zinzun's political choices help us to critically understand contemporary progressive Black diasporic politics?

Zinzun was a dear friend, someone i admired deeply and with whom i collaborated between 1995 and 2006, when he passed.[1] Since 2012, i have been conducting archival research on Zinzun's trajectory, including an analysis of the Coalition Against Police Abuse (CAPA) archives at the Southern California Library (SCL). This exposure to Zinzun's papers, many of which were unknown to me, generated new understandings on the competing political demands with which he grappled and the choices he made about the language, strategies, and ultimate goals of the organizations to which he dedicated his abundant energy, a considerable proportion of his financial resources, and his unbounded love.

Still, this essay is not so much about Zinzun as it is about the political blocs in which he participated. While Zinzun did make important strategic choices regarding how, with whom, when, and what battle front to engage, and despite the considerable influence he had on his fellow organizers, his evaluations reflected the political climate he inhabited, which included the institutional forces he and his organizations opposed, the political tendencies within his own blocs, and his beliefs and aspirations. It is therefore important to consider the demographic constitution of, and the range of the progressive convictions (and their corresponding theories) in Zinzun's political milieus. As we do so, we gain explanations for why certain agendas and strategies were chosen over others.

Specifically—and this is the essay's focus—via a critical reading of CAPA's archives, which i will juxtapose to the decade-plus of insight gained while participating in the organization, we attain insight into the reasons for the coalition's relatively muted public support for the utilization of the concept of genocide and the political groups that addressed it explicitly. Such silence is all the more puzzling given that CAPA's archives suggest that not only was Zinzun deep in his studies of antiblack genocide but that he also privately supported a 1996 Black-led charge of genocide against the US government. The charge was based on extensive research conducted by several individuals and organizations—some of which gained national attention, such as Gary Webb's investigative reporting contending that the US government, at the very least, had detailed knowledge of the drug trade in various inner cities.

The considerations i put forward are in the spirit of a concept Zinzun valued greatly, that of an unflinching self-critique. The constant analysis and calibration of political imagination and strategy were some of the most precious lessons i learned from him. This essay reflects both my respect for Zinzun and my attempt to put to work some of the epistemological principles on which he based his praxis, including the necessary constant reformulation of one's temporary truths. What would Michael think of a principled critique of his political work? i can hear him say it: "Right on!"

In what follows, 1) i submit and explain the proposition that CAPA's political imagination was based on the principle of *dialogical autonomy*. By providing a brief account of CAPA's programs and daily activities, 2) i then analyze Zinzun's relationship with the National Black United Front (NBUF) and its 1996 campaign against the genocide of Black people. Specifically, i ask, why didn't genocide become part of CAPA's conceptual universe and public intervention? I conclude by 3) drawing insights into the relationship between dialogical autonomy, non-Black episodic engagement with Black suffering, and the legitimization of the empire-state.

With B. Kwaku Duren and Anthony Thigpenn, Michael Zinzun was a cofounder, in 1975, of the Coalition Against Police Abuse in Los Angeles. Drawing on his seemingly indefatigable political energy, Zinzun became CAPA's main organizer, and in his daily practice reenacted and adapted many of the Black Power concepts and the Black Panther Party's orientations and symbology. Zinzun had joined the Southern California chapter of the BPP in 1970 but left about three years later due to the escalation of internal disputes and the dismantling of the party, in great measure a result of the FBI's counterintelligence operations. For over three decades, CAPA was active in a historical Black area of South Central Los Angeles whose racial demography was rapidly changing. Whereas South Central was about 80 percent Black in the 1970s, it was 50.3 percent Black in the 1990s, when Latinxs became 44 percent of its inhabitants.[2] There, Zinzun and his collaborators catalogued, investigated, and provided legal, logistical, and moral support to victims of police abuse. Yet the quotidian events of state violence, as predictable, time-consuming, and exacting as they were, constituted only one of CAPA's foci. Police abuse events were theoretically framed as opportunities to mobilize oppressed communities and inform them not only of their legal rights but also about local organizations and the types of support they offered. Like the Panthers, CAPA organized a series of survival programs intended to instruct, capacitate, and empower marginalized persons, specifically Black youths. The term "survival" was purposeful: the Panthers often verbalized that Black people in the US were under genocidal threat.[3] While CAPA organizers also studied the multiple facets of antiblack genocide, their actions, as i show below, were not as explicitly formulated against genocide.

I.

Inordinately dependent on Zinzun's strategic mind, committed energy, and financial resources, CAPA elaborated and practiced its programs based on the concept of *dialogical autonomy*. While the Black Power insistence on Black autonomy was evident in CAPA's emphasis on Black pride and Black political, logistical, legal, and mobilizing know-how, the dialogical orientation—one that sought collaboration with nonblack, civil society, and state political actors—was also accentuated. Dialogical autonomy meant the coexistence of two seemingly conflicting principles. On the one hand, it was manifested in the recurring attempts at, and successful realization of, Black-nonblack dialogue and practical collaborations. Such efforts included engaging with nonblack individuals and organizations, elected officials, news media personnel, courts, police departments, and other state apparatuses more generally. On the other hand, the *autonomy* component of dialogical autonomy required Black self-determination as a foundational and guiding principle, which in turn resulted from a critical recognition and an ensuing imperative. The critical recognition was that processes of exclusion and violence, vis-à-vis nonblack nonwhites, affected Black people disproportionately and distinctively, thus fundamentally. The ensuing imperative—the corollary of the critical recognition—was that Black people needed to assert their own analytical and political agendas. Both the critical recognition and its imperative drew from the concept of Black Power, exercised for generations in a variety of communities in the US and the Black diaspora. In Kwame Ture and Charles Hamilton's *Black Power*, the concept is presented as "a call for black people in this country to unite, to recognize their heritage, to build a sense of community. It is a call for black people to begin to define their own goals, to lead their own organizations and to support those organizations. It is a call to reject the racist institutions and values of this society."[4] Indeed, institutional racism, while operating independently of personal values and actions, "relies on the active and pervasive operation of anti-black attitudes and practices."[5] Ture and Hamilton go on to define the concept of Black Power: "Before a group can enter the open society, it must first close ranks. By this we mean that group solidarity is necessary before a group can operate effectively from a bargaining position of strength in a pluralistic society."[6]

CAPA activists did not often mention the term "antiblackness," yet their praxes suggested a comprehensive understanding of the concept: Black people's singular and fundamental place of exclusion in the constitution of the modern empire-staté.[7] Influenced by Black Power via Zinzun's experience with the Panthers, CAPA underscored Black autonomy, which was at the basis of the organization's theoretical and practical efforts. Theoretical efforts included seminars on the writings of Karl Marx, W. E. B. Du Bois, Mao Zedong, Frantz Fanon, and Assata Shakur about topics such as surveillance technologies, transnationalism, liberalism, health disparities, housing alternative materials, and self-help. They aimed at furthering a critical understanding of the empire-state apparatus, and how it affected, policed, and killed the oppressed in general and Black communities in particular. Practical efforts consisted of specific programs whose objectives were to mobilize, inform, and capacitate the people most affected by policies of marginalization.

A consequence of the adoption of *dialogical autonomy* is that, while recognizing the theoretical and practical validity of the Black-only orientation that was present in Black Power theoretical perspectives as well as endorsed strategically in formative moments of the BPP, CAPA's multiracial positioning, the result of tactical decisions accumulated over two decades of intensive activism, often overshadowed conceptual and organizing emphases on Black experiences and antiblackness.[8] Such decisions blunted, and often crowded out, CAPA's desires of Black autonomy, including Black theoretical autonomy. By Black theoretical autonomy i mean the will and capacity to zero in on Black experiences as the fundamental basis from which to critically understand the meta-theories, the elementary aspects, the modes of sociality, as well as the structural mechanics of the modern republic. Black theoretical autonomy requires a sustained focus on and a comprehensive grasp of blackness and antiblackness, which in turn informs the *possibility* of an analytical effort that considers nonblack experiences. I stress "possibility" to contrast Black theoretical autonomy to what, arguably, has become a canonical conceptual orientation in progressive political spaces, including Black Power–inflected blocs, namely, the *necessity* of engaging nonblack experiences.

When i make the distinction between these analytical perspectives, i do not want to negate the epistemological validity of studying Black experiences in conjunction with, and necessarily related to, nonblack experiences, and the ways in which they inform each other. The effort here is not to enact "oppression Olympics" and claim that Black experiences and antiblackness trump all other forms of oppression. It is analytically myopic to dismiss the manners by which distinct gendered/sexualized/racialized experiences are necessarily connected to (even though they may not be commensurable with) each other. Furthermore, it is politically naïve, perhaps even suicidal, especially in the US, where Blacks are just over 12 percent of the population, to preemptively negate multiracial alliances as a potentially effective strategy to pressure established forms of power and distribution of resources.[9] It goes without saying that political imagination and analysis are indissociable.

The effort, rather, is to engage the specificity of Black experiences. Which means being aware of the conceptual work that the canonical accusation of playing "oppression Olympics" performs, namely, the disavowal of the focus on antiblackness. To engage antiblackness is to recognize the diasporically multiple, ubiquitous, transhistorical, and persistent forms of dehumanization that affect Black people singularly (although of course not exclusively); the ways in which antiblackness impacts nonblacks; and the common societal forces that affect Blacks and nonblacks. In other words, while antiblackness is foundational, it engages differently situated subjects distinctively, and interacts with other forms of oppression, such as those related to cisheteropatriarchal forms of capitalistic exploitation and alienation.[10]

Hence the necessity of zeroing in on Black experiences, not only because of the pragmatic and indisputably singular social and ontological effects of antiblackness on the Black person, but also because her unique positionality is indicative of the myriad ways in which modern life and death worlds are constituted.[11] By focusing on blackness and antiblackness, we are compelled to substitute the progressive analytical dyad white-nonwhite, from which the people-of-color framework operates and the corresponding political blocs are formed, for the dyad Black-nonblack, which allows for an appraisal of the persistence, ubiquity, and intensity of antiblackness.[12]

Such considerations allow for an assessment of the ways in which CAPA, and its embodiment of BPP and Black Power visions, engaged nonblack political actors and sought the formation of multiracial collective blocs as strategies to influence cultural understandings, information media, the electoral process, and various apparatuses of the empire-state machinery. What explains such multiracial analytical and political drives? What prevented a more sustained focus on the specificities of Black experiences and Black autonomous forms of reflection and organization? By answering these questions, we will be able to better understand the successes and shortcomings of Black initiatives that, like those in which Zinzun played a prominent role, were inspired by Black Power and, more broadly, Black diasporic radical traditions.[13] These interrogations enable a comprehension of the reasons for CAPA's muted public support for Black-led initiatives explicitly denouncing antiblack genocide.

II.

To illustrate CAPA's relationship to Black autonomy as well as its tendency to accentuate multiracial common denominators, often at the expense of a more sustained focus on antiblack processes, i discuss Zinzun's relationship with the National Black United Front (NBUF), of which he was a founding member. NBUF was a left-leaning and nationalist organization formed in the late 1970s in Brooklyn and based in Chicago in the 1980s and 1990s. Specifically, i focus on NBUF's campaign against the state- and society-sanctioned genocide of Black people in the US. Although Zinzun was an active member of NBUF, a participant of its regional and national encounters, genocide was never part of CAPA's public vocabulary, much less of its organizational concepts. Such absence, i contend, was largely due to a model of multiracial organizing whose principle required the establishment of common experiences of oppression among Black and nonblack groups. The resulting multiracial blocs that formed around specific objectives, such as the 1987 campaign to prevent Zinzun's incarceration following his pacific involvement in a case of police brutality, were often energized by collective moral outrage at injustice and suffering inflicted on Black people.[14] Yet while such multiracial blocs were effective in generating public visibility and pressure, they prevented a deeper and more consequential engagement with the antiblack aspects of, in this case, police brutality specifically and social marginalization more generally. I am, thus, arguing that dialogical autonomy, though effective in agglutinating progressive multiracial constituencies around common social justice agendas, often required the bracketing of the focus on the specificities of Black experiences, *even when Black experiences of suffering galvanized the mobilizations.* The problem becomes even more complex when we notice that dialogical autonomy, as exercised by Black Power advocates and BPP members, often meant that the ensuing political bloc's leadership was composed mostly, if not exclusively, of Black persons. Zinzun's political efforts seldom escaped the conundrum, even though he seemed quite aware of it.

When CAPA emerged in 1975, it unapologetically continued several of the BPP's survival programs.[15] Many of its activities provided legal, logistical, and moral support to victims of police brutality. The coalition employed a constantly developing blueprint of activism that sought to rally the (rapidly changing but still) majority-Black residents of South Central Los Angeles. CAPA's manual of community organizing made it evident that cases of police brutality were to be transformed into mobilizing opportunities seeking long-term solutions to problems endemic to impoverished zones. "To this end," stated its Community Organization Manual, "CAPA has developed what it believes to be a highly effective organizing technique applicable to all communities. This technique is based on organizing in the wake of specific cases of police abuse. It can be done effectively in three steps: I. Document the case, II. Reach the people, and III. Mobilize the people."[16]

Endemic structural problems included unemployment; shortage of affordable housing; lack of daycare facilities and supervised leisure activities for youths; substandard formal education that lacked a recognition of Black people's complex historical and ongoing experiences; susceptibility to disease due to stress, malnutrition, exposure to environmental toxins, poor sanitation, and infestation by pests such as cockroaches, mice, and rats; and deficient public transportation, among others. For each of these problems, and continuing the BPP's survival programs, CAPA elaborated corresponding initiatives. To combat unemployment, CAPA offered training in various technical skills and job interview classes. Individuals received instructions on how to approach an employment interview, including appropriate clothing, which the organization would lend, rent, or help acquire. CAPA also housed many professionalization classes. For example, shortly after i joined the organization in 1995, i collaborated with Zinzun in developing a computer literacy program targeting youths who participated in the gang truce. With his own funds, Zinzun purchased several used computers. We then created a curriculum to be taught over eight weeks, at the end of which, for the students who demonstrated proficiency with the basic operation of the hardware and of word processing software, we issued course completion certificates. Some of those students started their own computer-related business, and following the communitarian responsibility perspective we stressed from the course's first day, insisted on participating in our classes as unpaid instructors. As well, CAPA invested in the formation and maintenance of the "Off the Roach" program. Reminiscent of a similar program Zinzun developed with the BPP, the "Free Pest Control," it was carried out by groups of youths who would, for donation fees, treat homes with boric acid guns. Before being deemed competent to work in the program, the youths underwent a rigorous course on pest control, including a graded final examination.[17] The boric acid guns were the result of Zinzun's long-term research on insects, including several conferences he had with entomologists at the University of California, Los Angeles. Zinzun's notes on this topic, as well as the various specialized academic articles on cockroaches, related diseases, and safe and environmentally sound methods of pest control, give us a sense of the groundbreaking work on health he and his collaborators conducted between the late 1960s and the 1990s. He often stated that "the Panthers were the first to come up with programs to test for sickle cell anemia before anyone could spell it."[18] The same was true for CAPA regarding the effective approach to eradicating domestic pests and thus reducing related illnesses.

Upon studying the CAPA papers at the Southern California Library, it became evident that the physical well-being of Black people was the fulcrum of Zinzun's preoccupations. The "Off the Roach" program was innovative not only due to the cutting-edge research conducted on the ways in which domestic insects caused or aggravated respiratory ailments such as asthma and a variety of debilitating infections, allergies, and chronic conditions among Black people. It was innovative also because, stressing the need to "TCB," or take care of business, as Black Power proponents insisted, it generated a source of autonomous income for local Black youths.[19] Such was the orientation behind other CAPA programs: silk screening, photography, video and filmmaking, computer literacy, public speaking, conflict resolution, and transportation for the elderly and incapacitated, among many others.[20]

This brief account of CAPA's daily activities and survival programs is meant as a contextualization for Zinzun's interest in the concept of genocide. Zinzun was aware of the 1951 publication of *We Charge Genocide*, and the mobilization that led to and followed it. He frequently mentioned the multiple factors that resulted in Black people dying prematurely (including suicide), and thus explained the Panthers and CAPA's multipronged approach of survival programs that focused on housing, nutrition, well-being, information, and technical skills. Even though Zinzun did not frequently employ the concept of genocide as developed in the Civil Rights Congress document William Patterson edited—and whose substance benefited from previous work by W. E. B. Du Bois and Paul Robeson, among many others.[21] Like them, he was acutely aware of the multiple and interrelated manners in which Black people were subjected to societal forces that resulted in a shorter collective life span relative to nonblacks. The concept of genocide was part of a critical analytical framework that recognized (a) the multiple and mutually reinforcing aspects of Black imposed marginalization, and (b) the ways in which it was part of a continuum. On this latter point, Zinzun often invited discussions on the relationships between collectively shared agreements, conscious and unconscious, and the elaboration and implementation of policy. For example, common tropes of "the urban youth," which paradigmatically referred to Black young people presumed to be violent and indeed nonhuman, served as justification, even if only tacit, for aggressive policing tactics as well as more severe sentencing guidelines.[22] Consequently, there existed a continuum—from popular representations to the elaboration and implementation of public policy—in which symbolic violence allowed for, and justified, quotidian forms of actual antiblack violence. In other words, for the Black to be continuously brutalized (actual violence), she has to be always and already rendered abject and less-than-human (symbolic violence).

In 1996, NBUF called on the United Nations to label an act of genocide the charges that the CIA had introduced crack cocaine to South Central

Los Angeles. In a newspaper clipping on which Zinzun had underlined several passages, Conrad Worrill, NBUF's chair, "said he believes there is a link between the introduction of crack cocaine in African American areas and the proliferation of imprisonment of African Americans, the three-strikes-and-you're-out policy and mandatory sentencing." In the article, Worrill is quoted as saying "We want the U.N. to affirm that genocide is taking place against Blacks in America."[23] Zinzun followed NBUF's genocide campaign closely. On May 14, 1997, for example, he received, by mail, in a manila envelope addressed to the Western Avenue CAPA office, notes from the NBUF's spring central committee meeting in Houston. Worrill signed the document by hand.

Why didn't Zinzun talk openly about the genocide campaign? Why didn't genocide become part of CAPA's conceptual universe and public intervention? The questions become intriguing when we notice that, at about the same time when NBUF's campaign against the genocide of Black people in the US was beginning, there were multiple newspaper articles, television programs, documentaries, and public events, in response to a 1996 series of articles by Gary Webb published in the *San Jose Mercury News*. Webb's articles suggested that CIA agents had facilitated the selling of drugs in Black neighborhoods in the US in order to generate revenue for anti-Sandinista, known as the Contras, military efforts, in Nicaragua.[24] Although dominant news media such as the *Los Angeles Times* and the *New York Times* claimed Webb's research overstated the government's involvement, there remained a strong consensus among Black people in the most affected areas, such as South Central Los Angeles, about the important role that the US government played in the so-called drug epidemic, at minimum because the state did not intervene to prevent its spread.

In response to the overwhelming negative response Webb's reporting garnered among Black people, on Friday, November 15, 1996, CIA director John Deutch spoke at a public event in Watts. Zinzun and other CAPA members attended the meeting at the Locke High School, on East 111st Street. It was an unusual occasion because public discussions are not part of the secretive CIA's mode of operation. Although the *Los Angeles Times* described the audience as "skeptical and irate," and stated that Deutch spent much of his time "fighting off hecklers," the thousand-person crowd, composed mostly of local residents, elected representatives, and activists, demonstrated a willingness to both listen to Deutch and affirm their belief that there was government collusion with the drug trade.[25] Rather than summarily negate

Webb's allegations, Deutch pledged to conduct a more extensive inquiry into the matter. "I ask you all," he said, "to keep your minds open until we have a thorough investigation."[26] One of the memorable moments in the Watts town hall happened when former Los Angeles police officer Mike Ruppert, stated, "I will tell you, Director Deutch, as a former Los Angeles Police narcotics detective, that the agency has dealt drugs throughout this country for a long time."[27]

In 1997, Zinzun aired an episode titled "Crisis of Cocaine" in his *Message to the Grassroots* weekly cable TV program, where he made similar claims about government involvement, if only due to inaction, in the rapid expansion of crack cocaine commerce in US Black communities starting in the early 1990s. Through his research, he amassed a sizeable archive of information about the drug smuggling and commerce in the inner cities: newspaper and magazine clippings, television news footage, and videotaped interviews with former dealers and law enforcement agents.

All of which is to say that Zinzun's decision not to make the so-called crack epidemic part of CAPA's activism, and, more generally, not to render the concept of genocide an element of the coalition's public political vocabulary is puzzling. What explains the decision? As someone who had spent most of his lifetime addressing the excesses of the empire-state and had personally suffered much violence and degradation at the hands of official bureaucracies such as local law enforcement and the FBI, Zinzun was no stranger to the government's role in perpetuating, at the very least by indecision, various forms of Black people's marginalization and early death by preventable causes. Indeed, while surveilling his every move since at least his time with the BPP, the FBI had deemed him "potentially dangerous," "subversive," as someone who presented "evidence of emotional instability (including unstable residence and employment record) or irrational or suicidal behavior," whose "prior acts (including arrests or convictions) or conduct or statements" indicated "a propensity for violence and antipathy toward good order and government"[28] Signed by J. Edgar Hoover, FBI director, on November 2, 1971, this memorandum, obtained via one of the many Freedom of Information Act requests Zinzun filed over the years, offers a brief window into the ubiquity of government presence in the lives of, not only those considered political threats but also, and more importantly, those inhabiting social spaces assumed to be incubators of discontent and opposition. Black social spaces were then, and remain, specifically targeted by intensive forms of surveillance, overtly and covertly.[29] As Zinzun liked to recount, CAPA had been infiltrated since its inception. Its own staff, occasional collaborators, allied protestors—and even the seemingly amiable woman next door to the office on Western Avenue who owned a small restaurant—all turned out to be paid LAPD informants.[30]

Zinzun's most severe experience of brutalization by the police happened in his own Pasadena neighborhood where, in the early hours of June 22, 1986, Steve Rivers, a Black man, was arrested on suspicion of burglary. As officers beat him with their batons, Rivers, already sprayed with Mace, handcuffed and lying on the ground, cried for help.[31] His shouts awakened many of the surrounding residents; to see what was going on, dozens of people poured out of their homes, including Frank Taylor and Michael Zinzun. When Taylor and Zinzun pleaded to get the officers' names and badge numbers, they were brutally beaten and arrested for "interfering with police."[32] Maced and struck with a flashlight, Zinzun suffered a severe gash on his head, which required forty stitches on his face and scalp. Such was the violence with which he was met that his skull was fractured. His left eye's optic nerve did not resist the flashlight blows and became detached, making him blind in that eye. Fifteen months after a protracted legal battle and mobilization effort, the city of Pasadena agreed to an out-of-court settlement that awarded $1.2 million to Zinzun, to be paid over thirty-five years. Legal victory notwithstanding, the physical and psychological damage was irreparable.[33]

It was not a lack of comprehensive experiential, shared, and intentionally accumulated knowledge about government actions in Black social spaces and their transgenerational negative consequences that prevented Zinzun and his local political blocs from embracing the concept of genocide.[34]

III.

The claim of antiblack genocide requires a suspension of accepted progressive wisdom that stresses experiential commonalities between Blacks and non-blacks. Instead, it affirms the specificity of Black experiences.[35] It dramatically alters the political stakes. Rather than reform, what is required under the aegis of antiblack genocide is a complete negation of formations of cognition, sociality, resource distribution, and indeed modes of political thought and action. Perhaps this is what Ture and Hamilton had in mind when they stated: "Of necessity, this means that the existing systems of the dominant, oppressive groups—the entire spectrum of values, beliefs, traditions and institutions—will have to be challenged and changed."[36] If the Black is to become whole, repossess her being, the structures of the mind and of the lifeworld that make her a necessary nonperson need to be annihilated. It is therefore unsurprising that, even though Zinzun was a consistent NBUF supporter, his political bloc's commitment to redeeming the imperial-state project of multiracial inclusion made it impossible to openly endorse anti-antiblack genocide agendas.

Dialogical autonomy, and the prize it puts on the need for Blacks to establish dialogues with the nonblack, can therefore be understood as a result of the imperative of multiracial translatability. A political calculation based on the principle of multiracial experiential common denominators, dialogical autonomy recognizes the singularity of gendered Black experiences, but opts to stress lines of experiential continuity between nonblack and Black social groups. The critique i draw here is not an a priori stance against the establishment of nonblack-Black translatability and political alliances. Rather, it is a plea to consider Black-nonblack alliances a possibility, and not a necessity, as it seems to be currently normative; and to linger on the uniqueness and fundamental cognitive and social role antiblackness plays in the constitution of our worldwide sociability. It is not to discount nonblack experiences or their connections to blackness. In the swiftness with which progressive Black and pro-Black fronts seek commonalities with the nonblack, they often relinquish an autonomous analysis that identifies—or, at the very least, considers—antiblackness as a central element of diasporic social formations. Indeed, Ture and Hamilton conclude *Black Power* by emphasizing the singularity of the Black experience, and how this experience of imposed abjection dialectically creates a unique critical angle, an epistemic privilege. "In this country," they stated, "we therefore anticipate that the oppressed black people are the most legitimate and the most likely group to put the system to the test, to put the hard questions. Professor Kenneth Clark wrote: 'The Negro in America, by virtue of the pervasive patterns of racial rejection, exclusion or a token and often self-conscious acceptance by a minority of white liberals, has been forced into a degree of alienation and detachment which has resulted in a pattern of social and personality consequences. *Among these consequences has been sharpened insights and increased sensitivity to some of the subtle forces which are significant in our complex social structure.*'"[37]

Black dialogical autonomy that emphasizes multiracial translatability not only was a defining aspect of CAPA, but also explains progressive efforts related to the diasporic Black Lives Matter movement. As it concerns such initiatives, it is not uncommon for mobilizations that arise from the death of an unarmed Black woman, man, or child, to swiftly claim that "police brutality impacts all of us," as if Black individuals are not the disproportionate target of institutionalized discrimination and police lethal intervention.[38] For example, the International Socialist Organization, a pro-Black multiracial progressive front, recently claimed that "following the murders of Michael Brown, Eric Garner, Aiyana Jones, Larry Jackson, and dozens of other innocent people of color, a new movement is finding its place in the fight for justice. To succeed, the Black Lives Matter movement needs a solid understanding of where this systemic racism comes from and how it supports the ruling class."[39] It is the seemingly normative ease with which this political bloc moves from the state-induced and extralegal murders of Black people to "dozens of innocent people of color" that is at the heart of the multiracial translatability imperative, the people-of-color framework, and the multiracial bloc it intends to bring together. An analysis of structural and foundational antiblackness as the source of Black death is pushed aside; systematic racism and capitalism become the common sources of suffering across lines of race, gender, sexuality, and nationality. From this blueprint, the pro-Black multiracial bloc emerges vibrant.

While the multiracial political blocs that congregated around the coalition often synthesized their political energy from the moral outrage at Black suffering, due to their driving principle—a people-of-color emphasis on common experiences of oppression—they were unable and unwilling to accentuate the singularity of Black experiences. To do so would not only force a reassessment of the terms under which the multiracial bloc came to being but also, and more importantly, the political strategies emanating from such terms. In the practice of CAPA activists, in line with Black Power theses, there existed a well-crafted multipronged approach to engaging, opposing, inhabiting, and eventually reforming the empire-state. This multipronged approach depended on the multiracial bloc's ultimate belief in the redemption of the entire formation of society, its worldviews, apparatuses, and modes of operation.

Such reformist orientation was quite evident in the Black Power theses. Kwame Ture bluntly affirmed that *Black Power* did not advocate for revolution: "It preaches reform."[40] Black Power had a clear anticapitalist vision and wanted a society free from exploitation. Yet it argued for political action within the law, action that sought to capture power through autonomous Black local organizing and the establishment of multiracial alliances. In a 1992 afterword, Ture reminded his readers that "all action proposed in the book is legal."[41] The absence of antiblack genocide in the progressive and even radical political vocabulary across the diaspora can be attributed, at least in part, to the symbiosis between (a) the principle of common experiences of oppression under cisheteronormative capitalist white supremacy according to which people-of-color political blocs converge, and (b) the legal and reformist agendas that seek to render the empire-state a tool of social justice and inclusion. According to this perspective, rather than an impossible project of multiracial integration, the empire-state, although reluctantly so, is porous to Black demands, and therefore salvageable.[42] The reformist Black-led multiracial bloc, although outraged by examples of antiblack brutality, is fundamentally optimistic; it embraces the future as the eventual realization of its dreams of inclusion.

Even avoiding the structural and foundational analysis of antiblackness, Michael Zinzun's lifelong efforts at building and sustaining multiracial blocs, which in turn sought to engage, inhabit, and transform the empire-state, showed that the possibility of *sustained* Black-nonblack collaboration was hardly actualized. Translation across Black-nonblack experiences, save for the moments of widespread indignation following well-publicized state-sanctioned brutality, seems like an unrealized project. CAPA's office remained predominantly Black throughout its two decades of existence, as did the staff and participants in key events to which Zinzun lent his energy and funds.[43] It is no accident that, as soon as Zinzun died, so did CAPA and the Community in Support of the Gang Truce, one of the many organizations housed in, related to, and dependent on the coalition. Similar insights can be drawn from the mobilizations that followed well-publicized acts of brutalization, including those against Zinzun.

Why don't similar mobilizations, including sustained study and research, happen around the *mundane expendability of Black life*? It is this quality of being unimaginable in times other than when there emerges multiracial episodic moral indignation, derived from activist efforts, and news and social media occasional evidence of inflicted terror on Black people, that renders unlikely the coming to terms with structural antiblackness. As long as Black pain is perceived as intermittent, rather than structural and foundational, antiblackness will remain unchallenged. Zinzun wanted to be ready for revolution. Yet the multiracial blocs that congregated around Zinzun were unwilling and/or unable to grasp that, above and beyond integration, social transfiguration requires an unapologetic confrontation with the very terms of this society's structuration, itself based on the unique, and perhaps untranslatable, dehumanization of Black people.

VI.

BLACK PANTHER LEGACIES IN A TIME OF NEOLIBERALISM

Southerners on New Ground (SONG), Durham chapter, and BYP100 calling for the end of pretrial detention at the 2018 Black Mama's Day Bailout Action. Since 1993 SONG has organized for Black and racial liberation, immigrant and undocumented rights, people with disabilities, working-class people, rural people, and LGBTQ people in the South. Photo courtesy of Serena Sebring

CHAPTER FIFTEEN

Black Queer Feminism and the Movement for Black Lives in the South: An Interview with Mary Hooks of SONG

Diane C. Fujino and Felice Blake

Mary Hooks is codirector of Southerners on New Ground (SONG), which began in 1993 as a queer liberation organization that struggles on many fronts for Black and racial liberation, immigrant and undocumented rights, for people with disabilities, working-class, and rural LGBTQ people in the South. Since the emergence of the current iteration of the Black liberation movement, SONG has joined the Movement for Black Lives (M4BL), composed of more than a hundred Black-led organizations. Hooks was on the planning committee for the inaugural conference for the M4BL in Cleveland in 2015. She cofounded the Black Lives Matter chapter in Atlanta. She is the originator and organizer of the Black Mama's Bailout campaign.

Diane Fujino: *The focus of this interview is to examine Black feminist and queer organizing with a focus on how the Black Panther Party and Black Power shape today's organizing. When I spoke with you earlier, you mentioned that the Black Panther Party was important to your own political development. Could you speak more about how the Panthers impacted you as well as other major influences on your own activism? I'm curious about their impact on SONG as well.*

Mary Hooks: I would say one of the watershed moments in my life was when Elaine Brown, the only woman to head the Black Panther Party, came to my very Lutheran, predominantly white college. This was probably 2003. I remember when she spoke, it literally blew my mind. It was the first time that I heard an analysis around the "war on drugs." The way she talked about revolution and the work of the Black Panther Party was deeply inspiring, but also left me feeling like there is so much that I hadn't been taught as a young person through high school and college as it relates to Black liberation struggles beyond the civil rights movement and the watered-down version that we got in public school. Elaine Brown ended up convening the few young Black students. I recall her giving us the mandate and charge around the next generation's role and work around Black liberation. After hearing her talk, I began deep personal research around the war on drugs and systemic oppression. That was my first opening to the Black Panther Party in such a visceral way.

I moved to Georgia in 2007 and met a woman, Paris Hatcher, at a bar one night who told me about the work she was doing to stop the shackling of Black women while giving birth. She introduced me to her political home, which was SONG. Southerners on New Ground (SONG) is a regional queer liberation organization made up of Black people, people of color, immigrants, undocumented people, people with disabilities, working-class and rural and small-town LGBTQ people in the South. We believe that we are bound together by a shared desire for ourselves, each other, and our communities to survive and thrive. We believe that community organizing is the best way for us to build collective power and transform the South. Out of this belief we are committed to building freedom movements rooted in Southern traditions like community organizing, political education, storytelling, music, breaking bread, resistance, humor, performance, critical thinking, and celebration.

SONG was started by three white lesbians and three Black lesbians, all who had come out of previous movements. Most of the founders were older—the youngest was like forty-five and maybe up to sixty—when they started the organization. Many had ties to the antiviolence movement, the traditional civil rights movement, and antiracist work exposing the Klan. Mandy Carter, for example, came out of the Quaker tradition and antiwar movements. That's how SONG started. Once I became a member, a lot of my political development came through Kai Lumumba Barrow, who came up through the Black Panther Party out of Chicago and found her way doing work in the South. She's also one of the founders of Critical Resistance. She was brought onto staff in 2011 to train up the few of us whom at the time they called the Raw Stallions because we were new or "green" organizers. Before the hiring of Kai and the Raw Stallions, SONG had only two staff members, codirectors Paulina Helm-Hernandez and Caitlin Breedlove, and they were building and rebuilding the organization and membership structure as well as beginning to position the membership and Raw Stallions to wage organizing campaigns. Kai came in and helped do some of the leadership and campaign development as well as transferring major historical and movement memory. She brought the analysis around Black liberation in a particular way and so in those earlier days, I deepened my understanding of the Black Panther Party platform and their programs. That helped us to think about how we would build our campaigns and how we understand issues to be widely and deeply felt.

Part of SONG's work has always relied on the historical memory, legacy, and past social movements that got us to where we are. We see ourselves within the lineage of the Black Radical Tradition that comes out of the South. When I think about other ways that we've been influenced, there's so much that continues to amaze me about the work of the Black Panther Party. Many of us grapple with how to support current political prisoners who have come out of that work and there are many organizations that provide us entry points into doing so. We also grapple with what is at stake and at risk for us who are now taking up this legacy of work. There are other comrades too in our generation standing trial or who are also political prisoners we work to hold down and lift up. I could go on, but those are some of the ways the Black Panther Party's influence resonates deeply with me inside my political home.

DF: *As you talk about the Black Radical Tradition, I'm thinking about W. E. B. Du Bois's ideas on abolition democracy, and Angela Davis on prison abolitionism, and the Black Panther Party working not only to dismantle unjust laws, but also to create these alternative institutions based on self-determination and Black power. I know SONG embraces a politic of abolitionism. Can you speak to what you mean by "abolition" and how it fits within this longer trajectory of Black radical organizing?*

MH: People believe that it's in our spirit, that for the descendants of Africans and those who made it through the Middle Passage the demand has always been abolition. Whether that's the system of chattel slavery, Jim Crow, or the prison-industrial complex, when we talk about abolition it's very much in the framework of Angela Davis. Many of us have given voice to making sure that we not just tear down the walls of prisons, but we actually have a cultural shift around the way we think about punishment and the way we embody different practices and processes to address harm, not just in the US, but globally. This thinking has guided our work as it relates to ending deportation and "melting ICE," as well as our work around ending money bail and pretrial detention. The long goal is abolition. It's not enough just to point out how flawed and how horrible this system is, but we're also responsible for taking on abolitionist reforms in order to tear it down brick by brick. That's our work in the Free from Fear campaigns that SONG is moving. We grapple with the question, "What do we need to be building in this time?" So even when we're bailing people out like we did a few weekends ago, we go back and forth, "Are we a bail fund?" We're trying to bring more political clarity around the need for direct service *and* organizing to be in better relationship with one another. Given the context of our social conditions and climate, we would be naïve to say that we could engage this prison-industrial complex without understanding that our folks have been deeply impacted by it for centuries and decades. This has to be a significant part of our work. Models like the Silicon Valley De-Bug, an amazing organization, [have] done a lot of work teaching our folks about participatory defense and providing resources to families and communities to help get their people out of jail. We just helped seed an organization in 2018 that grew out of our bailout work called the Center for Resilient Individuals, Families, and Communities. I just came back from New Orleans, and we're organizing an apprenticeship program for the moms that we bail out who get that taste of freedom once they get the dollar. They're like, "Hey, I want to organize! This is powerful work!" We want to be able to give folk the tools that they need to become leaders in their community as relates to grassroots organizing. I always try to bring the lesson from the decisions that we're making and try to sharpen our strategy as we continue to learn more about what it's going to take to get our people free.

Felice Blake: *Yeah, that's all so powerful. As you were talking I was just thinking about some of the work I do in teaching Black feminism, but also in teaching and connecting questions around gender and sexuality to the work that we do in relation to the jail and in the community. One of the things that happens* *when we think about the Panthers is that the history of Black feminist organizing and analysis doesn't always have a clear home within that history and what we see now. Of course, something like #MeToo was also started by and was about Black women. Yet even in our own moment we see how our understanding of the #MeToo movement and why it's happening needs to be informed by discussions about race, gender, sexuality, poverty, and so on. As you were just talking about the bailout campaign, I became interested in the way that, in the process, people are redefining what is a "mother," by looking at this long history of incarceration in relation to race, motherhood, and oppression, but also right now: how do we understand care giving, giving care, receiving, taking care of each other, and so on? So how do these questions about gender impact how we remember the Panthers? How have critical questions stemming from Black chauvinism or Black people's own investments in patriarchy shaped the way you work? How does SONG engage these issues?*

MH: SONG comes too out of a Black feminist tradition and practice, while simultaneously being a multiracial, cross-class, cross-gender organization. We don't see this as an organizational contradiction but an asset and understand Black feminist traditions, also often relegated to the historical sidelines, to be so profoundly politically life-giving. And one can adhere to or embody these principles of Black feminism across identity. One of the movement elders out of the South, our beloved Ruby Sales, comes out of SNCC actually. I don't know if she ever engaged in work around the Black Power movement explicitly. One of the things that strikes me as you were talking about #MeToo is something that she has laid on our hearts to grapple with. We saw the ways of the #MeToo movement as it relates to white women and their naming of being violated. Then we learned about Tarana Burke. One of the things that has been really amazing about Burke, as Mama Ruby was saying, "We as Black women who live at these intersections, we cannot take on the ways in which white women come out a tradition of saying, 'This person winked at me.' And then the next thing we knew someone is getting lynched or castrated." So we still have to hold these values of redemption, these values of truth telling. We have to be able to do so with due process whether that's inside of a courtroom or through community processes, to always speak the truth and not just anyone can say a thing happened and take it at face value. Not to interrogate the victim, but we also have to be in our integrity as we're talking about the ways in which harm has happened. So that's something we also carry inside of our work.

Oftentimes people ask, "Well, who do you bail out? Are you bailing out people with dangerous charges?" We're like, "Innocent until proven guilty. At this point in the game no one has been charged with anything. It is not our role and work to do that." But we should be trying to make more expansive the work we do outside of the court.

One of the goals for SONG, as it relates to how we're thinking about gender and caretaking, one of the things that we talked about when bailing out Black mothers was to make sure that when we talk about who's "mothering," we want to talk about the grandmothers who are taking care of second and third generations. We want to talk about the trans women who are raising up the girls in the clubs. They are caretaking and providing and raising up community, whether they bore them or not. Part of our mandate is to also to bail out Black trans women. We learned how spiteful the system is in how our people, and people in general, are categorized and caged. Oftentimes Black trans women are housed on the men's, side and it's based on the discretion of the officer that's processing them. Usually they're looking to see if this woman had top surgery, or if her wig can be taken off. This is a huge, contentious issue as it relates to queer nonbinary people. So these are all the things we're grappling with as we try to make sure that we are involved in the conversation, "Who are we talking about when we talk about who's mothering and who's raising children?"

DF: Mary, I have been so impressed with the ways that SONG works. Many people now use this term "intersectionality," but SONG seems to be practicing a radical intersectionality. On your website you have the Spanish language before English. You talk about Black people and people of color, about gender and sexuality, but you're also looking to undocumented people, ableism, so much more. I'm wondering if you can speak to what changes when Black feminist queer politics are put front and center?

MH: Oh my! I think that becomes the antidote, the solution to white supremacist heteropatriarchy. This is how we need to be moving. This is the politics, values that we should be adopting. My partner Charlene, she often talks about how the analysis of Black queer feminist politics helps people understand what it means to be a Black queer feminist. But then the ideology is an open invitation to everybody. Something that's really important, and Charlene stresses this a lot, just because you embody these identities does not make you inherently a Black queer feminist. That's something we have to continuously not be liberal around—the gendered movement—because our identity politics only get us so far.[1] We have to really ensure that folks are not only understanding the language and the analysis of Black queer feminism, but that it's also rooted in a practice. I would say that particularly because SONG's founders come out of movement, one of our foundational texts is the Combahee River Collective statement.[2] We have it in both Spanish and English. I remember stories Mandy Carter would tell—one of the first campaigns that SONG embarked on was to join the fight around the Mt. Olive pickle boycott in North Carolina being organized by farmworkers. They called many of the LGBTQ people to join this fight and many said, "This has nothing to do with us." But SONG saw the importance. We have inherited a legacy of work based on our insistence that many understand that our lives are interconnected but don't understand systems of oppression are deeply connected. Our strategies must reflect that analysis. If we think we can organize in silos or just for one issue, especially on the land where chattel slavery took place and is the current testing ground for right-wing strategies, we have a problem. With Black queer feminist politics—and it's beautiful that we have a language for it—we see that Black women, queer and trans people, poor people have shown up across many fights, which is a manifestation of that politic in action. At SONG we also have a formula for movement building that is Vision + Identity + Consciousness + Work. In other words all these elements are needed to be able to advance collective work. You can't just have one or two of them—all four are needed.

FB: *As you are doing the work, when you encounter obstacles to people listening to Black women or listening to queer Black women, what are the obstacles that people put in the way?*

MH: Oh, my God! In 2015 I helped start the Black Lives Matter chapter here in Atlanta. Immediately we began seeing signs of someone moving like a provocateur and eventually starting an off-brand chapter that they called Greater Atlanta Black Lives Matter. They started talking down about LGBTQ people and it was not in alignment with the principles and values of Black Lives Matter, which we know was started by two queer women, Patrisse Khan-Cullors and Alicia Garza, along with Opal Tometi. If you're undermining their work and not in alignment with the values and politics, then stop calling yourself Black Lives Matter. Call yourself something else.

Many people in Atlanta and across the country know about this person I'm speaking about.[3] I had a call one day, someone from SCLC [Southern Christian Leadership Council founded in 1957, with Dr. Martin Luther King as its first president] called and said: "We're really interested in investing in this guy's leadership. He could be the next Dr. King." It just blew my mind! Have they not seen all the dykes and lezzies and trans women who have stood down highways, who have stood before councils, who are going to the mat not just for our issues, but for all Black people? There is a refusal to acknowledge and the refusal to bear witness to this generation of movement and what folks of our particular experiences and politics bring to Black movement politics. It's also about ignoring the violence that happens to Black women and queer and trans women. One of the things that we refuse to do is to let anybody be invisible-ized. In a place like Atlanta where I do most of my organizing work, there's that long, open desire for another Dr. King, so much so that people are willing to get behind leaders that mean our people no good, just to be able to say we have a Black man who's leading.

FB: *Right, our own investment in patriarchy. I think that's a very internal conversation that has to be had among Black people.*

MH: I remember going back to Kai [Lumumba Barrow] when she joined the [SONG] staff, she talked about having to leave the Black Panther Party because the patriarchy was so real, "I could not survive being a Black lesbian woman in that organization." When we look at past movements we have to be critical, but not in a way that devalues what all the magic and all the beautiful work that previous formations have done. I think the refusal to have an honest read and to have the insight, hindsight, and foresight, as Mama Ruby said, around what current movements have done—if we don't grapple with those things, we will continue to perpetuate those same tensions. Many of us who are queer trans folk are oftentimes the ones relied on to be the truth tellers about it. And oftentimes we're seen as divisive or not prioritizing the "real issue," and unfortunately there are Black women who also subscribe to that as well. It's not just the Black men. It's going to take all of us to transform patriarchy, to transform our communities and transform our world.

DF: *This is what's so important about Black radical queer feminist politics. SONG was involved in the founding conference for the Movement for Black Lives in Cleveland [in July 2015], and you were on the planning committee. The*

Movement for Black Lives is simultaneously addressing a multitude of issues. Its members view militarism, a living wage, education, health care, and so forth, as all interconnected. Could you speak about what's happening since that time with the Movement for Black Lives (M4BL) and how SONG connects with it?

MH: It's important to name entry points. Before July 2015, circa the fall–winter of 2014, folks began convening. This was the Black leaders across the country saying, "Hey y'all, it's not just a moment, this is a movement! Let's bring the forces together." One of the things that kept radiating was this commitment to queer and trans leadership, a commitment to the South, understanding how the South had been ignored. So that's when SONG was brought to the table. We were clear, "We're a multiracial organization that has Black and Brown people." They were cool with that. When we began planning for Cleveland 2015, I remember being in the room with activists from at least ninety organizations. We talked about what the local campaigns meant for building a movement. Those discussions became the building blocks of the Vision for Black Lives Policy Platform that was released in August 2016.[4] We were really serious about holding the line around not picking sides in terms of Hillary and Trump. While people were trying to get us to support Hillary over Trump, we knew what Hillary had been responsible for in our communities. After Trump got into office, the strategy began reforming. We haven't gathered since the Cleveland conference.

We began writing up the M4BL 2021 Plan—what can we do together that we cannot do alone? What we knew to be true was that the political climate we find ourselves in grew out of the resistance that has been happening since 2013 with Black Lives Matter and even before that to the Occupy Movement [in 2011]. But for this generation of the Black liberation movement, it was 2013. We've been able to bring in more organizations to discuss how are we collectivizing our resources and sharing resources? How are we using our collective curriculum to train and develop other leaders? About 2017, we began to talk more about building rapid response strategies, a lot of that was being coordinated by Blackbird in Ferguson. So we agreed to meet for seven months, once a month, and we struggled, debated, and worked this plan for the M4BL's Vision for Black Lives. From that plan came the organizing table, we've been able to survey over a hundred Black-led organizations that are doing base building, intermediary work, to really understand what are the needs of grassroots organizers at this time. We're now planning a convening in February 2019, which will bring about five hundred people to Atlanta to think through new strategies. Which five to ten localities can we get up under and support the grassroots organizing that's happening there? What does it mean for Black people to build power and to take power? We're trying to do system change work, abolitionist work. We also want to convene folks to do some baseline training and skill up to make sure organizers have what they need so we can all do the work that we're called up to do. There are also very few programs—Blackbird is one of them—where about fifteen leaders of different organizations came together and got trained up on how we talk about the larger visions of the work that we're trying to move and to have spokespeople to make political interventions into the mainstream narrative about who we are, what the work is, and how we understand the political landscape today.

About the work that we've been doing around the Black Mama's Bailout, the ancestors brought it to me on my front porch one day. I brought it into SONG. Then we in SONG spoke about it at a Movement for Black Lives policy meeting that was specifically addressing bail. At that meeting, folks were like *yes, yes, yes!* We developed the National Bailout Collective to collectivize our resources to be able to do mass bailouts as part of a larger strategy to challenge the practice of money bail and pretrial detention. So the tentacles of work have spread widely.

In M4BL, we realize that we need to be doing the slower respectful work of organizing our people. Oftentimes people have an idea of what the M4BL is—resource, coalition—but we talk about it as an ecosystem. We try to connect the grassroots, local movements to a national movement and international movement. We're also very committed to not just doing the beck and response work, which we know is a need and also an opening to draw more people into organizations. About funders, we've always been clear—fund the movement, not just one organization. Organizations make up the movements. So we've been able to collectivize resources and to help support organizers who are moving initiatives that may be a few dollars short. I'm really proud of the work we've been able to do thus far.

FB: *We've been talking about the campaigns and dealing with policy, but I know the website states that SONG is rooted in a southern tradition that includes humor, music, performance. Can you say more about the creative, imaginative side and how that also works to bring people together?*

MH: SONG is rooted in the Black radical tradition, but it is also a queer liberation organization. I think about Audre Lorde and the "Uses of the Erotic" as part of some of the forces of energy that influences our work and how we show up to do change work. So for SONG we oftentimes talk about not just organizing from a place of righteous anger, which it is definitely righteous and necessary, but also from a place of longing and desire for something different. Over the past twenty-five years of SONG, a core part of how we do what we do is to impact the culture of the organization, the way we hold space and create collective alchemy. Organizing work is spirit work and is cultural work. Especially as southerners who have been regionally scapegoated and "marked as a lost cause" by others we know that any policy wins we advance need to be paired with profound culture change and that our work cannot, will not, and should not be solely quantified in policy wins. We have been taking care of each other—outside of the state for a long time and that is one of our profound assets. We center spirit work and communal work as some of the heartbeat of our organizing. A lot of it is the tradition of breaking bread, having altars to hold spirits, to make sure the place is welcoming for children, or just sitting on the front porch with someone and having a one-on-one, sipping tea. All of those things deeply impact how we're able to create transformative organizing work. When I was on the staff, we began holding a tradition called "Gaycation." Our people work really hard and struggle really hard, but if we're not also finding joy in it, then we shouldn't be doing it. So we began holding Gaycation once a year in the summertime. If you can pay $20, you pay $20; for someone else who can't, whatever. We might find ourselves in the woods and we take the time to actually embody beloved community. We take care of each other's babies. We collectively cook. We do the things we imagine will take place once revolution comes. So having spaces like that informs how we stay in the work and what we embody our gay sprinkle in the Black Radical Tradition. SONG has always been clear about desire and longing being the driving force of our work and also organizing from a place of vision. I'm thankful that one of our founders talks about how visionary organizing has been able to ascend above the trees and see the longing and where the horizon is, and be able to come down and take the beauty and magic of what is possible. So we can have the insight, hindsight, and foresight to make the strategic interventions where the vision is taking us and not just where our heartbreak would like to keep us.

DF: *Mary, when I attended SONG's roundtable at the American Studies Association conference [in Atlanta in November 2018], I was struck with that spirit that SONG has and the ways that you interacted. It was clear to me that you were self-consciously working to develop the humane, to prefigure the kinds of libera-tory social relations as they connect with creating structural change. As I hear you talk now, I also see that there's also a connection to nature and Mother Earth, a connection to the ancestors and spirituality. All of this—the social, the cultural, the spiritual, the political, the economic—is intertwined and somehow front and center for SONG. You were talking about where we need to take the movement, which is no easy question. I know we need to end, so I'd like to ask if you have any last remarks or anything you'd like to add.*

MH: One of the things that I'm grappling with as an organizer and as some-one who is always in a state of study. I'm always studying something, always reading something. One of the things the Black Panther Party offers this struggle of liberation is the manner in which they showed up. So much of their influence is in terms of the culture they developed, the way people dressed, the hair. I know today, we ask what's our swag look like? How are we showing up? The Black Panther Party really brought swag to the move-ment that identified that we are a force of people that are unified in struggle. In a lot of ways, their militancy gets devalued, but there was a certain level of rigor and discipline that came with that, a level of intention that I don't believe the current movement has yet embodied or figured out. It may not be the whole thing, but what is the dose of the Panthers that we need in our movement? There has always been a thread in Black liberation work, whether it's the Deacons for Defense or other organizations, not just those who car-ried arms, but also those who understood what is at stake in a different way. This is life or death, bodies are literally going to be killed, so there was a need for a different understanding of how we understood self-defense. We don't always see that tendency in this current iteration. I think about the young guy Joshua out of Ferguson who was sentenced to eight years after setting a trashcan on fire.[5] So in this generation, he is one of the first, I think it's fair to say, political prisoners of our time. How do we hold that dose of militancy that we need along with the desire, the longing, the spiritual, all of those things? And is there a place in the movement for it because that's something that the Black Panther Party modeled for us and that we have yet to figure out—how it fits into the movement at this point.

Representatives of the Afrikan Black Coalition and/or Black Student Union, UC Santa Barbara: Terron Wilkerson, Jordan Mitchell, Bianca Graves, Nia Mitchell, Edan Tessema, and Yoel Haile (left to right) presenting at the University of California (UC) Regents meeting in San Francisco in January 2016. ABC denounced the $425 million the UC system invested in Wells Fargo, a leading financier of private prisons, helping to force the UC system to divest. Photo courtesy of author.

CHAPTER SIXTEEN

Black Student Organizing in the Shadow of the Panthers

Yoel Yosief Haile

The Afrikan Black Coalition (ABC), a California statewide Black youth formation, is the largest Black student organization in the United States. It organizes Black student unions at sixteen colleges and universities. Before discussing the significant influence of the Black Panthers on ABC, it is imperative to trace the genesis of the organization.

The Afrikan Black Coalition began as a conference by a group of Black students at the University of California (UC) campuses in 2003. Between 2003 and 2012, it continued as an annual conference. In those years, it served as a great cultural institution and conference where Black students would gather over the course of a weekend, attend various workshops on issues about the Black world, and feel culturally affirmed and renewed in light of the categorically hostile and racist campus climate across all their campuses. However, politically, ABC was not able to achieve any significant victories or mount statewide organizing campaigns because its infrastructure was built around one annual event. It simply did not have the organizational structure to achieve anything but one annual conference. This is not to say that individual Black student unions (BSUs) throughout the various campuses were not politically active. To the contrary, many BSUs were engaged in many political struggles of their day and achieved important political victories. In this chapter, I will primarily refer to the time period between 2012 and 2018.

In 2012, the conference was hosted at UC Berkeley under the chairship of Brother Salih Muhammad. In 2013, the person who was elected to chair the conference resigned halfway through the year, prompting Brother Salih to jump back into the fray and assist the host campus with their conference planning. This incident exposed a serious weakness in the coalition, which was that there was no sustainable organizational structure to ensure the smooth year-to-year transition in putting together even one annual event. This revelation prompted Brother Salih to begin the process of transforming the coalition from a high-functioning conference planning committee into a well-structured organization with a staff structure that can ensure continuity and be a vehicle to improve the material conditions of the masses of our people. For the following year, Salih Muhammad and Rasheed Shabazz became interim executive director and communications director, respectively, and conducted many trainings and campus visits in order to establish the necessary relationships and buy-in to transform the loose coalition into an organization. Through this process, they established a central committee, similar in purpose to that of the Black Panther Party, that was comprised of the chairs of Black student unions of each member campus. The purpose of the central committee is to act as the highest governing body of the organization, set priorities, and direct the staff toward advancing the mission of the organization, which is the liberation of all Afrikan people.

Since the founding of the central committee and the relentless and tireless efforts of many comrades, too many to name here, the ABC was transformed from one annual conference into a formidable Black youth organization. The organization has six executive branches, which are as follows:

Executive Office: This branch is led by the executive director and includes the student affairs unit. It is primarily tasked with maintaining and supporting the BSUs and their leadership across all the member campuses. This includes regular communication with BSU leadership, field visits, ongoing support, and organizing training, among other things. One of its critical tasks is also to expand the organization's power by bringing in more BSUs into the coalition. As a result of their tireless work, what started as a coalition of BSUs at nine UCs now also includes BSUs at seven California State University (CSU) campuses.[1]

Political Bureau: This branch is led by the political director and is responsible for building up the organizing arm of the organization. Consequently, it creates and sustains relationships with freedom movements across the US, Africa, and Latin America to the extent possible. The political bureau also initiates and supports political campaigns to improve the material conditions of our people both on the campus level and throughout California. Lastly, this bureau is responsible for the internal security of the organization.

Black Community Programs (BCP) Bureau: The BCP, modeled and named after Steve Biko's programs during apartheid South Africa, is led by the BCP director. Its primary mission is to organize the Black communities in the cities of Oakland and Los Angeles and identify and deliver services that our people are in dire need of as a result of poverty and government neglect. The BCP is part of various social justice coalitions in Oakland and conducts various trainings and programs ranging from know your rights trainings and after school programs for students in continuation schools. For example, during the 2015–2016 academic year, we helped host after school programming for the mostly students of color attending Bunche Academy, a West Oakland continuation high school.

Business and Operations Bureau: This bureau is led by the business operations director of the organization and is tasked with several responsibilities. The primary task of this bureau is akin to the finance minister, which is to be in charge of the organization's financial health and accounting. It secures funding and administers it in a way that advances our mission. Part of this task includes identifying business opportunities that could be set up in order to establish the organization's financial independence and escape the trap of the nonprofit-industrial complex and the concerning level of dependence many social justice organizations have on foundation grants. Our fundamental belief is for us, by us.

Inclusion Bureau: This is a newly established bureau that is intended to help root out patriarchy and heteropatriarchy within the organization and conduct education efforts to achieve similar objectives both internally and externally. The staff, in response to both internal and external criticisms that the organization needs to do better in its practices to be more inclusive, voted unanimously to elevate this position to the executive level.

The ideas and organizing principles of the Black Panther Party are a central influence on the ABC and its organizers. We derived our ten-point plan from the Panthers, much like how the Panthers derived theirs from the Nation of Islam. Below is our plan:

1. We want freedom. We want power to determine the destiny of our Black community.
2. We want 40 acres of land for every Black person of adult age (18 and over). We believe the combined totality of those 40 acres per every

Black person over the age of 18 will constitute an independent and sovereign Black Republic.

3. We want the abolishment of patriarchy and heteropatriarchy.

4. We want financial reparations to Black people for the 250 years of unpaid labor that the US stole from our people.

5. We want an immediate end to police brutality, white terrorism and the gratuitous murder of Black people.

6. We want decent housing fit for the shelter of human beings and an immediate end to gentrification.

7. We want freedom for all Black people held in federal, state, county and city prisons and jails and released to the custody of the independent and sovereign Black republic.

8. We want the abolishment of the prison-industrial complex that has been erected to continue the enslavement of Black people.

9. We want the immediate cessation of Western interference in Africa, the Caribbean and other Third World continents and nations. We want an immediate cancellation of all World Bank and the International Monetary Fund loans to Africa, the Caribbean, and the rest of the Third World.

10. We want education for our people that exposes the true nature of this decadent American society. We want education that teaches us our true history and our role in the present-day society.

11. We call on Black people to not serve in any US enforcement institutions (armed forces, police, DEA, Homeland Security, Border Patrol...)

There are a few things worth noting about ABC's ten-point plan and the Panthers'. Our fundamental similarity is that we both believe in self-determination, identify the United States to be an illegitimate settler-colonial state, and are committed Pan-Africanists who support Third World decolonial struggles. We believe in African socialism and are ardent anticapitalists. We are students of Fanon and African revolutionaries the world over whom we study continuously. We believe that the Black Panther Party was one of the greatest and strongest organizations in the history of the Black freedom struggle in the continental United States.

There are some departures we take from the Panthers in our ideology. The Afrikan Black Coalition is a Black nationalist organization. We believe in separation and cessation from the United States into a sovereign Black nation. This is reflected in ABC's points #2 and #3 which read in their totality as follows:

#2. We want 40 acres of Land for every Black person of adult age (18 and over).

We believe that land is the basis of ALL independence. As such, we believe that the first demand of Black people in our quest for liberation must be the 40 acres per person that is owed to Black people by the US government. We believe the combined totality of those 40 acres per every Black person over the age of 18 will constitute an independent and sovereign Black republic. The establishment of a sovereign Black nation in North America will obviously be done with the consultation of the Indigenous people of this land.

#3. We want financial reparations to Black people for the 250 years of unpaid labor that the US stole from our people.

We believe that the US government owes Black people for the unpaid labor our ancestors provided to this country under chattel slavery and the subsequent underemployment of our people since the emancipation proclamation. There are already estimates ranging from $1.5 million each to $14.2 trillion in total due to the 40 million of Black people in America today who are descendants of enslaved Africans. We want total autonomy, sovereignty, and independence in the management of these funds.[2]

Our fundamental vision and dream of freedom is based in the establishment of an independent and sovereign Black nation in the continental United States. Of course, this idea is not new. The Honorable Elijah Muhammad and the Nation of Islam have long espoused this view and there were many activists in the 1960s and 1970s who sought to create the framework for the Republic of New Afrika. The idea was to combine the states of South Carolina, Georgia, Mississippi, Alabama, and Louisiana into one sovereign republic. We agree with this position.

Our dream of freedom is centered around land. A territory that belongs to our people, one that we can protect and defend militarily from all enemies. As Kwame Nkrumah stated, we believe land is the basis of all independence and that no people anywhere in the world can ever be free or independent without a land of their own. We believe that Black people are entitled to financial reparations from the United States government for the 250 years of unpaid labor during slavery. We envision for the combined funds of those reparations to constitute the national budget of a sovereign Black nation during its early years until the necessary infrastructures and industries can be set up and productive to the point of self-sufficiency. We believe in African socialism, akin to the Marxist-Leninist ideology of the Panthers. We believe in the nationalization of all the natural resources of the new republic and the use of its wealth to meet all the basic needs of its citizens—housing, food, health care, education, and full employment.

Furthermore, our ten-point plan emphasizes our desire to end patriarchy and heteropatriarchy. We seek a nation free of the oppression women and queer people face. We recognize that Huey Newton wrote in the 1970s about gay liberation and are simply elevating that point to one of the core principles and commitments of the organization.

Lastly, consistent with the Panthers' internationalist principles, our ten-point plan calls for the immediate cessation of Western interference in Africa, the Caribbean, and other Third World countries. We want an immediate cancellation of all World Bank and International Monetary Fund (IMF) loans to Africa, the Caribbean, and the rest of the Third World. This is a call similar to the one Captain Thomas Sankara of Burkina Faso made before the enemies of our people assassinated him through the treacherous Blaise Compare, who went on to betray all the principles of the Sankarist revolution and put the Burkinabe people under the mercy of French colonizers for the twenty-seven years he ruled Burkina Faso. Like Sankara, we believe these loans to be illegitimate and amount to nowhere near what the Western world has already stolen from Africans.

These are the visions of freedom and liberation the Afrikan Black Coalition has and seeks to bring into fruition. These ideas and ideologies are disseminated to the students we work with mainly through leadership trainings we host during the academic year. We host the following trainings throughout the year:

Camp Uhuru. This is a training that is usually held at the end of spring or early summer to onboard the newly elected BSU leadership throughout the state. We bring more than a hundred student leaders for a weekend to go through our political education and leadership development curriculum.

Black Student Leadership Training (BSLT). This training is held in early fall to delve deeper into our political education curriculum and develop work plans for the student leaders for the year. We bring more than a hundred student leaders for a weekend and conduct strategy and tactics sessions where we develop our statewide and campus level political campaigns.

Chairs' Retreat. This training is held in early winter and primarily trains the chairs of the BSUs throughout the state. We understand the burden of leadership, especially for youth who are elected to lead BSUs. It's a historic and awesome responsibility with many pitfalls and trials from all sides. For this reason, we bring all those leaders together for more political education, to help problem solve their challenges, and support them in meeting their great responsibilities.

Additionally, we still host, on an annual basis, the Afrikan Black Coalition Conference. The ABC Conference is the largest convening of Black youth in California and possibly in the nation. We bring anywhere from six hundred to nine hundred Black students from all over the state for a weekend to conduct political education, academic development, and career opportunity workshops. We also have multiple cultural shows and artists, as culture and art are fundamental components of political resistance and human development.

Lastly, members of the staff visit the campuses multiple times over the course of the year to conduct leadership training and political education. These are the mechanisms through which the ideology and principles of the organization are disseminated throughout its cadre and membership.

Our political analysis is developed through intense study of the history of our people and the freedom struggles of other Third World people. We have a long list of recommended books to read for people joining the staff of the organization as well as online lectures, documentaries, and videos that we believe are necessary in cultivating our development and knowledge. *It is important to note that experience and practice has also been a tremendous generator of knowledge, insight, and analysis for us. Our organizing campaigns over the last four years have taught us a tremendous amount about sustaining energy and discipline within the organization, working in coalitions, and surviving trials and tribulations both internally and externally.* These are things no book can teach but that organizers and organizations must learn through trial by fire. The important part here is that we make consistent efforts to apply all knowledge, test all assumptions and hypotheses, and create strategies that incorporate information and knowledge derived both from historical study and real-time developments. The synthesis of these knowledges has allowed us to wage some successful campaigns against mass incarceration within the UC system and survive as an organization during challenging times.

One of the lessons we have learned through both the historical study of the Panthers and our own experience is the critical importance of keeping internal disagreements of the organization internal. We have studied and witnessed the devastating and divisive impact of Eldridge Cleaver and Huey Newton's very public conflict. While the split was fostered by the FBI's infamous Counterintelligence Program (COINTELPRO), failing to keep internal differences private propelled the organization to a breaking point. As a result of this history, our ethos is to never attempt to resolve internal disagreements in the public sphere as we have never seen anything productive ever come out of such practice. The outcome of this ethos has been that even when we faced the painful experiences of having to suspend and expel former "comrades" from the organization for various transgressions, we never made public these decisions. One can only appreciate the restraint and discipline every member of the organization demonstrated in these decisions when one takes into account the sheer volume of the slander that was aimed at our organization through social media. In the age of Twitter, where people simply make outrageous claims within 140-240 characters in a false attempt to have nuanced discussions, only to conclude with hyperbolic statements that are neither here nor there, many organizers and organizations have fallen victim to the practice of attempting to have serious discussions over that medium. What has become clear over the last three to four years is that some of these "twittertionaries" (Twitter revolutionaries) use hyperbolic and blanket statements to gain more followers, likes, and retweets without contributing to the task of building lasting Black institutions that can withstand the test of time in order to serve the people "mind, body, and soul." This is in many ways similar to what many bourgeois Black "intellectuals" do on the academic scene: relentlessly criticize Black people who are actually engaged in the dialectical struggle of building organizations and institutions to serve the people, their shortcomings and contradictions notwithstanding, while drawing nice salaries from state institutions (colleges and universities) with no useful or material contribution toward those efforts. Perhaps unbeknownst to them, what their actions and constant search for more likes, retweets, and followers reflect is perhaps the single worst cultural trait of Western bourgeois societies—self-aggrandizing rugged individualism and white validation. Of course, the first task of any revolutionary organization is "to go back to the source," as Amilcar Cabral teaches us, and ground its resistance in African collectivism. This means we must root out any and all tendencies of individualism; for individualism is one of the central characters of traitors and reactionaries and should not be allowed to exist and fester within any organization that damages the struggle for collective freedom. This is precisely why Frantz Fanon, when speaking about the bourgeois elements of underdeveloped nations, stated, "The bourgeoisie should not be allowed to find the conditions necessary for its existence and its growth."[3]

The Afrikan Black Coalition has been immensely fortunate that many of its members and leaders have been mentored and brought up by movement veterans. This includes people who were organizers with the Student Non-Violent Coordinating Committee (SNCC), the first founders of BSUs in the late 1960s and early 1970s, and most importantly, leaders within the Black Panther Party. One of our mentors and elders is Elaine Brown. Elaine Brown first became a member of the Los Angeles chapter of the Black Panther Party, which was led by John Huggins and Bunchy Carter, who were martyred on the UCLA campus. She was recruited to the party by John Huggins himself. Over the course of time, she rose to the role of minister of information, and later, chair of the Black Panther Party while Huey Newton was in exile in Cuba. Sister Elaine has been a mentor of many in ABC since its inception. She has consistently participated in every panel and speaking event that we have asked of her and has held private sessions with us to impart her battle-tested wisdom. For our latest statewide ABC conference in January 2018, we invited the legendary Eddie Conway, high-ranking member of the Baltimore chapter of the Black Panther Party, to speak as one of our keynote speakers. Eddie Conway was framed for murder by the state and was held as a political prisoner for forty-four years before being released in 2014. We have been building a relationship with Brother Eddie and will continue to do so.

Fundamentally speaking, we envision for the ABC to function in structures similar to those of SNCC and the Black Panther Party. The mantra of the Black Panther Party, "Serve the People, Mind, Body, and Soul," is what we strive to embody in both our personal and organizational ethos. We deeply appreciate the discipline among most of the members of the party and the centralized paramilitary leadership infrastructure of the BPP. This is not to say that we avoid dealing with real weaknesses, both internal and external, that led to the destruction of the party. However, knowing what we know about the depth and extent of the war the FBI and all the intelligence agencies of the United States government waged on the Black Panther Party, we are not naïve enough to conclude the party was destroyed by its own internal weaknesses and discord. This point is critical to emphasize because some so-called historians and filmmakers seem to be engaged in a revisionist rewriting of history that exaggerates and highlights mistakes and failures of some members of the party to the point of assigning the blame for the destruction of the party to those internal problems. Such bourgeois historiography masks the calculated, brutal, and merciless ways through which the United States government sought to systematically destroy organizations of Black resistance, assassinate our leaders, and make lifelong political prisoners of those they decided not to or could not murder.

There is an ongoing discussion and reaction among contemporary organizations in the Black freedom struggle about what leadership structure is appropriate and can help us get to freedom. There are many in the present iteration of our freedom struggle who seem to favor a "horizontal leadership structure" or a "decentralized" organizational structure. People are using phrases like "leaderless or leader-full" movements to describe some of what we are currently witnessing within movement spaces. I believe a lot of this is really in reaction to the fact that during the civil rights and Black Power movements of the 1960s and 1970s, we had clearly identified and stellar leaders such as Malcolm X, Dr. Martin Luther King Jr., Medgar Evers, Fred Hampton, Kwame Ture (formerly Stokely Carmichael), John Huggins, Bunchy Carter, Huey Newton, Assata Shakur, and countless others who were clearly identifiable and targeted for assassination by the US government. Part of the current thinking is that if we elevate people to become such leaders as those, we will also be providing our enemies with a clear list of people to target in order to cripple our movements. There is of course serious merit to this argument in the context of a freedom struggle that is aboveground. However, a brief survey of freedom struggles in Africa, Latin America, and Asia show us that freedom struggles that are underground do a much better job of sustaining a hierarchical leadership structure to lead the vanguard party. What we have seen in liberation struggles the world over is that the vanguard party wages an armed struggle and conducts clandestine military missions within cities behind enemy lines. Its leadership is hierarchical and able to withstand enemy infiltration and assassination for much longer than aboveground movements have in the United States for various reasons.

Within ABC, the six-member executive staff (heads of each bureau) have equal voting power in matters regarding organizational positions and direction. In this manner, our practice is egalitarian. However, in times of disagreement, decisions are reached by majority vote. Once a decision is reached, every member of the organization is expected to abide by that decision regardless how they individually may have voted in the decision-making process. In this manner, we very much believe in democratic centralism. That is, we believe in the decision-making process to be democratic and robust in discussion, but once a decision is reached, it is central and should guide the actions of every member of the organization. We believe this process is the one that will help us achieve our goals and improve our effectiveness as an organization without being bogged down by bureaucratic processes while allowing sufficient space for robust discussion and input from members of the organization. In the final analysis, we believe a certain level of hierarchy is necessary in the leadership structure of organizations to ensure accountability and effectiveness.

The natural question that follows here is how effective has ABC been in advancing its mission and the campaigns it has waged. To answer that question, a brief synopsis of our campaigns is necessary.

Statewide BSU Demands Campaign

Starting in the fall of 2014, the Afrikan Black Coalition launched a multi-campus BSU demands campaign. This campaign attempted to replicate the successful organizing model of the BSU at UC Santa Barbara in 2013. The BSU at UC Santa Barbara successfully organized and secured the following wins in 2013:

a. Secured a commitment to raise over $2 million to hire four (4) endowed chairs in the field of Black Studies across the academic divisions with an agreement to complete within the next five years. .

b. Secured funding ($414,012) for the hiring of two psychologists who have extensive experience working with Black students and office space for Counseling and Psychological Services.

c. Secured funding ($217,000) for the hiring of an admissions counselor for diversity initiatives, four student interns, and a series of initiatives aimed to recruit Black students to UC Santa Barbara

d. Secured funding ($150,000–200,000) for the creation of the Ella Baker Visiting Professorship in Undergraduate Research in the Department of Black Studies to serve as recruitment tool for Black faculty

e. Secured funding ($200,000) for a two-year postdoctoral fellowship in the Center for Black Studies Research for two terms, with renewal based on meeting certain research criteria

f. Secured funding ($32,000) for a permanent student-activism centered display in North Hall in honor of the Black students involved in the 1968 takeover.

Based on this successful organizing campaign by the Black Student Union at UCSB, the Afrikan Black Coalition secured more victories across the state. Below are some highlights. At UC Berkeley:

1. The creation of the Fannie Lou Hamer Black Resource Center with two full-time staff, nearly a dozen student workers, and a full programming budget to serve the Black students at the campus
2. A commitment to raise a $20 million endowment for scholarships to Black students
3. The hiring of Black psychologists to serve Black students' well being

At Cal State LA:

1. Cal State LA agreed to divest from all private prison corporations
2. The creation of a Black scholars' floor in the dorms for Black students
3. The allocation of $200,000 to the Cross Cultural Center to support Black students and other students of color and to staff efforts and programs to recruit more Black students
4. The creation of a requirement to take a race and ethnicity course as well as a diversity course for all incoming students beginning in fall 2016.

There were other modest victories achieved through campaigns in other campuses such as the creation of a Black Scholars' Hall at Sonoma State University. This work is ongoing until such time Black students are able to thrive and be successful in their academic pursuits such that they can be of best service to the masses of our people.

ABC Prison Divestment Campaign

After a protracted two-year campaign that included media, organizing, research, and grassroots political education components, the ABC was able to successfully push the University of California to divest nearly $30 million from private prison corporations (CoreCivic, formerly Corrections Corporations of America, the GEO group, and G4S) in December 2016. After another year of agitation, we were also able to successfully push the UC system to terminate $475 million worth of contracts with Wells Fargo for its financing of private prisons and longstanding discriminatory lending practices against Black people and other communities of color.

Our assessment of the campaigns we have is that they have been relatively successful in terms of achieving the intended objectives as discrete projects with clear outcomes and are all the more impressive in this period of economic austerity. However, given that the mission of our organization is the liberation of all Afrikan people, we take no joy or respite in any victories that do not clearly advance us toward that objective. As such, we believe the real benefit in these campaign victories for us as an organization was the training ground it provided for many young people in the practice of organizing, power building, and leadership development. The real success for us in these campaigns was that many young Black people learned what it means to build and exercise power, create and execute strategies and tactics to achieve a set of objectives that we believed were helpful in our struggle forward toward freedom.

Conclusion

The impact of the Black Panther Party on all resistance movements in the United States that came after it has been indelible and widely acknowledged. Certainly the influence of the Black Panther Party, both as a historic organization and through individual Panthers who have mentored and supported ABC, has been deep and wide within the organization. We hold the Black Panther Party in the highest reverence for all the amazing things it did and inspired. This is a party that helped produce and mold some of our very best leaders, including the slain Fred Hampton, John Huggins, Bunchy Carter, and many others. The party's deliberate focus on organizing the "lumpenproletariat," or "brothers on the block" as Huey Newton called them, accounts for its wide and deeply felt impact both in the racial and class politics of Black communities throughout the continental United States. Its internationalist politics has been instructive in our own conception and development of our policies and efforts to stay connected with and closely follow the present-day iterations of freedom struggles in Africa, Latin America, and Asia. Our reverence and praise of the Black Panther Party is not uncritical, for it is only through a sober and clear-eyed analysis of history, organizations, and their strengths and weaknesses, without clouding emotionalism, that we can arrive at the correct antidotes of our movement weaknesses in order to advance our liberation mission.

Blake Simons standing outside UC Berkeley's Fannie Lou Hamer Black Resource Center, which the Black Student Union fought to have along with nine other demands. Photograph by Tashya Jones, 2019

CHAPTER SEVENTEEN

The Impact of the Panthers: Centering Poor Black Folks in the Black Liberation Movement

Blake Simons

B lack history is often hidden despite being right in front of us. My own history and ties to the Black Panther Party (BPP) were something I did not discover until my early twenties. When I was an organizer with the Black Student Union at UC Berkeley, I began a path to self-discovery and part of that was learning my own family's history. I learned that I was related to Jalil Muntaqim, former Black Panther and Black Liberation Army member, who is one of the longest held political prisoners in the United States. I began to write to him, and we've built a relationship through letter writing. At times, this is painful. Jalil should be free, and no one should have to build a relationship solely through letter writing. I began to take part in helping with his case, mainly spreading the word about his upcoming parole hearings. I also began researching his case, combined with studying the BPP and its community programs. I read Huey Newton's *To Die for the People*, which served as a foundational text for my politicization as a young Black organizer. The work of the party and Jalil Muntaqim's life and sacrifices had a transformative effect on my political ideology. My investigations have taught me to center Black folks most marginalized by this white supremacist capitalist state. The BPP and its community programs have served as a great inspiration in how we do community work today. I, along with Delency Parham, who also had family in the BPP, cofounded People's Breakfast Oakland, a free breakfast program in the town. This essay is a personal account of my transition from being a Black student organizer into becoming a Black community organizer and how studying the BPP helped this transition. I will then examine the current state of Oakland's politics and argue why it's important for organizers to embody the Black Marxist "serve the people" ideology of the BPP today.

Black Student Activism

I came into politicization after the murder of Oscar Grant. Oscar Grant was killed New Year's morning in 2009 by a BART police officer while he was handcuffed At the time, I was a junior in high school and a student athlete playing football and rugby. I matriculated to UC Berkeley where I was recruited to play rugby. During my senior season, I experienced a second coming of politicization. I was scrolling on Twitter and saw the dead body of Michael Brown Jr., who was executed via police lynching. As Black student athletes, we are programmed and instructed to stay quiet on major social issues. But I could no longer stay silent. I joined the Black Student Union (BSU) and participated in and helped orchestrate the 4.5-hour shutdown of UC Berkeley's most popular campus eatery in solidarity with Ferguson.[1] About a month later, I was back in training camp for rugby, but, facing intimidation from the athletics department for the BSU protest, I decided to quit. Though this was before Colin Kaepernick's taking the knee, the way the NFL ostracized Kaepernick shows that the white power structure only tolerates Black athletes when they play ball and keep quiet.[2]

While I was a BSU organizer, we led a successful demands campaign that led to the creation of the Fannie Lou Hamer Black Resource Center at UC Berkeley.[3] Some of the actions involved shutting down the main entrance on the campus on Cal Day as well as painting campus symbols such as the BIG C in the red, black, and green colors of the Pan African flag. Black students put their bodies on the line to fight for the center as well as nine other demands. This political fight was a militant nonviolent uprising of Black students on campus. After the shutting down of Cal Day, UC Berkeley administrators agreed to the BSU demands. Shortly after, I graduated and was hired by UC Berkeley to serve as the project manager for the newly created Fannie Lou Hamer Black Resource Center.

I also served as the communications director for the Afrikan Black Coalition, which was a statewide organization of BSUs in California. As comms director, I worked on a prison divestment campaign that led to the UC divesting $25 million from private prisons.[4] This was undoubtedly a big win, however, after many disagreements I eventually left the organization. At this time, I also began to intensively study the BPP, learning about their Black Marxist politics as well as their sixty-plus community survival programs.[5]

Gentrification in Oakland

The gentrification of Black Oakland was a major reason we created the People's Breakfast Oakland. Gentrification, as I define it, is the recolonization of historically colonized communities. This includes not only the extraction of existing resources, but also the implementation of resources that only the settlers and the petit bourgeois class can access. Gentrification is not new in Oakland, but it has intensified in relation to the war on Black Power. In the early 1970s, for example, Merritt College was moved from North Oakland to the Oakland Hills. Viewing this as resource extraction, Melvin Newton, chair of the Black Studies Department at Merritt and BPP national minister of finance, warned that if Merritt moved to the Hills it would not serve the community. He said, "By definition the hills are white folks country, and unless something is done here, the move to the hills may be the death of Merritt."[6] The Bay Area Rapid Transit (BART) was also a key part in the extraction of existing resources from the Black community. BART opened in 1972 and brought devastating effects to the Black community in Oakland. As Robert Self describes in his book on Oakland history, the construction of BART "eviscerated what was left of Seventh Street, once the heart of the city's black business district."[7] Again, this is the resource extraction that gentrification commits. It destroys Black economic development in the city and creates poorer conditions for the people. It also allows speculators to buy property for cheap and then raise rents. Today Oakland is still feeling the effects of these resource extractions caused by the early onslaught of gentrification in the 1960s, resulting in devastating displacements. New resources come in which are often only available to the invaders. For instance, the Bay Area is seen as a tech hub. These high-paying jobs are one of the reasons why the rent has increased rapidly in the Bay Area. However, Black people who are from Oakland and the broader Bay Area aren't reaping the benefits of this new economy. As the *San Francisco Chronicle* recently noted, tech companies still "struggle" to hire Black people. Facebook has only 3 percent Black workers, and only 2 percent of Google's employees are Black. The technification of the Bay Area has further contributed to the displacement of Oakland's Black population. Since 2000, Oakland has lost nearly 25 percent of its Black population.[8] Since 2015, the houseless population has increased 25 percent.[9]

People's Breakfast Oakland

The BPP's first community program, the free breakfasts for schoolchildren, inspired our People's Breakfast Oakland. Our program was built to address the current conditions of swiftly gentrifying Black Oakland. Our goal was to serve those most impacted by this white supremacist capitalist state, while also creating an inclusive space for the Black community to organize. This program centers Black houseless people in our organizing efforts. We argue that if we can't organize the Black community to provide free warm meals to the houseless, how can we even talk about revolution? It is impossible to expect the people to organize on a hungry stomach. Also, as organizers if we can't provide for our people and show them that there's an alternative to the ways this capitalist state operates, how can we expect the process of revolution to begin?

Some might criticize free food programs as "charity"; however, we believe this is a process of radical transformative change in the community. It is important to show people and captivate the people's imagination about what freedom can look like. Do we think that feeding people alone will start revolution? No. But revolution starts with valuing the humanity of those whose humanity the state strips away. Since creating the organization in 2017 we have fed more than ten thousand houseless people in West Oakland. Our program runs twice a month and as we grow we will increase the days we build with the people. Not only do we serve food, we also provide clothing, hygiene packs that include menstruation products, first aid products, and tents. We don't take a top-down approach. Instead, we center the needs of those we are serving and with whom we are building. For instance, after our first program, we asked leaders of the houseless camps about what they want to see from the program. We then adjusted the program based on the requests of the people. In addition, when the city of Oakland was attempting to evict one of the largest camps in West Oakland, leaders of the houseless camp asked us to help organize a protest. We brought out many community members and helped stop the eviction. We also know that feeding breakfast and organizing the houseless isn't the only goal we have. Taking inspiration from the Panthers, we want to create more programs in the community that address the Black community's material needs and thus we founded People's Programs as an LLC, a limited liability company, which oversees People's Breakfast Oakland.

Structurally, we reject the nonprofit-industrial complex. In order to stay true to our authentic voice and to avoid having to appeal to the moral compasses of foundations, we decided to form our program outside of the nonprofit-industrial complex. We organize from the politic that the white supremacist settler-colonial state has no right to exist. Many nonprofits are funded by the state; for example, "in 2011, one-third of revenue for 501(c)3 public charities came from the government through formal contracts and grants."[10] How can we be antistate and then take money from the government? It's an inherent contradiction. Other ways of funding are through foundations that are often centrist or slightly left of center. For instance, one of the biggest foundations, the Ford Foundation, rescinded funding from INCITE!, "a network of radical feminists of color organizing to end state violence and violence in our homes and communities," because INCITE! believed Palestine should be free.[11]

However, we do know that movement building requires raising funds. We are grassroots funded, and we also know from our history that the government will keep close tabs on revolutionary organizing groups and the IRS will attempt to decimate organizations. Therefore, we have set up People's Programs as part of an LLC in order to stay financially afloat and not have the IRS knocking at our door. We use this structure to file taxes on the money we bring in that is used to support our organizing. While some might say that this is a replication of a corporate model, it's solely for tax purposes and for the ability to embody self-determination within our organization. Since we are an LLC, we aren't tied to any foundations that would seek to curb radical activism and political thought. While our goal is not to make it a corporation, we feel this model allows us to serve the people as we build toward revolution.

We also created People's Programs as we noticed a gap in organizing in Black student spaces. Even as I see limitations in working at the university, there are radical subordinate spaces in universities and we should invest in them. Following Huey Newton and Bobby Seale's decision to move off campus into the community, BSUs or similar Black campus groups ought to create university-funded programs that support Black communities. For example, I am one of the founders of the Fannie Lou Hamer Black Resource

Center at UC Berkeley, born out of Black student struggle, and currently help run it. We developed two community programs within the first two years of our existence as a center. The first program is the Berkeley Black Scholars Program, which works with local Berkeley High Black students and brings them up to campus and provides students with research and organizing skills that they can take back to their community. The students have funds to research a problem in their local community and to create solutions. The other program is a community garden. Half of the garden's produce goes to Black students who are food insecure and the other half goes to the People's Breakfast Oakland. Berkeley BSU members regularly volunteer at the People's Breakfast Oakland. In addition, BSUs should have political education sessions where they bring in local organizers to speak about Black community issues as well as organizing trips to these communities to find ways to work together.

In conclusion, it is clear that there has been a war on the Black community in Oakland and throughout the united states. It is clear that capitalism is the enemy and that Black capitalism is not a solution to our oppression. Liberation requires a grassroots not a top down approach. It is one that must center those most impacted. Liberation comes from building each other up. Not a talented tenth petit-bourgeois approach that centers bringing resources solely to those in the academy. The Black Panther Party provides a good model in which serving the people to build them up for revolution is at the core of organizing. If we are to all be free, we must center those most marginalized and impacted in our community by this white supremacist settler colonial state.

Chinese Progressive Association organizers join the Asians Rise for Climate contingent at the historic March for Climate, Jobs and Justice in San Francisco, 2018. Author Alex Tom on right behind stroller. Photograph by Connie Hsu, 2018

CHAPTER EIGHTEEN

The Chinese Progressive Association and the "Red Door"

Alex T. Tom

Author's note: To begin, this is my own perspective developed over time. In my fifteen years at CPA, I've formally and informally interviewed many of the founders who were directly or indirectly connected to the Black Panther Party, the Red Guards, I Wor Kuen, and the League of Revolutionary Struggle. I am grateful to be living in and building from the legacy of such wisdom, struggle, and optimism for a world of peace and justice. This brief chapter is just the beginning of many more conversations.

The Black Panther Party made a hegemonic shift in politics that influenced the Asian American and broader social movements. This chapter will illustrate its overall influence on the Chinese Progressive Association (CPA), founded in San Francisco in 1972. Over the decades, CPA has evolved and transformed with the community, lifting the voices of oppressed communities, the poor and working class, and contributing toward the liberation of all people.

Born out of the 1970s people power movements, CPA had two major influences that are embedded in its DNA: 1) the elders from the 1930s Chinese Worker Mutual Aid Association (CWMAA) and 2) the young radicals, notably from the I Wor Kuen (IWK), a group inspired and influenced by the Black Panther Party (BPP).[1] Both lineages are intrinsic to the development of CPA and contribute to the unique role of being the "left pole" within the community, while simultaneously building a base of working-class leadership.

CPA has become the "Red Door" to connect our leaders and community to other movements.[2] In fact, CPA's first office at the International Hotel had a red door.

This chapter will focus on the influences of the Black Panther Party, however, it is critical to briefly discuss the influence of the Chinese elders, otherwise known as the "Lo Wah Que," who mentored CPA's founders. As historian Him Mark Lai notes, the Chinese Marxist left had a rich history during the Great Depression in the US and anti-imperialist movement in China.[3] This history laid the foundation for our role in the movement today. In 1938, the CWMAA formed to unite Chinese workers and worked to raise the status of Chinese workers in labor unions and improve their working conditions. The CWMAA led the effort to break into American Federation of Labor (AFL)–affiliated trade unions at the San Francisco waterfront. The AFL was notoriously racist and anti-Chinese, and the CWMAA was one of the only working-class Chinese organizations to directly challenge the AFL's racial exclusionary policies. It was also connected to international struggles. CWMAA cofounder Eva Chan Lowe was the secretary to Madame Sun Yat Sen in Hong Kong during the anti-imperialist war in China. Many of their leaders were jailed or repressed during McCarthyism in the 1950s. By the 1960s and 1970s, many were released and saw the reemergence of a new and radical social movement. These leaders lived in Chinatown and eventually cofounded CPA with the new generation of young Chinese American radicals. The Lo Wah Que brought wisdom, experience, patience, and a working-class perspective. The young radicals brought optimism, fire, determination, and fearlessness for revolutionary change. This was an intergenerational effort, a deliberate unity of immigrant and American born.[4]

Black Panther Influences

From Serve the People and survival programs to the Ten-Point Program, the BPP had a profound influence on the IWK founders who, along with the Lo Wah Que, helped to form CPA. The late 1960s and 1970s was a moment in US history when countries worldwide were fighting for self-determination and liberation from foreign domination. The US imperialist war of aggression in Southeast Asia had particular significance for the Asian American community. The Panthers helped provide clarity about the importance of opposing the war. The Panthers, unlike narrow Black nationalists, linked their cause with the domestic antiwar movement and anti-imperialists abroad.[5] The Panthers were about building a political trend of anti-imperialist and socialist politics in the community. The fates of our paths came together in the late 1960s.

Our histories are interconnected and distinct at the same time. In the late 1960s, CPA founders were part of multiple Asian revolutionary formations including the Red Guards and I Wor Kuen. Much of their journey and politicization began in the pool halls located on the border of Chinatown and Manilatown. In 1968, some of the young radicals were dissatisfied with the direction of youth organizations and wanted to model themselves after the Black Panther Party. This small group, which eventually became the Red Guards in 1969, engaged in political education with Panther leaders Bobby Seale and David Hilliard. Later, these youth were invited to the national headquarters in Oakland to continue their study and began to "show up" for each other. This process of building a deeper relationship, an explicit exchange between Black and Chinese radicals, transformed the characteristics of the community and the movement. Showing up for each other at "Free Huey Rallies" and I-Hotel[6] picket lines made Black and Asian solidarity visible and real. In the beginning, this group wanted to name themselves the "Red Dragons," but BPP cofounder Bobby Seale suggested they call themselves the Red Guards.[7]

In 1971, there were members of the Red Guards who wanted to continue as an underground organization much in the tradition of the Black Liberation Army and others who wanted to do mass work.[8] Those who wanted to engage in aboveground mass work joined I Wor Kuen, which had just moved its national headquarters from New York to the Bay Area. In early 1972, IWK cadre initiated many community projects including childcare programs, women's health clinics, the Bay Area Asian Coalition Against the War, and mass organizations like CPA. For eight months, members engaged in a community process to form CPA. By December 26, 1972, CPA was launched with the union of young radicals, workers, tenants, and the Lo Wah Que. CPA became the left pole and a leading voice of the poor and working-class community in Chinatown, including efforts to normalize US and China relations. This represented a seismic shift in Chinatown politics as the KMT and Chinese Six Companies virtually controlled everything from the garment factories and restaurants where workers worked to single-room occupancy housing where workers lived.[9]

With the dissolution of the organized left in the early 1990s, CPA stayed true to our roots and evolved through changing political tides over the last twenty-five years. From some of the most reactionary and neoliberal periods to the current period of explicit white nationalism and intensified austerity, CPA's organizational form has transformed while maintaining our principles and values. In our current form, CPA's Tenant Worker Center focuses on workforce development, outreach, and leadership development programs for low-wage workers, and Youth MOJO (Movement of Justice and Organizing) provides youth leadership development programs for Chinese and Asian American youth under eighteen.[10] Both programs have organizing campaigns and provide community education on the political moment and "wedge" issues that divide the community. In the last decade, CPA has built one of the most robust year-round citywide Chinese voter outreach programs, the Political Empowerment Campaign, which is integrated with San Francisco Rising, a multiracial citywide alliance of grassroots people of color–led organizations.

The Panthers were the catalyst for many on the left and believed in the self-determination of each community to define their issues, approach, and method. The following stories illustrate CPA's approach to building power and grassroots working-class leadership in the Chinese immigrant community. CPA continues to be a key voice in the community and the Red Door to other national minority communities and progressive movements.

Meeting People Where They Are At

In our organizing work, we often say, "meet the people where they're at." But this is easier said than done. I first met Xiu Zhen Li (Ms. Li) in 2004, while organizing workers at the King Tin Restaurant in Chinatown. I never imagined that she would become a key worker leader of the largest wage settlement in the state of California.

In 2004, the King Tin Restaurant became the first case to test the new San Francisco Minimum Wage Ordinance that was passed by voters in 2003. Originally, the workers only wanted what they were promised—$1,200 a month or $4 to $5 an hour for most workers, significantly lower than the $8.50 minimum wage. We had to organize workers around collecting what they were legally owed, not just what they were promised. Many feared losing their jobs or being blacklisted. In the end, it took three years of organizing and working with the Office of Labor Standards and Enforcement to collect $85,000 of wages owed and penalties.

Ms. Li worked two jobs at King Tin Restaurant, one as a janitor and the other as a kitchen worker. She worked over a hundred hours a week, fifteen hours a day and seven days a week. After the restaurant closed at 11 p.m., she would continue as the janitor working until 2 a.m. and return the next day at 11 a.m. She was barely paid $3 an hour. Ms. Li was one of the most exploited workers in the restaurant. She was also one of the least active workers in the campaign. In fact, she showed up only twice to our campaign meetings, once to complete the lost wages forms and the second time to pick up her check. Since she was the sole breadwinner in the family, she was too afraid to participate. However, after the campaign, Ms. Li began coming to CPA events. In the beginning, she never went to the marches or protests but enjoyed our annual picnics and Lunar New Year celebrations. Eventually, she participated in our Leadership Institute and built relationships with other leaders. Slowly, she began to speak publicly at CPA gatherings and encouraged other workers to stand up for their rights.

In 2008, Ms. Li began working as a dishwasher at the Yank Sing Restaurant, a Michelin-rated high-end dim sum restaurant on the waterfront. Again, she was not paid the minimum wage, but it was "better" and more stable than working in Chinatown. Just as before, she had a lot at stake. Her husband had just lost his job, and her daughter had just started college. In 2013, when CPA started organizing the Yank Sing Restaurant workers, she was reluctant to join the campaign. This was hard on the CPA organizers who had worked with her for over a decade, especially knowing that many of her coworkers trusted her. But we knew that we needed to continue meeting her where she was at and respect her position.

The organizing drive began with a mere six workers. For months, we talked to workers, but most were afraid of losing their jobs. Many were the sole breadwinners in their family. We needed Ms. Li.

One day, before a community and worker delegation went to the restaurant, we were giving an update to a room full of our community allies and partners. After a couple of speakers, Ms. Li emerged out of the crowd and began to tell her story of how she got involved and how it was important to stand up as workers. At that moment, I knew that we would win. Eventually, over a hundred workers signed on to the demand letter, and after continuous organizing for a year and in partnership with Asian Americans Advancing Justice—Asian Law Caucus, the Yank Sing Restaurant workers reached the largest settlement in California at a single restaurant with the Labor Commissioner—$4.2 million for over 280 workers. With that settlement, the workers, Ms. Li among them, could finally go back to China to visit family, send their children to college, or put down a payment on a new home.

When Ms. Li entered CPA's doors in 2004, we did not expect her to keep coming back for over a decade, and while she was initially scared to join the Yank Sing Restaurant worker campaign, she found her voice and helped other workers take their stand.

As a community organization, we create many pathways and roles for everyone. From services and campaigns to social and cultural events. Along the way we've learned the importance of "keeping your ear to the ground" to learn and understand the needs of the community. With the Red Door, we uplift the voices and roles of working people and plant the seeds of solidarity with other communities and progressive movements. For example, during the course of the campaign, worker leaders met other tenants and workers who were fighting on other fronts including anti-eviction struggles and other labor strikes including those at AT&T Ballpark and BART (Bay Area Rapid Transit). After the campaign, in 2014, some Yank Sing worker leaders decided to do voter outreach to support Proposition F, San Francisco $15 Minimum Wage Ordinance and Proposition G, the Anti-Speculation Tax. The "Red Door" is the bridge for the working class to connect their oppression to larger systems of oppression and to believe that another world is possible and necessary.

With Doors Wide Open

In 2012, CPA was preparing to celebrate our fortieth anniversary. It brought back a lot of joy and for some, some painful memories as well. Steve Lew, a member from the 1970s, who became a prominent leader in the LGBTQ movement, approached me and said he wanted to come "back" to CPA to make peace after twenty years. I did not completely understand at the time, but I willingly accepted the offer. With his support, we grew our grassroots fundraising and sustainer program, which is crucial as foundations tend to have their own priorities and deliverables. Grassroots donations are our "self-determination" fund in the truest sense.

After the successful anniversary event, we held an intergenerational dialogue with CPA organizers spanning five generations of leadership, from high school youth to our founders. This was the first time I had been in a room with elders who were part of the Asian American left of the 1960s and '70s, including IWK, League of Revolutionary Struggle, the Line of March, the Communist Workers Party, and the Communist Party USA.

After the opening panel, we split into small groups. One group had all the youth and some elders. It was silent at first, then one of the elders jumped in and shared a reflection, "Everything we did in the 1970s was great, but

I have one regret. . . . We shouldn't have kicked out the gays! My daughter is a lesbian and just got married. I'm so proud of her." That sent chills in the room. Then another elder spoke up and said, "Let's look on the bright side, we needed to make mistakes to be stronger today!" Finally, Steve Lew responded and said, "I was one of the gays you are talking about." He shared about his own internalization of homophobia and the alienation he felt in the movement during those times.

The dialogue continued. We were listening, watching, and learning how our elders were sharing and healing from past mistakes and past pain. It was a beautiful and powerful experience. The youth were speechless. Many were shocked to learn about CPA's and the movement's homophobic history and simply did not know how to respond.

Shortly after the event, one of the youth leaders and founders of Youth MOJO pushed us to or rather demanded that we establish a queer space, queer programs, and queer staff at CPA. They said that CPA was *already* their home and they should not have to go elsewhere to have a "queer" space. In fact, there were no other spaces for Asian and Chinese American high school youth at the time. It was a moment of reflection. Is this our role in the community? Do we have the ability to hold space for queer youth? Looking into our past, we have always had our ear to the ground and responded to the needs of the community. Thus in early 2013, CPA formed Gender, Sexuality and Diversities (GSD) and ran our first queer Alternative Spring Break, which was a four-day overnight retreat that included exchanges with other queer organizations in the Bay Area, workshops on queer liberation history, heteropatriarchy, transphobia, and an intergenerational community dinner. Now in its fifth year, GSD is one of the only spaces for queer and questioning Asian American high school youth in San Francisco.

This was merely the beginning of our transformation. It was no surprise that some of the most developed and politicized leaders in our youth program were queer or questioning. GSD made all of us stronger. GSD created space to discuss gender and sexuality within the Asian American community and broader society. Slowly, we began to hear stories of depression, isolation, and suicide among the many layers of our young people. We started BREATHE, a summer program to give our youth tools to address mental health issues for themselves and their friends. With Trump's election in 2016 and the hypervisibility of gun violence in school, this year, Youth MOJO is launching a campaign to increase mental health resources in San Francisco Unified School District for all students. This is not without challenges. Mental health continues to be a stigma in many immigrant communities, including in the Asian community, but our youth are showing us how to boldly enter with mutuality and love. From the intergenerational dialogue, our elders and youth transformed the Red Door. Our doors are wide open for the entire community.

These stories show how we respond to community needs and build working-class leadership at the same time. There are similarities with the Panthers' Serve the People programs but we also address the particular conditions in our community. The BPP understood that meeting the immediate needs of the community is based on a larger vision of self-determination. For example, CPA started one of the first English as a second language/citizenship classes in the 1980s and fought for recycling services in the 1990s; these services were responding to community needs and connecting people to the Red Door and other social movements.

Also, these services and programs meet the needs of the whole person and entire community. Members of CPA are not just "workers" or "youth," they are also mothers, queer, and disabled. This is the power we are building. Under the system of US capitalism, there are many challenges and contradictions within the people and community. We are struggling *together* with people and the community toward the broader mission and vision; we are not furthering the alienation and isolation they already face daily. Over time, we are building their leadership, consciousness, and collective power and, at the same time, connecting them to other movements through the Red Door.

Building Black and Chinese Solidarity

The working-class Black community has been massively displaced the last couple of decades. Currently, Blacks comprise less than 5 percent of San Francisco residents, a decrease of 50 percent since 1990. At the same time, with migration pressures, Chinese immigrants have been moving into San Francisco and into traditionally Black communities, causing increased tensions among Blacks and Chinese. In the early 2000s, the Lennar Corporation proposed a major housing development in the Bayview-Hunters Point Shipyard, the largest land grab in San Francisco history on one of the most polluted Superfund sites in the country.

In 2006, I spoke at POWER's (People Organized to Win Employment Rights) Community Cookout in the Bayview during Black History Month.[11] This launched some of CPAs most important solidarity work in the face of the massive displacement of the working-class Black community. At the cookout, I shared the need for solidarity and origins of the Rainbow Coalition, a story that was told to me by our elders. The Rainbow Coalition was started in Chicago in the late 1960s by Fred Hampton, deputy chairman of the Illinois BPP, to build a coalition with the Young Lords, Red Guards, and the Young Patriots as an alliance of poor and working-class Blacks, Puerto Ricans, Chinese, and whites. CPA and POWER had already spent years building relationships and learning about each other's communities, but we began to go deeper.

For years, POWER had been organizing around housing and environmental justice in historically Black Bayview-Hunters Point neighborhood, demanding that Lennar clean up the shipyard before building any housing. With the disproportionate rates of cancer and asthma in Bayview-Hunters Point, this was a critical issue for the entire community.[12]

With the increase of the Chinese population in the community, divisions deepened among Blacks and Chinese. In May 2010, there were three high-profile cases of young Blacks attacking Chinese seniors, which, in two cases, led to their deaths. CPA worked with POWER to hold a community dialogue. There was a lot of pain and misperceptions about why Blacks "don't care about their children's behavior" and why so many Chinese were "buying up the block." At the end of the day much remained unresolved, but a couple issues became clear: (a) our communities rarely had actual dialogue about our histories and community conditions and (b) both communities were living under structural poverty and fighting each other for small crumbs.

In 2008, POWER launched a grassroots ballot measure campaign (Proposition F) to mandate that 50 percent of housing be affordable. To undercut this effort, the Lennar Corporation produced an opposing ballot measure (Proposition G) and developed a Community Benefits Agreement (CBA) with the San Francisco Labor Council, San Francisco ACORN, and San Francisco Organizing Project (SFOP). Proposition G allowed Lennar to develop an 800-acre parcel in Bay View-Hunter's Point. Lennar made promises to make 33 percent of the units designated as affordable housing and to provide job training and other community benefits. But there was tremendous community opposition. CPA was the only Chinese immigrant–based organization among those who opposed Lennar and supported POWER's campaign. CPA voiced concern about the horrific level of toxic contamination left by the navy at this Superfund site. But many in the Chinese community were desperate for housing. One community member told me that they don't mind living on toxic land, stating that "Nothing is as bad as the conditions in China." We were seen as "anti-development" and "anti-progress." To this day, I remember CPA being called the "Chinese Regressive Association" on Chinese radio.

After the Lennar Corporation threw millions of dollars into the election, Proposition F lost and Proposition G won.[13] In 2010, the City and County of San Francisco approved the Environmental Impact Report, the final step for the development to move forward, by a vote of 8–3.

Nearly ten years later, a whistleblower revealed that Tetra Tech EC, which was contracted by the Lennar Corporation, had falsified the tests to show that the Superfund site had been cleaned. There are now three hundred homes built on toxic land, many occupied by Chinese immigrant families. An important lesson was that we followed the leadership of our trusted ally POWER, who had an organized and politicized base in the Bayview. We responded to the needs of the community to not pit jobs and housing against the health of the entire community. We know the real solutions come from the community.

Through this struggle, our position strengthened, our relationship deepened, and we learned a lot about how to exercise community power. However, for CPA and our allies, this also raised many questions about how working-class people of color community organizations were building political power. In 2010, the same year, we formed San Francisco Rising Alliance, the only multiracial, multisector, movement electoral vehicle of across the city. Today, it is a new center of gravity that builds solidarity within working-class communities of color and with progressive labor unions. Through the years, we have embodied the Red Door by cocreating an ecosystem of citywide coalition and alliances for our members to connect with other communities and movements. We are in "one struggle, on many fronts," as our elders would say.[14]

Our stand against the Lennar Corporation's development plan, as difficult as it was, shows how a small progressive bloc can transform relations and city politics more broadly. Even small fights like that at the King Tin Restaurant in the six blocks that is now Chinatown can uplift conditions across the city. Finally, it is never so simple as just building "Black and Chinese" unity. Instead we must ask critical questions: Who in the Black community, who in the Chinese community, who in community and labor are we uniting with? We are building unity among poor and working-class communities across the city.

Asian Americans as a Critical Force in the Twenty-First Century

In 2012, CPA hosted a celebration for Grace Lee Boggs in San Francisco Chinatown. It was a homecoming for Grace, an embrace, as most of her activism was in the Black liberation movement. In a room of over three hundred people, probably her largest Asian American audience, she said, "Asian Americans, particularly Chinese Americans, have an important role to play in challenging the dominance of China in the twenty-first century."[15] She asserted that with the climate catastrophe, the role of China in the global economy, and the decline of US imperialism, Asian Americans in the US will have a critical role in confronting Chinese capital and fighting racism in the US.

China is no longer a champion of self-determination as it was during the founding of CPA. Instead China is locked in competition with the United States to dominate regions of the world, including parts of Africa. With the United States' "Pacific pivot," where over 67 percent of military resources has shifted from the Middle East to the Asia Pacific, the region will be the site of many devastating battles and wars, which will also impact the future sovereignty of indigenous people and nations in the Pacific. Asian Americans and Pacific Islanders in the US will also need to forge a new form of solidarity within to confront and lead a broad working-class, multiracial, and internationalist front in the new times ahead.

From the Red Guards to the Red Door, we are taking to heart Grace Lee Boggs's call to action. Her favorite question to the movement was always, "What time is it on the clock of the world?" The Panthers could always tell time, and many would say they were ahead of their time. When the Panthers came to the Chinatown pool hall to do study groups with that group of young Asian radicals, they knew the important role of Asian Americans in the US in the current and future. They helped this group of radicals see the role they could play in their community, and since then, it has never stopped.

This moment is no different. With Trump's election, there has been a rise in explicit white nationalism and white supremacy; there has also been a rise in right-wing ethnic nationalism, especially in the Chinese community, otherwise known as the "Chinese Tea Party." By 2055, Asian immigrants will be the majority of immigrants in the US.[16] Asian Americans in the US will become the bridge in the movement to understand and challenge China's role in the global economy. At our core, regardless of the political moment, the task ahead is to maintain the vision and values, to respond to emerging needs, and to be the Red Door for the working-class community for decades to come.

Conclusion

Although the Panthers and CPA didn't work directly together, the legacy of the Panthers is deeply felt in our work today. We've been fortunate to make connections with former Panthers, including Emory Douglas, the Panther's minister of culture, and Kiilu Nyasha, who recently passed. Their stories as activists, organizers, and San Franciscans have helped to shape our young leaders. Every summer, Emory speaks to our Eva Lowe and Seeding Change fellows about art and activism. Kiilu lived in Chinatown and came to gatherings at CPA's office, including the talk by Grace Lee Boggs. Kiilu also spoke to our youth and broke bread with them at her home. At her celebration of life, one CPA youth shared Kiilu's profound impact. This is what movements are made of. The spirit of the Panthers lives on today and we are proud to be a part of it.

Acknowledgments

G iving thanks to our Creator, our Ancestors and our Indigenous Chumash Hosts, we want to acknowledge some of the help we received producing this book.

Matef:

My dad Lin Barker is still the most encouraging person I know. His love of studying history is infectious. And even though Prince and I have the same mother—she's never satisfied—Syd Nowell Barker is my first and still one of my most important teachers. I never learned anything in school 'til the eighth grade that my parents had not already taught me. My parents not only gave me the foundation of the three Rs of reading, writing and 'rithmatic, they also constructed within me the basis for the other three Rs; resistance, rebellion and revolution.

Both my Sisters have taught me more than I can list. Sandee Dunbar-Smalley and Lori Barker have so many talents and skills, which they employ for the uplift of humanity, that I have learned from them to always put people first when deciphering any and all situations.

Major gratitude to: Marcus Lopez Sr for guiding me to think deeply about everything, especially fascism; the All-African People's Revolutionary Party, including Dedon Kamathi, Macheo Shabaka and Munyiga Lumumba, who put theory into practice daily; Tony Jackson and Liz Bush, for more and more education; John Munro who gave excellent edits, advice and questions regarding my writing; and Diane—whose idea this book was in the first place.

Special thanks to Amit Singh, Faith Magdalena and Robert Landheer for watching my back while I was busy writing and editing.

Diane:

My deepest gratitude to the many activist-organizers and scholars who have profoundly changed the world and demanded liberation for Black people across many decades and in this new moment of Black struggle. Though, joyfully and sadly, too many to name, please know that you have transformed my life. With appreciation to: Matef, a fierce fighter and learned intellectual for Black liberation. Friends in struggle: Gloria Liggett, Marcus Lopez, Elizabeth Robinson, Sara Bazan, Zaveeni Khan-Marcus, Marisela Marquez, Raquel Lopez, George Lipsitz, Ralph Armbruster-Sandoval, Jonathan Gomez, Claudine Michel, Douglas Daniels, Nadège T. Clitandre, Chris McAuley, David Pellow, Lisa Park, and Charmaine Chua. Movement learning across the generations: Yuri Kochiyama, Fred Ho, Mo Nishida, Dedon Kamathi, Ramona Africa, Claude Marks, Diana Block, Linda Evans, Eve Goldberg, Rabab Abdulhadi, Adolfo Matos, Hank Jones, Mitsuye Yamada, Rev. Michael Yasutake, Robyn Rodriquez, Karen Umemoto, Chimaway Lopez, Casmali Lopez, Fabiola Gonzalez, Ana Rosa Rizo Centino, Chelsea Lancaster, and Angela Marks, and Marcelino Sepulveda. Constants in my life: Robyn, Don, Wendy, Janet, Elaine, Karina, Sandee, Lori, Bev, Jaden, Azriel. To my late parents, Yasuo and May Fujino, who taught me about unconditional love, and to my other parents, Lin Barker and the late Syd Nowell Barker, for their example of service and learning. To new possibilities, especially the amazingly talented activists in Cooperation Santa Barbara and with thanks to Cooperation Jackson.

Diane and Matef:

We want to express appreciation to all who made this book project possible, especially the incredible contributors and the terrific people at Haymarket Press—Anthony Arnove, Nisha Bosley, Charlotte Heltai, Rachel Cohen—for being just as excited about this project as we are. Special thanks to Emory Douglas, Akinsanya Kambon, Hank Jones, Shaka At-Thinnin, Sekou Odinga, Tama-sha Kambon, Felice Blake, Rosa Pinter, Mahsheed Ayoub, Rose Elfman, Zaveeni Khan-Marcus, Sepideah Mohsenian-Rahman, the UCSB Center for Black Studies Research, the UC Consortium for Black Studies in California, and the UCSB MultiCultural Center for supporting a series of talks and an art exhibit on which this book is based, and to the UCSB Academic Senate and the UCSB Office of Research, for supporting the development of this book project. To Kano and Seku Fujino-Harmachis for all their love, the most important element of the Black Radical Tradition and the main prophylactic against racial capitalism.

Endnotes

Introduction: The Enduring Significance of the Black Panther Party

1. The influence of the BPP and his knowledge of Black radical history are evident in Ta-Nehisi Coates's writings, including his National Book Award-winning *Between the World and Me* (New York: Spiegel & Grau, 2015) and "The Case for Reparations," *Atlantic*, June 2014.

2. The approach of this book to examine the impact of activism across generations is underused in studies of social movements. Nonetheless, studies that examine intergenerational continuity show the longer historical arc of social movement activity and impact. Donna Murch's prehistory of the Black Panther Party shows that people entering the BPP also had an activism history with previous organizations. Glenda Gilmore shows the radical roots of the civil rights movement. Erik McDuffie and Dayo Gore examine early Black left feminism as a forerunner to the development of more widely known Black feminism. Diane Fujino examines the Japanese American progressive activism in the early Cold War as predecessor to the Asian American movement. See Donna Murch, *Living for the City: Migration, Education, and the Rise of the Black Panther Party* (Chapel Hill: University of North Carolina Press, 2010); Glenda Elizabeth Gilmore, *Defying Dixie: The Radical Roots of Civil Rights, 1919–1950* (New York: W. W. Norton & Co., 2008); Erik McDuffie, *Sojourning for Freedom: Black Women, American Communism, and the Making of Black Left Feminism* (Durham, NC: Duke University Press, 2011); Dayo F. Gore, *Radicalism at the Crossroads: African American Women Activists in the Cold War* (New York: New York University Press, 2011); Diane C. Fujino, "Cold War Activism and Japanese American Exceptionalism," *Pacific Historical Review* 87 (2018): 264–304.

3. We acknowledge that the question of membership is contested. Some sold the newspaper and regularly attended Panther programs but may not have officially joined. The Panthers never kept formal membership rolls. Most estimates in the 1960s and 1970s state between 1,500 and 2,000 members; Bobby Seale estimated 5,000 at its peak in late 1968 and early 1969. See Ollie A. Johnson III, "Explaining the Demise of the Black Panther Party: The Role of Internal Factors," in *The Black Panther Party Reconsidered*, ed. Charles E. Jones (Baltimore: Black Classic Press, 1998), 391, 410; Joshua Bloom and Waldo E. Martin, *Black against Empire: The*

History and Politics of the Black Panther Party (Berkeley: University of California Press, 2013), 2; Jama Lazerow and Yohuru Williams, eds., *In Search of the Black Panther Party* (Durham, NC: Duke University Press, 2006), 4; United States Senate, *Supplementary Detailed Staff Reports of the Intelligence Activities and the Rights of Americans*, Book III, known as the Church Committee Report (Washington, DC: US Government Printing Office, 1976), 214; Philip S. Foner, ed., *The Black Panthers Speak* (Philadelphia: J. B. Lippincott, 1970), xiii–xiv; "Panther Supporters: Many Black Americans Voice Strong Backing for Defiant Militants," *Wall Street Journal*, January 13, 1970.

4. Michael L. Clemons and Charles E. Jones, "Global Solidarity: The Black Panther Party in the International Arena," in Kathleen Cleaver and George Katsiaficas, *Liberation, Imagination, and the Black Panther Party* (New York: Routledge, 2001), 20–39; John T. McCartney, "The Influences of the Black Panther Party (USA) on the Vanguard Party of the Bahamas, 1972–87," in *Liberation, Imagination and the Black Panther Party*, ed. Cleaver and Katsiaficas, 156–63; Judy Tzu-Chun Wu, *Radicals on the Road: Internationalism, Orientalism, and Feminism during the Vietnam Era* (Ithaca, NY: Cornell University Press, 2013), 110; Elbert "Big Man" Howard, *Panther on the Prowl* (BCP Digital Printing, 2002), 34–53; Polynesian Panthers post on Emory Douglas's Facebook page, November 11, 2014, at www.facebook.com/photo.php?fbid=10205690094558033&set=a.1634685913424.2094381.142; Douglas, conversation with Fujino, October 17, 2018. Cuba became a site of political asylum for Black radicals, including former Panthers William Lee Brent, Eldridge Cleaver, and Huey Newton as well as Robert F. Williams, Nehanda Abiodun, and others. See Teishan A. Latner, *Cuban Revolution in America: Havana and the Making of a United States Left, 1968–1992* (Chapel Hill: University of North Carolina Press, 2018), 221–51.

5. Jeffrey L. Judson, ed., *Comrades: A Local History of the Black Panther Party* (Bloomington: Indiana University Press, 2007), 1; Bloom and Waldo, *Black Against Empire*, 2; Katsiaficas, introduction, in *Liberation, Imagination, and the Black Panther Party*, ed. Cleaver and Katsiaficas, vii.

6. Alondra Nelson, *Body and Soul: The Black Panther Party and the Fight against Medical Discrimination* (Minneapolis: University of Minnesota Press, 2011); David Hilliard, ed., *The Black Panther Party: Service to the People Programs* (Albuquerque: University of New Mexico Press, 2008).

7. Barbara Ransby, *Making All Black Lives Matter: Re-imagining Freedom in the Twenty-First Century* (Berkeley: UC Press, 2018).

8. Erik S. McDuffie, *Sojourning for Freedom: Black Women, American Communism, and the Making of Black Left Feminism* (Durham, NC: Duke University Press, 2011); Dayo F. Gore, *Radicalism at the Crossroads: African American Women Activists in the Cold War* (New York: New York University Press, 2011); Ashley D. Farmer, *Remaking Black Power: How Black Women Transformed an Era* (Chapel Hill: University of North Carolina Press, 2017); Carole Boyce Davies, *Left of Karl Marx: The Political Life of Black Communist Claudia Jones* (Durham, NC: Duke University Press, 2008); Jeanne Theoharis, *The Rebellious Life of Mrs. Rosa Parks* (Boston: Beacon Press, 2013).

9. Diane C. Fujino, *Heartbeat of Struggle: The Revolutionary Life of Yuri Kochiyama* (Minneapolis: University of Minnesota Press, 2005); Diane C. Fujino, *Samurai among Panthers: Richard Aoki on Race, Resistance, and a Paradoxical Life* (Minneapolis: University of Minnesota Press, 2012); Diane C. Fujino, "The Indivisibility of Freedom: The Nisei Progressives, Deep Solidarities, and Cold War Alternatives," *Journal of Asian American Studies 21* (2018 June): 171–208.

10. Keeanga-Yamahtta Taylor, *From #BlackLivesMatter to Black Liberation* (Chicago: Haymarket Books, 2016); Charlene Carruthers, *Unapologetic: A Black, Queer, and Feminist Mandate for Radical Movements* (Boston: Beacon Press, 2018); Patrisse Khan-Cullors and asha bandele, *When They Call You a Terrorist: A Black Lives Matter Memoir* (New York: St. Martin's Press, 2018); Naomi Klein, *This Changes Everything: Capitalism vs. the Climate* (New York: Simon & Schuster, 2014); Naomi Klein, *No Is Not Enough: Resisting Trump's Shock Politics and Winning the World We Need* (Chicago: Haymarket Books, 2017); Bikem Ekberzade, *Standing Rock: Greed, Oil and the Lakota's Struggle for Justice* (London: Zed Books, 2018); Sarah van Gelder, ed., *This Changes Everything: Occupy Wall Street and the 99% Movement* (San Francisco: Berrett-Koehler Publishers, 2011).

11. Movement for Black Lives, "Platform," https://policy.m4bl.org/platform/, accessed October 19, 2018.

12. Movement for Black Lives, "About," "Platform," and "Policy Demands," https://policy.m4bl.org/, accessed August 21, 2016; Ransby, *Making All Black Lives Matter*, 3.

13. Clyde Woods, "Les Misérables of New Orleans: Trap Economics and the Asset Stripping Blues, Part 1," *American Quarterly* 61 (2009): 769–96; Walter Johnson, "What Do We Mean When We Say 'Structural Racism'?: A Walk Down West Florissant Avenue, Ferguson, Missouri," *Kalfou* 3 (Spring 2016): 36–62.

14. George Katsiaficas, "Organization and Movement: The Case of the Black Panther Party and the Revolutionary People's Constitutional Convention of 1970," in *Liberation, Imagination, and the Black Panther Party*, ed. Cleaver and Katsiaficas, 141–55; Black Panther Party, "Ten Point Platform and Program," October 1966, in *The Black Panthers Speak*, ed. Philip S. Foner (Philadelphia: J.B. Lippincott, 1970), 2–4.

15. Movement for Black Lives, "Platform."

16. BYP100, "Frequently Asked Questions and Glossary," https://byp100.org/faq/, accessed October 5, 2018; Kimberlé Crenshaw, with Priscilla Ocen and Jyoti Nanda, *Black Girls Matter: Pushed Out, Overpoliced, and Underprotected*, African American Policy Forum report, at www.aapf.org, accessed February 10, 2017.

17. Movement for Black Lives, "Platform"; Akasha (Gloria T.) Hull, Patricia Bell-Scott, and Barbara Smith, *All the Women Are White, All the Blacks Are Men, But Some of Us Are Brave: Black Women's Studies* (Old Westbury, NY: Feminist Press, 1982).

18. Movement for Black Lives, "Policy Demands"; Black Panther Party, "Ten-Point Platform and Program."

19. Ward Churchill and Jim Vander Wall, *Agents of Repression: The FBI's Secret War Against the Black Panther Party and the American Indian Movement* (Boston: South End Press, 1988).

20. "Herstory," blacklivesmatter.com, http://blacklivesmatter.com/a-herstory

-of-the-blacklivesmatter-movement/, posted December 6, 2014; Carruthers, *Unapologetic*; Vision Statement of the Movement for Black Lives.

21. Kimberlé Crenshaw introduced and developed the term intersectional in a 1989 critical race theory article to refer to the complex ways that Black women's oppression is shaped by the intertwining and inseparability of race and gender. The idea was developed in analyses by women of color of the 1980s, as in Hull, Bell-Scott, and Smith's *All the Women Are White, All the Blacks Are Men, but Some of Us Are Brave*, but in fact has a longer history dating back to long-sixties struggles by the Combahee River Collective, Black Panther women, Chicana and Asian American feminists, and before that to Claudia Jones and Esther Cooper Jackson in the 1930s and 1940s, and before that to Sojourner Truth in the 1870s.

22. Huey P. Newton, "The Women's Liberation and Gay Liberation Movements," August 15, 1970, in *The Huey P. Newton Reader*, ed. David Hilliard and Donald Weise (New York: Seven Stories Press, 2002), 157–59.

23. Robert Sandarg, *Jean Genet in America* (Huey P. Newton Papers, Stanford University, series 2, box 60) 58–59, cited in Ronald K. Porter, "A Rainbow in Black: The Gay Politics of the Black Panther Party," *Counterpoints* 367 (2012), 370.

24. Cited in Porter, "A Rainbow in Black," 370.

25. Cited in Charles E. Jones and Judson L. Jeffries, "'Don't Believe the Hype: Debunking the Panther Mythology," in *The Black Panther Party Reconsidered*, ed. Jones, 35.

26. Trystan Reese, "Lessons Learned from the Black Panther Party," thetaskforce.org, www.thetaskforce.org/lessons-learned-from-the-black-panther-party/, accessed October 22, 2018.

27. Cedric J. Robinson, *Black Marxism: The Making of the Black Radical Tradition* (London: Zed Books, 1983); Gerald Horne, *Communist Front? The Civil Rights Congress, 1946–1956* (Rutherford, NJ: Fairleigh Dickinson University Press, 1988); Robin D. G. Kelley, *Hammer and Hoe: Alabama Communists during the Great Depression* (Chapel Hill: University of North Carolina Press, 1990); George Lipsitz, *Rainbow at Midnight: Labor and Culture in the 1940s* (Urbana: University of Illinois Press, 1994); Penny M. Von Eschen, *Race against Empire: Black Americans and Anticolonialism, 1937–1957* (Ithaca, NY: Cornell University Press, 1997); Nikhil Pal Singh, *Black Is a Country: Race and the Unfinished Struggle for Democracy* (Cambridge, MA: Harvard University Press, 2004); Glenda Elizabeth Gilmore, *Defying Dixie: The Radical Roots of Civil Rights, 1919–1950* (New York: W. W. Norton, 2009).

28. Jacquelyn Dowd Hall, "The Long Civil Rights Movement and the Political Uses of the Past," *Journal of American History* 91 (2005): 1233–63; Peniel E. Joseph, ed., *The Black Power Movement: Rethinking the Civil Rights–Black Power Era* (New York: Routledge, 2006). While the origins of the Black Power movement are commonly dated to 1966, ideologies of Black Power certainly had earlier and global antecedents rooted in Africa as well. Matt Meyer and Dan Berger, "The Pan-Africanization of Black Power," in *We Have Not Been Moved: Resisting Racism and Militarism in Twenty-First Century America*, ed. Elizabeth Betita Martinez, Matt Meyer, Mandy Carter, et al. (Oakland, CA: PM Press, 2012), 137; and Gwendolyn Zoharah Simmons,

"Truly Human: Spiritual Paths in the Struggle against Racism, Militarism, and Materialism," in *We Have Not Been Moved*, ed. Martinez, Meyer, and Carter, 351–52; Komozi Woodard, "Rethinking the Black Power Movement," New York Public Library website, http://exhibitions.nypl.org /africanaage/essay-black-power.html, accessed December 9, 2018.

29. Diane C. Fujino, "Writing against the Grain: Biography, History, and the Long Freedom Movements," *American Quarterly* 69 (2017): 935–45; Peniel E. Joseph, *Stokely: A Life* (New York: Basic Civitas, 2014); Timothy Tyson, *Radio Free Dixie: Robert F. Williams and the Roots of Black Power* (Chapel Hill: University of North Carolina Press), 1999.

30. Grace Lee Boggs, *Living for Change: An Autobiography* (Minneapolis: University of Minnesota Press, 1998), 136.

31. Gerald Horne, *Black Revolutionary: William Patterson and the Globalization of the African American Freedom Struggle* (Urbana: University of Illinois Press, 2013); Gerald Horne, *Race to Revolution: The United States and Cuba during Slavery and Jim Crow* (New York: Monthly Review Press, 2014); Brenda Gayle Plummer, *In Search of Power: African Americans in the Era of Decolonization, 1956–1974* (New York: Cambridge University Press, 2013); Yuichiro Onishi, *Transpacific Antiracism: Afro-Asian Solidarity in Twentieth-Century Black America, Japan, and Okinawa* (New York: New York University Press, 2013); Robeson Taj Frazier, *The East Is Black: Cold War China in the Black Radical Imagination* (Durham, NC: Duke University Press, 2015); Sean L. Malloy, *Out of Oakland: Black Panther Party Internationalism during the Cold War* (Ithaca, NY: Cornell University Press, 2017); Cleaver and Katsiaficas, eds., *Liberation, Imagination, and the Black Panther Party*; Elaine Mokhtefi, *Algiers, Third World Capital: Freedom Fighters, Revolutionaries, and Black Panthers* (New York: Verso Books, 2018).

32. Singh, *Black Is a Country*; Jeanne F. Theoharis and Komozi Woodard, eds. *Groundwork: Local Black Freedom Movements in America* (New York: New York University Press, 2005); Hall, "The Long Civil Rights Movement."

33. Rickey Vincent, *Party Music: The Inside Story of the Black Panthers' Band and How Black Power Transformed Soul Music* (Chicago: Chicago Review Press, 2013); Ryan Lindsay, "West Oakland Finally Gets a Black Panther Mural: Two Black Artists Paint History into the Neighborhood," www.refa1.com/blog, posted November 11, 2017.

34. Todd Gitlin, *The Twilight of Common Dreams: Why America Is Wracked by Culture Wars* (New York: Metropolitan Books, 1995).

35. Robert L. Allen, *Black Awakening in Capitalist America: An Analytic History* (Garden City, NY: Doubleday Anchor Books, 1969); Robinson, *Black Marxism*; Rod Bush, *We Are Not What We Seem: Black Nationalism and Class Struggle in the American Century* (New York: New York University Press, 1999); Robin D. G. Kelley, *Freedom Dreams: The Black Radical Imagination* (Boston: Beacon Press, 2002); Peniel E. Joseph, *Waiting 'Til the Midnight Hour: A Narrative History of Black Power in America* (New York: Henry Holt, 2006); Rhonda Y. Williams, *Concrete Demands: The Search for Black Power in the Twentieth Century* (New York: Routledge, 2015).

36. Hilliard, ed., *The Black Panther Party: Service to the People Programs*; Murch, *Living for the City*; Nelson, *Body and Soul*; Robyn C. Spencer, *The Revolution Has Come: Black Power, Gender, and the Black Panther Party in Oakland* (Durham, NC: Duke University Press, 2016).

37. Tracye Matthews, "'No One Ever Asks What a Man's Place in the Revolution Is': Gender and the Politics of the BPP, 1966–1971," in *The Black Panther Party Reconsidered*, ed. Jones, 267–304; Angela LeBlanc-Ernest, "'The Most Qualified Person to Handle the Job': Black Panther Party Women, 1966–1982," in *The Black Panther Party Reconsidered*, ed. Jones, 305–34; Spencer, *The Revolution Has Come*; Ashley D. Farmer, *Remaking Black Power: How Black Women Transformed an Era* (Chapel Hill: University of North Carolina Press, 2017).

38. Donald Freed, *Agony in New Haven: The Trial of Bobby Seale and Ericka Huggins and the Black Panther Party* (New York: Simon & Schuster, 1973); Peter L. Zimroth, *Perversions of Justice: The Prosecution and Acquittal of the Panther 21* (New York: Viking, 1974); Judson, *Comrades*; Yohuru Williams and Jama Lazerow, *Liberated Territory: Untold Local Perspectives on the Black Panther Party* (Durham, NC: Duke University Press, 2008); Judson Jeffries, ed., *On the Ground: The Black Panther Party in Communities across America* (Jackson: University of Mississippi Press, 2010); Omari L. Dyson, *The Black Panther Party and Transformative Pedagogy: Place-Based Education in Philadelphia* (Lanham, MD: Lexington Books, 2014); Jakobi Williams, *From the Bullet to the Ballot: The Illinois Chapter of the Black Panther Party and Racial Coalition Politics in Chicago* (Chapel Hill: University of North Carolina Press, 2015); Lucas N. N. Burke and Judson L. Jeffries, *The Portland Black Panthers* (Seattle: University of Washington Press, 2016); Judson Jeffries, ed., *The Black Panther Party in a City Near You* (Athens: University of Georgia Press, 2018).

39. Stephen Shames, *The Black Panthers: Photographs by Stephen Shames* (New York: Aperture Foundation, 2006); Emory Douglas, *Black Panther: The Revolutionary Art of Emory Douglas*, ed. Sam Durant (New York, Rizzoli, 2007); Howard L. Bingham, *Black Panthers 1968* (Pasadena, CA: AMMO Books, 2009); Vincent, *Party Music*.

40. Lazerow and Williams, eds., *In Search of the Black Panther Party*; Fujino, *Samurai among Panthers*.

41. Bobby Seale, *Seize the Time: The Story of the Black Panther Party and Huey P. Newton* (New York: Random House, 1970); Huey P. Newton, *To Die for the People: Selected Writings and Speeches* (New York: Random House, 1972); Huey P. Newton, *Revolutionary Suicide* (New York: Harcourt Brace Jovanovich, 1973); Foner, *The Black Panthers Speak*.

42. Gene Marine, *The Black Panthers* (New York: New American Library, 1969); Earl Anthony, *Picking Up the Gun* (New York: Dial Press, 1970); George Jackson, *Soledad Brother: The Prison Letters of George Jackson* (New York: Bantam, 1970); George Jackson, *Blood in My Eye* (Baltimore: Black Classic Press, 1971); Angela Y. Davis, ed., *If They Come in the Morning: Voices of Resistance* (New York: Verso Books, 1971); Freed, *Agony in New Haven*; Zimroth, *Perversions of Justice*; G. Louis Heath, *Off the Pigs! The History and Literature of the Black Panther Party* (Metuchen, NJ: Scarecrow Press, 1976); G. Louis Heath, ed. *The Black Panther Leaders Speak* (Metuchen, NJ: Scarecrow Press, 1976).

43. Bobby Seale, *A Lonely Rage: The Autobiography of Bobby Seale* (New York: Times Books, 1978); Assata Shakur, *Assata: An Autobiography* (Chicago: Lawrence Hill Books, 1987); Churchill and Wall, *Agents of Repression.*

44. Diane C. Fujino, "Who Studies the Asian American Movement?: A Historiographical Analysis," *Journal of Asian American Studies* 11 (2008): 127–69.

45. Jones, ed. *The Black Panther Party Reconsidered*; Cleaver and Katsiaficas, eds. *Liberation, Imagination, and the Black Panther Party*; Hugh Pearson, *The Shadow of the Panther* (Reading, MA: Addison-Wesley, 1994); Huey P. Newton *War Against the Panthers: A Study of Repression in America* (New York: Harlem River Press, 1996); Jim Haskins, *Power to the People: The Rise and Fall of the Black Panther Party* (for young readers) (New York: Simon & Schuster, 1997); Judson L. Jeffries, *Huey P. Newton: The Radical Theorist* (Jackson: University of Mississippi, 2002); Curtis J. Austin, *Up Against the Wall: Violence in the Making and Unmaking of the Black Panther Party* (Fayetteville: University of Arkansas Press, 2006); Lazerow and Williams, *In Search of the Black Panther Party*; Jane Rhodes, *Framing the Black Panther Party* (Urbana: University of Illinois Press, 2007); Judson, *Comrades*; Paul Alkebulan, *Survival Pending Revolution: The History of the Black Panther Party* (Tuscaloosa: University of Alabama Press, 2007); Williams and Lazerow, *Liberated Territory.*

46. Elaine Brown, *A Taste of Power: A Black Woman's Story* (New York: Anchor Books, 1992); David Hilliard and Lewis Cole, *This Side of Glory: The Autobiography of David Hilliard and the Story of the Black Panther Party* (Boston: Little, Brown & Co., 1993); Dhoruba Bin Wahad, Mumia Abu-Jamal, and Assata Shakur, *Still Black, Still Strong: Survivors of the U.S. War against Black Revolutionaries*, eds. Jim Fletcher, Tanaquil Jones, and Sylvère Lotringer (New York: Semiotext(e), 1993); Mumia Abu-Jamal, *We Want Freedom: A Life in the Black Panther Party* (Cambridge, MA: South End Press, 2004); Earl Anthony, *Spitting in the Wind* (Malibu, CA: Roundtable, 1990) (in this book, Anthony reveals his work as an FBI informant); Marvin X (Jackmon), *Somethin' Proper: The Life and Times of a North American African Poet* (Castro Valley, CA: Black Bird Press, 1998); Lori Andrews, *Black Power, White Blood: The Life and Times of Johnny Spain* (Philadelphia: Temple University Press, 1999); Jack Olsen, *Last Man Standing: The Tragedy and Triumph of Geronimo Pratt* (New York: Anchor Books, 2000); Howard, *Panther on the Prowl*; Jasmine Guy, *Afeni Shakur: Evolution of a Revolutionary* (New York: Atria Books, 2004); Flores A. Forbes, *Will You Die with Me? My Life and the Black Panther Party* (New York: Atria Books, 2006); Reginald Major, *A Panther Is a Black Cat: An Account of the Early Years of the Black Panther Party* (Baltimore: Black Classic Press, 2006); Steve D. McCutchen, *We Were Free for a While: Back to Back in the Black Panther Party* (Baltimore: Publish America, 2008).

47. Hilliard and Weise, eds., *The Huey P. Newton Reader*; David Hilliard, ed., *The Black Panther: Intercommunal News Service, 1967–1980* (New York: Atria Books, 2007); Hilliard, *The Black Panther Party: Service to the People Programs*; Shames, *The Black Panthers*; Bingham, *Black Panthers 1968.*

48. See www.itsabouttimebpp.com/; Sandhya Dirks, "Preserving the History of the Black Panthers Close to Home," www.kqed.org/news/10868172/preserving-the-history-of-the-black-panthers-close-to-home, February 17, 2016.

49. Murch, *Living for the City*; Jeffries, *On the Ground*; Jeffrey Haas, *The Assassination of Fred Hampton* (Chicago: Chicago Review Press, 2010); Christian Davenport, *Media Bias, Perspective and State Repression: The Black Panther Party* (Cambridge: Cambridge University Press, 2010); Nelson, *Body and Soul*; Fujino, *Samurai among Panthers*; Bloom and Martin, *Black against Empire*; Vincent, *Party Music*; Dyson, *The Black Panther Party and Transformative Pedagogy*; Williams, *From the Bullet to the Ballot*; Herb Boyd, *Black Panthers for Beginners* (Danbury, CT: For Beginners LLC, 2015); Spencer, *The Revolution Has Come*; Bryan Shih and Yohuru Williams, eds., *The Black Panthers: Portraits from an Unfinished Revolution* (New York: Nation Books, 2016); Burke and Jeffries, *The Portland Black Panthers*; Malloy, *Out of Oakland*; Farmer, *Remaking Black Power*; Jeffries, *The Black Panther Party in a City Near You*.

50. Howard, *Panther on the Prowl*; Safiya Bukhari, *The War Before: The True Life Story of Becoming a Black Panther, Keeping the Faith in Prison, and Fighting for Those Left Behind* (New York: Feminist Press, 2010); Aaron Dixon, *My People Are Rising: Memoir of a Black Panther Captain* (Chicago: Haymarket Books, 2012); Jamal Joseph, *Panther Baby: A Life of Rebellion and Reinvention* (Chapel Hill, NC: Algonquin Books of Chapel Hill, 2012); Wayne Pharr, *Nine Lives of a Black Panther: A Story of Survival* (Chicago: Lawrence Hill, 2014); Jo-Ann Morgan, *The Black Arts Movement and the Black Panther Party in American Visual Culture* (New York: Routledge, 2019); Don Cox, *Just Another Nigger: My Life in the Black Panther Party* (Berkeley: Heyday, 2019).

51. Douglas, *Black Panther*; Russell Maroon Shoatz, *Maroon the Implacable* (Oakland, CA: PM Press, 2013); Stephen Shames and Bobby Seale, *Power to the People: The World of the Black Panthers* (New York: Abrams, 2016); Sekou Odinga, Dhoruba Bin Wahad, Shaba Om, and Jamal Joseph, *Look for Me in the Whirlwind*, eds. déqui kioni-sadiki and Matt Meyer (Oakland, CA: PM Press, 2017); Marc James Léger and David Tomas, eds., *Zapantera Negra: An Artistic Encounter Between Black Panthers and Zapatistas* (New York: Common Notions, 2017); Mokhtefi, *Algiers, Third World Capital*.

52. Kekla Magoon, *The Rock and the River* (New York: Aladdin, 2009); Rita Williams-Garcia, *One Crazy Summer* (New York: Amistad, 2010).

53. Bukhari, *The War Before*, 139–53.

54. Stokely Carmichael, "Pan-Africanism" (quoted from 202, 192, 200; also 183–220) and "From Black Power Back to Pan-Africanism" (221–27), both in *Stokely Speaks: From Black Power to Pan-Africanism* (New York: Lawrence Hill, 2007, orig. 1971); Huey P. Newton, "On the Middle East: September 5, 1970," in *To Die for the People: The Writings of Huey P. Newton*, ed. Toni Morrison (New York: Writers and Readers, 1973), quoted from 191; also 191–96.

55. "Chairman" is the term that was used to reference David Brothers for years, so we use it here, despite its gendered nature.

56. Foner, *The Black Panthers Speak*, xxvi; Spencer, *The Revolution Has Come*, 89. Panthers killed by police include Arthur Morris in Los Angeles in March 1968, Bobby Hutton in Oakland in April 1968, Steve Bartholomew, Robert Lawrence, and Tommy Lewis in Los Angeles in August 1968, Fred Hampton and Mark Clark in Chicago on December 1969; Carl Hampton in Houston in July 1970; Zayd Shakur in New Jersey in May 1973; Twymon Myers in New York in November

1973, and many others.

57. United States Senate, *Supplementary Detailed Staff Reports of the Intelligence Activities and the Rights of Americans*, Final Report of the Select Committee to Study Governmental Operations with Respect to Intelligence Activities, April 23, 1976; Churchill and Jim Vander Wall, *Agents of Repression*; "COINTELPRO 101," documentary (San Francisco: Freedom Archives, 2010).

58. Mumia Abu-Jamal, *Have Black Lives Ever Mattered?* (San Francisco: City Lights Books, 2017); Mumia Abu-Jamal, *Live from Death Row* (New York: Perennial, 1995); Albert Woodfox, *Solitary* (New York: Grove, 2019).

Chapter One
Assata Shakur: The Political Life of Political Exile

1. FBI / New Jersey State Police reward poster, May 2005. Author's collection.

2. John Rice, "Castro Defends American Militant Murderer Hiding Out in Cuba," Associated Press, May 11, 2005. Although Castro's speech did not refer to Shakur by name, he left no doubt about whom he was speaking.

3. For a history of these proceedings, see Evelyn Williams, *Inadmissible Evidence: The Story of the African-American Trial Lawyer Who Defended the Black Liberation Army* (Chicago: Lawrence Hill Books, 1993); Assata Shakur, *Assata: An Autobiography* (London: Zed Books, 1987).

4. See Betty Medsger, *The Burglary: The Discovery of J. Edgar Hoover's Secret FBI* (New York: Knopf, 2014); Ward Churchill and Jim Vander Wall, *The COINTELPRO Papers: Documents from the FBI's Secret Wars against Dissent in the United States* (Boston: South End Press, 1990).

5. Oscar Ferrer, "Political Prisoners in the United States," *Granma*, English edition, December 31, 1978.

6. Teishan A. Latner, *Cuban Revolution in America: Havana and the Making of a United States Left, 1968–1992* (Chapel Hill: University of North Carolina Press, 2018).

7. FBI/New Jersey State Police reward poster, May 2013. Author's collection.

8. Latner, *Cuban Revolution in America*, 251–63.

9. For instance, in 2015, *Havana Times*, an online blog and magazine that often features pieces critical of the Cuban government, initially published the unsubstantiated claim that the Cuban government had agreed to return "individuals on the island sought by US justice to the United States," before editing and correcting the story. Gabriela Radfar, "Cuba–US Talks and the Fate of Assata Shakur and Nehanda Abiodun," *Havana Times*, February 2, 2015, www.havanatimes.org /?p=109064.

10. Roberto Zurbano, author's interview, Havana, June 27, 2015.

11. See Christian Parenti, "Postmodern Maroon in the Ultimate Palenque," *Peace Review: A Journal of Social Justice* 10, no. 3 (1998): 419–26.

12. Source anonymous. Author's interview, Havana, June 28, 2013.

13. Charlie Hill and Nehanda Abiodun, US political exiles who have lived in Cuba

since 1971 and 1990, respectively, also maintain that the Cuban government never sought to limit their associations with either Cubans or foreigners.

14. The Black Liberation Army has received little sustained scholarly attention, despite the significance of the formation. Studies that have examined it include Akinyele Omowale Umoja, "The Black Liberation Army and the Radical Legacy of the Black Panther Party," in *Black Power in the Belly of the Beast*, ed. by Judson L. Jeffries; and Akinyele Omowale Umoja, "Repression Breeds Resistance: The Black Liberation Army and the Radical Legacy of the Black Panther Party," in *Liberation, Imagination, and the Black Panther Party*, ed. Cleaver and Katsiaficas.

15. For Cuban internationalism see, for instance, Margaret Randall, *Exporting Revolution: Cuba's Foreign Policy* (Durham, NC: Duke University Press, 2017); Isaac Saney, "Homeland of Humanity: Internationalism within the Cuban Revolution," *Latin American Perspectives* 36, no. 1 (January 2009): 111–23. For the internationalism of the Black Panthers, and the relationship between the Panthers and the Cuban Revolution, see Anne Garland Mahler, *From the Tricontinental to the Global South: Race, Radicalism, and Transnational Solidarity* (Durham, NC: Duke University Press, 2018); Sean L. Malloy, *Out of Oakland: Black Panther Party Internationalism during the Cold War* (Ithaca, NY: Cornell University Press, 2017) and *Black against Empire*, ed. Bloom and Martin Jr. See also Ruth Reitan, *The Rise and Decline of an Alliance: Cuba and African American Leaders in the 1960s* (East Lansing: Michigan State University Press, 1999).

16. Tyson, *Radio Free Dixie*.

17. Van Gosse, *Where the Boys Are: Cuba, Cold War America, and the Making of a New Left* (New York: Verso Books, 1993).

18. Devyn Spence Benson, *Antiracism in Cuba: The Unfinished Revolution* (Chapel Hill: University of North Carolina Press, 2015); Frank Andre Guridy, *Forging Diaspora: Afro-Cubans and African Americans in a World of Empire and Jim Crow* (Chapel Hill: University of North Carolina Press, 2010); Lisa Brock and Digna Castañeda Fuertes, eds., *Between Race and Empire: African-Americans and Cubans before the Cuban Revolution* (Philadelphia: Temple University Press, 1998).

19. See Ada Ferrer, *Insurgent Cuba: Race, Nation and Revolution, 1868–98* (Chapel Hill: University of North Carolina Press, 1999); Alejandro de la Fuente, *A Nation for All: Race, Inequality, and Politics in Twentieth-Century Cuba* (Chapel Hill: University of North Carolina Press, 2001); and Danielle Pilar Clealand, *The Power of Race in Cuba: Racial Ideology and Black Consciousness During the Revolution* (Oxford: Oxford University Press, 2017).

20. Bloom and Martin Jr., *Black against Empire*.

21. See, for instance, William Lee Brent, *Long Time Gone: A Black Panther's True-Life Story of His Hijacking and Twenty-Five Years in Cuba* (New York: Times Books, 1996).

22. Bloom and Martin, *Black against Empire*, 195.

23. Shakur, *Assata: An Autobiography*, 268.

24. Shakur, *Assata: An Autobiography*, 268.

25. See Isaac Saney, *Cuba: A Revolution in Motion* (London: Zed Books, 2004).

26. Shakur, *Assata: An Autobiography*, 267.

27. Shakur, *Assata: An Autobiography*, 268. Lowercase in the original.

28. Assata Shakur, in conversation with Pastors for Peace and recorded by Karen Lee Wald, in Paul Davidson, "Interview with Assata Shakur," *Flame* 6, November 6, 2000, www.fantompowa.net/Flame/assata_interview.htm.

29. The origin of the Venceremos Brigade is examined by the author in *Cuban Revolution in America: Havana and the Making of a United States Left, 1968–1992* (Chapel Hill: University of North Carolina Press, 2018).

30. Latner, *Cuban Revolution in America.*

31. Yuri Kochiyama, *Passing It On* (Los Angeles: UCLA Asian American Studies Center Press, 2nd ed., 2004).

32. Shakur interviewed by Davidson.

33. See Audre Lorde, *A Burst of Light and Other Essays* (Ithaca, NY: Firebrand Books, 1988).

34. Shakur interviewed by Davidson.

35. Evelyn C. White, "Prisoner in Paradise," *Essence,* June 1997.

36. Nehanda Abiodun, author's interview, Havana, June 19, 2018.

37. Alicia Garza, "A Herstory of the #BlackLivesMatter Movement," *Feminist Wire*, October 7, 2014, www.thefeministwire.com/2014/10/blacklivesmatter-2.

38. See, for instance, Donna Murch, *Assata Taught Me: State Violence, Mass Incarceration, and the Movement for Black Lives* (Chicago, IL: Haymarket Books, 2020).

39. Assata Shakur, "Letter from Assata on the Prison Industrial Complex," September 25, 1998. Republished by Afrocubaweb.com, www.afrocubaweb.com/assata2.htm#Prison.

40. See, for instance, Dan Berger, *Captive Nation: Black Prison Organizing in the Civil Rights Era* (Chapel Hill: University of North Carolina Press, 2014).

41. FBI / New Jersey State Police reward poster, May 2013. Author's collection.

42. Although the statement's authenticity cannot be verified, it is regarded by a number of Shakur's comrades in Cuba as fraudulent, a view reportedly shared by representatives of Cuban state intelligence personnel. Interview sources anonymous. Available at www.news24.com/Archives/City-Press/Listen-up-The-European-is-not-your-friend-20150429.

43. Nehanda Abiodun, interview with author, Havana, July 15, 2018.

44. Charlie Hill, interview with author, Havana, July 23, 2018.

45. Anonymous, interview with author, Havana, June 2013.

46. Joy James, "Framing the Panther: Assata Shakur and Black Female Agency," in *Want to Start a Revolution? Radical Women in the Black Freedom Struggle*, ed. Dayo F. Gore, Jeanne Theoharis, and Komozi Woodard (New York: New York University Press, 2009), 155.

47. Nehanda Abiodun, author's interview, Havana, July 23, 2018. Abiodun died in Havana on January 30, 2019.

Chapter Two: "We Had Our Own Community": Hank Jones, Spaces of Confinement, and a Vision of Abolition Democracy

1. Ruth Wilson Gilmore, *Golden Gulag: Prisons, Surplus, Crisis, and Opposition in*

Globalizing California (Berkeley: University of California Press, 2007), 28.

2.   W. E. B. Du Bois, *Black Reconstruction in America: Toward a History of the Part which Black Folk Played in the Attempt to Reconstruct Democracy in America, 1860–1880* (New York: Touchstone, 1935/1995), 182.

3.   Du Bois, *Black Reconstruction*, 184–89; George Lipsitz, "Abolition Democracy and Global Justice," *Comparative American Studies* 2 (2004): 271–86.

4.   Angela Y. Davis, *Abolition Democracy: Beyond Empire, Prisons, and Torture* (New York: Seven Stories Press, 2005); Michelle Alexander, *The New Jim Crow: Mass Incarceration in the Age of Colorblindness* (New York: New Press, 2010); Ava DuVernay, *13th* (documentary, 2016). The fields of critical race theory and critical legal studies were created to contest the ways the law, far from being neutral, often work to reproduce racist and capitalist structures, policies, and practices. These fields interrogate the relationship between law and power that results in racial and class subordination (Kimberlé Crenshaw, Neil Gotanda, Gary Peller, and Thomas Kendall, eds., *Critical Race Theory: The Key Writings That Formed the Movement* (New York: New Press, 1995).

5.   On Black movement armed struggle, see Umoja, "Repression Breeds Resistance, 3–19; Akinyele Omowale Umoja, *We Will Shoot Back: Armed Resistance in the Mississippi Freedom Movement* (New York: New York University Press, 2013); also see note 22.

6.   After Hank's paternal grandmother died when Hank was three years old, his step-grandfather continued to live with his family. Department of Commerce, Bureau of the Census, Fourteenth Census of the United States: 1920—Population, information on Tommie Rose Taylor and George Taylor; Department of Commerce, Bureau of the Census, Sixteenth Census of the United States: 1940—Population Schedule, information on Hank W. Jones, Sr. and Annie Jones; Hank Jones, interview by Diane C. Fujino and Matef Harmachis, January 31, 2016, Santa Barbara, CA.

7.   Jones, interview by Fujino and Harmachis, January 31, 2016.

8.   Cedric J. Robinson, *Black Marxism: The Making of the Black Radical Tradition* (Chapel Hill: University of North Carolina Press, 2000).

9.   Henry Watson Jones Sr., teaching public school (US Census, 1930; US Census, 1940).

10. Panther Emory Douglas also lived for a couple of years in San Francisco's Chinatown, where his mom could afford "a cheap hotel." He "got along well with the other kids," but also "felt out of place" and unwelcomed in his friends' homes. See Elton C. Fax, *Black Artists of the New Generation* (New York: Dodd, Mead & Co., 1977), 261.

11. Hank Jones, interview by Fujino and Harmachis, January 31, 2016.

12. House Committee on Armed Services, "Universal Military Training and Services Act," Public Law 51, June 19, 1951; House Committee on Armed Services, "Reserve Forces Act of 1955."

13. In public talks and private discussions, Jones repeatedly dates his political awakening to August 28, 1955, the date of Till's murder. But as he recounts, it was actually the photos of the funeral in *Jet* magazine that triggered his response ("Nation Horrified by Murder of Kidnapped Chicago Youth," *Jet*, September 15, 1955, 4, 7–9).

14. Hank Jones, interview with Fujino and Harmachis, January 31, 2016.

15. "Parents Boycott Busses, Hold Freedom School," *Movement*, published by SNCC of California, February 1966, 1; "Campus Politicians," *Franciscan*, 1964, at https://diva.sfsu.edu/bundles/235673, accessed Aug. 23, 2017; Mike Miller, Veterans of the Civil Rights Movement oral history, Dec. 2012, at www.crmvet.org/nars/millerm.htm, accessed Jan. 26, 2020; Karen Umemoto, "'On Strike!' San Francisco State College Strike, 1968–1969: The Role of Asian American Students," *Amerasia Journal* 15 (1989): 28.

16. SNCC of California, "Rent Strike Wins Contract with Slumlord," *Movement* 2 (March 1966): 1; Clayborne Carson, *In Struggle: SNCC and the Black Awakening of the 1960s* (Cambridge, MA: Harvard University Press, 1981), 28–30, 142–44. Saul D. Alinsky's *Reveille for Radicals* (Chicago: University of Chicago Press, 1946) anticipated Alinsky's widely popular, *Rules for Radicals: A Pragmatic Primer for Realistic Radicals* (New York: Random House, 1971).

17. Jordan Klein, "A Community Lost: Urban Renewal and Displacement in San Francisco's Western Addition District" (master's thesis, UC Berkeley, 2010); Gary Kamiya, *Cool Gray City of Love: 49 Views of San Francisco* (New York: Bloomsbury, 2013), 294–311; *The Fillmore*, directed by Peter L. Stein, aired on KQED, 1999; "Ribbon Cutting and Grand Opening of Mary Helen Rogers Senior Community," www.chinatowncdc.org, accessed August 23, 2017; Clement Lai, "The Racial Triangulation of Space: The Case of Urban Renewal in San Francisco's Fillmore District," *Annals of the Association of American Geographers* 102 (2012): 151–70; Meredith Oda, "Rebuilding Japantown: Japanese Americans in Transpacific San Francisco during the Cold War," *Pacific Historical Review* 83 (2014): 57–91; Hank Jones, interview by Fujino and Harmachis, January 31, 2016.

18. Stokely Carmichael, "Power and Racism," *New York Review of Books*, September 22, 1966; reprinted in *Stokely Speaks* (New York: Lawrence Hill Books, 2007/1971), 23.

19. bell hooks, *Teaching to Transgress: Education as the Practice of Freedom* (New York: Routledge, 1994), 3, 24.

20. Hank Jones, conversation with Diane Fujino, October 16, 2018; Hank Jones, interview by Fujino and Harmachis, January 31, 2016.

21. Bloom and Martin, Jr., *Black against Empire*, 48–50, 56; Emory Douglas, interview with Diane Fujino and Matef Harmachis, August 7, 2017, San Francisco, CA.

22. Ward Churchill and Jim Vander Wall, *Agents of Repression: The FBI's Secret War Against the Black Panther Party and the American Indian Movement* (Boston: South End Press, 1988); Bloom and Martin, *Black against Empire*, 200–203, 209–10; Curtis J. Austin, *Up Against the Wall: Violence in the Making and Unmaking of the Black Panther Party* (Fayetteville: University of Arkansas Press, 2006), 169.

23. Austin, *Up Against the Wall*, xvii–xxiii; Umoja, "Repression Breeds Resistance"; Tyson, *Radio Free Dixie*, 214; Malcolm X, *Malcolm X Speaks*, ed. George Breitman (New York: Grove, 1990/1965), 7–8.

24. Umoja, "Repression Breeds Resistance," 5–19; Don Cox, "The Split in the Party," in *Liberation, Imagination, and the Black Panther Party*, 118–22; Bloom and Martin, *Black against Empire*, 341–71; Philip S. Foner, ed., "Introduction," *The Black Panthers Speak* (Philadelphia: J. B. Lippincott, 1970), xxvi.

25. Note that Jones did not consider himself to be a BLA member; I provide the larger context of clandestine Black liberation activity. Umoja, "Repression Breeds Resistance," 12; "Charges in Killing of S.F. Officer/A History of Conflict," *San Francisco Chronicle*, January 24, 2007.

26. Hank Jones, interview with Fujino and Harmachis, January 31, 2016.

27. Hank Jones, interview with Fujino and Harmachis, July 31, 2017, Altadena, CA.

28. Hank Jones, interview with Fujino and Harmachis, July 31, 2017.

29. Anne-Marie Cusac, "You're in the Hole: A Crackdown on Dissident Prisoners," *Progressive*, December 2001; Nora K. Wallace, "Inmate Questions Post-Sept. 11 Treatment," *Santa Barbara News-Press*, July 1, 2002; Dan Berger, "Two Prisoners Named Williams," *Nation*, December 14, 2005; Dan Berger, "Rescuing Civil Rights from Black Power: Collective Memory and Saving the State in Twenty-First Century Prosecutions of 1960s-Era Cases," *Journal for the Study of Radicalism* 3 (2009): 1–27.

30. Claude Marks, "Black Panther Veterans Jailed in San Francisco," *San Francisco Bay View*, October 26, 2005; Hank Jones, interview with Diane Fujino and Matef Harmachis, January 31, 2016, Santa Barbara, CA.

31. Jaxon Van Derbeken, "Ex-militants Charged in S.F. Police Officer's '71 Slaying at Station," *San Francisco Chronicle*, January 23, 2007; Kiilu Nyasha, "The San Francisco 8 and the Ongoing War against the Black Panther Party," *San Francisco Bay View*, April 21, 2007; Demian Bulwa, "Bail Cut in 1970s Cop-killing Conspiracy Case," *San Francisco Chronicle*, August 22, 2007.

32. Hank Jones, interview with Fujino and Harmachis, July 31, 2017, Altadena, CA.

33. Claude Marks, "Black Panther Veterans Jailed in San Francisco," *San Francisco Bay View*, October 26, 2005. The FBI regularly visited family members of Black Panthers as a tactic of harassment and intimidation (Robyn Spencer, *The Revolution Has Come: Black Power, Gender, and the Black Panther Party in Oakland* [Durham, NC: Duke University Press), 95; Diane C. Fujino, "Art that Flows from the People": Emory Douglas, International Solidarity, and the Practice of Co-creation," this volume].

34. Hank Jones, interview with Fujino and Harmachis, July 31, 2017, Altadena, CA.

35. "Former Black Panther Details Brutal Police Torture to Extract Confession in 1971 Murder Case," *Democracy Now!*, November 30, 2007.

36. Quoted in *Legacy of Torture: The War against the Black Liberation Movement*, directed by Andres Algeria, Claude Marks, and the Freedom Archives, 2006.

37. The descriptions of their torture given by Bowman and Taylor to the filmmakers of *Legacy of Torture* closely match the statements by Scott in a taped interview with a radio journalist in 1975, according to an article in the *San Francisco Chronicle* (Jaxon Van Derbeken, "Ex-militant Seen as Likely to Testify at Cohorts' Trial," *San Francisco Chronicle*, January 25, 2007); Hank Jones, interview with Diane Fujino and Matef Harmachis, January 31, 2016, Santa Barbara, CA.

38. Committee for the Defense of Human Rights, "Free the San Francisco 8!" website, at www.freethesf8.org; Van Derbeken, "Ex-militants Charged"; Marcus Wohlsen, "Activists Back Suspects in Cop's Death," *Mercury News*, January 28, 2007.

39. Hank Jones, interview with Fujino and Harmachis, July 31, 2017, Altadena, CA.

40. Herman Bell, letter to supporters, July 2, 2009, posted at http://freethesf8.

blogspot.com/2009/06/herman-bell-pleads-guilty-to-reduced.html.

41. Demian Bulwa, "Bail Delayed for Black Liberation Suspects," *San Francisco Chronicle*, August 8, 2007; Demian Bulwa, "Bail Cut in 1970s Cop-killing Conspiracy Case," *San Francisco Chronicle*, August 22, 2007; Jonathan Curiel, "Alleged Cop Killers Accuse Prosecutors of 'Vendetta,'" *San Francisco Chronicle*, September 24, 2007; Demian Bulwa, "Conspiracy Charges Dropped in 1971 Slaying of S.F. Police Officer," *San Francisco Chronicle*, January 11, 2008.

42. Bulwa, "Conspiracy Charges Dropped"; John Koopman, "Plea Deal, Probation in '71 Killing of Officer," *San Francisco Chronicle*, June 30, 2009; John Koopman, "2nd Guilty Plea in 1971 Killing of S.F. Officer," *San Francisco Chronicle*, July 7, 2009; John Koopman, "Charges Dismissed against Four in Ingleside Cop Murder Case," *San Francisco Chronicle*, July 7, 2009.

43. The monthly breakfast has been called "The Marvin Jackson Roland Freeman Breakfast" on a website documenting the history of the Los Angeles Panthers, though this is most commonly referred to as "the Panther breakfast"; see http://ultrawav0.wixsite.com/41central/monthly-reunion, posted circa late 2013.

44. Hank Jones, interview with Diane Fujino and Matef Harmachis, July 31, 2017, Altadena, CA.

45. Hank Jones, interview with Diane Fujino and Matef Harmachis, July 31, 2017, Altadena, CA.

46. Following Ra Un Nefer Amen, Jones uses the spelling "Kamitic," also commonly spelled Kemetic. Ra Un Nefer Amen, *Metu Neter*, vol. 1 (New York: Khamit Corp., 1990).

47. Hank Jones, interview with Diane Fujino and Matef Harmachis, July 31, 2017, Altadena, CA; Hank Jones, conversation with Diane Fujino, October 16, 2018.

48. Hank Jones, interview with Diane Fujino and Matef Harmachis, July 31, 2017, Altadena, California. Unbeknown to Jones, other Panthers were engaging meditation, yoga, or other spiritual practices in prison, including Ericka Huggins and Huey Newton (see Fujino, "A Spiritual Practice for Sustaining Social Justice Activism: An Interview with Ericka Huggins," this volume; Huey P. Newton, *Revolutionary Suicide* (New York: Penguin Books, 2009/1973, 106).

49. See, for example, Agnessa Kasumyan, "Social Justice Panel at GCC," *El Vaquero*, April 19, 2013; "LA Progressive Live! From Emmett Till to Black Panthers to Black Lives Matter," January 19, 2015, https://www.laprogressive.com/black-panthers/; "Possessive Investments: Systems of Power, Possibilities of Dissent," conference, UCLA, March 7, 2015, fsrn.org/2015/03/black-lives-matter-activists-move-forward-while-looking-back/; The Undercommons speakers series, UCLA, February 2016, https://theundercommons.wordpress.com/tag/hank-jones/; Frank Carber, "'Showing Up for Black Lives, Part II' Panelists Discuss Love and Revolution," *Occidental Weekly*, March 21, 2017.

50. Rhyston Mays, "First National M4BL Convention a Beacon of Hope," posted July 29, 2015, http://progressivepupil.org/tag/black-panther-party/.

51. Movement for Black Lives, "About Us," https://policy.m4bl.org/about/; Mays, "First National M4BL Convention."

52. Movement for Black Lives, "About Us."

53. See the Vision Statement of the Movement for Black Lives at https://policy.m4bl.org.

54. Hank Jones spoke with Sekou Odinga on "Prisons, Black Panthers, and Abolition Democracy: A Conversation with Sekou Odinga and Hank Jones," UC Santa Barbara, February 1, 2016, in a program organized by Diane Fujino and others, at www.research.ucsb.edu/cbs; video in author's possession.

55. "We Stand with Palestine in the Spirit of "*Sumud*": The U.S. Prisoner, Labor and Academic Solidarity Delegation to Palestine, March 24 to April 2, 2016, at samidoun.net/2016/04/on-palestinian-prisoners-day-anti-prison-labor -academic-delegation-takes-stand-against-israeli-state-violence-affirms -solidarity-with-palestinian-people/.

56. Ali Abunimah, "Parents Relieved at Conviction of Settler Who Burned Their Son Alive," Electronic Intifada, April 19, 2016.

57. Delegation member Diane Fujino spoke alongside Jones at the Panther breakfast on May 8, 2016, and the Black August program on August 21, 2016.

58. Jimmy O'Balles and Hank Jones, conversations with Diane Fujino and Matef Harmachis, at the "RISE" BPP art exhibit, Los Angeles, March 15, 2014; Rosalind McGary of RISE Arts Collective, conversation with Diane Fujino, Panther breakfast, Los Angeles, March 9, 2014; Rosalind McGary, email to Diane Fujino, March 9, 2014; "RISE: Love. Revolution. The Black Panther Party," press release, February 5, 2014; video posts about the RISE exhibit at www.youtube.com/ watch?v=8QrYes1NQdc and www.youtube.com/watch?v=UL6RFzJEIMA, accessed October 12, 2018.

59. At Yuri Kochiyama's memorials in Oakland on August 3, 2014, and in Los Angeles on August 31, 2014, Diane Fujino was witness to and helped to facilitate the exchanges among Hank Jones, Shuji Nakamura, and the Kochiyama family. On Kochiyama, see Diane C. Fujino, *Heartbeat of Struggle: The Revolutionary Life of Yuri Kochiyama* (Minneapolis: University of Minnesota Press, 2005).

60. Odinga and Jones, "Prisons, Black Panthers, and Abolition Democracy."

61. Robinson, *Black Marxism*.

Chapter Three: Kiilu Taught Me: Letters to My Comrade

1. Kiilu was known by her given name, Pat Gallyot, during this time. Kiilu's own account of joining the Panthers can be found on the official website of Black Panther Party alumni: itsabouttimebpp.com/Our_Stories/Chapter1/A_Chapter _In_The_Life.html.

2. Much of her print and television work since 2000 is archived on her blog, kiilunyasha.blogspot.com.

3. Mao, *Quotations from Chairman Mao Tse Tung* (Peking: Foreign Language Press, 1972).

4. Mao, *Quotations from Chairman Mao*, 195.

5. "PE" stands for Political Education.

6. Fanon, *The Wretched of the Earth* (New York: Grove Press, 1968), 206.

7. Mao, *Quotations from Chairman Mao*, 15.

8. Kiilu's goddaughter.

9. "A Disability Justice framework understands that all bodies are unique and essential, that all bodies have strengths and needs that must be met...that we are powerful not despite the complexities of our bodies, but because of them . . . that all bodies are caught in these bindings of ability, race, gender, sexuality, class, nation state and imperialism, and that we cannot separate them. These are the positions from which we struggle." Patricia Berne, *Skin, Tooth, and Bone: The Basis of Movement Is Our People: A Disability Justice Primer* (San Francisco: Sins Invalid, 2016).

Chapter Four: A Spiritual Practice for Sustaining Social Justice Activism: An Interview with Ericka Huggins

1. The Oakland Community School was nationally recognized for excellence in community-based education, with at different times, 27 full-time accredited teachers and a $450,000 federal grant. The school was based on holistic approaches to education that included "discipline with freedom, to allow flexibility and creativity," and included daily meditation (Robyn C. Spencer, *The Revolution Has Come: Black Power, Gender, and the Black Panther Party in Oakland* (Chapel Hill: North Carolina Press, 2016, 183–186).

2. Lesley Oelsner, "Deadlock by Jury Results in Seale-Huggins Mistrial," *New York Times*, May 25, 1971; Lesley Oelsner, "Charges Dropped in the Seale Case; 'Publicity' Cited," *New York Times*, May 26, 1971; Catherine Roraback Collection of Ericka Huggins Papers, Yale University Beinecke Library.

3. The first sentence of the quote is slightly modified for clarity, per Ericka Huggins's request and with Mary Phillips's consent. Mary Phillips, "The Power of the First-Person Narrative: Ericka Huggins and the Black Panther Party," *Women's Studies Quarterly* 43 (2015): 38; also see Tony Platt and Cecilia O'Leary, "Two Interviews with Ericka Huggins," *Social Justice* 40 (2014): 54–71.

4. Ericka, born January 5, 1948, in Washington, DC, had turned twenty-one just days before John Huggins was killed. See Fiona Thompson, "An Oral History with Ericka Huggins" (Oral History Center, Bancroft Library, University of California, Berkeley, fall 2007), 1, 31.

5. Huggins's sensitivity, vulnerability, and ideas are revealed in the poems she wrote inside Niantic State Farm for Women. See Huey P. Newton and Ericka Huggins, *Insights and Poems* (San Francisco: City Lights, 1975); Amy Washburn, "The Pen of the Panther: Barriers and Freedom in the Prison Poetry of Ericka Huggins," *Journal for the Study of Radicalism* 8 (2014): 51–78.

6. John Eligon, "Black Stress Matters," *New York Times*, March 29, 2018; also see Jenna Wortham, "Black Health Matters," *New York Times*, August 27, 2016.

7. Erika Garner was an activist on behalf of her father, Eric Garner, who was famously choked to death by a New York City police officer.

Chapter Five: Serving the People and Serving God: The Everyday Work and Mobilizing Force of Dhameera Ahmad

1. Thank you to the Ahmad and Simon families, especially Saadat and Nisa Ahmad and Timothy Simon for sharing your life with and memories of Hajja Dhameera. Additional thanks to Naima Jameson, Imam Zaid Shakir, Sundiata Rashid, Su'ad Abdul Khabeer, Tahir Abdullah, Diane Fujino, Matef Harmachis, and Junaid Rana. The title "Hajja" or "Hajj" is given to someone who has performed the Islamic pilgrimage, or hajj, to Mecca (in contemporary Saudi Arabia) in the prescribed month of the lunar year. Dhameera and her husband Saadat were among the first African Americans from the Bay Area community to make hajj, which they did in the 1980s. Hajja Dhameera transitioned to the next life on July 24, 2017, in San Francisco. May Allah have mercy on her.

2. Maryam Kashani, "Habib in the Hood Mobilizing History and Prayer towards Anti-Racist Praxis," *Amerasia Journal* 44, no. 1 (2018): 61–84.

3. "San Francisco State University College of Ethnic Studies, Interview with Striker Dhameera Ahmad," San Francisco, 2008, https://diva.sfsu.edu/collections/coes/bundles/218203. This is one of the few interviews of Dhameera that is available online. It is an interview she conducted with students of San Francisco State University as part of an oral history of the Third World Strike. In it, Dhameera discusses balancing Black Panther and student life, as well as the legacy of this student movement to change the ways we think about the transmission of knowledge.

4. Dhameera Ahmad, interview with the author, March 20, 2017.

5. Dhameera Ahmad, interview with the author, January 10, 2017.

6. Dhameera Ahmad, interview with the author, March 20, 2017.

7. Dhameera Ahmad, interview with the author, March 20, 2017.

8. The predominantly female presidium of the SF State Black Student Union was a committee that worked with and advised the predominantly male central committee.

9. Manning Marable, *Malcolm X: A Life of Reinvention* (New York: Viking, 2011); Jared Ball and Todd Steven Burroughs, eds., *A Lie of Reinvention: Correcting Manning Marable's Malcolm X* (Baltimore: Black Classic Press, 2012). See also Maryam Kashani, "The Audience Is Still Present: Invocations of El-Hajj Malik El-Shabazz by Muslims in the United States," in *With Stones in Our Hands: Writings on Muslims, Racism, and Empire*, eds. Sohail Daulatzai and Junaid Rana (Minneapolis: University of Minnesota Press, 2018), 336–53.

10. Frantz Fanon, *Wretched of the Earth*, trans. Richard Philcox (New York: Grove Press, 2004); Vijay Prashad, *The Darker Nations: A People's History of the Third World* (New York: New Press, 2007); Sohail Daulatzai, *Black Star, Crescent Moon: The Muslim International and Black Freedom beyond America* (Minneapolis: University of Minnesota Press, 2012); Malcolm X and George Breitman, *Malcolm X Speaks: Selected Speeches and Statements* (New York: Grove Weidenfeld, 1990).

11. Safiya Bukhari, *The War Before: The True Life Story of Becoming a Black Panther, Keeping the Faith in Prison, and Fighting for Those Left Behind* (New York: Feminist Press at CUNY, 2010); Imam Jamil Al-Amin, *Revolution by the Book (The Rap Is*

Live) (Beltsville, MD: Writers' Inc. - International, 1994); Sekou Odinga et al., *Look for Me in the Whirlwind: From the Panther 21 to 21st-Century Revolutions*, eds. déqui kioni-sadiki and Matt Meyer (Oakland, CA: PM Press, 2017).

12. Abdul Raoof Nasir, interview with the author, September 4, 2017. See also Murch, *Living for the City*. Prior to the founding of the Black Panthers, both Huey Newton and Bobby Seale participated in reading groups in which the Qur'an was read. They briefly considered joining the Nation of Islam, which had chapters in both San Francisco and Oakland at the time.

13. Upon the death of the Honorable Elijah Muhammad in 1975, his son Wallace Muhammad began "the Transition" in which he moved a majority of the community toward an "orthodox" Sunni Islam; these communities mostly refer to themselves as Warith Deen Muhammad communities. Minister Louis Farrakhan separately reorganized the Nation of Islam toward its former theological and ideological premises in 1978. Today, depending on location and leadership, the different NOI mosques range in how closely they resemble the NOI pre-1975 or Sunni Islam. I qualify "orthodox" because what is considered orthodox or traditional is subject to debate and sociopolitical context.

14. Dawn-Marie Gibson and Jamillah Karim, *Women of the Nation: Between Black Protest and Sunni Islam* (New York: NYU Press, 2014); Ula Yvette Taylor, *The Promise of Patriarchy: Women and the Nation of Islam* (Chapel Hill: University of North Carolina Press, 2017); Carolyn Moxley Rouse, *Engaged Surrender: African American Women and Islam* (Berkeley: University of California Press, 2004). I use a lower-case "black Muslim," to distinguish from "Black Muslim," which is an appellation put upon members of the Nation of Islam by C. Eric Lincoln; they simply called themselves "Muslim." C. Eric Lincoln, *The Black Muslims in America* (Boston: Beacon Press, 1961).

15. Gibson and Karim, *Women of the Nation*.

16. Nisa Ahmad in "Africa Today/Transitions on Traditions, Dhameera Special," KPFK (Berkeley, 2017), https://kpfa.org/episode/africa-today-september-11-2017/.

17. Murch, *Living for the City*, 169.

18. "Africa Today/Transitions on Traditions, Dhameera Special."

19. Timothy Simon, interview with the author, August 16, 2018. Dhameera once told me that regardless of their theology, she had initially joined the Nation because they were doing something for the Black community.

20. Diane C. Fujino, "Grassroots Leadership and Afro-Asian Solidarities: Yuri Kochiyama's Humanizing Radicalism," in *Want to Start a Revolution? Radical Women in the Black Freedom Struggle*, ed. Dayo F. Gore, Jeanne Theoharis, and Komozi Woodard (New York: New York University Press, 2009); Barbara Ransby, *Ella Baker and the Black Freedom Movement: A Radical Democratic Vision* (Chapel Hill: University of North Carolina Press, 2003); Ruth Wilson Gilmore, "Abolition Geography and the Problem of Innocence," in *Futures of Black Radicalism*, ed. Gaye Theresa Johnson and Alex Lubin (New York: Verso Books, 2017), 225–40.

21. Sundiata Rashid, interview with the author, August 26, 2018.

22. *Masjid* is the Arabic term for mosque.

23. See the "#IslamophobiaIsRacism syllabus," https://islamophobiaisracism

.wordpress.com/.

24. Qur'an translations are from Abdullah Yusuf Ali, *The Meaning of the Holy Qurān*, 10th ed. (Beltsville, MD: Amana Publications, 2002).

25. Ahmad, interview with the author, March 20, 2017.

26. Imam Zaid Shakir, author interview, July 26, 2018.

Chapter Six: Ecosocialism from the Inside Out

1. In particular, my contribution was to the International Campaign to Free Russell Maroon Shoatz. In this I worked with Fred Ho to coedit Maroon's book *(Maroon the Implacable*, copublished by PM Press and Ecosocialist Horizons in 2013), which I was then honored to take on a national book tour together with his daughter, Theresa Shoatz. For the month of April 2014, we "rode the Maroon wave," as Theresa said, through about twenty events in seventeen cities, meeting with dozens of organizers and hundreds of activists to push for Maroon's release from solitary confinement. Our strategy was successful; Maroon was released into general population in February 2014.

2. Thanks to Kanya D'Almeida, Joel Kovel, Paul Bermanzohn, Salvatore Engel-Di-Mauro, Mike Frank, Lutie Spitzer, Matef Harmachis, Diane Fujino, the late Fred Ho, and especially to all the political prisoners ("real and potential") with whom I've had the honor to correspond over the last five years: Russell Maroon Shoatz, Kempis Songster aka Ghani, Todd Hyung-Rae Tarselli, Kevin Rashid Johnson, David Gilbert, Herman Bell, and Andre Shabaka Gay.

3. "The Real Walking Dead" by Russell Maroon Shoatz, November 2015, http://ecosocialisthorizons.com/2016/01/the-real-walking-dead/.

4. Ashley Dawson, *Extinction: A Radical History* (New York: OR Books, , 2016), 66.

5. Masanobu Fukuoka, *Sowing Seeds in the Desert: Natural Farming, Global Restoration, and Ultimate Food Security* (White River Junction, Vermont: Chelsea Green Publishing, 2012), 47.

6. "Each generation must discover its mission, fulfill it or betray it, in relative opacity." Frantz Fanon, *The Wretched of the Earth*, trans. Richard Philcox (New York: Grove Press, 2004), 45.

7. Safiya Bukhari, *The War Before: The True Life Story of Becoming a Black Panther, Keeping the Faith in Prison, and Fighting for Those Left Behind*, ed. Laura Whitehorn (New York: The Feminist Press at CUNY, 2010), 131.

8. George Jackson, *Soledad Brother: The Prison Letters of George Jackson* (New York: Lawrence Hill Books, 1994), 26.

9. "Revolutionary Target: The American Penal System: Report by the Committee on Internal Security," House of Representatives, Ninety-Third Congress, First Session, December 1973.

10. "Former warden of United States Penitentiary Marion, the prototype of modern supermax-style solitary confinement, Ralph Arons, has stated: 'The purpose of the Marion Control Unit is to control revolutionary attitudes in the prison system and in the society at large.'" Quoted in Kanya D'Almeida and Bret Grote, "Solitary

Confinement: Torture Chambers for Black Revolutionaries," Al Jazeera, August 2012.

11. Assata Shakur, *Assata: An Autobiography* (London: Zed Books, 1987), 147.

12. Praise for Russell Maroon Shoatz, *Maroon the Implacable: The Collected Writings of Russell Maroon Shoatz*, ed. Fred Ho and Quincy Saul (Oakland, California: PM Press and Ecosocialist Horizons, 2013), ii.

13. "Class political consciousness can be brought to the workers *only from without*, that is, only from outside the economic struggle, from outside the sphere of relations between workers and employers." V.I. Lenin, *What Is to Be Done: Burning Questions of Our Movement,* (Stuttgart, Germany: Verlag von J. H. W. Dietz Nachf, 1902) (emphasis in original).

14. "African state after African state has gained political independence with a tumultuous rush that was not envisaged even by the most sanguine of the early advocates of independence . . . . What is to be noted is that Kenyatta, Nkrumah, Banda, to take the best-known names, were all imprisoned by the British Government and *had to be released to head the independent states.* The colonial mentality having been broken, the only way to restore some sort of order or, to reject a word now corrupted and offensive, the only way to have a viable society was to transfer the man in jail to be head of state. In no other way could the African people once more accommodate themselves to any social structure." C. L. R. James, *A History of Pan-African Revolt* (Oakland, California: PM Press, 2012), 116 (emphasis in original).

15. "One of the most important characteristics of any group that is developing towards dominance is its struggle to assimilate and to conquer 'ideologically' the traditional intellectuals, but this assimilation and conquest is made quicker and more efficacious the more the group in question succeeds in simultaneously elaborating its own organic intellectuals." *Selections from the Prison Notebooks of Antonio Gramsci,* ed. and trans. Quintin Hoare and Geoffrey Smith (New York: International Publishers, 1971), 10.

16. "Word Play," in *Ho Chi Minh on Revolution, Selected Writings 1920–66*, ed. by Bernard Fall (Kolkata, West Bengal, India: Signet, 1967), 137.

17. Marvin Gaye, "Save the Children" on the album *What's Going On?* 1971.

18. Immanuel Wallerstein, "The Current Conjuncture: Short-Run and Middle-Run Projections" *Monthly Review*, December 2009.

19. "The First Ecosocialist International: Combined Strategy and Plan of Action," December 2017: http://ecosocialisthorizons.com/2017/12/the -first-ecosocialist-international-combined-strategy-and-plan-of-action/.

20. Quincy Saul, "From the Plan of the Homeland to a Plan for the Planet," Telesur, December 2017.

21. "Again, and maybe the last time on this earth, I recall the great vision you sent me. It may be that some little root of the sacred tree still lives. Nourish it then, that it may leaf and bloom and fill with singing birds. Hear me, not for myself, but for my people; I am old. Hear me that they may once more go back into the sacred hoop and find the good red road, the shielding tree!" *Black Elk Speaks,* as told to John Neihardt (New York: State University of New York Press, 2008), 221.

22. The other categories of potential political prisoners that he lists include: "death row convicts, those with three-strike and mandatory sentences, those serving life

without parole, juveniles sentenced as adults, immigrants, environmental/ecological defenders, Muslims and 'suspected' foreign terrorists, gang members, right-wingers, and Mariel Cuban migrants (boat people) from the 1980s . . . [and] all of those jailed as a result of the parts they played in 'the drug game.'" Shoatz, *Maroon the Implacable*, 47–48.

23. Mumia Abu-Jamal, "What's a Jailhouse Environmentalist?" prison radio broadcast, March 2013, www.prisonradio.org/media/audio/mumia/whats-jailhouse -environmenalist-358-mumia-abu-jamal.

24. Joel Kovel, *The Enemy of Nature: The End of Capitalism or the End of the World?* (London: Zed Books, 2007).

25. On the concept of species-being, see *Economic and Philosophic Manuscripts of 1844*, by Karl Marx. This point, and the connection to *ubuntu*, was made by former political prisoner Tim Blunk (editor of *Hauling Up the Morning*, 1990) at a conference on solitary confinement in 2012. This talk is available online here: www.youtube .com/watch?v=Ub5NRBmpz3w.

26. Jack Henry Abbot, *In the Belly of the Beast: Letters from Prison* (New York: Random House, 1981), 50 (emphasis in original).

27. It is worth noting that these two political prisoners who have never communicated, who both once upheld an ideology of revolutionary nationalism, have after years of studies in solitary confinement, renounced their previous views and arrived at nearly identical political conclusions, involving the centrality of women's liberation and ecological practices.

28. Karl Marx and Frederick Engels, *The Communist Manifesto* (London: Workers' Educational Association, 1848).

29. "The Future" by Leonard Cohen, Columbia, 1992.

30. Joel Kovel, "The Future Will Be Ecosocialist—Because without Ecosocialism There Will Be No Future," Ecosocialist Horizons, November 2011, http:// ecosocialisthorizons.com/2011/11/the-future-is-ecosocialist/.

31. Ho and Saul, *Maroon the Implacable*, 270.

32. Abbot, *Belly of the Beast*.

33. Rose Braz and Craig Gilmore, "Joining Forces: Prisons and Environmental Justice in Recent California Organizing," *Radical History Review 96* (2006): 95–111.

34. Prison Ecology Project: https://nationinside.org/campaign/prison-ecology-/; Fight Toxic Prisons conference: https://fighttoxicprisons.wordpress.com/; Candice Bernd, Zoe Loftus-Farren, and Maureen Nandini Mitra, "America's Toxic Prisons: The Environmental Injustices of Mass Incarceration," *Truthout*, June 2017.

35. Salvatore Engel-DiMauro, "Prison Abolition as an Ecosocialist Struggle," *Capitalism Nature Socialism*, March 2012.

36. Eduardo Galeano, interviewed by Amy Goodman, *Democracy Now!* November 5, 2008, www.democracynow.org/2008/11/5/uruguayan_writer_eduardo _galeano_on_barack.

37. Quincy Saul and the Ecosocialist Horizons editorial collective, *Truth and Dare: A Comic Book Curriculum for the End and the Beginning of the World* (New York: Autonomedia, 2013).

Chapter Seven: The (R)evolution from Black Power to Pan-Africanism: David Brothers and Dedon Kamathi at the Bus Stop on the Mountaintop of Agitprop

1. Cleveland Sellers, *The River of No Return: The Autobiography of a Black Militant and the Life and Death of SNCC* (Jackson, MS: University Press of Mississippi, 1990).

2. *Eyes on the Prize II: America at the Racial Crossroads 1965–1985*, episode 7, "The Time Has Come (1964–66)" (USA: Blackside/PBS).

3. Ekwueme Michael Thelwell, *Ready for Revolution: The Life and Struggles of Stokely Carmichael (Kwame Ture)* (New York: Scribner, 2003); Peniel Joseph, *Stokely: A Life* (New York: Basic Civitas, 2014).

4. Kwame Nkrumah, *Handbook of Revolutionary Warfare: A Guide to the Armed Phase of the Revolution* (London: Panaf Books Ltd., 1968).

5. Hakim Adi, *Pan-Africanism: A History* (London: Bloomsbury Academic, 2018).

6. Huey Newton, "on Pan-Africanism or communism: December 1, 1972," in *The Huey Newton Reader*, ed. David Hilliard and Donald Weise (New York: Seven Stories Press, 2002). See also Hakim Adi, *Pan-Africanism and Communism: The Communist International, Africa and the Diaspora, 1919-1939* (Trenton, NJ: Africa World Press, 2013).

7. C. L. R. James, "Reflections on Pan-Africanism," part 1, www.columbia.edu/itc /english/edwards/Reflections%20of%20Pan-Africanism.pdf. Accessed October 24, 2018.

8. Vincent Bakpetu Thompson, *Africa and Unity: The Evolution of Pan-Africanism* (New York: Humanities Press, 1969).

9. Kwame Nkrumah, *Ghana: The Autobiography of Kwame Nkrumah* (London: Panaf Books Ltd., 1957); *Challenge of the Congo: A Case Study of Foreign Pressures in an Independent State* (London: Panaf Books Ltd., 1967).

10. Adi, *Pan-Africanism.*

11. For the role of culture in revolution, see *Return to the Source: Selected Speeches of Amilcar Cabral*, ed. Africa Information Service Staff (New York: Monthly Review Press, 1973).

12. Thompson, *Africa and Unity.*

13. J. E. Casely-Hayford, "Address to the 4th Session of the National Congress of British West Africa," Lagos, Nigeria, December 1929, quoted in Thompson, *Africa and Unity.*

14. Eldridge Cleaver, "Culture and Revolution: Their Synthesis in Africa," *Black Scholar* 3 (1971): 33–39; also Eldridge Cleaver, "On Lumpen Ideology," *Black Scholar* 4 (1972): 2–10.

15. Fred Ho, "Notes on the National Question: Oppressed Nations and Liberation Struggles within the U.S.A.," in *Wicked Theory, Naked Practice: A Fred Ho Reader*, ed. Diane Fujino (Minneapolis: University of Minnesota Press, 2009).

16. Fred Ho, "Fists for Revolution: The Revolutionary History of I Wor Kuen/League of Revolutionary Struggle," in *Legacy to Liberation: Politics and Culture of Revolutionary Asian Pacific America* (New York: Big Red Media; San Francisco: AK Press, 2000); see also Matt Meyer and Dan Berger, "The Pan-Africanization of Black

Power: True History, Coalition-Building and the All-African People's Revolutionary Party: An Interview with Bob Brown, Organizer for the All-African People's Revolutionary Party (GC)," in *We Have Not Been Moved: Resisting Racism and Militarism in 21st Century America*, ed. Elizabeth "Betita" Martinez, Matt Meyer, and Mandy Carter (Oakland: PM Press, 2012); and Gwendolyn Zoharah Simmons, "Truly Human: Spiritual Paths in the Struggle Against Racism, Militarism, and Materialism," in Martinez, Meyer and Carter, eds, *We Have Not Been Moved*.

17. Tony Thomas, "Black Nationalism and Confused Marxists," *Black Scholar* 4 (1972): 47–52.

18. Amiri Baraka, "Black Nationalism: 1972," *Black Scholar* 4 (1972): 19–22.

19. Stokely Carmichael, "Marxism-Leninism and Nkrumahism," *Black Scholar* 4 (1973): 41–43.

20. Stokely Carmichael, "We Are All Africans," *Black Scholar 1* (1970): 15–19.

21. Charles V. Hamilton, "Pan-Africanism and the Black Struggle in the U.S.," *Black Scholar* 2 (1971): 10–15; Stokely Carmichael and Charles V. Hamilton, *Black Power: The Politics of Liberation in America* (New York: Vintage Books, 1967).

22. While Ture provides an *ideological* trajectory, all three movements have much longer and more complicated *histories*. For the civil rights movement, see Jacquelyn Dowd Hall, "The Long Civil Rights Movement and the Political Uses of the Past," *Journal of American History* 91 (2005): 1233–1263; Peniel E. Joseph, ed., *The Black Power Movement: Rethinking the Civil Rights–Black Power Era* (New York: Routledge, 2006). For Black Power before 1966 see Adam Ewing, "The Challenge of Garveyism Studies," *Modern American History* 1 (2018): 399–418; Peniel Joseph, *Waiting 'Til the Midnight Hour: A Narrative History of Black Power in America* (New York: Holt Paperbacks, 2007); Ashley Farmer, *Remaking Black Power: How Black Women Transformed an Era* (Chapel Hill: University of North Carolina Press, 2017); Nikhil Singh, *Black Is a Country: Race and the Unfinished Struggle for Democracy* (Boston: Harvard University Press, 2005); James Smethurst, *The Black Arts Movement: Literary Nationalism in the 1960s and 1970s* (Chapel Hill: University of North Carolina Press, 2005). For the lengthy history of Pan-Africanism, see Adi, *Pan-Africanism*; C. L. R. James, *A History of Pan-African Revolt*, reissue (Oakland, CA: PM Press, 2012).

23. Ahmed Seku Ture, *Strategies and Tactics of the Revolution*, vol. 21 (Conakry, Guinea: State Press Office, 1977). Also see Ernesto Che Guevara, *Socialism and Man in Cuba* (New York: Pathfinder Press, 1989).

24. Robert Chrisman, "Aspects of Pan-Africanism," *Black Scholar 4*, The Pan-African Debate (1973): 2–8; see also Eric Williams, *Capitalism and Slavery* (Chapel Hill: University of North Carolina Press, 1944); most importantly see Cedric Robinson, *Black Marxism: The Making of the Black Radical Tradition* (London: Zed Press, 1983) for explanation of "racial capitalism."

25. John Munro, *The Anticolonial Front: The African American Freedom Struggle and Global Decolonisation, 1945–1960* (Cambridge: Cambridge University Press, 2017).

26. "Reflections of a Revolutionary Pan-Africanist Freedom Fighter," AAPRP statement for Chairman David Brothers's funeral, June 2007, in author's possession.

27. Rooted in its view that the students are the spark of the revolution, the AAPRP

focuses on creating study circles on college campuses as a base for the broader political education and organizing of the masses of African people.

28. "Free the Panther 21," ed. Wayne Sailor, *Reconstruction 1* (Lawrence, KS: Reconstruction Press, Inc, 1969); "Press Conference of N.Y. Panthers," ed. Eldridge Cleaver, *The Black Panther Extra* (Oakland, CA: Black Panther Party, 1968); Peter L. Zimroth, *Perversions of Justice: The Prosecution and Acquittal of the Panther 21* (New York: Viking Press, 1974).

29. All quotes in this article are from personal conversations and interactions between the speaker and author across many years, unless otherwise noted.

30. Tejvir Grewall, "Tribute to Dedon Kamathi," marking three years since Bro Dedon's transition, August 25, 2018; Dedon Kamathi, "Biographical Statement of Dedon Kamathi," for AAPRP Cultural Workers Bureau, 2003 (both documents in author's possession).

31. All-African People's Revolutionary Party, "Thirty Years of African Liberation Day: A Brief Overview of Its Rich and Powerful History," 1988, pamphlet in author's possession.

32. Gary Webb, *Dark Alliance: The CIA, the Contras, and the Crack Cocaine Explosion* (New York: Seven Stories Press, 1998); Keven Booth, *American Drug War: The Last White Hope* (Studio City, CA: Sacred Cow Productions, 2008); K. Connie Kang, "Distrust Greets CIA Promise of Crack Probe; Cocaine: South-Central Residents Doubt Director's Assurance That the Agency Will Investigate Itself," *Los Angeles Times*, November 17, 1996.

33. Jack Olsen, *Last Man Standing: The Tragedy and Triumph of Geronimo Pratt* (New York: Anchor Books, 2001); Matef Harmachis, "Dedon Kamathi: Making the Airwaves Safe for Revolution at High Noon," *Kalfou* 3 (2016): 302–306.

34. Dr. Nkrumah wrote, "The total liberation and unification of Africa under an All-African Socialist government must be the primary objective of all Black revolutionaries throughout the world. It is an objective which, when achieved, will bring about the fulfillment of the aspirations of Africans and People of African descent everywhere. It will at the same time advance the triumph of the international socialist revolution and the onward progress towards world communism, under which, every society is ordered on the principle of from each according to his ability, to each according to his needs."

35. Quote from a letter dated September 14, 2013, but found after Bro Dedon's transition. Former congresswoman Cynthia McKinney wrote that "[this was the] letter that Dedon wrote in the case of his demise during the trip that he and I took together to Syria while it was under attack from US imperial forces."

Chapter Eight: States of Fugitivity: Akinsanya Kambon, Pan-Africanism, and Art-Based Knowledge Making

1. Frederick Douglass, *Life and Times of Frederick Douglass* (New York: Collier Books, 1962; orig. 1881), 912–13; Celeste-Marie Bernier, "Frederick Douglass: The Story of the Slave and the Black Radical Tradition," presentation at the Black Radical

Tradition symposium, University of California, Santa Barbara, April 18, 2018.

2. Faizah Alim, "Sad Surrender of Artist Fugitive," *Sacramento Bee*, May 8, 1987.

3. Alim, "Sad Surrender of Artist Fugitive"; William Hinckle, "An Eerie Visit to the Secret Gallery of a Black Artist on the Lam," *San Francisco Examiner*, c. 1987; "Akinsanya Kambon: The Fugitive Returns," *Suttertown News*, June 25–July 2, 1987; Akinsanya Kambon, interview by Diane Fujino, June 27, 2018, Long Beach, CA; Kevin Coyle, "The Fugitive Returns," *Suttertown News*, June 25–27, 1987.

4. Angela Davis, *Angela Davis: An Autobiography* (New York: International Publishers, 1974), 5.

5. "Akinsanya Kambon: The Fugitive Returns."

6. "Akinsanya Kambon: The Fugitive Returns."

7. Hinckle, "An Eerie Visit."

8. Richard Price, ed. *Maroon Societies: Rebel Slave Communities in the Americas* (Baltimore: Johns Hopkins University Press, 1996; report 1979).

9. See, for example, Assata Shakur, *Assata: An Autobiography* (London: Zed Books, 1987); Safiya Bukhari, *The War Before: The True Life Story of Becoming a Black Panther, Keeping the Faith in Prison, and Fighting for Those Left Behind*, ed. Laura Whitehorn (New York: The Feminist Press, 2010); Russell Maroon Shoatz, *Maroon the Implacable*, ed. Fred Ho and Quincy Saul (Oakland: PM Press, 2013); Frank B. Wilderson, III, "The Vengeance of Vertigo: Aphasia and Abjection in the Political Trials of Black Insurgents," in *Afro-Pessimism: An Introduction* (Minneapolis: Rackled and Dispatched, 2017), 127; chapters, this volume, by or about Sekou Odinga, Jalil Muntaqim, Assata Shakur, and Hank Jones.

10. "Akinsanya Kambon: The Fugitive Returns."

11. Barbara Tomlinson and George Lipsitz, "Insubordinate Spaces for Intemperate Times: Countering the Pedagogies of Neoliberalism," *Review of Education, Pedagogy and Cultural Studies* 35 (2013): 3–26.

12. At the time of her death in 2017, Akinsanya's mother was known as Laura Ella Houston, taking on her third husband's last name ("Laura Ella Houston, 94, Remembered," obituary, *Sacramento Observer*, August 24, 2017).

13. Kambon, interview by Fujino, June 27, 2018.

14. Kambon, interview by Fujino, June 27, 2018.

15. Kambon does research, whether through reading or listening to the oral stories of African and Indigenous elders, in order to create his art. His storytelling about the Buffalo Soldiers is straightforward, absent critique. But when asked, he is clear that he neither condemns nor celebrates the Buffalo Soldiers, but views them, not unlike himself as a US Marine in Vietnam, doing the work to advance US colonial expansionism; in the case of the Buffalo Soldiers by killing Indigenous peoples and for invading Cuba and the Philippines in the aftermath of the Spanish-American War (Kambon, interview by Fujino, June 27, 2018; Akinsanya Kambon, conversation with Diane Fujino, March 12, 2019).

16. Leon Waters, historian and chair of the Louisiana Museum of African-American History (LMAAH), has long been conducting research and giving historical tours of the 1811 slave revolt, with the LMAAH beginning their commemorations of the 1811 revolt in 1995. Leon A. Waters, "Jan. 8, 1811: Louisiana's Heroic Slave

Revolt," *San Francisco Bay View*, July 1, 2013, at https://sfbayview.com/2013/07 /new-orleans-1811-slave-revolt-tour-raises-funds-to-rebuild-libraries-in-haiti /leon-waters-speaks-on-1811-slave-revolt-largest-in-us-2011/; "New Orleans: The Struggle for Recognition of the Historic 1811 Slave Revolt," *The Louisiana Weekly*, Jan. 10, 2011, posted at https://revolutionaryfrontlines.wordpress.com /2011/01/17/new-orleans-the-struggle-for-recognition-of-the-historic-1811 -slave-revolt/; Albert Thrasher, *On to New Orleans!: Louisiana's Heroic 1811 Slave Revolt* (New Orleans: Cypress Press, 1996); Daniel Rasmussen, *American Uprising: The Untold Story of American's Largest Slave Revolt* (New York: HarperPerennial, 2011); Kambon, interview by Fujino.

17. Alessandro Portelli, *The Death of Luigi Trastulli and Other Stories: Form and Meaning in Oral History* (Albany: State University of New York, 1991), 2.

18. In Chela Sandoval's decolonial feminist pedagogy, the greatest power lies not in the speaking, but rather in the witnessing back to the speaker or text the meaning of the work/words to the participants (Eddy Francisco Alvarez, Jr., "Jotería Pedagogy, SWAPA, and Sandovalian Approaches to Liberation," *Aztlán: A Journal of Chicano Studies* 39 (2014): 215–27); also Diane C. Fujino et al., "A Transformative Pedagogy for a Decolonial World," *Review of Education, Pedagogy, and Cultural Studies* 40 (2018): 69–95.

19. In his widely influential *Wretched of the Earth*, Frantz Fanon speaks not only to the "cleansing force" that violence against oppression can animate among the oppressed, but also about the tremendous costs of violence—for the victims and for the perpetrators of brutality (New York: Grove, 1991/1963).

20. Kambon, interview with Fujino.

21. Diana Griego Erwin, "Two War Stories—Vietnam and Personal Pain—Become One in Art," *Sacramento Bee*, November 9, 2003; Carol Kino, "With Sketchpads and Guns, Semper Fi," *New York Times*, July 14, 2010; Kambon, interview by Fujino. F. Hampton Livingston posted online at 562 CityLife some of Kambon's speeches and interviews on the Vietnam War, including "Detroit Blue" Part 1 at www.youtube.com/watch?v=ccEfMvDuLgk (3:46), posted May 29, 2011; "Detroit Blue" Part 1 at www.youtube.com/watch?v=itJSvZwKXuw (3:26), posted May 29, 2011; and "Reflections of the Vietnam War: Racism and Long Binh Jail," www.youtube.com/watch?v=ukbFTnapBsE (4:15), posted May 29, 2016.

22. Dorothy Korber, "Students Rally in Support of Lecturer Who Was Fired for Being Late," *Sacramento Bee*, August 15, 1987.

23. "Mark Teemer Sentenced," *Sacramento Observer*, November 7, 1973; Kambon, interview with Fujino. These cities represent police killings of Michael Brown, Freddie Gray, Philando Castile, Stephon Clark, and women Rakia Boyd and Shelley Frey (African American Policy Forum, *Say Her Name: Resisting Police Brutality Against Black Women*, 2015).

24. "Youths Chase, Beat Ball Team in Oak Park," *Sacramento Bee*, July 9, 1968; Curtis R. Burau, "Stabbing, Fire-Bombings Erupt in Sacramento," *Sacramento Bee*, July 10, 1968.

25. Kambon, interview with Fujino.

26. "Black Panther Teaches at SSC," *Sacramento Observer*, January 30, 1969; "'Free

Huey' Rally of Panthers Attended by 300," *Sacramento Observer*, May 8, 1969; "Oak Park Defense Fund Investigates Slaying," *Sacramento Observer*, October 1, 1970; "Sacramento Chapter of the Black Panther Party," at www.itsabouttimebpp. com, accessed July 26, 2018; Kambon, interview by Fujino. The free breakfast program in Oakland began on January 20, 1969 (*Black Panther*, December 21, 1968; January 4, 1969; February 17, 1969) and the Sacramento BPP breakfast program on May 7, 1969, at the Oak Park United Church of Christ ("Hot-Breakfast for Oak Park," *Sacramento Observer*, May 8, 1969).

27. Huey P. Newton, *War Against the Panthers: A Study of Repression in America* (New York: Harlem River Press, 1996).

28. "Sacramento Chapter of the Black Panther Party," Kambon, interview with Fujino.

29. "Black Panther Coloring Book," copy in author's possession; George Lardner Jr., *"Panthers: A Recital of Fear and Crime," Washington Post*, June 19, 1969; George Lardner Jr., "Panther Book Shows Dead Police 'Pigs,'" *Washington Post*, June 25, 1969; "Inflaming Tracts Hit by Agnew," *Washington Post*, June 27, 1969; Marjorie Hunter, "City Detective Terms SDS a 'Dangerous' Group," *New York Times*, June 27, 1969; "Black Panther 'Propaganda' Hit by Agnew," *Los Angeles Times*, June 27, 1969.

30. Memo, FBIHQ to SAC San Francisco and 39 field offices, May 10, 1969; Memo, Dir. FBI, to SAC San Francisco, May 27, 1969; both cited in Ward Churchill, "'To Disrupt, Discredit and Destroy' The FBI's Secret War Against the Black Panther Party," in Kathleen Cleaver and George Katsiaficas, eds., *Liberation, Imagination, and the Black Panther Party* (New York: Routledge, 2001), 87–89.

31. "Oak Park Four: The Controversial Trial of Four Young Men of Protest," *Sacramento Observer*, October 1, 1970; Robert Fairbanks, "Mayor of Sacramento Deplores Police Action," *Los Angeles Times*, June 19, 1969; "Police Arrest, Charge 7 in Slaying of Officer," *Sacramento Bee*, May 27, 1970; "7 Jailed in Slaying of Sacramento Officer," *Los Angeles Times*, May 27, 1970; "Teemer, Artist, to Teach Art," *Sacramento Observer*, October 1, 1970; "Jack Strivers, Youngest of 'Oak Park Four,'" *Sacramento Observer*, October 1, 1970; "Conspiracy Arraignment Today," *Sacramento Union*, May 28, 1970; Alicia Denise Harris, "Mediated Memory: The Case of the 'Oak Park Four,'" master's thesis, California State University, Sacramento, 2011, 41–64.

32. Besides Teemer, the Oak Park Four were Jack Strivers, nineteen, Caeriaco Cabrallis, twenty-three, and Booker T. Cooke, twenty.

33. "Oak Park Defense Funds Investigates Slaying," *Sacramento Observer*, Oct. 1, 1970.

34. Archy Lee, living in Sacramento, refused to be returned to his slave master in the South and won his freedom in the courts. Clarence Caesar, "An Historical Overview of the Development of Sacramento's Black Community, 1850–1983" master's thesis, California State University, Sacramento, 1985, 225; cited in Harris, "Mediated Memory," 66; also 31–33.

35. "Oak Park Defense Funds Investigates Slaying," *Sacramento Observer*, October 1, 1970; "Defense Fund Goes through Changes," *Sacramento Observer*, October 1, 1970.

36. "Defense Ask for Witness Test," *Sacramento Observer*, August 6, 1970; "Evidence Seized Illegally," *Sacramento Observer*, September 24, 1970; "'Oak Park Four' Decision: All Freed!" *Sacramento Observer*, January 28, 1971; Harris, "Mediated

Memory," 54, 63–64.

37. "'Oak Park Four' Decision: All Freed!" *Sacramento Observer*.

38. Melvin Whitaker, "Reflections on Injustice," *Sacramento Observer*, February 4, 1971.

39. Ruth Wilson Gilmore, *Golden Gulag: Prisons, Surplus, Crisis, and Opposition in Globalizing California* (Berkeley: University of California Press, 2007), 28.

40. Coyle, "Fugitive Returns."

41. "Citizens Rally to Aid Black Artist, Mark Teemer," *Sacramento Observer*, October 31, 1973; Akinsanya Kambon, "Bio," www.thegallerykambon.com, accessed October 11, 2016.

42. Tom Johnson and Austin Lewis, "Revolutionary Thoughts: A Sacramento Panther Speaks"; Kambon, interview by Fujino.

43. "Why the Free Breakfast?" *Black Panther*, October 4, 1969. Huey Newton differentiated reformist gains from a Marxist critique of capitalist production: "I don't think black people should be fooled by their come-ons because everyone who gets in office promises the same thing. They promise full employment and decent housing; the Great Society, the New Frontier...No effects are felt in the black community, and the black people are tired of being deceived and duped. The people must have full control of the means of production" ("Huey Newton Talks to The Movement...," *The Movement*, August 1968).

44. Cedric J. Robinson, *Black Marxism: The Making of the Black Radical Tradition* (Chapel Hill: University of North Carolina Press, 2000/1983).

45. Akinsanya Kambon, presentation at University of California, Santa Barbara, November 14, 2016.

46. Peniel E. Joseph, *Stokely: A Life* (New York: BasicCivitas, 2014); Stokely Carmichael, with Ekwueme Michael Thelwell, *Ready for Revolution* (New York: Scribner, 2003).

47. "All-African People's Revolutionary Party (GC): Origins," posted on May 12, 2010, www.a-aprp-gc.org/party-3/origins/, accessed August 2, 2018.

48. Grace Douglas, "Akinsanya Captures Spirit of the People," *Black Market*, March 1982.

49. Bryan Hill, "Elmina Castle and Its Dark History of Enslavement, Torture, and Death," July 23, 2018, www.ancient-origins.net/ancient-places-africa/elmina-castle-and-its-dark-history-enslavement-torture-and-death-003450, accessed August 5, 2018; elminacastle.info, accessed August 28, 2018; Diane Fujino, tour of Elmina, c. July 1997.

50. Kambon, interview by Fujino.

51. Akinsanya Kambon, presentation at University of California, Santa Barbara, November 14, 2016; Akinsanya Kambon, as told at the Gallery Kambon in Long Beach, March 15, 2014; slighted edited by author.

52. In 1998, a *Sacramento Observer* article reported that Kambon had create more than 900 oil paintings and more than 200 bronze and ceramic sculptures in the past 20 years (Mosi Reeves, "Artist with a Message," *Sacramento Observer*, February 11, 1998).

53. Kambon, interview with Fujino; Akinsanya Kambon and Tama-sha Kambon, conversation with Diane Fujino, March 17, 2019.

54. "Akinsanya," by Akinsanya Kambon, unpublished manuscript, no date.

55. "Akinsanya," by Akinsanya Kambon, unpublished manuscript, no date.

56. Daryl Kelley, "Activist Remnant Hits Shift in Campus Blacks," *Los Angeles Times*, November 24, 1985; Susan Pack, "'System' Shuts Free Art School," *Press-Telegram*, August 12, 1992; Wayne Wilson, *Sacramento Bee*, August 15, 1987.

57. Danifu Bey, interview by J. R. Valrey, *P.O.C.C. Block Radio*, Los Angeles, November 2005, cited in George Percy Barganier, III, "Fanon's Children: The Black Panther Party and the Rise of the Crips and Bloods in Los Angeles (PhD diss., UC Berkeley, 2011), 64, 50, 72; also Genoa Barrow, "Anti-Gang Warfare Summit Held Locally," *Sacramento Observer*, August 25, 2005; Alex Alonso, "Territoriality Among African-American Street Gangs in Los Angeles" (master's thesis, University of Southern California, 1999), 90.

58. Alonso, "Territoriality Among African-American Street Gangs in Los Angeles," 90–91; Barganier, "Fanon's Children," 83.

59. Kirsten Lee Swartz, "Teacher Helps Youths Find an Escape from the Streets," *Los Angeles Times*, October 11, 1992; Genoa, "Anti-Gang Warfare Summit;" Kambon, interview with Fujino; Michelle Alexander, *The New Jim Crow: Mass Incarceration in the Age of Colorblindness* (New York: New Press, 2010).

60. Kambon, interview with Fujino; Genoa, "Anti-Gang Warfare Summit;" "Stopping the Violence," *Sacramento Observer*, April 21, 2011.

61. Rick Vanderknyff, "African History, Prodded, Rewrites Itself Art," *Los Angeles Times*, May 13, 1994.

62. Swartz, "Teacher Helps Youths."

63. Swartz, "Teacher Helps Youths;" Mosi Reeves, "Artist with a Message: Akinsanya Kambon Reflects on His Activism," *Sacramento Observer*, February 11, 1998.

64. George Lipsitz, *How Racism Takes Place* (Philadelphia: Temple University Press, 2011), 149–66; *Third Ward TX* (documentary, New Day Films, 2007).

65. Swartz, "Teacher Helps Youths;" Ward Churchill and Jim Vander Wall, *Agents of Repression* (Boston: South End Press, 1988).

66. "Fund-raiser to Help Pay Medical Expenses of Ailing Black Activist," *Los Angeles Times*, April 11, 1997; the author's observant participation at this event.

67. Richard Fausett, Manny Fernandez, and Alan Blinder, "Micah Johnson, Gunman in Dallas, Honed Military Skills to a Deadly Conclusion," *New York Times*, July 9, 2016; Louis Sahagun and Jaweed Kaleem, "A Study in Anger: How Gavin Long Went from Decorated Iraq Veteran to Cop Killer," *Los Angeles Times*, July 19, 2016.

Chapter Nine: Art That Flows from the People: Emory Douglas, International Solidarity, and the Practice of Cocreation

1. Emory Douglas as told to Courtney Yoshimura, *Art Forum*, www.artforum.com/words/id=64411, posted November 1, 2016.

2. George Lipsitz, quoted in Andrea Estrada, "UCSB Black Studies Scholar Examines Improvisation as a Tool for Social Change," www.news.ucsb.edu/2013/013580/ucsb-black-studies-scholar-examines-improvisation-tool-social-change, posted July 10, 2013; also see George Lipsitz, "Not Just Another Social Movement: Poster

Art and the Movimiento Chicano," in *American Studies in a Moment of Danger* (Minnesota: University of Minnesota Press, 2001), 181.

3. Emory Douglas, *Black Panther: The Revolutionary Art of Emory Douglas*, ed. Sam Durant (New York: Rizzoli, 2007); Marc James Léger and David Tomas, ed, *Zapantera Negra: An Artistic Encounter between Black Panthers and Zapatistas* (Brooklyn, NY: Common Notions, 2017).

4. Emory Douglas, interview with Diane Fujino and Matef Harmachis, August 7, 2017, San Francisco, CA; Léger and Tomas, *Zapantera Negra*, 9.

5. Daniel Fischlin, Ajay Heble, and George Lipsitz, *The Fierce Urgency of Now: Improvisation, Rights, and the Ethics of Cocreation* (Durham, NC: Duke University Press, 2013), xii, xi–xxxiv; Estrada, "UCSB Black Studies Scholar Examines Improvisation as a Tool for Social Change."

6. Emory Douglas and Akinsanya Kambon, interview with Felice Blake and Diane Fujino, November 14, 2016, Santa Barbara, CA.

7. The OSPAAL poster featuring Douglas's images of Black men in berets was designed by Lazaro Abreu and shown in Douglas, *Black Panther*, on page 100; also Douglas, interview with Fujino and Harmachis.

8. While acknowledging that Douglas included women in his artwork more than most in his times, Ericka Doss critiques his use of normative gendered representations. She writes: "But by casting black women within conventional and limited roles, as salesgirls and mothers, for instance, Douglas reinforced the patriarchal conceits that largely dominated the Black Panthers' political image and program" [Ericka Doss, "'Revolutionary Art Is a Tool for Liberation': Emory Douglas and Protest Aesthetics at the *Black Panther*," in Kathleen Cleaver and George Katsiaficas, ed., *Liberation, Imagination, and the Black Panther Party* (New York: Routledge, 2001), 182]. While many of his images depict women with either babies or guns—thus reinforcing or rejecting the association of femininity with domesticity—I contend that exceeding domestic or revolutionary representations, many of Douglas's images show Black women in struggle, in celebration, and in otherwise humanizing depictions. These include his renditions of Black women singing, "Hallelujah!," throwing out a large rat, playing a tambourine "to keep on struggling for brighter days," and shouting for "freedom." Beyond his artwork, Panther women saw Douglas as a man who showed respect to women in his lived practice as well. Ericka Huggins spontaneously offered: "Why do we love Emory? Because he's always been aware of the importance of health and wellness; always, always, always compassionate; always aware of women and gender. He doesn't make a big word about it. He's a gentle soul, a humble person." (Ericka Huggins, interview with Diane Fujino, Oakland, CA, April 17, 2018).

9. Douglas, interview with Fujino and Harmachis.

10. Douglas, interview with Fujino and Harmachis; Elton C. Fax, *Black Artists of the New Generation* (New York: Dodd, Mead & Co., 1977), 257–58.

11. Fax, *Black Artists of the New Generation*, 258; Douglas, interview with Fujino and Harmachis; Emory Douglas, interview by Marc Steiner, *Marc Steiner Show*, November 14, 2014, http://therealnews.com/t2/index.php?option=com _content&task=view&id=31&Itemid=74&jumival=12658, January 7, 2018.

12. Douglas, interview with Fujino and Harmachis; Sam Lefebvre, "Without Charles Sullivan, There'd Be No Fillmore as We Know It," KQED.org, June 14, 2017, www.kqed.org/arts/13414955/without-charles-sullivan-thered-be-no-fillmore -as-we-know-it, accessed July 9, 2018. On Yori Wada's work at the Booker T. Washington Center and Buchanan YMCA, see "Yori Wada: Working for Youth and Social Justice," interviews by Frances Linsley and Gabrielle Morris, 1983 and 1990, https://oac.cdlib.org/view?docId=hb7r29p1vn&brand=oac4&doc .view=entire_text.

13. Clyde Woods, in his ambitious study of the Mississippi Delta from the 1830s to the 1980s, developed the term "blues epistemology" to refer to "the working-class African American community-centered tradition of development thought and practice and its critiques of the plantation bloc, its political economy, and its tradition of social explanation." See Clyde Woods, *Development Arrested: The Blues and Plantation Power in the Mississippi Delta* (London: Verso, 1998), 247.

14. Warden asserts that the Afro-American Association was among the first to use the term "Afro-American," to exclude whites from their organization, and to "really talk about Black is beautiful." Don Warden, interview by Robert E. Martin, July 25, 1969, Howard University, Moorland-Spingarn Research Center. BPP founders Huey Newton and Bobby Seale were members of the AAA, as were Ernest Allen Jr., Marvin X, Cedric Robinson. Newton left the group, as did many others, critical of Warden's dominating style and rather conservative politics of Black sufficiency and Black enterprise. See James Edward Smethurst, *The Black Arts Movement: Literary Nationalism in the 1960s and 1970s* (Chapel Hill: University of North Carolina Press, 2005), 256–61; Huey Newton, *Revolutionary Suicide* (New York: Ballantine Books, 1973), 66–71; Bobby Seale, *Seize the Time* (New York: Vintage Books, 1968), 14, 21–22; Robin D. G. Kelley, foreword, in *Black Marxism: The Making of the Black Radical Tradition*, Cedric J. Robinson (Chapel Hill: University of North Carolina Press, 2000/1983), xv–xvi.

15. "Afro-American Studies at Merritt," *Peralta Colleges Bulletin*, December 8, 1967; Rick Heide, "Faculty OK's New Black Department," *Merritt College Reporter*, November 21, 1968; "Afro-American Department at Merritt College," *Peralta Bulletin Colleges*, January 24, 1969—all from Merritt College and Peralta District archives; David Dupree and William McAllister, "A Campus Where Black Power Won," *Wall Street Journal*, November 18, 1969; Jeffrey Heyman and Michelle Lee, "Merritt College: Home of the Black Panthers," documentary, Peralta TV, 2008.

16. Larry Neal, "The Black Arts Movement," *Drama Review* (Summer 1968); Kalamu ya Salaam, "Historical Overviews of the Black Arts Movement," in *The Oxford Companion to Women's Writing in the United States* (New York: Oxford University Press, 1995), at www.english.illinois.edu/maps/blackarts/historical.htm; Marvin X (Jackmon), *Somethin' Proper: The Life and Times of a North American African Poet* (Castro Valley, CA: Black Bird Press, 1988), 115–27; Samuel A. Hay, *Ed Bullins: A Literary Biography* (Detroit: Wayne State University Press, 1997), 24–25.

17. Amiri Baraka, "Emory Douglas: A 'Good Brother,' a 'Bad Artist,'" in *Black Panther*, Douglas; Smethurst, *Black Arts Movement*, 277–85.

18. Smethurst, *Black Arts Movement*, 274–85; Douglas, interview with Fujino and

Harmachis, August 7, 2017, San Francisco, CA; Emory Douglas, phone conversation with Diane Fujino, October 1, 2018.

19. Douglas, interview with Fujino and Harmachis, August 7, 2017, San Francisco, CA. The masthead and titles were written by hand in the first issue of the *Black Panther* newspaper (April 25, 1967), but by the second issue (May 15, 1967), the entire paper had a professional look and layout, owing to the work of Emory Douglas.

20. Bobby Seale, foreword, to Douglas, *Black Panther*, 13; Mumia Abu-Jamal, in *Black Panther*, Douglas, 4; St. Clair Bourne, "An Artist for the People: An Interview with Emory Douglas," in Douglas, *Black Panther*, 199–205; Douglas, interview with Fujino and Harmachis, August 7, 2017, San Francisco, CA.

21. In forming the BPP, Huey Newton had stated: "We have to have a program for the people. A program that relates to the people. A program that the people can understand. A program that the people can read and see." Seale, *Seize the Time*, 59.

22. Emory Douglas, "The Battle Cry: 'Culture Is a Weapon,'" posted on Emory Douglas' Facebook, April 5, 2012; Colette Gaiter, "What Revolution Looks Like: The Work of Black Panther Artist Emory Douglas," in Douglas, *Black Panther*, 94, 96; Baraka, "Emory Douglas: A 'Good Brother,' a 'Bad Artist,'" 181; Mulvey, quoted in Gaiter, "What Revolution Looks Like," 96; Frantz Fanon, *The Wretched of the Earth* (New York, Grove Press, 1963), 94.

23. Smethurst, *Black Arts Movement*, 283.

24. Cox, "The Split in the Party," 118–22; Joshua Bloom and Waldo E. Martin, *Black against Empire: The History and Politics of the Black Panther Party* (Berkeley: University of California Press, 2013), 358–71.

25. All quotes are from Douglas, interview with Fujino and Harmachis. On Algeria, see Kathleen Cleaver, "A Picture Is Worth a Thousand Words," in *Black Panthers*, Douglas, 59–63; Elaine Mokhtefi, *Algiers: Third World Capital* (New York: Verso, 2018), 91, 104.

26. Douglas, interview with Fujino and Harmachis. The East Coast BPP started the *Right On!* newspaper in spring 1971, after the televised Newton-Cleaver conflict; see Safiyah Bukhari, *The War Before: The True Life Story of Becoming a Black Panther, Keeping the Faith in Prison, and Fighting for Those Left Behind* (New York: Feminist Press, 2010), xliii, 61; Bloom and Martin, *Black against Empire*, 369.

27. Cox, "Split in the Party," 121.

28. According to Emory, after the Panthers' Sacramento protest his mother, Lorraine Douglas, was "harassed by the FBI" and "constantly hounded by the fear that her son might be among those singled out for 'liquidation.'" Her fears intensified after the police killed Bobby Hutton on April 6, 1968, but Emory persisted, and his mother eventually accepted his commitment (Fax, *Black Artists of the New* Generation, 275).

29. Donna Jean Murch, *Living for the City: Migration, Education, and the Rise of the Black Panther Party in Oakland, California* (Chapel Hill: University of North Carolina Press, 2010), 178–83, 225; Bloom and Martin, *Black against Empire*, 389.

30. Jane Rhodes, *Framing the Black Panther Party* (Urbana: University of Illinois Press, 2007), 85–87; Gerald Horne, *Black Revolutionary: William Patterson and the Globalization of the African American Freedom Struggle* (Urbana: University of Illinois

Press, 2013), 207–210; Douglas, interview with Fujino and Harmachis; Douglas, conversation with Fujino.

31. By the early 1990s, top party leaders, including Douglas, spoke to Geronimo ji Jaga Pratt's lawyer to admit that Pratt was at a BPP meeting in Oakland at the time the murder for which he was convicted was committed 400 miles away in Santa Monica. Based on a 147-page petition, with 300 pages of exhibits, Pratt's conviction was overturned in 1997, after twenty-seven years in prison for a crime he did not commit (Jack Olson, *Last Man Standing: The Tragedy and Triumph of Geronimo Pratt*, New York: Anchor, 2000), 333; Edward Boyer, "Pratt Strides into Freedom," *Los Angeles Times*, June 11, 1997).

32. Douglas, interview with Fujino and Harmachis, August 7, 2017, San Francisco, CA. In the early morning police raid on the Philadelphia BPP in late August 1970, the police made the Panthers strip down to their underwear and line up against the wall—a photographed image of harassment and humiliation that Douglas well remembers. The police raid occurred just days before the BPP's Revolutionary People's Constitutional Convention taking place in the "City of Brotherly Love" (Omari L. Dyson, Kevin L. Brooks, and Judson L. Jeffries, "'Brotherly Love Can Kill You': The Philadelphia Branch of the Black Panther Party," in *Comrades: A Local History of the Black Panther Party*, ed. Judson L. Jeffries (Bloomington: Indiana University Press, 2007), 235; Mumia Abu-Jamal, *We Want Freedom* (Cambridge: South End Press, 2004), 195–96).

33. Subcomandante Marcos, "The Fourth World War Has Begun," trans. Nathalie de Broglio, *Nepantla: Views from South 2* (2001): 559-572.

34. Quotes from Léger and Tomas, *Zapantera Negra*, 102–103, 53–54; also 1–9, 105; "The Black Panthers and the Zapatistas: An Encounter," *Whenua Fenua Enua Vanua: Revolutionary Anti Colonialism & Anti Capitalism in the Pacific*, posted October 21, 2012, http://uriohau.blogspot.com/2012/10/, accessed on January 11, 2018.

35. To see the artwork, see Zapantera Negra-En Donde Era La Onu, www.edelo.org/zapantera-negra/4571745556, accessed January 10, 2018.

36. Léger and Tomas, *Zapantera Negra*, 18–19.

37. Linda Tuhiwai Smith, *Decolonizing Methodologies: Research and Indigenous Peoples*, 2nd ed. (London: Zed, 2012; 1999).

38. Cedric J. Robinson, *Black Marxism: The Making of the Black Radical Tradition* (Chapel Hill: University of North Carolina Press, 2000; reprinted 1983), xii–xiv, 121–22.

39. Roger Peet, "Zapatista Murals," posted January 10, 2014, at https://justseeds.org/zapatista-murals/.

40. Chiapas Support Committee, at https://chiapas-support.org/ and www.facebook.com/CSCzapatistas/, accessed July 10, 2018.

41. Douglas, *Black Panther*; Sam Durant, introduction, in *Black Panther*, Douglas, 21–22.

42. Emily Hill, "Emory Douglas: Art's Rebel without a Pause," *Dazed and Confused*, November 2007, www.dazeddigital.com/artsandculture/article/20981/1/emory-douglas-arts-rebel-without-a-pause; Emory Douglas, "Position Paper No. 1: On Revolutionary Art," *Black Panther*, January 24, 1970.

43. Michael L. Clemons and Charles E. Jones, "Global Solidarity: The Black Panther Party in the International Arena," in *Liberation, Imagination and the Black Panther*

Party, Cleaver and Katsiaficas, 20–39; John T. McCartney, "The Influences of the Black Panther Party (USA) on the Vanguard Party of the Bahamas, 1972–87," in *Liberation, Imagination and the Black Panther Party*, Cleaver and Katsiaficas, 156–63; Judy Tzu-Chun Wu, *Radicals on the Road: Internationalism, Orientalism, and Feminism during the Vietnam Era* (Ithaca, NY: Cornell University Press, 2013), 110; Bloom and Waldo, *Black against Empire*, 319–21; Elbert "Big Man" Howard, *Panther on the Prowl* (BCP Digital Printing, 2002), 34–53; Polynesian Panthers on Emory Douglas's Facebook page, November 11, 2014, www.facebook.com/photo.php?fbid=10205690094558033&set=a.1634685913424.2094381.142; Douglas, conversation with Fujino. Cuba became a site of political asylum for Black radicals, including former Panthers William Lee Brent, Eldridge Cleaver, and Huey Newton as well as Robert F. Williams, Nehanda Abiodun, and others; see Teishan A. Latner, *Cuban Revolution in America: Havana and the Making of a United States Left, 1968–1992* (Chapel Hill: University of North Carolina Press, 2018), 221–51.

44. Emory Douglas, bio and resume, sent to author, October 2016; Mokhtefi, *Algiers, Third World Capital*, 91.

45. "New to the Collection: Richard Bell/Emory Douglas," https://uqartmuseum.wordpress.com/2016/08/31/new-to-the-collection-richard-bellemory-douglas/, posted August 31, 2006; "Richard Bell—"Enfant Terrible," at www.aboriginalartonline.com/art/bell.html, accessed January 11, 2018; "A Peace Offering to White Australia," *Black Noise: Exploring Australian Indigenous Art in Melbourne*, https://bnmelb.wordpress.com/2012/08/03/basil-sellers-art-prize-2012-artist-talks-with-richard-bell/, accessed on January 11, 2018; Richard Bell's website, www.kooriweb.org/bell/article13.html; "Emory Douglas and Richard Bell, All Power to the People," www.milanigallery.com.au/about-us, accessed January 11, 2018.

46. "We Can Be Heroes, with Richard Bell and Emory Douglas," www.artgallery.nsw.gov.au/collection/works/117.2015/, accessed January 14, 2018; Emory Douglas, Facebook, 2011, www.facebook.com/photo.php?fbid=2200783465509&set=a.1634685913424.2094381.1424975446&type=3&theater, accessed December 18, 2017.

47. At Norman's funeral in 2006, with Smith and Carlos present as pallbearers, in his eulogy, Carlos said, that he "had expected to see fear in Norman's eyes. 'I didn't. I saw love.'" See Rupert Cornwell, "Great Olympic Friendships: John Carlos, Peter Norman and Tommie Smith—Divided by Their Colour, United by Their Cause," *Independent*, August 4, 2016; also Christine Milne, "An Activist Life," (St. Lucia, Queensland, Australia: University of Queensland Press, 2017), 209.

48. "A Peace Offering to White Australia," *Black Noise: Exploring Australian Indigenous Art in Melbourne*, https://bnmelb.wordpress.com/2012/08/03/basil-sellers-art-prize-2012-artist-talks-with-richard-bell/, accessed on January 11, 2018.

49. Harry Edwards, *The Revolt of the Black Athlete* (Urbana: University of Illinois Press, 2017, 1969), 46–47, 76–86, 142–46; Dave Zirin, *What's My Name, Fool? Sports and Resistance in the United States* (Chicago: Haymarket Books, 2005), 73–78; John Branch, "The Awakening of Colin Kaepernick," *New York Times*, September 7, 2017, www.nytimes.com/2017/09/07/sports/colin-kaepernick-nfl-protests.html.

50. "Bell Invites," www.smba.nl/en/exhibitions/bell-invites/index.html, accessed January 11, 2018.

51. "Oakland Palestine Solidarity Wall," http://artforces.org/projects/murals/usa /oakland-palestine-solidarity-mural/, accessed May 24, 2018; "Oakland Unveils Mural in Solidarity with Palestine," *Electronic Intifada*, August 10, 2014.

52. "Israel-Gaza Conflict: 50-Day War by Numbers," *UK Independent*, August 27, 2014; "Palestine Mural Is Unveiled in Oakland, and Activists Gear Up to 'Block the Boat,'" *Mondoweiss*, August 11, 2014; also Kristian Davis Bailey, "Black-Palestinian Solidarity in the Ferguson-Gaza Era," *American Quarterly* 67 (2015): 1017–1026.

53. "Third World Round Up: The Palestine Problem: Test Your Knowledge," *SNCC Newsletter*, June–July 1967, 4–5; Keith P. Feldman, *A Shadow over Palestine: The Imperial Life of Race in America* (Minneapolis: University of Minnesota Press, 2015), 59–86; Alex Lubin, *Geographies of Liberation: The Making of an Afro-Arab Political Imaginary* (Chapel Hill: University of North Carolina Press, 2014), 121–40. It is Douglas's distinct recollection that Newton had planned to travel to Israel but was denied entry into Israel (Douglas, conversation with Fujino).

54. "We Stand with Palestine in the Spirit of "Sumud": US Prisoner, Labor, and Academic Solidarity Delegation to Palestine, March 24 to April 2, 2016, http:// samidoun.net/2016/04/on-palestinian-prisoners-day-anti-prison-labor-academic -delegation-takes-stand-against-israeli-state-violence-affirms-solidarity-with -palestinian-people/, posted April 16, 2016.

55. Emory Douglas's Facebook, 2010, www.facebook.com/photo.php?fbid=1779495 893583&set=a.1634685913424.2094381.1424975446&type=3&theater, accessed December 18, 2017.

56. "Child among Three Palestinians Shot Dead by Israeli Army," *Guardian*, October 5, 2018, www.theguardian.com/world/2018/oct/05/child-among-three-palestin-ians-shot-dead-by-israeli-army; World Bank, "Cash-Strapped Gaza and an Econ-omy in Collapse Put Palestinian Basic Needs at Risk," press release, September 25, 2018, www.worldbank.org/en/news/press-release/2018/09/25/cash-strapped -gaza-and-an-economy-in-collapse-put-palestinian-basic-needs-at-risk; David M. Halbfinger and Isabel Kershner, "Israeli Law Declares the Country the 'Nation-State of the Jewish People,'" *New York Times*, July 19, 2018. The day before Douglas's talk, a University of Michigan professor was disciplined for refusing to write a letter of recommendation for a student to study in Israel, in solidarity with the academic boycott of Israel (Kim Kozlowski, "UM Disciplines Prof over Israel Letter Controversy," *Detroit News*, October 9, 2018, www.detroitnews.com /story/news/local/michigan/2018/10/09/university-michigan-disciplines-professor -over-israel-letter-controversy/1580969002/).

57. Rigo 23, email to Chrisstina Hamilton, October 9, 2018; "Required University of Michigan Lecture Included Slide Comparing Netanyahu to Hitler," www.haaretz .com/us-news/required-university-of-michigan-lecture-compared -netanyahu-to-hitler-1.6534977, October 8, 2018.

58. Emory Douglas, "Position Paper No. 1: On Revolutionary Art," *Black Panther*, January 24, 1970, emphasis mine.

59. Woods, *Development Arrested*; George Lipsitz, "Challenging Neoliberal Education at the Grassroots: Students Who Lead, Not Students Who Leave," *Souls: A Criti-cal Journal of Black Politics, Culture, and Society* 17 (2015): 303–21; Diane C. Fujino

et al., "A Transformative Pedagogy for a Decolonial World," *Review of Education, Pedagogy, and Cultural Studies* 40 (2018): 69–95.

60. Emory Douglas, "Art in Service for the People," *Black Scholar* 9 (1977): 55–57; Douglas, "Revolutionary Art;" Emory Douglas, interview with Diane Fujino and Matef Harmachis, August 7, 2017, San Francisco, CA.

61. Douglas's philosophy of walking with the people is also reflective of his political ideology: "There can only be true love of humanity when class distinctions have been done away with, all over the world" (Emory Douglas, "To All Progressive Artist [*sic*] Who Are Struggling against the Racist U.S. Government . . . World Enemy Number One," *Black Panther*, August 29, 1970). On *preguntando caminamos*, see John Holloway, "Dignity's Revolt," in John Holloway and Eloina Palaez, ed., *Zapatista! Reinventing Revolution in Mexico* (London: Pluto Press, 1998). I thank Esther Lezra for her interpretation of "make our way by asking."

62. Woods, *Development Arrested*, 247.

63. Marcy Rein, "The More Times Change . . . the Bay Area Alternative Press '68–'98," *Media Alliance* 17 (1998), cited in Colette Gaiter, "Visualizing a Revolution: Emory Douglas and the Black Panther Newspaper," AIGA, the Professional Association for Design, June 8, 2005, www.aiga.org/visualizing-a-revolution -emory-douglas-and-the-black-panther-new, accessed December 18, 2017.

64. Emory Douglas, "Political Artist Manifesto: Food for Thought," Emory Douglas's Facebook, posted April 5, 2012, www.facebook.com/photo.php?fbid=10200209728 432305&set=a.1634685913424.2094381.1424975446&type=3&theater.

65. Martin Luther King, Jr., "Letter from Birmingham Jail" (1963).

66. Emory Douglas, "The Battle Cry: 'Culture Is a Weapon,'" Emory Douglas's Facebook, posted April 5, 2012, www.facebook.com/photo.php?fbid=1020020972843 2305&set=a.1634685913424.2094381.1424975446&type=3&theater, created in support of a benefit for political prisoners and prisoners of war in New York and a tribute to Gil Scott Heron and Tupac Shakur.

67. Emory Douglas, "On Revolutionary Culture," in the *Black Panther* newspaper; reprinted in *New Black Voices: An Anthology of Contemporary Afro-American Literature*, ed. Abraham Chapman (New York: New American Library, 1972), 489–90.

68. The Sandra Bland quote is verbatim, with minor grammatical edits by the author; see Emory Douglas, Facebook, posted December 22, 2015. The "police terror" image was posted October 24, 2015; both at www.facebook.com/photo.php?fbid =10208156962508190&set=a.1634685913424.2094381.1424975446&type =3&theater, accessed January 14, 2018.

Chapter Ten: Poetic Justice: The Dialectic Between Black Power Politics and Fred Ho's Revolutionary Music

1. Kat Chow, "Iconoclastic Musician Takes Measure of His Life: 'I Became a Fighter,'" *Code Switch*, NPR, February 22, 2014, www.npr.org/sections/codeswitch /2014/02/22/279169546/iconoclastic-musician-takes-measure-of-his-life-i-became -a-fighter, accessed November 10, 2017.

2. Herb Boyd, "Political Prisoner Russell Maroon Shoatz Out of Solitary Confinement," *Amsterdam News*, March 20, 2014, http://amsterdamnews.com/news/2014/mar/20/political-prisoner-russell-maroon-shoatz-out-solit/.

3. Chow, "Iconoclastic Musician Takes Measure."

4. Fred Ho, interview with author, September 30, 2011.

5. Wei-hua Zhang, "Fred Wei-Han Ho: Case Study of a Chinese-American Creative Musician," *Asian Music* 25, no. 1–2 (1994/1993): 356.

6. Fred Ho, "For Revolutionary Firespitter Sister Jayne Cortez (May 10, 1934–December 28, 2012)," *Black Scholar* 43, no. 1–2 (2013): 5.

7. Cynthia Ann Young, *Soul Power: Culture, Radicalism, and the Making of a U.S. Third World Left* (Durham, NC: Duke University Press, 2006).

8. Fred Ho and the Afro Asian Music Ensemble, *Yes Means Yes, No Means No, Whatever She Wears, Wherever She Goes!* (Big Red Media, 1997).

9. Magdalena Gómez, "Machete and Chopsticks," in *Yellow Power, Yellow Soul: The Radical Art of Fred Ho*, ed. Tamara Roberts and Robert N. Buckley (Champaign: University of Illinois Press, 2013), 54.

10. Tamara Roberts, *Resounding Afro Asia: Interracial Music and the Politics of Collaboration* (Oxford: Oxford University Press, 2016), 125.

11. Vijay Prashad, *The Darker Nations: A People's History of the Third World* (New York: New Press, 2007), 10.

12. Timothy Tyson, *Radio Free Dixie: Robert F. Williams and the Roots of Black Power* (Chapel Hill: University of North Carolina Press, 1999); Richard Wright, *Black Power: Three Books from Exile: Black Power; The Color Curtain; and White Man, Listen!* (New York: HarperCollins e-books, 2010), 45.

13. Fred Ho and Bill Mullen, *Afro Asia: Revolutionary Political and Cultural Connections between African Americans and Asian Americans* (Durham, NC: Duke University Press, 2008), 5.

14. Prashad, *The Darker Nations*, xvii.

15. Newton, *Revolutionary Suicide*, 70.

16. Robin D. G. Kelly, "Black Like Mao," in *Afro Asia*, ed. Ho and Mullen, 105.

17. Michael L. Clemons and Charles E. Jones, "Global Solidarity: The Black Panther Party in the International Arena," *New Political Science* 21, no. 2 (1999): 177–203.

18. Wadado Leo Smith, "Creative Music and the AACM" in *Keeping Time: Readings in Jazz History*, ed. Robert Walser (Oxford: Oxford University Press, 2014), 274.

19. Smith, "Creative Music and the AACM," 274.

20. Ingrid Monson, *Freedom Sounds: Civil Rights Call out to Jazz and Africa* (Oxford, England: Oxford University Press, 2010), 227–30.

21. Christopher J. Lee, *Making a World After Empire: The Bandung Moment and Its Political Afterlives* (Athens: Ohio University Press, 2010).

22. Vijay Prashad, "Foreword," in *AfroAsian Encounters: Culture, History, and Politics*, ed. Heiki Raphal Hernandez and Shannon Steen (New York: New York University Press, 2006), xxi.

23. Loren Kajikawa, "The Sound of Struggle," in *Jazz/Not Jazz: The Music and Its Boundaries*, ed. David Ake, et al., (Oakland: University of California Press, 2012), 141.

24. Amiri Baraka, *Blues People: Negro Music in White America* (New York: William

Morrow, 1963).

25. See for instance Leonard Brown, *John Coltrane and Black America's Quest for Freedom: Spirituality and the Music* (Oxford: Oxford University Press, 2010), 140. [T]he music made by the classic quartet [of Coltrane] still modeled an ethos more in line with King's ethic of love and social democracy than it did the separatist ideology of Elijah Muhammad or the cries of Black Power by Stokely Carmichael or H. Rap Brown.

26. Peter Lavezzoli, *The Dawn of Indian Music in the West* (London: Continuum International Publishing Group, 2006), 293.

27. Quoted in Ben Ratliff, *Coltrane: The Story of a Sound* (New York: Farrar, Straus and Giroux, 2007), 157.

28. Edward Brathwaite, *The Development of Creole Society in Jamaica* (Oxford: Oxford University Press, 1971).

29. See Robin D. G. Kelley, *Freedom Dreams*, for more discussion on the concept of the "polycultural" as opposed to multicultural.

30. James Smethurst, *The Black Arts Movement: Literary Nationalism in the 1960s and 1970s* (Chapel Hill, NC: University of North Carolina Press, 2005), 113.

31. Smethurst, *Black Arts Movement*, 188.

32. Smethurst, *Black Arts Movement*, 193.

33. Amiri Baraka (LeRoi Jones), *Black Music* (New York: Quill, 1967), 183.

34. Scott Saul, *Freedom Is, Freedom Ain't: Jazz and the Meaning of the Sixties* (Cambridge, MA: Harvard University Press, 2005), 229.

35. Fred Ho, *Wicked Theory, Naked Practice: A Fred Ho Reader*, ed. Diane C. Fujino (Minneapolis: University of Minnesota Press, 2009), 165.

36. Susan M. Asai, "Cultural Politics: The African American Connection in Asian American Jazz-Based Music," *Asian Music* 36, no. 1 (2005) and Kajikawa, "The Sound of Struggle."

37. Gómez, "Machete and Chopsticks."

38. Ho, *Wicked Theory*, 180.

39. Kimberly W. Beston, *Performing Blackness: Enactments of African-American Modernism* (Abingdon-on-Thames, GB: Routledge, 2000), 165.

40. Fred Ho, "For Revolutionary Firespitter Sister Jayne Cortez (May 10, 1934– December 28, 2012)," *Black Scholar* 43 (2013): 5.

41. Quoted in Ho, "For Revolutionary Firespitter," 5.

42. Ho, *Wicked Theory*, 171.

43. Jessica Gordon Nembhard, *Collective Courage: A History of African American Cooperative Economic Thought and Practice* (University Park: Penn State University Press, 2014), 218.

44. Julian Ellison, "Cooperation and Struggle: The African American Cooperative Tradition," *Scoop Newsletter* 50 (September 1980): 2.

45. Fred Ho, press kit, *The Black Panther Suite*, 1999, accessed at the Fred Ho Archive at UConn Storrs, June 1, 2018.

46. Kalamu ya Salaam, *Magic of Juju: An Appreciation of the Black Arts Movement* (Chicago: Third World Press, 1998).

47. Ho, *Wicked Theory*, 79.

48. Fred Ho, "Revolutionary Asian American Art," in *Legacy to Liberation: Politics and*

Cultures of Revolutionary Asian Pacific America, ed. Fred Ho et al. (San Francisco: AK Press, 2000), 387.

49. Kevin Fellezs, "Enter the Voice of the Dragon: Fred Ho, Bruce Lee, and the Popular Avant-Garde," in *Yellow Power, Yellow Soul*, 39.

50. Ho, "Revolutionary Asian American Art," in *Legacy to Liberation*, 383.

51. Ho, "Revolutionary Asian American Art," in *Legacy to Liberation*, 383.

52. Amiri Baraka, liner notes to *The New Wave in Jazz*, John Coltrane, Albert Ayler, Archie Shepp, et al., Impulse AS-90, Vinyl, LP 1966.

53. Susan M. Asai, "Cultural Politics: The African American Connection in Asian American Jazz-Based Music," *Asian Music* 36 (2005), 86.

54. Salim Washington, "Fred Ho's Ethical Aesthetic," in *Yellow Power, Yellow Soul*.

55. Michael C. Heller, *Loft Jazz: Improvising New York in the 1970s* (Oakland, CA: University of California Press, 2017), 69.

56. Ho, *Wicked Theory*, 172.

57. Ho, *Wicked Theory*, 172.

58. Heller, *Loft Jazz*, 89.

59. Will Friedwald, "Big Bands and Deft Duos," *Wall Street Journal*, February 24, 2012.

60. Ho, *Wicked Theory*, 129.

61. Ho, *Wicked Theory*, 138.

62. On the Ecosocialist International in Venezuela in 2017, see http://ecosocialisthorizons.com/2017/12/the-first-ecosocialist-international-combined-strategy-and-plan-of-action/and http://ecosocialisthorizons.com/about/. On the Afro Yaqui Music Collective, see http://afroyaquimusiccollective.com/.

63. See Fred Ho, "From Banana to Third World Marxist," in *Wicked Theory, Naked Practice*.

64. Assata Shakur, *Assata: An Autobiography* (Chicago: Laurence Hill, 1987), 241.

65. Fred Ho, "Preface: FIRE IN THE HOLE! WHY RUSSELL MAROON SHOATZ IS IMPORTANT TO CREATIVE REVOLUTIONARIES!" in *Maroon the Implacable: The Collected Writings of Russell Maroon Shoatz*, ed. Fred Ho and Quincy Saul (Oakland, California: PM Press, 2013).

66. Fred Ho, *The A to Z Characteristics and Qualities of Being a Revolutionary*, self-published essay, 1.

Chapter Eleven: Legacy: Where We Were, Where We Are, Where We Are Going

1. The authors intentionally spell "Afrika" with a "k" because few Afrikan languages contain the letter c. They intentionally spell "amerikkka" in lowercase and with a "kkk" to signal the historical overlap of white supremacist philosophies of the United States and the Ku Klux Klan. This terminology is common in the New Afrikan and Black Power movements.

2. The authors use lowercase to refer to the "united states" to contest the legitimacy of the nation-state and reveal its settler colonial historical formation.

3. Peter L. Zimroth, *Perversions of Justice: The Prosecution and Acquittal of the Panther*

21 (Viking Press: New York, 1974).

4. Delivered on October 16, 1963, as "The Negro Child – His Self-Image"; published in *Saturday Review*, December 21, 1963. Reprinted in James Baldwin, *The Price of the Ticket, Collected Non-Fiction 1948–1985* (New York: St. Martin's Press, 1985).

Chapter Twelve: Black August: Organizing to Uplift the Fallen and Release the Captive

1. Judson Jeffries, ed., *Comrades: A Local History of the Black Panther Party* (Bloomington and Indianapolis: Indiana University Press, 2007), 278.
2. Shaka At-Thinnin, chair, Black August Organizing Committee, interview with Matef Harmachis and Diane Fujino, Oakland, CA, August 9, 2017.
3. On August 12, 2015, reportedly one day after he came out of solitary confinement, Hugo "Yogi" Pinell, aka Dahariki, was assassinated under cover of a "prison riot." He had been in prison for forty-six years, the majority of that time in solitary confinement.
4. Jitu Sadiki, Black Martyr's Tour, August 25, 2018.
5. Min Sun Yee, "Death on the Yard: The Untold Killings at Soledad and San Quentin," *Ramparts*, April 1973.
6. Mama Ayanna Mashama, "Black August: The True History, Culture, and Practice," www.mxgm.org/black-august-2018-1, accessed July 31, 2018).
7. Soledad Brothers Defense Committee, "Support the Soledad Brothers!" freedomarchives.org/Documents/Finder/DOC513_scans/Soledad_Brothers/513. Soledad.Brothers.Support.the.Soledad.Brothers.pdf, accessed September 23, 2018.
8. Associated Press, "Courtroom Escape Attempt/Convicts, Trial Judge Slain/Two Others Wounded," August 8, 1970.
9. Lori Andrews, *Black Power, White Blood: The Life and Times of Johnny Spain* (Philadelphia: Temple University Press, 1999).
10. At-Thinnin, interview with author, July 2017.
11. For more information on SSU operations see California Department of Corrections and Rehabilitation, www.cdcr.ca.gov/search/?q=special+service+unit, accessed February 18, 2020. See also Christian Parenti, "Rural Prison as Colonial Master," *Prison Legal News* at www.prisonlegalnews.org/news/1998/apr/15/rural-prison-as-colonial-master/, posted April 15, 1998. For how SSU is used against nonprisoners see Kendra Castaneda Perez, "Corrections Dept. Agents Bang on Activist's Door at 8 a.m. over a Postcard She Wrote to a Prisoner," Prison Watch Network, prisonwatchnetwork.org/category/cdcr-special-service-unit-cdcr-ssu/, posted October 28, 2014.
12. Federal Bureau of Investigation, "Black Guerilla Family," archive.org/stream/BlackGuerillaFamily/Black%20Guerilla%20Family%2003_djvu.txt, accessed September 21, 2018.
13. At-Thinnin, interview with author, July 2017.
14. Mama Ayanna Mashama, "Black August."
15. Ajamu Nangwaya, "Why Black August Should Be Celebrated across the

Americas," www.telesurtv.net/english/opinion/Why-Black-August-Should-Be-Celebrated-Across-the-Americas-20160820-0009.html, posted August 1, 2018; Upstate Chapter of Northeast Political Prisoner Coalition, "The Spirit of Black August in Solidarity with Venezuela," venezuelanalysis.com/analysis/14030, posted September 4, 2018.

16. Federal Bureau of Investigation, "Black Guerilla Family," archive.org/stream/BlackGuerillaFamily/Black%20Guerilla%20Family%2003_djvu.txt, accessed September 21, 2018.

Chapter Fourteen: Dialogical Autonomy: Michael Zinzun, the Coalition Against Police Abuse, and Genocide

1. See, for example, joão h. costa vargas, *Never Meant to Survive: Genocide and Utopias in Black Diaspora Communities* (Lanham, MD: Rowman & Littlefield, 2008). The author intentionally uses the lowercase "i" and the lowercase in his name to show the importance of the collective over the individual.

2. See joão h. costa vargas, *Catching Hell in the City of Angels: Life and Meanings of Blackness in South Central Los Angeles* (Minneapolis, MN: University of Minnesota Press, 2006).

3. See Huey Newton's statement to that effect in Donald Weise and David Hilliard, *The Huey Newton Reader* (New York, NY: Seven Stories Press, 2002), 279.

4. Kwame Ture (Stokely Carmichael) and Charles Hamilton, *Black Power: The Politics of Liberation in America* (New York, NY : Knopf, 1967), 44.

5. Ture and Hamilton, *Black Power*, 5.

6. Ture and Hamilton, *Black Power*, 44. This quotation exemplifies the only reference to antiblack processes explicitly named as such in *Black Power*, which, given the many examples about Black people's singular experiences that appear in the book, indicates a vocabulary choice rather than a conceptual awareness.

7. The concept of empire-state draws from Moon-Kie Jung, *Beneath the Surface of White Supremacy: Denaturalizing U.S. Racisms Past and Present* (Stanford, CA: Stanford University Press, 2015), especially chapter 3. Proposing that "we see less like the state and more like the ruled," Jung reminds us of the following: "For the indigenous peoples, the United States immediately became one more empire-state with which they had to contend" (61). From its very beginning, the formation of the US state "comprised not only the states but also other political spaces, which were to be ruled ultimately as Congress saw fit and would not have voting representation in the federal government" (62).

8. Ture and Hamilton, *Black Power*; Diane Fujino, *Samurai among Panthers: Richard Aoki on Race, Resistance, and a Paradoxical Life* (Minneapolis: University of Minnesota Press, 2012), chapter 6.

9. Hamilton, *Black Power*, 216–17, where he states, in his afterword, "The larger the political arena—town, city, county, state, national—one attempts to play in, the more allies organized into coalitions will one need."

10. The analysis of residential segregation, school disciplining practices, and youth

imprisonment, for example, suggests dynamics by which antiblackness impacts in particular manners (a) differently racialized groups and (b) within the same racialized group, persons differently positioned by gender, sexuality, nationality, and social class, among others. See, for example, joão h. costa vargas, *The Denial of Antiblackness: Multiracial Redemption and Black Suffering* (Minneapolis: University of Minnesota Press, 2018), chapters 2 and 3.

11. For an instructive essay on the centrality of blackness in the constitution of modern and US subjectivities, see James Baldwin, "My Dungeon Shook: Letter to my Nephew on the One Hundredth Anniversary of the Emancipation," in *James Baldwin: Collected Essays*, ed. Toni Morrison (New York: Library of America, 1998), 5–10. On the pragmatic effects on antiblackness and the ways by which nonblack subjectivities, particularly Asian and Latino, are constituted in the contemporary US in opposition to Blacks, see, for example, George Yancey, *Who Is White? Latinos, Asians, and the New Black/Nonblack divide* (Boulder, CO: Lynne Rienner, 2004). One of the pioneering philosophical studies on antiblack racism is Lewis R. Gordon, *Bad Faith and Antiblack Racism* (Amherst, NY: Humanity Books, 1999). See also vargas, *The Denial of Antiblackness.*

12. For a sociological study that supports the utilization of the dyad Black-nonblack, see Yancey, *Who Is White?*

13. The reference here, of course, is Cedric Robinson, *Black Marxism: The Making of the Black Radical Tradition* (Chapel Hill: University of North Carolina Press, 2000). By Black radical traditions i mean the accumulated knowledge, over generations, of both the structures and protocols of Western civilization and the African worldviews that provided compelling alternatives to the necessary dehumanization encoding modernity and its attending processes such as colonialism and slavery. In *The Denial of Antiblackness*, i draw parallels between, rather than distinguish, (a) an emphasis on the specific historical and collective experiences of Black people and antiblackness, and (b) Robinson's perspective on Black revolt, imagination, the stress on the metaphysical and the fantastic (the "structures of the mind"), and the ontological totality.

14. See vargas, *The Denial of Antiblackness.*

15. For analyses of BPP's survival programs, see, for example, Kathleen Cleaver and George Katsiaficas, eds., *Liberation, Imagination, and the Black Panther Party: A New Look at the Panthers and Their Legacy* (New York, NY: Routledge, 2001).

16. joão h. costa vargas, *Catching Hell in the City of Angels: Life and Meanings of Blackness in South Central Los Angeles* (Minneapolis, MN: University of Minnesota Press, 2006), 239.

17. See aspects of the program on SCL's website, www.socallib.org/newyear-support2/.

18. On the Panther's health programs, see, for example, Alondra Nelson, *Body and Soul: The Black Panther Party and the Fight against Medical Discrimination* (Minneapolis: University of Minnesota Press, 2011).

19. In Zinzun's archives at the SCL there were several notes on pest control services performed by youths, in Los Angeles and in Pasadena. The fee was voluntary, but most receipts showed that the youths were almost always paid.

20. The photography, computer, and film editing classes were connected to Zinzun's

decade-long hosting of the cable TV program *Message to the Grassroots*, which aired weekly for sixty minutes until 1998. As well, CAPA was an early advocate of cooperative solutions to homelessness and its associated problems.

21. For an analysis of the genealogy of *We Charge Genocide*, see Carol Anderson, *Eyes Off the Prize: the United Nations and the African American Struggle for Human Rights* (New York: Cambridge University Press, 2003). For a detailed account of the ways in which William Patterson's political trajectory intersected with the publication of *We Charge Genocide*, see William Patterson, *The Man Who Cried Genocide: An Autobiography* (New York: International Publisher, 1971), and Gerald Horne, *Black Revolutionary: William Patterson and the Globalization of the African American Freedom Struggle* (Urbana, Ill.: University of Illinois Press, 2013).

22. See, for example, the so-called gang injunctions in Los Angeles, starting in 1987. Although these legal mechanisms aimed at restricting the movement of supposed gang members, it criminalized entire neighborhoods. See vargas, *Never Meant to Survive*.

23. Chinta Strausberg, "Worrill Says CIA Drug Plot "Genocide," Calls for UN Probe." *Chicago Defender*, September 23, 1996.

24. The *San Jose Mercury News'* series of article was then expanded in Gary Webb, *Dark Alliance: The CIA, the Contras, and the Crack Cocaine Explosion* (New York: Seven Stories Press, 1998).

25. John Mitchell and Nora Zamichow, "CIA Head Speaks in L.A. to Counter Crack Claims," *Los Angeles Times*, November 16. 1996. The *New York Times* painted a more balanced picture by noting that there were boos, shouts, and curses, but ultimately the crowd was pacific, well aware of the heavily armed security police that visibly moved around the auditorium, and thus in no moment minimally threatened the director.

26. B. Drummond Ayres Jr., "C.I.A. Chief Visits Watts to Counter Crack Talk," *New York Times*, November 16, 1996.

27. "Former LA Police Officer Mike Ruppert Confronts CIA Director John Deutch on Drug Trafficking," www.youtube.com/watch?v=UT5MY3C86bk, accessed February 6, 2018. It is worth noting that both Webb, in 2004, and Ruppert, in 2014, allegedly committed suicide, the former with two gunshots to the head.

28. US Department of Justice, "Michael Zinzun: Extremist Matters."

29. It is telling that democratic New York City mayor Bill de Blasio's policing program is called Omnipresence. It is supposed to be an improvement over the policy of stop-and-frisk. See vargas, *The Denial of Antiblackness*.

30. I analyzed various examples of empire-state hypersurveillance, and CAPA's response to them, in previous publications. See, for example, vargas, *Catching Hell*, *Never Meant to Survive*, and *The Denial of Antiblackness*.

31. Michael Zinzun Defense Committee. "Free Speech is on Trial," no date.

32. Kwaku Duren, "Police and Courts Clobber Pasadena Black Activists," *National Alliance*, February 27, 1987.

33. "It's all over, and now I can begin picking up the pieces of my life," Zinzun said after the court victory. "The money will . . . send a clear message to the city and the Police Department that they can no longer act like judge, jury and executioner."

Ashley Dunn, "Police Injury Suit Settled for 1.2 Million: Pasadena Agrees to Pay Community Activist Blinded in One Eye," *Los Angeles Times,* February 3, 1988.

34. For a description and analysis of the various local political blocs in which Zinzun participated, such as the Community in Support of the Gang Truce (CSGT), and The Peace and Freedom Party (PFP), see vargas, *The Denial of Antiblackness.*

35. A few organizations in the US have framed as genocide the current and historical state-sanctioned brutality against Black people—the Malcolm X Grassroots Movement in New York City and We Charge Genocide in Chicago. On the hegemonic and potentially transformative uses of the concept of genocide, see Dylan Rodriguez, "Inhabiting the Impasse: Racial/Racial-Colonial Power, Genocide, Poetics, and the Logic of Evisceration." *Social Text* 33, n. 3, (September 2015), 19–44. See also joão h. costa vargas and Joy James, "Refusing Blackness-as-Victimization: Trayvon Martin and the Black Cyborgs," in *Pursuing Trayvon Martin: Historical Contexts and Contemporary Manifestations of Racial Dynamics,* George Yancy and Janine Jones, eds., (Lanham, MD: Lexington Books, 2013), 193-204, and Frank Wilderson, *Red, White, and Black: Cinema and the Structure of U.S. Antagonism* (Durham, NC: Duke University Press, 2010).

36. Ture and Hamilton, *Black Power,* 179.

37. Ture and Hamilton, *Black Power,* 180. My emphasis.

38. For example, the 2015 Civil Rights Division of the Department of Justice report on its investigation of the Ferguson Police Department (FDP), in the wake of the police assassination of Michael Brown, was unambiguous in its findings about the FDP's antiblack orientation: "Ferguson's law enforcement practices overwhelmingly impact African Americans. Data collected by the Ferguson Police Department from 2012 to 2014 show that African Americas account for 85% of vehicle stops, 90% of citations, and 93% of arrests made by FPD officers, despite comprising only 67% of Ferguson's population." United States Department of Justice Civil Rights Division, *Investigation of the Ferguson Police Department* (Washington, DC, 2015), 4.

39. University of Texas, "Capitalism and The New Jim Crow," February 2015. https://utexas.collegiatelink.net/organization/ISO/calendar/details/585779. I thank Connor Healy for this reference, used in his undergraduate honors thesis, which at the time of this writing was in draft form. See Connor Healy, "Kill the Boer: Anti-Blackness and the (Im)possibility of White Revolutionary Praxis," Honors Thesis, Austin: University of Texas, 2016, 48.

40. Ture and Hamilton, *Black Power,* 187.

41. Ture and Hamilton, *Black Power,* 188.

42. joão h. costa vargas, "Gendered Antiblackness and the Impossible Brazilian Project: Emerging Critical Black Brazilian Studies," *Cultural Dynamics* 24, no. 1 (2012): 3–11.

43. For example, my own ethnographic witnessing as well as available documentation show only a sprinkling of Latinx, White, and Asian involvement in the planning of and participation in the 1996 commemoration of the gang truce's fourth anniversary. Out of about twenty participants in a planning meeting, including Zinzun, there were three Latinxs, among them one woman. vargas, *The Denial of Antiblackness,* chapter 6.

Chapter Fifteen: Black Queer Feminism and the Movement for Black Lives in the South: An Interview with Mary Hooks of SONG

1. On Charlene Carruthers's ideas, see Charlene Carruthers, *Unapologetic: A Black, Queer, and Feminist Mandate for Radical Movements* (Boston: Beacon Press, 2018).
2. Combahee River Collective, "A Black Feminist Statement," in *This Bridge Called My Back: Writings by Radical Women of Color*, ed. Cherríe Moraga and Gloria Anzaldúa (New York: Kitchen Table Press, 1981), 210–18; Keeanga-Yamahtta Taylor, *How We Get Free: Black Feminism and the Combahee River Collective* (Chicago: Haymarket Books, 2017).
3. Mo Barnes, "Why There Is a Beef with Black Lives Matter Activists in Atlanta, Part 1," *Rolling Out*, March 23, 2018.
4. On the Movement for Black Lives, see https://policy.m4bl.org.
5. Rebecca Rivas, "Community Leaders Gather to Plead for Ferguson Protestor Joshua Williams' Release from Prison," *St. Louis American*, August 3, 2018.

Chapter Sixteen: Black Student Organizing in the Shadow of the Panthers

1. The California public higher education system includes ten University of California campuses, 23 California State University campuses, and 115 community college campuses.
2. Thomas Creamer, "Estimating Slavery Reparations: Present Value Comparisons of Historical Multigenerational Reparations Policies," *Social Science Quarterly 96:* 639–655; Denis Rancourt, "Calculating Reparations: $1.5 Million for Each Slave Descendant in the U.S." *Black Agenda Report*, January 23, 2013, at www.blackagendareport.com/content/calculating-reparations-15-million-each-slave-descendant-us.
3. Frantz Fanon, *Wretched of the Earth* (New York: Grove Press, 1963), 174.

Chapter Seventeen: The Impact of the Panthers: Centering Poor Black Folks in the Black Liberation Movement

1. Kimberly Verklov, "Black Students Stage Protest at Golden Bear Cafe against Police Killings," *Daily Californian*, www.dailycal.org/2014/12/04/black-students-stage-protest-golden-bear-cafe-police-killings/, accessed October 19, 2018.
2. Reese Renford, "The Lack of Political Activism among Today's Black Student-Athlete," *Journal of Higher Education Athletics and Innovation* 1, no. 2 (2017): 123–31, https://journals.shareok.org/jheai/article/view/950.
3. Tracey Taylor, "After Long Fight, Black Students at UC Berkeley Celebrate Opening of Their Own Center," *Berkeleyside*, www.berkeleyside.com/2017/02/23/long-fight-black-students-uc-berkeley-celebrate-opening-center, accessed October 19, 2018.
4. Anthony Williams, "Afrikan Black Coalition Accomplishes UC Prison

Divestment," Afrikan Black Coalition, http://afrikanblackcoalition.
org/2015/12/18
/afrikan-black-coalition-accomplishes-uc-prison-divestment/, accessed October
19, 2018.

5. *A Huey P. Newton Story*, "Community Survival Programs" (Luna Ray Films: PBS,
2001), www.pbs.org/hueypnewton/actions/actions_survival.html, accessed October
19, 2018.

6. David Dupree and William McAllister, "A Campus Where Black Power Won,"
Wall Street Journal, DATE.

7. Robert Self, *American Babylon: Race and the Struggle for Postwar Oakland*, rev. ed.
(Princeton, NJ: Princeton University Press, 2005).

8. Matthai Kuruvila, "25% Drop in African American Population in Oakland,"
San Francisco Gate, www.sfgate.com/bayarea/article/25-drop-in-African-Ameri-
can-population-in-Oakland-2471925.php, accessed October 19, 2018.

9. Mark Hedin, "Survey Confirms Oakland Homeless Crisis Growing Worse," *East
Bay Times*, www.eastbaytimes.com/2017/06/02/survey-confirms-oakland-home-
less-crisis-growing-worse/, accessed October 19, 2018.

10. Sarah Pettijohn, Elizabeth Boris, Carol De Vita, and Saunji Fyffe, "Non-
profit-Government Contracts and Grants: Findings from the 2013 National
Survey," Urban Institute, www.urban.org/sites/default/files/publica-
tion/24231/412962-Nonprofit-Government-Contracts-and-Grants-Find-
ings-from-the-National-Survey.PDF, accessed October 19, 2018.

11. INCITE!, *The Revolution Will Not Be Funded: Beyond the Non-profit Industrial
Complex* (Durham, NC: Duke University Press, 2017).

Chapter Eighteen: The Chinese Progressive Association and the "Red Door"

1. Many in the CWMAA were members of the Communist Party USA - Chinese
Unit and were also part of the Chinese Revolution in China.

2. The "Red Door" is a concept that came out of CPA's 2008 strategic planning
discussions with staff and board members. Since then, we have embraced this
symbolism in our work.

3. Him Mark Lai, "To Bring Forth a New China, to Build a Better America: The
Chinese Marxist Left in America to the 1960s," *Chinese America: History & Perspectives 6* (1992): 3–72.

4. Pam Tau Lee, Chinese Progressive Association Board Chair, 40th Anniversary
Booklet (2012).

5. Bloom and Martin, *Black against Empire*, 12.

6. The International Hotel housed more than 100 low income Filipino and Chinese
seniors and was the storefront for many Asian radical organizations. In the late
1960s their campaign against the evictions sparked a citywide and multiracial
struggle that lasted over 10 years. After nearly three decades of continued struggle,
the I-Hotel was reopened with 100 units affordable housing for seniors.

7. "Legacy to Liberation: Interview with Alex Hing, Former Minister of Information for the Red Guard and the Founding Member of I Wor Kuen," interviewed by Fred Ho and Steve Yip, 296.

8. Mass work is a principle from Mao Tse Tung that describes the activity of building the deepest and broadest revolutionary unity among the "masses" in the community within a broad united front of mass organizations and movements.

9. The KMT, otherwise known as the "Kuomintang," and the Chinese Six Companies were powerful conservative forces that typically represented the business interests in Chinatowns across the United States.

10. When CPA was established in 1972, the founders protected CPA legally by forming as a 501(c)3. However, it wasn't until 1991 that CPA began to function more formally as a 501(c)3 with paid and full-time staff.

11. In 2014, POWER merged with Causa Justa :: Just Cause to build the power of Black and Latinx communities across the Bay Area.

12. A 1995 study showed that breast cancer rates among women under the age of fifty who lived in Bayview-Hunters Point were twice the normal level; see www.sfdph.org/dph/files/reports/StudiesData/DiseaseInjury/bvhuntca.pdf, January 1998.

13. Robert Selna and Heather Knight, "Prop. G Winning Big; Prop. F Losing Big," *San Francisco Chronicle*, June 4, 2008, www.sfgate.com/news/article/Prop-G -winning-big-Prop-F-losing-big-3210500.php#photo-2352785.

14. "One Struggle, Many Fronts" was a slogan that was started by the "Bay Area Asian Coalition Against the War (BAACAW)," a formation founded by IWK members to oppose the US war on Vietnam.

15. Celebration of Life for Grace Lee Boggs in San Francisco Chinatown, 2012.

16. "Modern Immigration Wave Brings 59 Million to U.S., Driving Population Growth and Change through 2065," www.pewhispanic.org /2015/09/28/modern-immigration-wave-brings-59-million-to -u-s-driving-population-growth-and-change-through-2065 /ph_2015-09-28_immigration-through-2065-05.

Index

Page numbers in *italic* refer to illustrations. "Passim" (literally "scattered") indicates intermittent discussion of a topic over a cluster of pages.

Abbott, Jack Henry, 107
Abdulhadi, Rabab, 175
Abdulmumit, Jihad, 231
Abiodun, Nehanda, 28, 33, 35, 37–38, 39, 226, 309–10n13
Aboriginal Australian artists, *150*, 171–73
Abu Jamal, Mumia, 68, 106, 161, 165, 168, 215–16, 225
Acoli, Sundiata, 53, 206, 215
Africa, 115–23 passim, 141–48 passim, 208, 321n14; exiles, *152*, 164. *See also* Algeria; Pan-Africanism; South Africa
Africa, Debbie, 209
Africa, Mike, 209
African Blood Brotherhood, 50
Afrikan Black Coalition (ABC), 267–79, 282–83
Afro-American Association, 159, 332n14
Afro-Asian Unity Conference, Bandung, 1954. *See* Bandung Afro-Asian Unity Conference, 1954
Ahmad, Dhameera, *90*, 91–97
Algeria, 93; BPP in 117, 163–64, 171, 175, 208
Ali, Laila, *112*
Ali, Muhammad, *112*, 173
Alinsky, Saul, 47

All-African People's Liberation Party (AAPRP), 114, 118, 121–23, 141–42, 148–49
Alston, Ashanti, 61, 212
American Federation of Labor (AFL), 290
American Indians. *See* Native Americans
Anderson, Marian, 119
antiblackness, 238–40, 247, 248, 249
armed resistance and self-defense, 43, 50–51, 114, 210; Sacramento BPP protest, 114, 165, 222n28
Arons, Ralph, 320n10
art and artists: Douglas, 137, *152–54*, 155–81; exhibits, 64, 167, 172; Kambon, *124–26*, 127–49. *See also* murals; sculptures and statues
Asai, Susan, 196
Asian-Afro Unity Conference, Bandung, 1954. *See* Bandung Afro-Asian Unity Conference, 1954
Asian Americans, 198. *See also* Chinese Americans; Japanese Americans
At-Thinnin, Shaka, *220*, 223, 224–25
Ausar Auset Society, 59
Australian Aboriginal artists. *See* Aboriginal Australian artists

bailout campaigns, 253, 256, 258, 262, *266*
Baldwin, James, 205, 217
bandele, asha, 96
Bandung Afro-Asian Unity Conference,

About Haymarket Books

Haymarket Books is a radical, independent, nonprofit book publisher based in Chicago. Our mission is to publish books that contribute to struggles for social and economic justice. We strive to make our books a vibrant and organic part of social movements and the education and development of a critical, engaged, international left.

We take inspiration and courage from our namesakes, the Haymarket martyrs, who gave their lives fighting for a better world. Their 1886 struggle for the eight-hour day—which gave us May Day, the international workers' holiday—reminds workers around the world that ordinary people can organize and struggle for their own liberation. These struggles continue today across the globe—struggles against oppression, exploitation, poverty, and war.

Since our founding in 2001, Haymarket Books has published more than five hundred titles. Radically independent, we seek to drive a wedge into the risk-averse world of corporate book publishing. Our authors include Noam Chomsky, Arundhati Roy, Rebecca Solnit, Angela Y. Davis, Howard Zinn, Amy Goodman, Wallace Shawn, Mike Davis, Winona LaDuke, Ilan Pappé, Richard Wolff, Dave Zirin, Keeanga-Yamahtta Taylor, Nick Turse, Dahr Jamail, David Barsamian, Elizabeth Laird, Amira Hass, Mark Steel, Avi Lewis, Naomi Klein, and Neil Davidson. We are also the trade publishers of the acclaimed Historical Materialism Book Series and of Dispatch Books.

About the Editors

DIANE C. FUJINO is an activist-scholar teaching and writing about Asian American radical struggles, Black Power struggles, and Afro-Asian solidarities, and is professor of Asian American Studies and former director of the Center for Black Studies Research at the University of California, Santa Barbara. She has long participated in political prisoner, education, and US Third World liberation solidarity struggles and is active with the Ethnic Studies Now! Santa Barbara Coalition and a founding member of Cooperation Santa Barbara. She is author of *Heartbeat of Struggle: The Revolutionary Life of Yuri Kochiyama* (2005); *Samurai among Panthers: Richard Aoki on Race, Resistance, and a Paradoxical Life* (2012); and *Nisei Radicals: The Feminist Poetics and Transformatice Ministry of Mitsuye Yamada and Michael Yasutake* (forthcoming); and editor of *Wicked Theory, Naked Practice: A Fred Ho Reader* (2009).

MATEF HARMACHIS is a social scientist teaching high school, a former journalist, and a long-time activist working in pan-African and Third World decolonization solidarity, education, labor, and political prisoner liberation movements. He is active with the Ethnic Studies Now! Santa Barbara Coalition, which recently won the passage of an ethnic studies course requirement for high school graduation in the Santa Barbara school district.

Photos by Kano Fujino-Harmachis

About the Contributors

BEN BARSON works at the intersection of the academic, activist, and performing arts worlds. He is an ASCAP award-winning composer and protégé of the late Fred Ho. He is unrelenting in his commitment to make music that fights racism, capitalism, patriarchy, and planetary destruction. He has been acknowledged as a "Pittsburgh arts innovator" (*Pittsburgh Post-Gazette*) and a "groundbreaking artist." (Madison *Isthmus*); his compositions have been called "utterly compelling" (*I Care if You Listen*), "fully orchestrated and magnificently realized" (*Vermont Standard*), and "pushing boundaries in a well-conceived way" (*Midwest Review*).

TINA BARTOLOME was born and raised in San Francisco, the daughter of working-class immigrants from the Philippines and Switzerland. Somewhere between unlearning the lie of Columbus, facing eviction, writing on walls, and fighting racist propositions, she joined the movement and never looked back. Over the past twenty-five years, she has trained thousands of emerging organizers and activists across the country, striving to continue the legacies of Paulo Freire, Ella Baker, June Jordan, Yuri Kochiyama, and Kiilu Nyasha. She works at School of Unity and Liberation in Oakland, California.

FELICE BLAKE is an associate professor in the English Department at the University of California, Santa Barbara. She has published work on racism, culture, and resistance in *Al Jazeera*, *Ethnic and Racial Studies*, *African American Review*, and *SOULS: A Critical Journal of Black Politics, Culture, and Society*. Dr. Blake is the author of *Black Love, Black Hate: Intimate Antagonisms in African American literature* (Ohio State University Press) and coeditor of *Antiracism Inc.: Why the Way We Talk About Racial Justice Matters* (Punctum Books).

YOEL YOSIEF HAILE is a criminal justice program manager with the ACLU of Northern California, where he works to end mass incarceration. As the founding political director of the Afrikan Black Coalition, a statewide Black youth organization, Yoel helped lead campaigns that resulted in the University of California divesting all of its nearly $30 million in holdings from private prison companies and terminating $475 million in contracts with Wells Fargo. Yoel received his master's degree in public policy from the Goldman School of Public Policy at UC Berkeley in 2016.

MARY HOOKS is a thirty-eight-year-old, Black, lesbian, feminist, mother, organizer, and codirector of Southerners on New Ground, a political home for LGBTQ liberation across all lines of race, class, abilities, age, culture, gender, and sexuality in the South. Mary joined SONG as a member in 2009 and began organizing with SONG in 2010. Mary's commitment to Black liberation, which encompasses the liberation of LGBTQ folks, is rooted in her experiences growing up under the impacts of the War on Drugs.

ERICKA HUGGINS is a human rights activist, poet, educator, Black Panther Party leader, and former political prisoner. During her fourteen years as a BPP leader, the longest of any woman in leadership, she was director of the Oakland Community School (1973–81), a groundbreaking community-run child development center and elementary school founded by the BPP, and created the vision for its innovative curriculum. Based on her extraordinary life experiences, she speaks widely on the physical and emotional well-being of women, children, and youth, whole-being education, over-incarceration, and the role of spiritual practice in sustaining activism and promoting change.

MARYAM KASHANI is a filmmaker and assistant professor in gender and women's studies and Asian American studies at the University of Illinois at Urbana-Champaign. Her work focuses on theories and theologies of liberation, geography, race, Islam, and visual culture. Her current project *Medina by the Bay* is based on ethnographic research and filmmaking with Muslim communities in the greater San Francisco Bay Area. She is part of the leadership collective of Believers Bail Out, a community-led effort to bailout Muslims in pretrial and immigration incarceration towards abolition.

DÉQUI KIONI-SADIKI is a Black feminist, educator for liberation, artist, human/prisoner rights activist working on behalf of/with u.s.-held political prisoners and prisoners of war (PPOWs) in the fight for their release. She cohosts/produces *Where We Live*, a listener-sponsored weekly public affairs show and is coeditor/contributing essayist of *Look for Me in the Whirlwind: From the Panther 21 to 21ˢᵗ-Century Revolutions* with essays, interviews, and articles published in the *Amsterdam Newspaper, San Francisco Bayview, Huffington Post*, and the *Journal of the Research Group on Socialism and Democracy*.

TEISHAN A. LATNER is an assistant professor of history at Thomas Jefferson University. He is the author of *Cuban Revolution in America: Havana and the Making of a United States Left, 1968–1992* (2018).

JALIL A. MUNTAQIM is a former member of the Black Panther Party, the Black Liberation Army, and is one of the world's longest-held political prisoners, having been imprisoned since 1971. He is the author of *We Are Our Own Liberators*, a compilation of prison writings. Many of his essays have been published in anthologies. His articles have appeared in several newspapers and progressive publications. For more information on Jalil's case and fight for parole, see www.freejalil.com.

SEKOU ODINGA, born in Jamaica Queens, New York, is a founding member of the Black Panther Party in New York, a founding member of International Section of the Black Panther Party, and a soldier in the Black Liberation Army. He spent thirty-three years as a political prisoner and came home in November 2014. He is a public speaker, writer, political activist, and a founding member of the Northeast Political Prisoner Coalition. He is a loving father of ten, grandfather of thirty-one, and great grandfather of three.

QUINCY SAUL is a musician, organizer, and a cofounder of Ecosocialist Horizons. He is the author of *Truth and Dare: A Comic Book Curriculum for the End and the Beginning of the World*, *Maroon Comix: Origins and Destinies*, and the coeditor of *Maroon the Implacable: The Collected Writings of Russell Maroon Shoatz*.

BLAKE SIMONS is cofounder of the Fannie Lou Hamer Black Resource Center at UC Berkeley. At UC Berkeley, he was a political science major and African American studies minor and worked with the Black Student Union on gaining demands for institutional change. He is a founding member of People's Breakfast Oakland and cohost of Hella Black Podcast. Blake is also family to Jalil Muntaqim, a Black Panther Party and Black Liberation Army political prisoner.

ALEX T. TOM is a former executive director of the Chinese Progressive Association in San Francisco and cofounder of Seeding Change. Currently, he is the executive director of the Center For Empowered Politics, a new project that aims to train and develop new leaders of color and grow movement building infrastructure. In 2019, Alex received the Open Society Foundation Racial Justice Fellowship to develop a toolkit to counter the rise of the new Chinese Right Wing in the US.

joão costa vargas works at the University of California, Riverside plantation.